# THE BABY BOOMER'S HANDBOOK FOR WOMEN

To Bobbie
Hope you Like the Book
Bonnie Basara

Edited by Linda Ellis Eastman

Professional Woman Publishing
Prospect, Kentucky

THE BABY BOOMER'S HANDBOOK FOR WOMEN


Published by:
Professional Woman Publishing
Post Office Box 333
Prospect, KY 40059
(502) 228-0906
www.pwnbooks.com

Please contact the publisher for quantity discounts.

ISBN 13: 978-0-9799711-6-7
ISBN 10: 0-9799711-6-0

Library of Congress Cataloging-In-Publication Data

Cover Design and Typography by:
Sential Design, LLC — www.sentialdesign.com
Cover photo: Dreamstime.com

Printed in the United States of America

*"Dedicated to the wonderful people who touched our lives."*

# TABLE OF CONTENTS

## TABLE OF CONTENTS
### -CONTINUED-

## TABLE OF CONTENTS
-CONTINUED-

## TABLE OF CONTENTS
-CONTINUED-

# TABLE OF CONTENTS
-CONTINUED-

# ABOUT THE AUTHOR

## LINDA EASTMAN

Linda Ellis Eastman is President and CEO of The Professional Woman Network (PWN), an International Training and Consulting Organization on Women's Issues. She has designed seminars which have been presented in China, the former Soviet Union, South Africa, the Phillipines, and attended by individuals in the United States from such firms as McDonalds, USA Today, Siemens-Westinghouse, the Pentagon, the Department of Defense, and the United States Department of Education.

An expert on women's issues, Ms. Eastman has certified and trained over two thousand women to start consulting/seminar businesses originating from such countries as Pakistan, the Ukraine, Antigua, Canada, Mexico, Zimbabwe, Nigeria, Bermuda, Jamaica, Costa Rica, England, South Africa, Malaysia, and Kenya. Founded in 1982 by Linda Ellis Eastman, The Professional Woman Network is committed to educating women on a global basis regarding, self-esteem, confidence building, stress management, and emotional, mental, spiritual and physical wellness.

Ms. Eastman has been featured in USA Today and listed in Who's Who of American Women, as well as Who's Who of International Leaders. In addition to women's issues, Ms. Eastman speaks internationally regarding the importance of human respect as it relates to race, color, culture, age, and gender. She will be facilitating an international conference where speakers and participants from many nations will be able to discuss issues that are unique to women on a global basis.

Linda Ellis Eastman is also founder of The Professional Woman Speakers Bureau and The Professional Woman Coaching Institute. Ms. Eastman has dedicated her businesses to increasing the self-esteem and personal dignity of women and youth around the world.

*Contact:*
The Professional Woman Network
P.O. Box 333
Prospect, KY 40059
(502) 566-9900
lindaeastman@prodigy.net
www.pwnbooks.com
www.protrain.net

# INTRODUCTION

**Linda Ellis Eastman**

The majority of chapters in this book were written by professional women, coaches and consultants who were born between 1946-1962, the Baby Boom years. Each of these women lived during a period of time that witnessed the birth of Elvis Presley, The Beatles, Rock & Roll, the Hoola Hoop, the Pill, women's liberation, the assertive woman, The Civil Rights Movement, the deaths of President John Kennedy and Rev. Dr. Martin Luther King, the Challenger space shuttle explosion, men on the Moon, AIDS, women living into their 80's and 90's as the norm, the Polio vaccine, the Poodle Skirt, the Mini Skirt, and freedom of choice for women. The list could go on and on.

This book is written for ALL women by Baby Boomers who share their life's journey and strategies for dealing with stress, independence, grief, self-acceptance, and avoiding toxic relationships.

With age comes experience and lessons learned. May the reader glean much confidence and support from the writing of each chapter contained within. The Baby Boomers, the largest generation in history, have much to share from the trials, challenges, successes and obstacles presented to women since 1946 to the present.

Women have indeed 'come a long way'. But there is more work to be done. Take the ideas and advice from the authors and reach for the stars, no matter your age.

# THE BABY BOOMERS HANDBOOK FOR WOMEN

# ABOUT THE AUTHOR

## Shirley A. Williams

Shirley A. William is President and CEO of ***Leadership in Action, LLC***. Her mission is "Developing the workforce of today". She conducts workshops and seminars that have been presented throughout the United States and abroad. The workshops and seminars conducted by the institute consist of topics such as: Women as Leaders, Leadership Skills and The Superwoman Syndrome. Ms. Williams has been certified by The Professional Woman Network as a Professional Coach and Diversity Consultant.

Ms. Williams' knowledge of business and professionalism is supported by over 20 years of real world and practical leadership experience acquired from the telecom and staffing industries, non-profit, university and faith based organizations. She has over 12 years experience in employee recognition, training recruiting, and change and knowledge management.

Among her many accomplishments, Ms. Williams has co-authored one book and is working on the second book. She has been recognized by the Lydia Circle of Christian Business and Professional Women with the ***Spirit of Deborah Leadership Award*** and ***Leadership Advancement Award*** by Wayne State University Relations.

**Books**

- Co-Author of "***The Baby Boomer's Handbook For Women***" (August 2008)

**Certifications**

- Certified Professional Coach
- Registered Corporate Coach
- Certified Diversity Consultant
- Certified DISC Behavior Model Consultant

**Professional Spotlight**

- The Magnolia Radio Show, Baby Boomer's Handbook for Women "***Reinventing Yourself at Any Age***" (August 2008)

**Professional Organizations**

- Professional Woman's Speakers Bureau
- Professional Woman's Authors Institute
- National Association of Female Executives
- Lydia Circle of Christian Business and Professional Women
- National Association of Baby Boomer Women
- ASTD (Association of Training and Development)

*Contact:*
Shirley A. Williams
(888) 926-9911
www.leadershipinaction.info
swilliams@leadershipinaction.info

**ONE**

# REINVENTING YOURSELF AT ANY AGE

**By Shirley A. Williams**

*"If outrageous imagination is the wine of madness, then come and fill my cup."* —Sheldon Kopp, Psychologist and Writer

I will begin by saying that I believe life is a temporary assignment that requires us to possess the gift of an open mind. As a result of this belief, I personally have never found any comfort in driving through life in the "we always did it this way" lane. Reinventing myself has been a life- long journey that started with parents in Detroit, Michigan who had the courage to reinvent themselves by migrating to Detroit from Thomaston, Georgia, because of the rumors about job opportunities up north that were paying $5.00 an hour. That was their reason for packing up the family, their faith, a few belongings, and heading north. Having the audacity to make such a radical change in those days came with great risk, but would later prove to be a positive life-altering event. I'm proud to say the same spirit for change is in my DNA.

Word was rapidly spreading throughout the south about the "good factory jobs, good pay and lifestyles to match." Even though the jobs were not glamorous and would require heavy lifting and agility, the people were coming north in droves. Despite the fact that the work was hard, working conditions were undesirable and hours were long, this was nothing new for them because their liberation was worth it. To them, the move symbolized an improved quality of life and an answered prayer. It was a move built upon faith, family, hope, change and a spirit of community. The move for my parents occurred in the mid 40's, post WWII, and long before blacks would even hear or become acquainted with the words "civil rights". My parents, like the others, dared to dream about the possibility for a better quality of life for their family that was only a few hundred miles away.

As families became more economically stable, there was newfound pride and understanding of community; block clubs were formed, families attended PTA meetings and participated in neighborhood cookouts. The new community environment gave them more confidence and hope in the promise of the American dream.

The neighborhoods became more diverse and offered a chance to develop cross-cultural relationships, appreciation and respect. It was the V.A. home loans and pilot programs introduced during the 50's that provided access for many of these first time buyers. The "motor city" (Detroit) was on the move and considered a desired place to raise a family.

The neighborhood I grew up in was very diverse and segregation was something my parents and grandmother were familiar with; however, it was not a concept that was easy for me to understand. After all, my circle of friends and schoolmates were Black, Polish, Spanish and Greek. Even though the community was diverse and many of our parents were co-workers, my parents continued to be guarded and humble in their presence. At the time, I didn't quite understand why, to me it appeared that my parents sort of treated them like they were special; however, growing older increased my understanding. The 1967 riots also had something to do with my gaining insight. As I reflect upon the time that some of us fondly refer to as "back in the day", I will confess that my journey as a "Baby Boomer" was a path that I am blessed to have traveled, because for me it was truly the "good ole days".

Growing up during that time greatly contributed to the value system that I have used as the standard for living my adult life. From the very beginning, we were taught that church was mandatory and not an option. In fact, on Sunday mornings my grandmother would simply say, "As for me and my household, we will serve the Lord." We grew up knowing: family was everything, children were seen and not heard, adults ruled, school clothes and play clothes were not the same, homework was done as soon as you came home from school, there were no after- school snacks because there was dinner instead, and then jello, cake or cookies as dessert. Kool-aid was our only beverage of choice and streetlights were our cue that playtime was over.

I have deep appreciation and love for my parents; it is because of their bravery, willingness to embrace change, and giving their fears to God. Because of them, I can say that I am a woman with a heart for change. Reinventing ourselves provides us with a platform for showcasing our value, self-confidence and capacity to rock the world.

I once overheard one of my daughters describe me to one of her friends as being progressive.

I remember wondering what that meant to her. I later realized that she was paying me a compliment. I was different from many of my family and friends; pension, gold watches and seniority were never on my radar screen. However, the next adventure was. In my mind, change represented a new adventure leading to my true destiny. The infamous subjective performance review was my motivator for movement; the reviews always shared a common theme that opened my eyes, the words flexible, resilient and adaptable, which represents a spirit of change. Although those traits were recognized as strengths the recognition and or reward for displaying a "team player" behavior was often overlooked by the rationale that doing so would undermine the team performance concept.

Reinventing you begins with a ***heart for change***; after all, change is the driving force for reinventing you, as "they" would say the only constant in life is change. Do you have a heart for change? By the end of this chapter you will know. My stumbling block when it comes to change is patience. To overcome this weakness, I remind myself of an excerpt from a sermon I once heard; the Bishop said, "Work patience until it works." It took me a minute, but I finally got it. Change also requires commitment, patience with yourself, faith in yourself, and hard work.

Reinventing you is typically inspired as a result of an impactful life event. It is usually an event that is often times accompanied by something or someone causing a change or a shift in our comfort zones. Our response to the shift is either positive or negative. How we deal with it is what sets the stage for the end result. The bottom line is that reinventing yourself is mostly about empowering yourself by ***giving you the permission*** to do what you do.

I recall in the 70's getting fired from a secretarial job. That experience forced me into what I call the corner of honesty. My revelation was that typing 15 words per minute, not counting errors, was indeed a valid reason for termination. Despite the pain and embarrassment, it motivated me to reinvent myself. I always wanted to learn more about fine jewelry, so instead of basking in sorrow, I applied for a job at fine jewelry store and became a certified gemologist. That experience gave me the confidence to move on to reinvent me again and again. Below are a couple examples of circumstance that may be the stimulus for the reinventing of you. After you read it, think about a time when you had to reinvent yourself.

1. The children are all grown up, the nest is empty, the loneliness and lack of sound in the house is deafening, and all the free time is driving you crazy. Do all of these changes have you questioning your purpose? To determine what your hidden dream is, stop for a moment, relax, be still and open your mind, now focus on tasks, hobbies or activities that bring you peace, joy and self-fulfillment. To discover your new purpose, pull out your personal unfulfilled dreams, use them as your launching pad, and do some mind storming.

2. The loss of a spouse leaves you empty, confused and regretful for the small things you overlooked before. Something as simple as walking into a dark house or entering an empty room that would normally be occupied can become a challenge. To assist with getting through this difficult period, take as much time as you need for healing you. Once you're ready, say okay self, you were a master at being ***a we***, and because of that you can trust that God will also let me master being ***a me***. Also be assured, the time will come when you will find the courage, desire, strength and mindset to go

on with life. Only when you reach this point can you give yourself permission to dust off those dreams you placed on hold and begin entertaining thoughts of giving birth to those dreams.

***When you are ready make your move, dare to dream BIG, dare to put your dream in writing.***

As baby boomer women (born 1945-1965), we were groomed from birth to re-invent ourselves. We have had more choices than our mothers; we are women who are more educated, politically astute, outspoken, wealthy, healthy and active in our communities. We are women who have reinvented lifestyles and made a difference in the world.

The disadvantage with only focusing on giving and doing for others resulted in our overlooking the obvious question: what do we do with ourselves now? I am hopeful this chapter will help to remind you of how creative, talented and resourceful we are, and that it encourages you to dust your dreams off and do something with them.

According to the National Association for Baby Boomer Women, there are 38 million baby boomer women and they are blooming across lifestyles and reinventing retirement.

It is also predicted that by 2010, we will be the richest market segment with no desire to slow down, and therefore we are reinventing careers and the traditional job. We also represent the largest number of new business owners; we're opting for the position of entrepreneur.

After I was forced to join the ranks of the commonly displaced baby boomers due to corporate downsizing, I recognized that the customary "*package*" would not sustain us during our retirement years.

We really hadn't done a great job at saving for retirement. We believed we were still young enough to work a few more years and correct our oversight. The concern prompted me to begin researching the subject of retirement planning and the projected income requirements to determine any necessary budget modifications. While investigating, I came across an article about retired executive men. It talked about how they were reinventing themselves and becoming business process consultants (that was an ah-ha moment for me). I recall thinking to myself, these men are selling knowledge aka intellectual capital they imported from previous work experiences. I began to think about the knowledge or intellectual property I had stored in my head. But even more importantly, was it something others could see as having value?

At this point, I retreated to my "closet of honesty" to do a self-inventory (being real). I began with my *thinking inside the box, a Shirley concept.* Here is where you retreat to chart life/professional experiences to determine how to shape your dream based upon your related competencies. I spent an entire day home alone working on this, and it is difficult for me to describe how enlightening and encouraging it was to sit and focus on me and my skills and talent. I used this technique because it forces you to think about what you have imported from the different job descriptions, tasks and life/skills we acquired over the years. I also factored in the various positions I held: computer sales, staffing branch manager, recruiting director, trainer, national account manager, management and regional operations manager. ***Embracing my self worth***, allowed me an inroad to see my own value by taking inventory of my skills, talents and previous experience, and revisiting each experience made me ask myself these questions:

1. What did I do best?

2. Which position gave me the greatest satisfaction?

3. Is it something I wouldn't mind doing until it's time to reinvent me again?

4. Who would be my clients?

5. How do I expand my net, *aka network?*

6. What don't I want to do?

Reinventing yourself may sound intimidating. If it does, just look at it as a do over with multiple personalities.

To really get a handle on reinventing yourself, try the ***thinking inside the box*** technique. Doing this exercise will help you to gain clarity and visualize your value; it also gives you a point of exploration for potential outside the box. What if you also discover that your skills and talents have the potential for being your gateway to building your own glass ceiling? Remember that tucked away inside your box is a lifetime of talent, skills and knowledge that has been generated from both our professional and personal life experiences.

Let's look at the typical roles in the box and the potential portability of those skills and talents and what will work outside your box. Portability works like this: I am the oldest daughter, (*leadership & accountability*) big sister, *(managing others)* the wife, *(operations manager & decision maker)* mother, (*communications specialist, finance manager and law enforcement*) social coordinator, *(event planner and facilitator)* chauffer, *(transportation specialist)*, cook *(nutritionist and restaurateur/ caterer*). These are additional roles we have had to fill at some point in our lives. Play with them and see what you come up with; nurse, babysitter, project manager for science fairs and the caregiver for aging parents. (Multi-tasking really should have been our hallmark.)

The following example reminds me of a friend who had lost her job and had to get creative to make ends meet. She loved baking, so she made two cakes and took them to the local Coney Island restaurant in her neighborhood. The sales pitch she used was interesting; she agreed to leave the cakes for two days to see if they would sell. If they did, the cakes would cost $25.00 each. If they did not sell, nothing was owed. She reinvented herself six years ago and is now known as the cake lady and has about thirty clients ordering an average of nine cakes per week. (A home based business.)

Doing my own inventory was the motivator I used to envision myself as an entrepreneur. The end result was starting my own training and performance development company. Reinventing yourself is about changing course and staying charged up to stay the course.

The following exercise is intended to help you picture reinventing you. Think of it as a passport to pursue your interest, fulfill your dreams, and your tool to turn hobbies into something more. Take a moment to reflect upon your options, consider the skills, talents and resources required to do the job, and then consider other enterprises you can transfer them to.

*It's inventory time; use both categories and think inside the box. Imagine how you can reinvent you by combining the two lists:*

***My Job Descriptions/Titles:***

1. ______________________________

2. ______________________________

3. ______________________________

4. ______________________________

5. ______________________________

6. ______________________________

***My Life Roles:***

1. ______________________________

2. ______________________________

3. ______________________________

4. ______________________________

5. ______________________________

6. ______________________________

***Parting thoughts:*** Dreams do not come with an expiration date, and reinventing you has no age limit. Begin today by giving yourself permission to pursue your dreams.

Our potential is unlimited when we merge life and professional skills, as demonstrated by the women below. If you are armed with a dream and the courage to reinvent yourself, the world is yours to conquer. I encourage, implore, and expect you to make your dream your reality.

I wonder what talents or skills life/professional experiences each of these women may have had to capitalize on to achieve their dreams?

Marie Callander—Frozen Foods and Restaurants

Ms. Fields—Cookies

Mary Kay—Cosmetics

Rachel Ray—Cooked her way into TV and Books

Paula Dean—Restaurants, TV and Books

Oprah Winfrey—TV, Magazines and Movies

***Dedication***

*To my mother, I say thank you for teaching me to be my own cheerleader. To my daughters, thank you for giving me so many reasons to be your #1 cheerleader and allowing me to do so. To the other special women in my life, thank you for your encouragement, prayers and love.*

# ABOUT THE AUTHOR

## ALICE J. MAXIN

Alice J. Maxin is President and Founder of **Panorama Coaching**, a company dedicated to helping clients achieve success through vision and planning. She is a professional life coach, certified by the Professional Woman Network (PWN), an international consulting and training organization.

With a Master's degree in education from Clarion University of PA, Alice taught in public schools for over twenty-five years before changing careers in 1995. She became a labor relations specialist for Pennsylvania State Education Association (PSEA/NEA), negotiating and advocating for school employees across southwestern PA. Proficient in assertive behavior and communication skills, Alice exhibits expertise in facilitation, training, coaching, problem solving and trust within the workplace environment. This led to the origination of **Panorama Coaching.** Alice is a certified trainer for Basic Leadership Skills, Women's Leadership, Assertiveness, Women's Issues, Emotional Wellness, Organizational Skills (including time management), and Training the Trainer. Her customize-designed programs for both businesses and individuals provide the foundation for **Panorama Coaching.**

In addition to being a member of the PWN International Advisory Board, Alice belongs to the PWN Speakers Bureau and the National Association for Female Executives. She received recognition for her professional successes in Who's Who Among American Teachers, Who's Who in American Education, and Who's Who of American Women and Women's Business Network. Alice co-authored three PWN books: *Woman's Journey to Wellness: Mind, Body, and Spirit* and *Beyond the Body: Developing Inner Beauty, The Baby Boomer's Handbook.*

Alice enjoys spending time with her granddaughter Erin and volunteering for the Armstrong County Community Foundation's early literacy initiative. She also organized the first support group for the Restless Legs Syndrome Foundation in western PA, Pittsburgh North.

Her company, **Panorama Coaching**, achieves widespread respect for its useful applications in the professional environment and for continued relevance in its clients' lives. Whether you are an individual seeking guidance from a personal coach or a business, hospital, or school searching for just the right program, let your horizons expand and the view will become clearer by contacting **Panorama Coaching** for all of your training and coaching needs.


*Contact:*
**Panorama Coaching**
Alice J. Maxin
143 Sportsman Road
Leechburg, PA 15656
(724) 295-4121
E-Mail: alice@panoramacoach.com
Website: www.panoramacoach.com

## TWO

# OVERCOMING THE "WHAT IF" SYNDROME

**By Alice J. Maxin**

*"The only known cure for fear is faith."*
—Lena Kellogg Sadler, American Physician (1875 – 1939)

Much of the anxiety within of our lives begins with the words ***What If***. As we approach the great milestones of ages 60, 65, 70 and older, we may tend to look at the world through foggy bifocals more often than the rose-colored glasses of our youth. Instead of letting ourselves relax and enjoy the richness of the life we've worked so hard to achieve, some women get caught up in the ***What If*** syndrome.

Have you ever heard yourself saying or even thinking any of the following?

1. What if my spouse gets seriously ill or dies?
2. What if my children move far away?
3. What if my medical coverage is terminated?
4. What if I have not saved enough for retirement?
5. What if I suffer the loss of my best friend?
6. What if I become terminally ill?
7. What if the Earth collides with the sun?

(I added the last one just to illustrate how we can worry about the future being as awful as we can imagine.)

Imagining the best-case scenario instead of the worst one does not come naturally for many women. From the time we were young, being raised in the era of blond furniture and black and white television, scores of women were being admonished with awful predictions. Put a check mark beside the exclamations below that you remember hearing in your formative years.

________ Do not stick out your tongue. Your face will freeze like that.

________ Laugh before sunrise; cry before sunset.

________ Get your feet wet and you will catch your death of cold.

________ Be careful what you wish for; you just might get it.

________ If you pull out a gray hair, two more will grow in its place.

________ Swallow that seed and a watermelon will grow in your belly.

________ Step on a crack; you'll break your mother's back.

________ Eat the crusts of your bread so your hair will be curly.

________ Keep pouting and a birdie will land on your lip to do his business.

________ Do not eat standing up; you will get fat legs.

While these sayings were meant to foster good practices, another message was loud and clear: if bad things happen to good people, it is their own fault. Predictions of gloom and doom sometimes overshadowed the lessons we were to learn.

Fast forward to present day. Acting like a victim before an event even happens develops from the habit of expecting unfair, unwanted, and unwarranted events to be inevitable. It focuses on the negative rather than the positive aspects of our lives. One equation learned in algebra states that a negative multiplied by another negative equals a positive. However, compounding negative thoughts and expectations in our lives will NOT produce an optimistic result.

Letting the ***What Ifs*** take over our thinking is handing our future over to ***If Only I Had.*** Read below to see the correlation.

1. **What if** my spouse/partner dies? **If only I had** said I love you more often...

2. **What if** my children move far away? **If only I had** spent more time with them when they were here...

3. **What if** I do not have enough money to retire? **If only I had** followed a sound financial plan…

4. **What if** my medical coverage is terminated? **If only I had** attended the company's meeting about…

5. **What if** I get terminally ill? **If only I had** followed my doctor's advice…

6. **What if** I lose my best friend? **If only I had** made time for the girlfriends' trip we always talked about…

7. **What if** the Earth collides with the sun? (No one will have to worry anymore!)

Missed opportunities can result from the negative ***What Ifs.*** We need to take ownership of our lives: our emotions, our thoughts, our words, and our actions. Once we take responsibility for ourselves, our vision for the future will become clearer. If we walk around in fear with our eyes shut tight, more obstacles than pathways will be ahead of us. Both our sighted vision and our mental vision will suffer.

Think of the toddler just learning to walk. If she spent her time sitting in her diaper on the floor, sucking her thumb, and thinking – ***What if*** (1) I fall; (2) I go backwards; (3) I don't know which way to go; (4) people laugh at me; (5) I get hurt; (6) no one likes me anymore… I imagine she would be crawling on all fours for years to come! Short of having a physical disability that prevents us from walking upright, we do not want to be the toddler who never experiences the extraordinary independence of walking on her own.

As Baby Boomers, we don't want to be like the 'What if' toddler when approaching our golden years. To be paralyzed by the ***What Ifs*** is to turn our lives over to our fears. Keep in mind that FEAR can stand for False Evidence Appearing Real. No other person can live your life for you; likewise, no one has ever walked in your shoes. Your life and your outlook on life are solely your responsibility.

"What?" you might say. "But, I did not choose to have overbearing grandparents, an absent father, mean sisters, a lazy brother, or a lack of money growing up. I did not choose to be short, to be the youngest sibling, or to have cancer. How can you possibly say that my life is my responsibility? Look at the hand I've been dealt!"

Fair enough – let's look at the hand you may have been dealt. How have you reacted to circumstances beyond your control: negatively and without hope, or with faith that you can make the best of any situation? In the scenarios below, mark which statement best describes how you would react if it happened to you.

1. My parents never encouraged me and always put me down.

   A. I give up easily on most things. I know I am not very capable because my parents always told me that.

   B. I strive to do my best and encourage others to do the same.

2. My siblings are selfish, lazy or absent from my everyday life.

   A. It's no wonder my kids are the way they are. They are cut from the same cloth. Nothing ever changes.

   B. I live my life with integrity and forgiveness. I set a good example for others.

3. I lived in poverty as a child.

    A. My life was scarred by early living conditions. I'll never have anything better. What's good enough is...well... good enough.

    B. I work hard to provide for my family to assure our financial future.

4. I have been diagnosed with cancer.

    A. I am going to die. So why bother with anything?

    B. I am going to follow my doctor's plan of treatment and do all that I can to feel good about myself.

The first response in each of these four examples is a negative one. It exemplifies the thinking of a person who sees herself as a victim. She feels no motivation to change her circumstance and improve her future because she blames her past or something that is outside of her control.

The second responses demonstrate how a positive outlook on life can be a harbinger of a hopeful future. This person takes responsibility for her life without blaming others. Which person are you? How you deal with your past will determine how you approach your future.

Now let's change our pessimistic ***What ifs*** to optimistic ***What ifs***?

For example: What if my spouse/partner becomes terminally ill?

1. Could be changed to: What if my spouse/partner and I still have 20 more wonderful, healthy years to enjoy?

How would you personally change the gloomy ***What Ifs*** below to present an idealistic viewpoint?

1. What if it rains when I go to the beach?

______________________________________________

2. What if no one likes the menu at my dinner party? __________

______________________________________________

3. What if my Social Security check arrives too late to pay off my charge accounts? ______________________________

4. What if no one wants to publish the book I've been working on for three years?______________________________

______________________________________________

Performing exercises like this one is first-rate practice for changing internal frowns into promising thoughts of the future.

That is one of the ways to overcome the ***What If*** syndrome: practice. Practice does not make perfect, but it can make your new thinking into a better and healthier habit. And once a certain way of thinking becomes a habit, it becomes automatic. If you keep telling yourself that things will not turn out well, you will believe it. Even if events are positive, your mind will focus on the one minuscule part that could be interpreted as not being perfect. Remember, your perception is your reality!

Turn that thinking around. Repeat over and over any of the following sentences that currently are not automatic for you.

1. I am a good person. Good things will happen in my life.

2. I am an intelligent person who is able to think, plan and make courageous decisions that are right for me.

3. I am a strong person. I can handle whatever turn my life takes.

4. I have a valuable support system. Friends and family will help me through the rough times and will celebrate the good times with me.

5. My belief in a Higher Power is undeniable. Faith will accompany me through the uphill times and will not allow me to coast too quickly downhill during the easy times.

Make one or more of those statements your mantra – a thought that you chant to yourself every day. Make it part of the positive thinking that will become a permanent aspect of your life. Have faith in the outcome.

Faith. That is one word to remember when you want to ward off the ***What Ifs***. List a few other words that you think of when you hear the word *faith*.

________________________________________

________________________________________

You might have included: confidence, trust, reliance, assurance, conviction, belief. Each person's point of reference will determine the response. There are no wrong answers.

People sometimes view faith only as an attribute of religion. Faith in a Higher Power is not so much a religion as it is a belief. Faith can also mean confidence in yourself to make choices that are right for your life. Wherever your faith lies and whatever assurance it gives you does not matter as much as the fact that you have faith. Faith will enable you to overcome the ***What Ifs***.

Where we focus our attention is where our energy goes. In a song from days gone by, listeners are advised to accentuate the positive and eliminate the negative. It is not possible to eliminate everything that is harmful, depressing, and disheartening around us. However, it is feasible to change our perspective.

To walk around with a silly grin on our faces is to invite scorn and disbelief from others. However, living our lives with an upbeat point of view will usually ensure a constructive reaction from others. And when we surround ourselves with helpful, engaging people, our lives are less likely to incur the ***If Only I Had***s.

Abraham Lincoln declared that most folks are about as happy as they make up their minds to be. Does it mean that nothing will ever go wrong for us? No. It simply means we make our own life story from what happens to us, by us, for us, and around us. Living life with a positive attitude produces more happiness than shrouding ourselves in negativity, waiting for something to go wrong.

**What if** the light at the end of the tunnel is NOT a train coming toward you? Then, do not stand on the tracks waiting for one. Instead - see the light of faith leading you out of the darkness. CELEBRATE!

**Dedication to My Daughter, Kim**

Of all the things in my life for which I am thankful, you hold a special place in my heart. You were my first child. I was young, but still realized what a gift I had been given. We grew up together – each in our own way. And now we share even more: respect, friendship, trust and faith. May you experience the incredible joys that I have known as a mother as you watch your own daughter become a young lady. And always let the ***What Ifs*** bring happiness into your life!

*Notes:*

# ABOUT THE AUTHOR

## ANISE KEY BROWN

Anise Key Brown brings more than 20 years of professional experience in human development, transformation and community empowerment. She possesses a Bachelor's degree in Sociology and has received two Master Degrees; one from the State University of New York at Albany and the other from Miami University in Oxford, Ohio. She has pursued post-graduate studies at Howard University in Washington, D.C. and has obtained certifications in Management from the American Management Association. She has also studied at the John F. Kennedy School of Government at Harvard University. She is a certified ESOL (English for Speakers of Other Languages) instructor and an Adult Literacy Tutor.She has received certification as a Life Coach from the Empowerment Institute in Rhinebeck, New York.

Mrs. Brown has worked for the Los Angeles Department of Human Services and tenured as an Assistant Professor for a private University in North Carolina. Her most recent experiences include program development work for an international women's organization in Washington, D.C. where she lobbied on Capitol Hill for issues related to the well-being and empowerment of women from a global perspective. She is the founder of ANISE, Inc. (**A**nise **N**ewton **I**nstitute for **S**elf **E**mpowerment) which is an organization designed to help women realize their full potential in life. She currently serves as the Director of a local government agency in Silver Spring, Maryland.

As a civic activist, Mrs. Brown has held memberships and leadership positions in a number of organizations including the local chapter of the NAACP, the League of Women Voters, the National Political Congress of Black Women, the National Association of Female Executives and Women in Public Policy among others.

Considering herself to be a world traveler, Mrs. Brown's most recent ventures include an excursion to the People's Republic of China and a journey to the country of South Africa. Mrs. Brown currently resides in the suburbs of Maryland with her husband of 25 years, who is a local attorney. She is also the mother of two college-aged sons.

*Contact:*
Anise Key Brown
P.O. Box 524
Brookeville, Maryland 20833
(301) 682-6494
anise1@verizon.net

THREE

# THE SECOND HALF OF LIFE: MAKING THE DECISION TO RETIRE

**By Anise Key Brown**

It's scary! More frightening than any decision I have ever made; more scary than making the decision to get married or even have children. As a matter of fact, these were easy decisions compared to making the decision to retire. You see, I worked for forty years and was eagerly looking forward to receiving my forty acres and a mule and tiptoeing through the tulips of retirement freedom. I could not wait until I was eligible. Every time someone younger than 60 years of age said that they were retired, I turned light green with sweet envy. When I met a lady who told me that she had recently retired, I immediately invited her to lunch so that I could get all the details as to how to do this retirement thing right. I was eagerly looking forward to all the do's and don'ts of retirement planning. Boy! Was I ever so disappointed when she announced to my chagrin that she was back in the market looking for a JOB! Why retire and then go back to work, I wondered? Is it financial or is it sheer boredom? I simply did not want to stop one job only to start another unless there was some deep down passion to do so. I wanted my retirement to offer the ultimate choice of not having to return to work.

You see, my mother retired at age 62 after single-handedly raising five children without any government assistance. She had worked all her life having started at two years of age in my grandfather's cotton fields. But it was this steady accumulation of twenty years of dedicated service as a nurse in the intensive care unit of a large hospital that allowed her to garner some kind of pension and call it a day.

I thought that I was going to best her by 10 years by retiring at age 52 with a steady accruement of 18 years. I had a career that granted retirement eligibility for its employees at age 50 and 15 years of continuous service. I began to count the days and months when the magic hour would arrive. And when it arrived, I ran over to human resources to get my "golden parachute" in the form of a review of my retirement package. Was I ever shocked! (Floored, quite frankly.) I would get paid one third of my current salary and since I was accustomed to the other two thirds, I did not consider that this would be quite enough.

It would be early retirement because I did not quite have the full age and number of years and therefore the penalty, it had been whispered, would be quite severe. But I did not care. I was not about to allow a penalty to keep me from enjoying a respite from the 9 to

5, many weeknights and too many weekends. However, after visiting with human resources the reality set in. The penalty was more crippling than I had imagined and I could not see myself giving away that much money by retiring too soon. So, when the magic moment finally arrived, I hesitated. I simply was not ready. Besides, I told myself, my job wasn't bad. I had a lot to be grateful for and abundant blessings that people look for in a satisfying career. I had good pay, flexibility, benefits, a supportive staff, and a new boss that I simply admired. So I decided to settle in. I reflected on a quote from the book, *Get A Life-You Don't Need a Million to Retire* that stated, "No practical retirement plan will work if your heart is not a believer." And this was precisely how I was feeling. So, I started coming up with new ideas to reinvent my work plan and myself. I created new initiatives and implemented some exciting new projects. However, before long I was bored. Infused with my new ideas and energy were the same old songs that have long been played as a part of routine work. I did not feel like dancing to those tunes anymore. I wanted a new song, and what better time to do so than now. But still the lingering fact of one third of my salary as take home pay would not go away. On top of all that, the economic downturn of the nation's economy was becoming quite dismal. I did not want to add a shrinking salary to the already shrinking dollar.

As these doubts and fears mounted, the reality was that the state of the economy was getting worse. Gas and food prices were increasing at an alarming rate and unemployment statistics were at an all time high. Even in a normally safe environment of government work, the impact was being felt. Reductions in force and early retirement incentives became a normal part of reducing the budget deficit caused by a recessive economy. Since I did not qualify for early retirement, I began to ask myself, "Who in their right mind would walk away from a job in this kind of negative economic downturn?" As a responsible, sensible and logical person, the thoughts kept creeping up. And I answered, "Not you, certainly not you." It seemed everywhere I turned the media was telling me (and all the other baby boomers) that we had to have millions of dollars to retire. One full-size ad displayed in a national newspaper focused on the need to get ready for retirement investing. However, they only wanted to talk to people who had at least $500,000 to get started. My goodness, that's a half million dollars!

This ad and more like it certainly did not help, and I took on a scared and scarce mentality. When I came into contact with other women who boldly declared their freedom from the daily commutes, supervision of others, long boring meetings and other accouterments of work life, I wanted to congratulate them and ask, "Wow, how did you do it?" When a co-worker declared that she was going to retire in one year and ten months, I had the impression that she was very confident about her decision and knew exactly what she wanted to do. My thought was, "Why can't I get to that place?"

So I started to regroup. Nothing empowers a person more than knowledge. I began to do my research and turned a blind eye and deaf ear to scare tactics and thoughts. Even though my career had been promising, I had to acknowledge and recognize that deep down inside it was time for a change. It was time for me to share my talents, skills and services with the rest of the world. And so I began to prepare to cross the bridge from full-time career to full-time retirement (and thus the second half of my life). I asked myself, what are the main factors that I would need to consider and have answers to as I moved gracefully into the retirement arena? I narrowed it down to three main questions:

1. *What do I want to do with the rest of my life?*

2. *What kind of financial situation would I want to have in place to have a comfortable and worry-free retirement?*

3. *What kind of support network do I need to have in place to sustain me during my freedom years?*

It doesn't matter whether we call it the second phase of life, the last third, the afternoon of our life (as coined by spiritual guru Dr. Wayne Dyer), middle age, empty nest syndrome, or the fertile void, as defined by Ilana Rubenfied, which is a time when your old ways do not work or you don't have new ways of coping. The question still remains, **what do I want to do with the rest of my life?** Very few of us know exactly how we want to spend the second half of our lives. And for many, it creates an uncomfortable state of anxiety, confusion and uncertainty. One of the ways to cope with these questions is to first realize that these can be some of the best years of our lives. Never before have older baby boomer women enjoyed so much opportunity to continue our mental, emotional and spiritual growth. We're living longer, healthier, more productive lives, and though we may no longer be as young in body, many of us quite frankly are much younger in spirit and attitude than that of our more youthful selves. We know that we have earned the right to dance to a different drummer, make our own decisions, fulfill our forgotten dreams, voice our truth, and enthusiastically embrace all of the pain, joy, trials and triumphs that life has to offer.

As an individual who has worked all her life, I just couldn't wake up one day and have nothing to do. I have always been active and involved, and the "rocking chair" theory has never been my cup of tea. For me, I had already achieved another goal of mine and that was to start a non-profit foundation. However, it was lying dormant with very little activity, except to support similar organizations whose mission was to empower women. Not having to go to work everyday would provide me with the opportunity to work with the foundation full time. I have always loved politics, and the opportunity to become involved rather than just write checks to the candidate of my choice got me all excited again. I could travel not just to foreign and exotic lands, but also to visit my elderly relatives and spend some valuable and cherished moments with them.

So, the question begs. What do you really want to do with the rest of your life? Do you want adventure and exploration? Do you want to travel, go back to school, start a new business, leave a marriage, find a new love, relocate perhaps to a different city, state or country? Things have changed for the better for women, and we have infinite opportunities to live a different and more fulfilling kind of life; to actually do things that we once only dreamed of. These are tough questions that must be answered in order to make the most of the rest of our lives.

The other piece of the puzzle, as we contemplate the decision to retire, is to **ask about our financial status and how much money we need to comfortably retire into a secure financial future**. Even though I have been married for more than twenty-five years, I have always been financially independent to a certain degree. I started working a real job at the age of 13 and had to get a "worker's permit" from the state labor department in order to begin gainful employment. I felt like I was on my way to financial freedom forever. Furthermore, my mother had taught me well the adage, "God bless the child that's got it own", so I wanted to make sure that when I retired I was truly able to take care of myself. Every woman who has had the honor and privilege of earning her own money is familiar with and quite afraid of the "bag lady syndrome". No one wants to become so destitute that you imagine yourself being weighed down by layers of soiled clothing, pushing around a grocery cart and sleeping under a bridge. According to most recent studies, women still only earn 77 cents for every dollar that a man makes. Older women especially are three times as likely to be poor as men. Baby boomer women fear aging more than older men and have every reason to worry about their economic futures. We normally outlive men, and a major cause of poverty is the loss of a spouse. As we become older, we need to ensure that we have adequate income as we age, which means being accountable for planning our financial future, whether we are married or single. Whether we consult with a financial planner, accountant, bank officer, read how-to-books, or attend financial management workshops for women, it is important that we employ every opportunity to ensure our comfort and security before it's too late.

The challenge is certainly not going to be easy. It appeared that I chose the worse time ever to start seriously contemplating retirement. The decline of the dollar and the fears of recession were looming large. With the cost of living going up and the rate of inflation going out the window, the fear factor continued to resonate in my mind. I began to ask myself again, could I afford to retire? As soon as I thought that I could focus my financial attention on a real retirement savings plan, some unexpected demand would come along requiring expenditures that I had not planned for. Even though I consider myself to be fiscally conservative, I did not want to live my latter years as a cheapskate and defer all forms of luxury. And, I certainly did not want to have to look for a job every time I needed a little extra cash. In other words, I wanted to be able to afford to retire.

However, recent statistics reveal that only 18% of retirement age Americans are financially ready to retire. This was the lowest estimate in over 18 years, down from 27% in 2006. Financial considerations and restraints are two of the core reasons that many women continue to work, even when they desire to retire. Nevertheless, we can lessen the financial chains that bind us to a 9 to 5 job if we begin to put some things in place. I accepted that I would have to watch the dollars more and be less flexible in my spending. **First,** we should always take advantage of any retirement benefit or matching program that our company offers, and we should match this contribution at its maximum, such as the 401 plans. Those of you are self-employed should, of course, engage in the types of programs, such as Keoghs, that are available. The traditional IRA (Individual Retirement Account) and the Roth IRA cannot be overlooked as major retirement savings plans for our future. They are all affordable, and it encourages us to save towards retirement on a consistent basis. There are a number of financial planning resources such as websites, books and seminars that we can take advantage of, and it's never too late to start. The **second** thing that we can do is to engage in another stream of income. This can be some other way that we can earn additional income on a consistent basis. It can include turning a hobby into a profit-making engine, getting paid for outside consulting work, or speaking engagements. There are as many ways to obtain additional income as there is income. For me, I chose to invest in real estate in order to obtain properties for rental income. This also provided me with an opportunity to give back to the community by offering affordable housing. This supplement will add to my pension before I am eligible to receive social security and well after. Even though I did not want the headaches that come with being a landlord, the monthly income far outweighs the headaches that come with this venture. I also decided to hire property managers to assist with some of the responsibilities that come with real estate management and investment. All of the profits from these properties go towards my retirement savings plan.

**Third,** in order for women to save adequately for our freedom years, we have to say no. Of course, we would like to be able to fund our kids' college education and our retirement, but if it boils down to savings for retirement or college, many financial experts advise you to save for retirement. Our children can always get loans or scholarships to fund their college years, but we cannot get a loan or scholarship to fund our retirement.

**Fourth,** one of the best pieces of advice that I received regarding managing my finances towards retirement was to figure out how much money I would be receiving and then start narrowing down and adjusting my expenses and life style to meet that amount. If you find that you need more than the adjusted amount, then you should put some mechanism in place for that contingency, such as a part-time job or some other profit-making venture. Current predictions state that we will need 70% to 80% of our highest earning years to be able to comfortably retire. Whether you think you need more or less, there are a number of vehicles on line that can help to determine how much we will need to live comfortably in our dream years. We need to start getting rid of debt, downsizing our expenses, and paying off our credit cards. I do not believe that we need to live a life of total frugality in our younger years and defer any luxury now for the future. There can, however, be a happy medium so that we can realistically enjoy both.

And **last,** as we make the tough decision to walk away from the world of work, **we must create a social network and support system that will help to sustain us** as we move towards a different world called retirement. We should not, however, overwhelm ourselves with a million and one committees to sit on. If we choose to volunteer, it should be with an organization that we feel passionate about and thoroughly enjoy being involved in. As a civic activist, I think it 's important that we share our time and resources with the people and community that we live in. Service to people and our country is one of the most honorable things that we can do. However, often when we retire, we think that we have all the time in the world and find ourselves overworked. I've known people who became busier in their retirement years than they were when they were actually working. If that truly makes you happy, then by all means enjoy it; but if not, find a balance. And of course, the relationships with family and friends should be strengthened and enhanced to maintain a level of love and camaraderie.

In conclusion, retirement is a new world, but it can be a brave new world. As Eckhart Tolle says in his new bestseller, *A New Earth—Awakening to Your Life's Purpose,* "We evolve or we die." Change is sometimes painful, but it can also be healing. One thing that we know for sure is that it is inevitable. We know that the older we get, the more difficult change becomes, and we settle for the status quo, for the familiar, the security of that which we know. Retirement represents enormous change for many. However, change can be invigorating, enlightening, refreshing and exciting. In order to make an omelet, you must break an egg. How we propose to embrace change plays an important role in whether we laugh or cry, suffer pain or experience joy. As we get older, wiser and better (and yes, more beautiful) in deciding what we do with the rest of our lives as it relates to the concept of retirement, we must embrace change for the best that it will bring out in us. We can take control over our own lives and decide how we want to design the second half of our life. Envision the best. Live and be grateful every day for the gift of life. We should be committed to making the second half of our lives the model for other young women to aspire.

We should leave a legacy that shows what the best of life looks like in our latter years. Whether you decide to retire from the workplace now or wait a little longer, you can decide to retire from at least the negative attitudes and old thoughts that keep us stuck in a rut and not living our very best. Making the decision to retire is not an easy one, but once you make it, you should never look back. Enjoy every minute and finally live your heart's desire. Happy Retirement!

**Recommended Reading:**

*You Can Do It! The Boomer's Guide to a Great Retirement* by Jonathan D. Pond

*It's Only Too Late If You Don't Start Now—How to Create the Second Half of Your Life At Any Age* by Barbara Sher

*Reinventing the Rest of Our Lives—Women In Second Adulthood* by Suzanne Braun Levine

*Leap! What Will We Do With the Rest of Our Lives? Reflections from the Boomer Generation* by Sara Davidson

*Get a Life! You Don't Need a Million to Retire* by Ralph Warner

# ABOUT THE AUTHOR

## Cathy Holloway Hill

Cathy Holloway Hill is the proud owner of C. Holloway Hill Enterprises, a personal and professional career consulting company in Jeffersonville, Indiana. Her company's mission is to devise strategies that promote performance excellence and empower others to achieve their personal and professional best. Cathy provides her clients with the tools and knowledge to take action, discover potential, embrace change, and unleash their brilliance.

In addition to her entrepreneur role, Cathy is also a Network Engineering Manager for Brown-Forman Corporation in Louisville, Kentucky. In this role, Cathy is responsible for infrastructure projects, daily operations, and maintenance of the company's multi-million dollar global network infrastructure (voice, video, data, internet). Her professional experience in the male-dominated technology industry affords her the ability to speak from the heart on many topics related to career and life success. She has been recognized with numerous awards for outstanding leadership. She is a member of PWN, National Association of Women Writers, National Speakers Association, and National Association of Female Executives. Cathy is certified in Diversity Training, Professional Speaking, and Customer Service.

For two consecutive years, Cathy was recognized as the Black Achiever of the Year within the Community. This award recognizes African-American professionals for their career accomplishments and commitment to mentoring youth. She has also been recognized in the Who's Who Kentucky, Center for Leadership Development, and many other mentoring programs.

Cathy has a B.S. in Computer Science from Bellarmine University, Louisville, Kentucky. She began her career at IBM Corporation and has received numerous performance awards at both IBM and Brown-Forman Corporation.

Cathy's motto is; ***"Life is not about finding yourself, it's about creating yourself"***. She is working on her first book for women entitled "*Brilliant Women, Brilliant Careers*".


*Contact:*

Telephone: 502-387-7701

P. O. Box 1513

Jeffersonville, Indiana 47131

Email: cathy@chollowayhill.com

Website: www.chollowayhill.com

## FOUR

# JUST DO IT! OVERCOMING PROCRASTINATION

**By Cathy Holloway Hill**

There is one word that can bring feelings of anxiety and stress, causing you to put off saying it aloud. The dreaded word is procrastination. It is described as delaying, dilly-dallying, excuse making, postponement, delaying action, and even the dreaded word that we all hate to admit - laziness. We have all been guilty of procrastinating at one time or another in our lives, but there are some women who chronically and habitually put off what they need to do. Always delaying what we need to do NOW has consequences, both mentally and physically. We may not only feel stress, but also a sense of laziness and worthlessness. There are some women who live by the motto, "Why do today what I can put off 'til tomorrow?" The accumulating effects of this mindset can be very damaging to self, and also provides others with a sense of undependability.

A woman should be known for her word. If committing to something, she should follow through.

Procrastination comes down to two things – poor planning and poor time management. The good news is that both of these skills can be learned and mastered. How many times have you said, "I've got plenty of time to do that; it's not due until next week." As next week approaches, you scramble around at the last minute and ultimately suffer the consequences. (Even perpetual tardiness qualifies as procrastination.) Procrastination is an automatic habitual process that leads to needless postponement. It is automatic, and it happens seamlessly time and time again.

**Exercise:**

**Are you a procrastinator?** Review the following and ask yourself these questions:

- When you face an unpleasant or boring task (or have doubts about your abilities), you substitute a more pleasant, easier, lower-priority task.
- When you feel you can't begin a task because you don't have time to complete it, you avoid it altogether.
- You look for band-aids to "stop the bleeding", instead of long-term solutions.
- You make avoidable mistakes that cause time-consuming re-work.
- You wander aimlessly from one project to another.
- You say "yes" to any request with no regard to your existing busy schedule.
- You feel easily distracted and overwhelmed.
- You lack energy to complete even the smallest jobs/tasks.

**Procrastinator Styles**

Following are five procrastination behavioral styles that describe why and how we end up in the perpetual cycle over and over again:

- **Self-Doubt:** These people feel there are strict standards about how things should be done and they have a tremendous fear of failure. They constantly second-guess themselves and, therefore, delay taking action.

- **Discomfort-Dodging:** This group avoids activities that cause them discomfort, distress or anxiety. Unfortunately, what they fail to realize is that the act of dodging the task doesn't make it go away; therefore, tension builds due to the avoidance.

- **Driven by Guilt:** These people feel guilt over uncompleted tasks, but rather than correct the original lack of action, they continue to delay taking action, which continues a constant cycle of guilt. They live with this guilt, attempt to do the project, and then put it off again. Hence, more guilt.

- **Habitual (or Learned Behavior):** The habitual offender has procrastinated so many times it becomes an ingrained response. This person no longer thinks about why they do it; they feel it's just a part of their nature. They have learned the behavior from their environment (a parent or a spouse/partner), and it becomes an automatic response to say, "I'll do it later." Oftentimes, the habitual procrastinator is in denial of their behavior because their response to completing tasks is on autopilot, and they shrug it off as a character flaw.

- **Poor Time Management:** This group simply fails to prioritize. In their busy world, there are so many things to do that they reach a point when they can't determine which task is important. They may also feel that the needs of others are more important than their own. Many working mothers tend to fall into this category of procrastinators, as they place family and employers' needs ahead of their own. They put off taking care of themselves.

Once you recognize your style of procrastination, you can take steps to stop it. Additionally, understanding the effects is tremendous incentive to commit to putting the steps in place to overcome this daunting way of life.

**The Effects of Procrastination**

One of the most obvious effects of procrastination is the failure to reap the rewards that would come from taking action. Although you know what you want and how to get it, you still need to take action. It is at this point that the procrastination sets in. Because the results you desire are often bigger and better than what you currently have, you must step outside your comfort zone to get it. You may have to take actions to which your unconscious mind reacts by "protecting" you against that which is uncomfortable or unknown. Although the short-term effects of procrastination might appear as "positive", the long-term effects are most often negative.

Through your actions and your behavior, you create your life, which may be either positive or negative because actions (or lack thereof) lead to consequences. It not just your actions, but also your failure to take action that will have a greater effect on the rewards you reap from life. From this point of view, the effects of procrastination are not just a direct, but also an indirect loss of rewards. However, taking positive action opens you up to new opportunities.

The following is a categorized list of the negative effects procrastination can have on your life.

**Exercise: Negative Effects of Procrastination**

Check off those that apply to you.

1. Physical

   - Tension headaches
   - Increased blood pressure
   - Sleep disturbances
   - Fatigue
   - Agitation and restlessness
   - Intestinal disturbances
   - Muscle aches

2. Mental/Cognitive

   - Self-criticizing & low self-esteem
   - Obsessive thoughts
   - Rebelliousness
   - Perfectionism

3. Emotional

   - Frustration
   - Irritability

- Feelings of guilt
- Fear and anxiety
- Worry
- Tearfulness
- Anger
- Depression – sense of helplessness
- Envy of others who get things done

4. Work/Career

   - Reduced contribution to teamwork
   - Increased likelihood of mistakes, accidents, outbursts and burn-out
   - Missed career opportunities
   - Reduction in productivity

5. Personal Relationships

   - Nagging and frustration
   - Blaming and accusations
   - Isolation due to excessive worry over uncompleted tasks
   - Negative effect on family members

6. Quality of Life

   - Diminished creativity

- Sense of spiritual emptiness
- Loss of perception
- No sense of accomplishment
- Reduced ability to visualize a positive future
- Overwhelming sense of "time is passing too quickly and life is passing me by"
- Lack of personal growth

## Tips to Overcome Procrastination

New habits will be needed, and this takes time, commitment, and discipline. Making the decision to overcome procrastination will be less daunting if you keep the end result in mind, and realize that you will not only improve your time management, but you will also enhance your overall quality of life. The rewards and benefits are endless.

## 11 Steps for Overcoming Procrastination

1. **Only focus on the essential.** You may be so overwhelmed with tasks that you don't know where to begin. Take a few minutes and list your projects and tasks. Look over the list and decide which tasks are essential, and which will lead to the most benefit and have the most impact on your life. Put a star next to the essential projects and tasks. Now, look at the rest and determine what can be eliminated or delegated. Clear the deck for the essential tasks, so you'll actually have time to do them. And therein lies the key to this step: if you focus on the benefits, instead of the difficulties of a task, you will be motivated to get it done. Motivation is the key.

2. **Create accountability**. We may feel guilty procrastinating, but if we're the only one aware of the procrastination, it doesn't hurt us much. However, most of us hate to look bad in the eyes of others. We want others to think highly of us – it's human nature. So take advantage of that fact, and leverage it.

   Here's how: for every essential project and task on your list (see Step 1), assign someone to whom you can report your progress. Email a colleague or trusted friend and commit to providing them with a projected completion date for your project. The more people you have who are expecting you to complete a project, the more likely you are to finish the task. Create accountability and you'll get it done.

3. **Take baby steps**. Taking on an overwhelming task or project can stop us in our tracks. Imagine looking up at a mountain and deciding whether you're going to climb it today or if you're going to go to the store to buy some groceries instead. You'll go to the store each and every time. So instead of looking at the mountain, look only at the next signpost up the road. When you focus in this manner, it is achievable.

4. **Set deadlines**. This is where refocusing your approach with time management begins. Without deadlines it is difficult to get anything done. Deadlines give a sense of urgency that gets you working and moving.

5. **Create a reminder system**. There is a tremendous amount of technology available to set up reminders – cell phones, email, PDA's, etc. If you don't own one of these devices, get one. They are

very affordable and helpful while travelling, and they can be carried either in your purse or in your car. The benefits are immeasurable.

6. **Have realistic expectations.** Do you have unrealistic expectations? If you feel the need to be perfect, you will never get started. If you are painting a room, you may find yourself noticing an imperfection. But remember, nothing is perfect.

   Nothing is perfect. Lower your expectations and be satisfied with the implementation. Creativity is allowing yourself to make mistakes. You can revise, repaint, reread, rewrite, refinish and reconstruct.

7. **Keep it interesting.** Do you find the project boring? How can you propel yourself into action when you find a project empty and unrewarding? Don't vent, re-invent! Find a way to stimulate yourself, bringing enthusiasm to your task. You have a powerful imagination at your disposal! Use your creativity, your sense of humor, and your positive thoughts to infuse your task with creativity and fun. If you are working on a boring project, turn up the music!

8. **Visualize a positive outcome.** Use positive visualization techniques to ensure that you complete your task. See yourself finishing the task at hand successfully. Imagine all the details, even the problems and glitches. Rehearse the scene in your mind often. See yourself working it all out. Then take a bow and hear the resounding applause. Visualize your accomplishment, and by all means, reward yourself upon completion!

9. **Small rewards.** Rewards - we all love them. On a weekly basis, ask yourself, "What have I accomplished this week that is deserving of a special reward?" Pamper yourself. You deserve it.

10. **Don't sweat the small stuff.** Make sure to eliminate the small stressors in your life to minimize tension, unpleasantness and distraction. Those small stressors add up. Avoid stimulants like caffeine, nicotine, alcohol, processed white foods and sugars, which will physically stress your body and, therefore, your mind. Get adequate sleep. The better you treat your body and mind, the more energy you will have to complete your projects and not put them off until tomorrow.

11. **Learn to relax.** Whether it's listening to music or meditating, relaxation is essential in overcoming procrastination. You will encounter obstacles, and there will be times when you may want to give up and fall back into your old habits. Find a calm inner place within your spirit to meditate and reflect. This inner peace will allow you to become calmer, and not let life (and projects) overwhelm you.

Armed with a better understanding of procrastination, and how to reduce its influence on your life, the possibilities and rewards are endless for experiencing peace-of-mind and greater personal self-satisfaction through ending habits on procrastination. Keep working toward your goal. If you stay focused and remain committed to accomplishing your goals and not waiting until tomorrow to accomplish them, the rewards you gain from this new behavior will lead to enhanced physical, mental, and emotional well being. You have everything to gain. So what are you waiting for? Just do it!

**Recommended Readings:**

*The Now Habit* by Neil Fiore, PhD

*Self-Discipline in 10 Days: How to Go From Thinking to Doing* by Theodore Bryant

*Eat That Frog! 21 Great Ways to Stop Procrastinating* by Brian Tracy

# ABOUT THE AUTHOR

## Ruby M. Ashley, MBA

Ms. Ruby Ashley, is the Chief Executive Officer of Ruby Ashley & Associates. She is a leader in personal and professional development, specializing in the delivery of workshops, seminars, training programs and assessments. Her workshops and training programs are highly interactive and stimulating, with a focus on improving employee performance. She firmly believes that as long as individuals are willing to learn, change, and grow, they will always reach high levels of achievement.

Ms. Ashley is an accomplished motivational keynote speaker, facilitator, trainer, and consultant, Ms. Ashley has more than 29 years of experience in the corporate environment. As a Certified Customer Service Trainer, she delivers an outstanding Customer Service Excellence program.

Some of her other training programs include the topics of Personal and Professional Development, Women Issues, Self-Esteem, Leadership Development, Strategic Planning, Road Map to Retirement, and Team Building. The teen topics she addresses include: Leadership, Save Our Youth, and Teen Image.

Ms. Ashley earned a Bachelor of Science and Master Degree in Business from Brenau University in Gainesville, GA. She is a member of The Professional Woman Network (Advisory Board), American Business Woman Association, and Toastmasters International.

Ruby Ashley is also co-author of Becoming the Professional Woman, Self-Esteem & Empowerment for Women, The Young Woman Guide for Personal Success, Beyond The Body! Developing Inner Beauty, Women As Leaders: Strategies For Empowerment & Communication, The Christian Woman Guide For Personal Success, Overcoming The Superwoman Syndrome, and Emotional Wellness For Women Volume I, in the PWN Library.

Ms. Ashley is available to conduct seminars and workshops on a local, national, and international basis.

*Contact:*
Ruby Ashley & Associates
rbyash@aol.com
www.protrain.net
704-719-9637

## FIVE

# TAKE A RISK: FEEL THE FEAR BUT DO IT ANYWAY!

**By Ruby Ashley**

The *Merriam-Webster online dictionary* defines fear as "an unpleasant and often strong emotion caused by the anticipation or awareness of danger." Sometimes the threat of peril is real, while at other times it is only a perceived menace made worse by our imaginations. In either case, fear can cause us to feel uncomfortable, isolated, discouraged, and powerless. These feelings seem especially prevalent as we get older. Often, we become comfortable in our daily routines and regular habits, so much so that when we have to make a change, we feel afraid. The unknown is always a little scary – just because we don't know what to expect – good or bad, and unfortunately, most of us often fear the worse rather than hope for the best.

While fear is often associated with negativity, it is actually a very necessary emotion that can often be quite beneficial. Fear helps people recognize and respond to dangerous situations. Just think back to our ancestors. How would they have survived without feeling the fear associated with life-threatening encounters? If they didn't feel afraid, they would just have been oblivious to the many dangers around them and would probably now be extinct. Fear is an innate part of every individual. As such, we should recognize it as a natural part of life. The real key to effectively dealing with your fear is taking action. Think about a caveman being threatened by a wild animal. If that caveman takes action by running, climbing a tree, or hiding to escape from this dangerous situation, he is much more likely to survive. However, if he chooses to do nothing, then he could be seriously injured or killed by the predator. Fear, then, is really a call to action. It is a signal that you need to do something.

Unfortunately, many of us are paralyzed by our fears. Instead of recognizing this opportunity to take action, we feel the fear and then ignore it. Sometimes we make excuses for our inaction by saying things like: "I'm too old to change" or "I can't start over now" or "That's better left for young people." This negative self-talk is defeating. By affirming that you don't believe you can do something – for whatever reason – your age, your health, your physical abilities – you are making excuses and limiting yourself. Buying into the idea that you are too old to do something or that it is too late to start something new is giving up on yourself. Take Grandma Moses, for example. She took up painting when she was in her seventies because her arthritis prevented her from continuing to do embroidery. In this case, she didn't let her physical limitation stop her creativity. She just expressed it in another way. Lucky for us that she did because now we have some remarkable paintings that we would not otherwise have if she had simply decided to give up and not try something new.

**Fear Disorders**

Fears come in many shapes and sizes. In fact, according to the National Institute of Mental Health, 19 million people in the United States alone suffer from mental illnesses that involve irrational fear responses. These disorders include generalized anxiety disorder, panic disorder and post-traumatic stress disorder. Some of the more common types of fear are:

**Athazagoraphobia** – fear of being forgotten or ignored
**Claustrophobia** – fear of confined spaces
**Atychiphobia, Kakorrhaphiophobia** – fear of failure
**Metathesiophobia** – fear of changes
**Acrophobia** – fear of heights
**Phobophobia** – fear of being afraid
**Necrophobia** – fear of death

**Fear is Related to a Number of Emotional States**

There are several different types of fear that stop people from taking action to pursue their dreams. Some of these fears include fear of rejection, fear of failure, and fear of change.

**Fear of Rejection**

Have you ever wanted to pursue a dream, but you were afraid of what others would say about it? In the past, have well-meaning people discouraged you from going after things you wanted to achieve by telling you all the reasons why what you wanted to do wouldn't work? You should never let others' negativity instill fear in you. Just because they think they are being realistic and helpful doesn't mean they are right. You can't let the fear of rejection stop you; otherwise, you will never try to do anything you care about doing.

Did you know that statistics say that 10% of people will never like you? So, it's just not possible to please everyone and make them happy. In fact, we have all been rejected at some point in our lives, and I think we can all agree that it is a very negative experience. Emotions and character traits associated with rejection include embarrassment, low self-esteem, poor self-image, and an inferiority complex. However, like fear, rejection should be faced head on. You shouldn't let your imagination run wild with negative thoughts about yourself. If you feel embarrassed, admit it; hold your head up and learn from the experience. Realize that it may make you a better person in the long run.

When was the last time you felt rejected? ______________________

______________________________________________

How did this make you feel?______________________________

______________________________________________

When you overcame the rejection, how did you feel? ____________

______________________________________________

You have to take action in order to achieve what you want from life. Now is the time to begin pursuing a dream that you've had on hold for quite a while. Don't let the fear of rejection hold you back. Just realize that there will be people who will try to discourage you by criticizing what you are trying to accomplish.

It is important to understand that these people may feel the way they do because they are afraid you will succeed. Perhaps they are jealous that you have the guts to do something they won't – to try something new. While some will be genuinely happy for you, others may only be pretending to be supportive, and others will never want you to succeed. In the event that nobody you know has anything positive to say about your endeavor, and you have to stand alone, stand, never giving up on pursuing your goal. This is your dream, so take ownership of it. Take the risk! Decide how you are going to deal with any negativity you might experience, and then proceed in pursuing your goal. It's your dream or vision; you don't need someone else's approval to become a better person.

If you find that the criticism of others is very difficult to overcome, consider not sharing with other people what you are doing. Wait until you have already succeeded and accomplished your goal. After all, success is hard to argue with! If you can't keep what you are doing to yourself, for whatever reason, then simply ignore the naysayers. Have enough confidence in yourself to believe that what you are doing is important. Think about what this accomplishment will mean to you and stay focused on it, realizing that all you can do is try to succeed in turning your dreams into realities. Then you can be happy in knowing that you have not only helped yourself, but also possibly helped someone else.

**Fear of Failure**

As long as you are living, you have unlimited opportunities to do anything you want to do. The only limitations you have are the ones you impose on yourself. Life is full of possibilities. You just have to recognize what they are and then be brave enough to risk failing. And if you think about it, failure really isn't so bad. I'm sure you can think of many instances in your life when you failed at something. It didn't kill you, did it? In fact, it may have been as a result of your failure that something better happened that wouldn't have otherwise happened if you had succeeded. For example, let's say you didn't get into the college you wanted and ended up going to a different school. But as a result of going to the other school, you met your spouse. You would have never met this person if you had gotten into the college you had wanted to go to in the first place. Life is full of many paths, going in all different directions, and we can never know which one is the best for us. All we can do is enjoy the path we are on and be willing to go in a different direction, if that's where life takes us.

Many people don't begin new ventures because they are afraid of failing. They think that if they try to achieve their dream and fail, then they will be worse off than they are right now because their dream has now died. However, if they never try to reach their goals, they have also failed. Dreams cannot be achieved without some effort. You never know what is possible if you don't try. At least if you take action, you are actively involved in your life, rather than just sitting around passively waiting for something to happen to you. True, you may not achieve what you set out to do, but you will learn something valuable just by trying. You may discover what you are made of and how much character you have. You will find out how you respond to adversity and deal with obstacles in your way. You will ultimately discover what things work and what things don't, making you a wiser individual. By stretching yourself beyond your limitations, you may just discover capabilities you didn't know you had.

Of course, it's natural to be nervous on a new job or venture. There's no doubt you want to succeed because you're afraid that if you don't, you will be fired or considered a failure. You should recognize that the possibility of being criticized or humiliated is very real, but you have to overcome that fear in order to ultimately succeed. Let's look at a couple of people who are famous for doing great things. They both failed numerous times, but they continued to take the risk of trying again and again until they succeeded. For example, Walt Disney was fired from a newspaper company and went bankrupt several times before he built Disneyland. After facing many setbacks and places that refused to let her perform, Josephine Baker made a big comeback that included her successful Carnegie Hall and Paris performances. Both Walt Disney and Josephine Baker demonstrated confidence and perseverance. They refused to give up on their dreams. Learn from their example. Don't ever give up on your dream. Began taking action immediately to make it a reality!

Dream or goal: ______________________________

______________________________

Strategies for achieving: ______________________________

______________________________

Action to be taken:

________________________________________

________________________________________

You must face your fear of failure, recognizing that you will encounter difficulties along the way to achieving your dreams, but also realizing how important it is that you persevere. When you become fearful, you must stand up and face your fears by either saying something or doing something. Taking action is much better than simply doing nothing, even if it means making some changes in your life.

**Fear of Change**

Change is going to happen – whether you want it to or not. Children grow up and leave home, friends move away, and spouses will eventually pass on. Worrying about these things will not change them. Fearing something terrible will happen cannot prevent it from occurring. The only things you have to gain from worry and fear are unhappiness and misery. You cannot change the future, no matter how much you fret about it. All you can do is live in the present, and you have to decide if it is going to be a happy time or a miserable one. Try to picture yourself as others see you. Would they say you are a positive or negative person? Are you someone others want to be around? What you have in your life – whether positive or negative – is a direct reflection of your attitude. If you have a positive attitude, then you will be much more likely to see your failures as opportunities to learn. However, if you have a negative attitude, you are much more likely to be defeated when challenges occur. Living with chronic fear can be both physically and emotionally draining, making you feeble and weak. In order to live a happy and fulfilling life, you need to reach the point where your fears do not stop you from daring to think new thoughts, take risks, fail, and start again. This process may be repeated many times before you ultimately succeed. But the journey is well worth the effort because it is what gives you purpose in life. And without something to live for, life becomes a real bummer.

List two things that you fear will change and why.

________________________________________

________________________________________

Why? ____________________________________

________________________________________

Why? ____________________________________

________________________________________

Write what actions you would take to change the fears:
Action: __________________________________
Action: __________________________________

*"Fear makes the wolf bigger than what he is."* — German Proverb

While fear can manifest itself in many ways, there are some steps you can take to conquer your fears so that instead of being paralyzed by them, you can take action from a position of wholeness and strength.

1. Admit you are afraid and acknowledge why the situation has made you fearful. Once you recognize that you feel fear, then you can

decide how you are going to handle it. Determine the action you will take in order to improve your situation.

2. Imagine the worst. If you can think of the most terrible consequence of whatever you plan to do (like going bankrupt if you start your own business), then you will be mentally prepared, and you will also realize that the consequences are well worth the risk.

3. Identify the person or people causing you fear (write down their names). By being aware of those individuals who instill fear in you, you can make some decisions about whether you will choose to be around them in the future.

4. How do you feel about negative comments and projections? Knowing whether this type of negativity will affect you greatly or just "roll off your back" can help you determine whether you should share what you are doing with others.

5. Will your response be "Flight or Fight"? If you are ready to take a risk, then you should fight your way through you fear; but if not, will you just walk away and give up?

Can fear be healthy? Sometimes - when it alerts you to dangerous situations and/ or motivates you to take action. Just take comfort in knowing that whatever you fear, someone else has also felt the same feeling. Fear is universal; it touches everyone, but it doesn't stop people from achieving their dreams. Even ordinary people that accomplished extraordinary things felt fear. Know that when you try to succeed you, too, will feel some kind of fear.

Make sure you don't buy into the idea that your age prevents you from doing whatever you want to do. Age shouldn't be a barrier. The only thing that can stop you is your own doubts, and you can overcome those by having confidence in yourself. When you live in fear, you're isolated from your true self. You are trapped by your own fears, sending signals that you are incapable of having what you want to have, doing what you want to do, or being who you want to be. Expect more, don't conform yourself to minimum expectations, accepting less, thinking you don't have any other options. Because you do!

**Conclusion**

To you, the reader, think about your life being a journey that has taken you from an infant baby to where you are now. Perhaps you experienced many disappointments, and fearful moments along with your successes. But you are still here, and as long as you are here, you have the opportunity to take action to fulfill any dreams, visions, or goals that you have a desire to accomplish. I encourage you to take the risk, feel the fear, but do it anyway!

**Dedication**

I dedicate this chapter in memories of my loving grandmother Azzie Lee McCray, aunt Fannie M. Griggs, uncle Arthur Lee McCray, great aunt Martha Downing, great uncle Charlie B. Grimes, grandma Mary Jeter El, and my teacher and mentor, Lucille Smith.

*"Thank you, God, for all that I am and will become."*

**Recommended Readings:**

*On Becoming Fearless...in Love, Work, and Life* by Arianna Huffington

*Moving from Fear to Freedom* by Grace Fox

## ABOUT THE AUTHOR

### CLAUDIA WHITE

Born on the west side of Chicago, Claudia White graduated from Purdue University with a BS in Business and minors in Marketing and Psychology. Her extensive career as a sales representative began with American Hospital Supply. She then broke into the field of advertising with the Leo Burnett advertising agency in Chicago, IL. After Leo Burnett, Claudia White became a Marketing Communications Specialist for General Electric Medical Systems in Milwaukee, WI. Claudia then joined Bristol-Myers Squibb in the Princeton, NJ headquarters as a Marketing Communications Manager. In this role, Claudia was responsible for placing, originating, and evaluating print advertising and visual media advertising for ostomy, wound care, and specialty product lines. She is currently a Senior Hospital Sales Specialists for King Pharmaceuticals in the Columbus Ohio market. There, she is charged with penetrating teaching hospitals in the Columbus area, and orchestrating/executing sales agendas for multi-million surgical and infectious disease products lines. She gives thanks to her niece Whitney Clair White, an undergraduate at Northwestern University for contributing to this project.

*Contact:*
Positive Pathways Unlimited
1209 Hill Road North #249
Pickerington, OH 43147
(614) 570-2057
Wcdub11@aol.com
www.protrain.net

SIX

# CREATING THE LIFE YOU WANT NOW

**By Claudia White**

Have you ever seen a Georgia O'Keefe Painting? "Red Canna" is one in particular I find to be inspiring. It is a rich painting in oil of a detailed and vibrant red flower. When reflecting on her own work, O'Keefe explained it to represent the "wideness and wonder of the world that she lived in." Her paintings bring the viewer on a journey through intimate landscapes of petals, stems, and color. Each painting is a statement of two things, beauty and strength. It is no coincidence that these qualities contained within a work of art can be experienced in our daily lives. Let me make clear that I am not writing to critique modern art. Rather, I present the artwork of Georgia O'Keefe as a gateway into a way of thought that I firmly believe may change your life for the better: you can at any moment create the life that you want now. We have the power to create a life filled with beauty, strength, courage, and resilience. I am so excited to be writing about this topic because it has influenced my life and made many positive things possible.

It seems abstract or impossible even, but think how motivating, how empowering it could be if you only let yourself believe that your life is a blank canvas awaiting your first brush stroke to make it into a beautiful piece of art.

I am writing this chapter with the sincere hope that it will inspire you to pursue your most heartfelt dreams with all the determination you can muster. Positive change is possible, and achieving your dreams is possible. I hope to make this clear first by discussing a little of my own story, then by discussing how not looking back and believing that you are what you think can help you create the life you want now.

I would like to share with you a period in my life during which I underwent severe crises. It was a devastating period, and if it were not for my abiding faith and insurmountable desire to overcome my situation, I don't believe I would be here to share my story with you. My nightmare began March 13, 1995. This was the day I held my mother's hand in mine as she slipped from this world into the next. She had been battling many diseases over the course of her life, yet remained one of the strongest women I have ever met. March 13th began like every other day as she got herself together to go for her dialysis treatment. She was in good spirits that day, even though she knew what awaited her at the dialysis center. Little did she know that day would be her last dialysis treatment; she went into cardiac arrest while attached to the machine and slipped into a coma shortly after.

After my mother's funeral and attending to all the paperwork with my family, I returned home to Ohio to deal with my husband of ten years who was also battling health problems. As I slowly began to deal with my mother's loss, my husband's health seemingly began to improve. Then one day out of nowhere, my husband walked into our bedroom and told me he wanted a divorce. This was almost three months to the date after my mother's passing. I remember being there in that moment, hearing him mouthing the words; but it was as if I was having an outer body experience. I stood there frozen in time hoping that I was asleep, and upon wakening it would be a terrible nightmare.

But it was real. Shortly after, I began partying and living a life that was alien to me and the person I once was. I felt as if my life was spinning out of control; I struggled to function in a world that seemed to be moving on with or without my contribution to it. When my family gave me a major wake-up call, I realized I could not go on living this way. It was time to effectively deal with my grief and to stop masking my pain by partying and hanging out with friends that reinforced this behavior. I had to start anew. Slowly but surely I got my act together. I joined a gym. I found a church that I liked attending, I found truly supportive girlfriends to lean on, and found little ways to reward myself, like going to a spa once a month. I did things that made me feel strong and beautiful as the Red Canna Georgia O'Keefe painted, and looked for the good in my life. I had a good job and had many different options available to me. This is of course the most ironic part of all. I had been a successful black business woman long before I met my husband, I had my faith in God before my husband, and I had a loving family before my husband. Losing my mother was something that could never be changed; it altered the rest of my life. But there had always been good in my life. In other words, my canvas had already been filled with beauty and strength. However, it was up to me to rediscover these magnificent qualities and redirect my brush strokes.

I'm sure that you, the reader, can reflect on times of crises, as most of us have had to do. One thing to be considered is that people deal with crises differently. Thinking positively is not easy for everyone to do. The real crux of the matter is not how many times we fall down, but how many times we're able to get back up. I think Donnie McClurkin, the renown gospel singer, expressed it best when he sang, "We fall down but we get up." But why are some people more able to recover from crises than others? Why does one person face a crisis and not just survive, but actually grow from experiencing that calamity?

This is undoubtedly a very complex subject. However, I am convinced that one important factor in people's success is their strong desire and determination to not remain stuck in the past and wallow in self-pity. We sometimes become content with staying in our comfort zone out of fear of trying new things. We literally fear "thinking outside of the box" (See the PWN book *Survival Skills for the African American Woman*). After all, the beast we know is better than the one we don't know. The pain that is familiar to us may seem less threatening than vying for the unknown. This is an irrational cycle and way of living, but there are reasons for it. Such a tendency may be associated with some painful childhood memories that place us into a feeling of hurt and shame. But, you must realize that change is good. Art is change, and to live life as if it's a blank canvas destined for great things means to embrace the fact that routine and fear will not help you prosper.

Just take a moment to grasp the innate power that is attached to the following phrase: "Create the Life You Want Now." This very moment you can wipe clean the slate that is your life and create your first masterpiece. Or, you can make changes to an existing piece of canvas created a long time ago. We can and should do whatever is necessary to bring strength and beauty into our lives. Allow yourself to understand that your life is something you can shape, mold, and alter in whatever way that helps you achieve your dreams. Life is not a static process. To make my point more clear, consider the converse for a moment. What would it mean if life was static and that you could not create the life that you wanted? Where would that get you? Would you be able to be happy settling, staying in routine, and believing that positive change would never be possible?

Remember that your past does not have to dictate your future. I think believing this is a very important step to realizing your goals. There may have been times in the past when you were not the person you are now, times when you made poor decisions or did things to hurt yourself and others around you. These experiences are a part of you, but they cannot control you. You can overcome any obstacle, even if it is an obstacle of the past by thinking outside the box. All this means is trying new things, looking for new ways to make yourself feel empowered. This is possible, no matter where you are in life.

One step to take is to ask yourself how intuition and reflection speak to you. Do you slow down long enough to hear your own thoughts and desires, your own innate reactions to people and situations? If the answer is no, then you must ask yourself how to slow down long enough to consider these things. All this is about is getting in touch with yourself and knowing what it is you need and desire. A large part of creating the life you want is knowing what you want.

When I was in my 20's, I worked for Leo Burnett, a large ad agency in Chicago. The company had a slogan, which at the time I found rather corny. It read, *"When you reach for the stars, you might not get one, but you won't come up with a hand full of mud, either."* Now having spent a couple years around the bend, experienced crises and overcoming obstacles, I fully understand and embrace this concept. It speaks to the fact that you should always aim high. Even if you don't attain all of your dreams, you didn't just walk though life never having tried to accomplish them. So whatever you do, don't compromise on the things that are important to you; you get whatever it is that you settle for, so only settle for the best that life has to offer. Remember, successful people never stop dreaming. They make plans and set the goals that are necessary in place for accomplishing their dreams. If they don't have the specific knowledge needed to attain their dreams, they get the proper training necessary to accomplish them. They are unafraid to work hard and they refuse to quit.

As you pursue your dreams and passions, always remember that success, like life, is a journey. The paths to these things are indefinable and unique to every human being. Living your life as if it is a piece of art is an instrumental means of attaining your goals. The road to those goals may not always be clear, but nonetheless there are things that I believe can make the navigation of this path easier. At the most base level, do whatever is necessary to maintain good health, to have the material tools you need to prosper, to keep family and friends close, and to always trust yourself. Focus on what you want in your life, rather than what you don't. As stated earlier, you are what you think, so if you focus on negative things, rest assured you will have plenty of negativity in your life. Always strive for excellence and live life to the fullest. You want your canvas to be rich with color, texture, and imagination to make your piece of art memorable because you are a powerful person worthy of achieving your goals. No one else can make that clear for you. The points established in this chapter serve simply as a framework and strong aid toward positive change. But the power is innately in you, because your life is your masterpiece. You are more than capable of creating the life that you want now. Why not do whatever it takes to make it full of beauty and strength?

This chapter is dedicated to my loving parents: to my Mom who was unwavering in her love and support of her children throughout her life; and to my Dad who I was able to develop an incredible relationship with as an adult. Their impact on my life has lead to me becoming a person who is always striving to turn my life canvas into a masterpiece of beauty and strength.

Claudia White

## ABOUT THE AUTHOR

### AMICITIA MALOON-GIBSON

Amicitia Maloon-Gibson is the President and Founder of ATIC & MG Center For Excellence (MGC4E), Inc a non-profit community base global training and service institute. The focus is on Education, Empowerment, and Encouragement to Excel – E4 for human capital. Maloon-Gibson & Associates is the profit entity of the MGC4E. She has developed, implemented and delivered seminars and workshops in the United States and in International countries. Additionally, Cita brings 25 years of experience working with government and private organizations in the areas of leadership, training, motivation, team building, employee recruitment & succession planning, and organizational development. She has a Bachelor degree in Psychology and a Masters degree in Management and a Masters degree in Human Resources Development.

She is a member of the American Association of Christian Counselors (AACC), the Black African-American Christian Counselors (BAACC), the Marriage and Family Network (AACC) and she is a certified Mediator/Life Coach. She is a charter member of the Brevard County Business and Professional Women/USA/FL.; National Association of Female Executives, the Association for Conflict Resolution. She is a member of Women Speakers Bureau and a 29 years Veteran of the U.S. Armed Forces. She is a Board of Director member of Christian Services Charities for 2008-2009.

Cita Maloon-Gibson delivers exceptional seminars and keynotes, and is available for regional, national, and international travel engagements. Her international travels include the British Virgin Islands, US Virgin Islands, England, Germany, Prague, France, Belgium, Puerto Rico, Hawaii, Aruba and the Bahamas.

*Contact:*

Amicitia Maloon-Gibson
P.O. Box 411482
Melbourne, FL 32941
(321) 537-5002
Maloon57@aol.com
www.citagibson.com
www.mgc4e.org

SEVEN

# LEADERSHIP LESSONS: WHAT I LEARNED FROM MY FATHER

**By Amicitia I. Maloon-Gibson, MHR, MA, CSP**

*"If God has given you leadership ability, take the responsibility seriously."*
—Romans 12:8 (NLT)

The union of Claude and Juanita Maloon qualifies me as a product of the Baby Boomer's era. An era of change and "Yes, I can or No I won't." The evolution of women in new roles. Women were evolving in non-traditional roles and stepping out of the home into the workforce. The radio stations played songs with messages like, "You've come a long way baby to get where you got to today." Women sent messages through songs, like "Respect" and "I Will Survive" by the Queen of Soul, Aretha Franklin. Women were seen on billboards – for cigarettes ads…I remember the Virginia Slims commercials. Women in the movies of "leading roles" got the traditional parts, like June Cleaver in "Leave it to Beaver," the stay-at-home submissive mom; and "I Love Lucy" featured the American red haired actress Lucille Ball who was loved by her viewers, but was the opposite of June Cleaver – she never listened to her husband. Two other sitcoms I remember were "Good Times" with another stay-at-home mom who kept the family together during hard times, and the "Cosby Show". What I remember about female leadership and the Cosby Show was Claire Huxtable. She was a working professional, maintained the home, raised five children, and enjoyed life. My perception of these events contributed to part of my socialization process – good, bad, or blended together – they had some impact on my life.

In reflecting upon the role of women as I watched them on television, it brought to mind the question of women's leadership. Were women to follow, or did they dare step into leadership roles, such as Claire Huxtable. And what exactly is leadership? Throughout my career as a professional soldier and leader, I have read books on leadership that gave me many perspectives of leadership from various scholars who have studied the topic, such as John Maxwell, Stephen Covey, General Colin Powell, General Julius W. Becton, Jr., Miriam Langston Heard, Bishop Theodore Dexter Jakes, James McGregor Burns and many others. During my twenty-five plus years as a leader, I adapted to the many definitions of leadership based on the situation at that specific time. I embraced the definition, "Leadership is the art of accomplishing more than the science of management says is possible." This quote is from a leadership primer of eighteen lessons from General Colin Powell, Chairman (Ret), Joint Chiefs of Staff and former U.S. Secretary of State.

Leadership is for everyone – it is not for just those that make it to the top. I believe that anyone can learn to lead by discovering their purpose – their calling and preparing for the time they will be called to lead. In my role as a Transitional Life Coach, I believe that we must develop specific qualities to attain the success we want to see in ourselves. It is my job to coach clients to a higher calling of purpose, self-empowerment, self-awareness, and a sense of fulfillment that most times result in job satisfaction, increased compensation, and repositioning by using skill sets and abilities. The goals of Leadership Lessons is to help you pay attention to your expectations, and be mindful of what will get you to your purpose – your calling – your niche. I am sharing some leadership principles that worked for me during my Baby Boomers tenure, and continue to work for me.

Sometimes what you are looking for is within arms reach of you – you just have to reach out and get it. What I know for sure on this journey of life is that these **five key lessons** or **principles** that I learned worked for me in growing and moving up to the top of the Leadership Pyramid and my personal life. Leadership ladders sometimes tilt and you may fall. Assure yourself that you most definitely do get up and try again, as quitting is not an option in the success equation. Failure is acceptable, as we learn from our failures, but quitting is not acceptable if you are striving to be successful. A Leadership Pyramid is wider at the base and gives you a stronger foundation. If your foundation is strong at the base, you can build it upward without fear of falling as you would on a leadership ladder, which is somewhat unstable.

*"Trust in the Lord with all your heart and lean not on your own understanding; in all your ways acknowledge him, and he will make your path straight."*—Proverbs 3: 5-6 (NIV)

**Lesson #1: Follow the greatest leader of all. Choose ye this day whom you will serve, and put God first before anyone or anything in your life.**

Many times in my life, I have put too much of my focus on doing work, church, people and family, and not enough focus on my personal relationship with God. It is not a good habit to develop because our personal relationship with God gives us the spiritual strength imperative to pursue all of our callings and to maximize to our greatest potential. My Father was a member of the same church all his life (ninety-three years), Frederick Evangelical Lutheran Church, the oldest historical church on the island of St. Thomas. He led us to church and Sunday school every Sunday. He served as an usher and other ministry positions for over sixty years. I learned about commitment and service from him in this area. He would go every week to the sanctuary and hand fold the bulletins. Even when the church got an automatic folder, my father and the usher ministry continued with the process of folding by hand. At age ninety-one, he became visually impaired and could no longer do volunteer work as an usher, so he resigned. He was honored for his commitment and service for those years of service.

**Lesson #2: Be A Unique Leader.**

When I began leading as a company commander my first platoon of non-commission officers, I interacted with each soldier the same way. The challenge with this is that people are very different and very unique. Many personalities can interpret the same leadership style differently. What works well for leading one person may be less effective for leading another. One day, I called my father as I was in tears (across the United States) on the telephone, and I knew he would rescue me with some words of encouragement. I called him to say that I was quitting the

Army because there was one soldier who was getting on my last nerve. I told my father that all the other soldiers responded to my leadership style well except this young man. He was disrespectful, foul- mouthed and very racist. I commanded an all-male company, including my full-time staff. My father asked if I had presented the question to this difficult soldier as to why he has this behavior towards me. I said no, the others do what I ask and I don't ask them to do anything that is not part of their job description or that is not in compliance with the values of the Army and I assumed that this difficult solder would do the same. My father said I couldn't quit because I was there to make a difference in that soldier's life and that of many more. He suggested that I speak to the young man and find out what was bothering him. He is your "unique one." My father said that I was the shepherd and that I may have ninety-nine soldiers, *but the one that strays is the most important one*. Then, my father relayed the biblical story of the Prodigal Son. I was empowered with the principle of "the unique one" – the son that went astray. I spoke to the soldier and he explained why his behavior was such – he was taught the behavior by his father and thought it was right. His mother died at birth and he had some issues with women in leadership – in charge as a part of his upbringing and socialization process. No one confronted him about that behavior before or cared enough to take a risk and ask. I got him the professional counseling he needed through the chaplain and other counseling sources. His behavior turned around, and years later we ran into each other and he thanked me for caring and saving his career and his life. I applied this principle during my tenure years as a leader in the Baby Boomer years when women just started to evolve in positions of authority. It improved my ability to recognize different personalities and know how to best lead in each-one teach-one concept.

I'm still a leader being refined and reshaped. Whenever I have the opportunity to lead someone in a one-on-one consulting session, I customize a unique approach suited for the situation and for the best results of my client. (It is very important, especially if you are a mentor, coach or ministry counselor, to understand the "unique one" principle.) My father taught me a great lesson in this area as we spoke about life. He loved my siblings and me in a unique way. He displayed his love for each of us, even when we agreed to disagree. The lesson was that he loved unconditionally, and each of his children was his "unique one." From time to time I would put him to the test – I would ask who he loved the best, and he would say that he loved all of his children uniquely.

*"I can do all things through Christ who strengthens me."*
—Philippians 4:13

**Lesson #3: Know Your Limits.**

During the early stages of employment, I developed work plans for the week and set a daily agenda or to-do list. I ensured the plans were executed by the staff assigned, or outsourced certain tasks to get the best product or service for the agency. The work was challenging and complex, but we had a great team and we met our timelines. During my third place of employment, where I worked was deficient in personnel staffing and under-budget. I inherited a backlog of uncompleted projects from my predecessor. It immediately taught me my limitations. Although we had extended work hours and an increase in human capital, it was impossible to do what needed to be done. It was a decision I made of assuming that I could achieve unrealistic goals because I always met or exceeded challenging deadlines in the past. Understand that you are human and have limitations. Know your limitations. Plan realistically. Otherwise, you will burn yourself out – call it stress, whatever the case, it will impact your emotional wellness. One family member is usually tasked as the "strong one" or the one that you can depend on. My father was that person and I must have inherited this leadership trait, too. I watched him gracefully say no with a smile on his face, and recommended someone else that he knew was capable of taking on task. So, know your limitations and take appropriate actions not to over task yourself or others. Say no with a smile and mean it. The church program, the Parent Teacher Association, professional organizations and family members will still get what they need done without you.

*"When pride comes, then comes disgrace,*
*but with humility comes wisdom."*—Proverbs 11:2 (NIV)

**Lesson #4: Keep Your Pride In Your Pocket.**

As a young adult, we are quick to say, "old people" (anyone older than you at the time) don't know anything. For a while I didn't understand this principle, but when I got it – I got it. Looking at our society today, this may be one of the most challenging areas in our society. Pride can ruin good relationships of many, many years. I once attended a church where two beautiful, mature deaconesses had not talked to each other for over twenty-five years. They moaned and groaned at each other and rolled their eyes in church. Both of them looked miserable and eventually became very ill. I remembered this principle to keep your pride in your pocket every time I saw them. My father often stated that attitude is everything; respect your elders and love those who use you. He was always in the attitude of gratitude and humility. Sometimes he would say, to keep peace you must be humble and be the bigger person; put your pride in your pocket. As an EEO and Diversity Professional, I found this principle to be very helpful. As a senior manager who worked for Senior Executives that were not receptive to culture of a changing workforce, it opened doors inculcating change. You have to know when to be still and know that your pride may be stomped on, but it will work out in the long run. Most of the time it worked for me. It's called keeping your mouth shut, even when you know that what is being articulated is wrong and you are right. Eventually, you will see the results; your peers, supervisors and others will have a greater level of respect for you. Being a leader requires having these two words in your vocabulary: "**Thank-you**" and accepting responsibility for not only what went well, but what went wrong. And these four words, as well: **"I made a mistake."** Recently, I experienced this as a volunteer with a local non-profit, and I swallowed my pride, even thought I was right. I worked out to the favor of the organization in the long run, and others thanked me for my patience in dealing with a very nice, but short-tempered leader.

*"Give, and it shall be given unto you; good measure, pressed down, and shaken together and running over For with the same measure that ye mete withal it shall be measured to you again."* —Luke 6:38 (KJV)

**Lesson #5: Serving Others And Giving**

Serving and giving is a part of living. My father often said, "When much is given, much is required." He gave so much of himself in service and being a father to the fatherless, that most people called him "Pappie", or addressed him as Mr. Maloon. I can only remember four individuals during my father's life that called him "Claude," my mother, and his siblings, Hugo, Wally and Amy. Even his godchildren called him "Pappie." I can remember that our family was truly extended, and my father ensured that no one in the neighborhood (the widowed) went hungry or without anything. Consistently for years, my siblings and I took turns carrying food, fetching water, and running errands for the elders in our neighborhood. Not only at holidays, but also throughout the year, especially on Sundays, until they died. As I reflect on this now, I cry with Joy realizing we were a blessed family. I knew we were not poor; we were living in abundance. Maybe that's why my favorite poem is "My Cup Overfloweth." The author is unknown. I will share this gift with you at the end of this chapter. I use it just about every time I speak to young people.

Serving requires having a servant's heart. It requires sacrificing self-interest and not looking for rewards or a parade. My father was very humble. He was honored many times. And when I would tell him how proud we were of him, his reply would be, "To God Be the Glory." As for giving, my father gave his tithes and offering for as long as I can remember. He would teach us how to prepare our envelope for Sunday school and church. Many times, I didn't understand why kids had to give back to the church. As I got older, I realized that I could not afford not to give. This principle of serving and giving is a great gift and legacy that my father past on to many through his leadership.

Who was Claude D. Maloon? He was a 'talk strong' Dutch-American. He was a great leader in his community, both formally and informally. He was the "Unique one" who lived what he preached in his professional decorum. He was "Pappie" and Mr. Maloon to many, and had a servant's heart. He was the bigger one, for he kept his pride in his pocket and served in humility and the spirit of gratitude. He exemplified service and giving to his community and others. He was the biological father of five boys and five girls (only one preceded him in death, Claude (Butch) Maloon, Jr.). My father was proud of all of his children and all of us were proud of him. He would want me to say the most important thing about him, that he was a Christian and a child of God. He loved music (he played the violin) and singing, and one of his favorite songs was "He'll Understand" and say well done.

*"But thou shalt remember the LORD thy God: for it is he that giveth thee power to get wealth, that he may establish his covenant which he sware unto thy fathers, as it is this day."* — Deut. 8:18 (KJV)

**MY CUP OVERFLOWETH**

Author Unknown

*I've never made a fortune, and it's probably too late now.*
*But I don't worry about that much, I'm happy anyhow.*
*And as I go along life's way, I'm reaping better than I sowed.*
*I'm drinking from my saucer, 'cause my cup has overflowed.*
*Haven't got a lot of riches and sometimes the going's tough.*
*But I've got loving ones around me and that makes me rich enough.*
*I thank God for his blessings and the mercies He's bestowed.*
*I'm drinking from my saucer 'cause my cup has overflowed.*
*O' remember times when things went wrong,*
*my faith wore somewhat thin.*
*But all at once the dark clouds broke and the sun peeped through again.*

*So Lord, help me not to gripe about the tough rows that I've hoed.*
*I'm drinking from my saucer 'cause my cup has overflowed.*
*If God gives me strength and courage when the way grows steep and rough.*
*I'll not ask for other blessings, I'm already blessed enough.*
*And may I never be too busy to help others bear their loads.*
*Then I'll keep drinking from my saucer 'cause my cup has overflowed.*

## ABOUT THE AUTHOR

**HEIDI CIUZIO-SANTIAGO RN CLNC**

Heidi Ciuzio–Santiago was born in Bronx, New York, and currently resides in Monroe, New York with her four teenage children and two teacup poodles. She has been in the healthcare industry for over twenty five years and has spent most of that time in home care both in the role of field nurse and management.

In 2000 Heidi earned her certification as a Legal Nurse Consultant, and founded her own consulting business. She was featured in CLNC Success Stories from the Vicky Millazo Institute and is currently pursuing her Bachelors/ Masters in Public Health.

In her role as mother, Heidi has served as the President of the Parents Auxiliary for the New York Military Academy for four consecutive years, raising thousands of dollars for the student body. She considers her children her greatest achievement.

Heidi joined the corporate arena in 2005 and has since been a leader in sales of cutting- edge wound care, educating hundreds of physicians/nurses and home care management in top wound care techniques.

Heidi Ciuzio-Santiago considers her presentations to be honest, humorous and upbeat which she considers a reflection of her life philosophy.

*Contact:*
Heidi25@optonline.net

## EIGHT

# INTERNATIONAL TRAVEL MADE SIMPLE

### By Heidi Santiago

I absolutely LOVE to travel, and if it was always simple, I don't think it would be as much of an adventure. Part of the fun is the planning, preparing and deciding. I have been to four continents and over ten different countries (including the Caribbean), and I can truthfully say I have had almost as much fun in the planning as I have had in the traveling.

For me, the research is all part of the fun. It's my way of dreaming. However, it's also the first important step in a carefree vacation. For those of you unfamiliar with computers, I suggest you find a good travel agent. Although a dying breed, you can still find one, if you look. For those of you who are computer literate, there are dozens of sites to research. I want to caution you to be careful when booking online; many times there are hidden fees and restrictions. A little later on in the chapter I will list just a few of the many reputable websites.

What I also do is, once I have planned a vacation through a site, before I book the ticket, I go to the airline website and see if I can get a better deal through them. I also check directly with the hotel. Next, I religiously read the online reviews. I ignored the reviews once and was so sorry. I found out the hard way that what is considered a five-star resort in the Caribbean is probably a three-star here in the states.

But before you even get that far, you have a few things to decide: knowing what to *ask* a travel agent or *look* for online, which will make your planning easier.

1. A budget: decide how much you can afford to spend in total. Your budget will be a key factor in where and the type of vacation you take. Believe it or not, travel abroad can be done on almost any budget.

2. How much time do you have? If you only have a few days, Europe may not be the best choice. Consider travel time and jet lag before you get dead set on a locale to visit.

3. Are you limited to a certain time of year? If not and are on a budget, that's great. If you travel a little off-season, Europe can be very affordable.

4. Last, what kind of vacation do you have in mind? Do you just want to unwind, relax and vegetate on the beach, or do you want to see the sights. If relaxation is what you have in mind, a Caribbean island might be a good choice.

Knowing all this gives you a good starting point once you start planning your vacation. Now, when you go online or see your travel agent, you have options. Some websites that are reputable for travel planning are:

1. www.Sidestep.com
2. www.expedia.com
3. www.cheaptickets.com
4. www.kayak.com
5. www.yahootravel.com
6. www.travelocity.com

All of these sites have a vacation or "deals" tab. I usually go to those first to get an idea of what is out there. Then I take it from there. Many times they list destinations I would never have thought of. Keep your mind open to different places.

Now that you have planned your vacation, you will need to get organized. The first item on your list has to be your passport. Unless you are traveling within the United States, a passport is a requirement. You cannot leave or enter the United States without one. If you don't know how to obtain one go to www.travel.state.gov . This is probably the best web site for all your travel questions. It is a government site. As a matter of fact, if planning an overseas vacation, before you book, check here first. Not only does it tell you how to obtain a passport, it lists any travel advisories for every country, safe places to travel, and tips and guidelines. If you plan to travel abroad, especially if you plan to travel to a country where the culture is very different, you need to visit this site. Many a vacation has been ruined just because of an innocent gesture that was taken as an insult or slight. For example, in countries like Afghanistan or Turkey, women are expected to respect the Islamic culture. When in foreign countries, the law of the country prevails and you need to know what that is.

So now that you have researched your destination, booked your travel and have your passport, what now? Well, you may want to learn more about the weather forecast and interesting places to visit. I usually go to the website for the locale and try to find out what I can. Just Google the name of the country and city and you will find tourist information. If you are not a frequent traveler and need assistance, I have taken the liberty to list a few websites that can help.

1. www.travelistic.com
2. www.dontforgetyourtoothbrush.com
3. www.tripprep.com
4. www.weather.com
5. www.Xe.com
6. www.homeandabroad.com
7. www.travelandleisure.com

All of these are good sites; your preference will depend upon how much you want to plan. I do strongly recommend that you at least visit Xe.com to check the monetary exchange rate and weather.com to know what to pack.

I have just given you enough information to successfully plan your own vacation, but a chapter of mine would not be complete with me interjecting my own experiences and opinions.

**Heidi's Travel Philosophy**

One thing I have learned in all my travels is to be flexible. Flights get delayed, weather changes, and things happen. I strongly recommend NOT sweating the small stuff. If you have done everything in your power to pre-plan and something happens, just deal with it! Don't let it ruin your entire vacation. Be open to a new experience. I have met so many interesting people when stranded at an airport restaurant.

I believe there are basically two kinds of travelers, the VACATIONERS and the TOURISTS. Vacationers don't usually make plans; they are more of the lay-on-the-beach, fly-by-the-seat-of- your-pants kind of planner. If something interrupts their daily activities, no big deal. They tend to sleep in and forget time exists. Then there is the tourist. They get up early, and feel the need to get as many activities into their schedule as possible. They plan the day around meals and don't really have "down- time". Both types of travels are great, and depend on the person's personality. I am a cross between the two and it depends on where I am. When I vacation in the Caribbean, I am a true vacationer. I am happy to sit on the beach with a punch and a good book. When I travel abroad however, I do like to see some of the sights. I don't feel the need to see everything, but like to get a bit of local culture. To insure a good time, make sure when planning your vacation you travel with someone of a like mind.

If you are a true TOURIST, consider paying a little extra for one of the guided trips or cruises. They are more expensive; however the professional guide companies have set itineraries that afford you the most "bang for your buck".

**Packing Thoughts**

I would like to tell you how to pack lightly, but truth be told, I have not yet mastered that skill. To tell you the truth, I don't really try! My idea of packing lightly is 2- 65 lb bags. It must be a throwback to my Girl Scout days. I like to be prepared. Hey, everyone is allowed one minor flaw! I know that I will probably pay the excess baggage fee and am fine with it. I just build it into my expenses.

One last checklist before you go:

1. Make sure you have a valid passport.

2. Visit the www.travel.state.gov.com website to check on safety and register with them.

3. Leave a family member an itinerary and a way to contact you.

4. Take ALL valuables and medications on board with you.

5. Leave plenty of time to get to the airport. (Better you wait around a while than take a chance on missing your flight.)

6. Check in with your air carrier the day of travel.

7. RELAX and have a great time.

CIAO! AU REVOIR! ARRIVEDERCI! ALOHA! ADIOS! AUF WIEDERSEHEN!!

*Notes:*

# ABOUT THE AUTHOR

## Mary Paul

Mary Paul is owner of Mary Paul LLC, a consulting firm focused on providing excellent service to organizations in the areas of organization development and training. The firm specializes in building individual and team effectiveness through education and learning's using the Myers Briggs type indicator and the enneagram.

Mary is also the Organization Effectiveness Manager for Harley-Davidson Motor Company's Corporate Headquarters in Milwaukee Wisconsin. Mary's primary responsibilities include taking a leadership role in the design and development of organizational change efforts that are consistent with evolving organizational needs and business requirements. She also assists in the development of strategies for and provides coaching to Harley-Davidson Leadership to identify training needs and create appropriate actions to meet those needs to support the organization's strategic plan.

Prior to her current role, Mary has held several positions within Harley-Davidson including being a Program Manager for Rider's Edge Motorcycle Training program, plus various positions within the Organization Development and Training Department.

In the past, Mary has also held management positions with Anheuser-Busch Companies and Sara Lee in St. Louis, Missouri.

Committed to her profession, Mary is also a member of a number of professional business organizations including the Professional Woman Network, Professional Dimensions, Women in Networking, and the American Society for Training and Development.

Mary can be reached by email at marypaulllc@gmail.com

*Contact*
Organization Development and Training Manager
Harley-Davidson Motor Company
5801 S. Oak Road
West Bend, WI 53095
(414) 343-4652
mary.paul@harley-davidson.com

# NINE

# ENCORE CAREERS

## By Mary Paul

Ah…retirement, those golden years when you can just sit back and relax; this is not so for most baby boomer women. The vast majority of our generation has chosen to continue working for many reasons. The word retire comes from the French word *retirer*, which means to go into seclusion. Today, that's hardly how we think of moving into our retirement years. Many of us will go into an "encore career", which may be to do what we love to do, start our own business, or earn extra income. In addition, some of us may find ourselves in circumstances that call for us to work well into our senior years.

This chapter focuses on taking a look at current data about how baby boomer women are approaching retirement, interviews with baby boomer women who have moved into an encore career, and resources for finding information on moving into an encore career.

There are 38 million baby boomer women in the United States today. Middle age finds us pondering how we've lived the first half of our lives and what to do about the second half. Some of us are in the grips of a midlife crisis, going through menopause, or even considering cosmetic makeovers. Many are caring for elderly parents while parenting children and working full time.

The life expectancy of the baby boomer generation has significantly increased; most of us in reasonably good health will live into our 80's. Marc Freedman states in his book *Encore*, "*Although boomers will work longer for many reasons --- to earn money, stay healthy, maintain social connections, feel accomplished, keep busy, and maintain identity -- in the end, the real force driving people to find meaningful work is not economic or social, but personal. It's that inner voice calling for something as simple as a change of pace, as ambitious as changing the world, as profound as reclaiming a dream deferred before it is denied.*"

In a study of over 2000 baby boomers, conducted for investment firm Merrill Lynch by Harris Interactive®, most widely known for The Harris Poll®, shows that many baby boomers plan to keep working and earning money during their retirement years, but will alternate between periods of work and leisure.

- **Highlights of The New Retirement Baby Boomer Survey** While 76% of baby boomers intend to keep working and earning in retirement, on average they expect to "retire" from their current job/ career at around age 64, and then launch into an entirely new job or career.

- **Baby boomers reject a life of either full-time leisure or full-time work.** When asked about their ideal work arrangement in retirement, the most common choices among baby boomers in the survey would be to:

    - Repeatedly "cycle" between periods of work and leisure (42%)

    - Have part-time work (16%)

- Start their own business (13%)
- Work full time (6%)

  (Only 17% of the baby boomers in the survey reported that they hope to never work for pay again.)

- **Baby boomer women are better educated, more independent, are simultaneously juggling more work and family responsibilities and are more financially engaged than any generation in history.** According to the survey, married baby boomer women are more than six times more likely to share responsibility for savings and investments compared to their mothers' generation (33% now vs. 5% then).

- **Baby boomer women are dreaming of retiring to Mars while baby boomer men hope to retire to Venus.** Baby boomer men are looking forward to working less, relaxing more, and spending more time with their spouse. Baby boomer women view the dual liberations of empty nesting and retirement as providing new opportunities for career development, community involvement and continued personal growth.

- **The unpredictable cost of illness and healthcare is by far baby boomers' biggest fear.** They are three times more worried about a major illness (48%), their ability to pay for healthcare (53%) or winding up in a nursing home (48%), than about dying (17%).

- **Financial preparedness is the gateway to retirement freedom and the antidote to retirement phobia.** Accumulating the resources baby boomers believe they need for retirement freedom (81%), rather than age (56%) or any other variable, was cited as the most decisive factor for when they choose to retire.

Women in the full age range of baby boomers are moving into new areas of work. Since this is *The Baby Boomer's Handbook for Women*, I wanted to share some real life examples of women who have chosen encore careers as a matter of choice, happenstance, and circumstance. These women were successful in their own right, and could have chosen to retire in a more traditional way, but chose instead to take on new challenges that contribute to others.

**Interview Number One:**

*Jean Majewski*, age 62, Director of Organizational Services, Milwaukee School of Engineering, Milwaukee, WI, majewski@msoe.edu

1. ***Can you tell me about yourself?***

   I'm a life-long learner who's taken on various roles: teacher, counselor, facilitator, administrator, and consultant. I love being part of another's development and growth. I've worked in education, healthcare and manufacturing over the years. I also love to learn myself, so traveling, gardening, being outdoors, or in discussion groups are great ways for me to enrich myself.

2. ***What prompted you to move into a new direction?***

   I'm adding "care-giver" to my list of professions because my mom, while not sick, is no longer able to manage for herself. When she was 87, we both sold our houses and moved in together. Initially I thought we would be "room mates", but it soon became clear to me that she would need more care than I anticipated. Think broken hip, broken wrist, and need of a new knee! Caring for her is now central in my life and professional responsibilities fill in the gaps.

3. ***How do you see your career choice playing out in the future?***

   In addition to caring for my mom and learning about physical therapy, nursing, and activities for seniors, I work outside the home. I moved from my own consulting business to Director of Organizational Services of the business outreach arm of the Milwaukee School of Engineering. The position offers me the flexibility, professional contacts and context, a forum in which to be of service and creating and providing learning opportunities. I see myself moving forward in this career and "growing the business." Since I've never imagined myself in this role, it's rather exciting to see how I can influence the success of this business.

4. ***When do you anticipate actually retiring…or not working in some capacity?***

   I plan to continue in this work and caring for my mother as long as her health requires and until I am near 70. At that time, I hope to become more involved in feminine spirituality and becoming a personal coach in that area.

5. ***What else would you like to share with other Baby Boomer women who may be contemplating an encore career?***

   Do it! If you need to, rest for a period before engaging in the next possibility, but do it! It will keep you connected to other people, let you try things you haven't up to now, and open doors to places that you may not have gone otherwise.

**Interview Number Two:**

*Gail Maggraf*, age 56, business owner.

1. ***Can you tell me about yourself?***

   I was born into a dysfunctional family, alcoholic father, mother in denial, and married the same. After 24 years and two sons and two daughters, the light finally went on and I divorced. I had worked for Jewel-Osco Supermarket for many years and also baked specialty cakes for restaurants and clients. (Best cheesecakes you've ever tasted!)

2. ***What prompted you to move into a new direction?***

   I decided that as long as I would be working the rest of my life, it would be doing something that I truly loved! I went to dog/cat grooming school and purchased an established grooming salon. Two years later I sold my home and moved 90 miles from city life in Chicago to country life, population 320! (Norman Rockwell Land!) I don't even own a TV. I reside on twelve acres, still have the shop, which is managed for me, have a grooming and boarding business where I live, and started a foster program for the county that I live in.

   Prior to my arrival, animal control was the town veterinarian, who would keep stray animals for 10 days, try to locate their owners or other interested parties, and then euthanize them. Besides my own animal fostering program, I also foster for two other organizations, which independently foster animals and specialize in animals that are emaciated and have other issues. The rescue work I do is so rewarding! Currently, I have 7 dogs in my "pack" and 10 foster dogs.

3. ***How do you see your career choice playing out in the future?***

   I love my life and will continue on this path. My goal is to expand and build the best boarding facility/humane society, working to educate the humans and rehabilitate the animals indefinitely.

4. ***What else would you like to share with other Baby Boomer women who may be contemplating an encore career?***

   Follow you instinct! (When I was 13, we went looking for a puppy at a kennel/boarding facility. I walked around looking at all the dogs and told my parents, "When I finish school, I am going to do this! I am going to work with dogs!" My father looked at me and laughed saying, "That isn't a career!")

Go with your heart, don't give up! You will have road blocks, you will lose money, and you will question yourself! Don't let other people dissuade you; it's not their path, it's YOURS! I have several sayings posted in my office:

"There is no shortcut to winning and success. There is only getting started and sticking with it!" I don't know the author.

The second is by Robert Browning: "Why stay on Earth except to grow?"

And, "Don't pray to have an easy life; pray to be a strong person!"

**Interview Number Three:**

*Kim Maggraf*, age 59. (Yes, they are sisters.)

1. ***Can you tell me about yourself?***

My younger sister, Gail and I grew up in Chicago, Illinois. Our father was an angry, emotionally distant alcoholic. Family life was filled with his unpredictable outbursts of anger. I learned at an early age that my expression of opinion that was counter to my father's, or expression of any independent thought, would incur my father's wrath. I went to college in the early sixties, when postsecondary institutions had begun to recruit low-income urban youth, such as me. I attended college in rural central Illinois and then Northwestern University, but had no educational or career goal. After almost three years, I dropped out and worked at a public aquarium, where I met my husband, who was from Milwaukee, Wisconsin. I married and moved to Milwaukee in the mid-seventies, worked for an association management company, a mortgage insurance company, and a technical college. Through these jobs, I gained extensive meeting, convention and special event planning experience, and non-profit management experience. Eventually, I started working as an independent meeting planner—first on a part-time basis while still holding my day job, and then as a full time meeting and event planning consultant. I am an active volunteer in several community organizations.

2. ***What prompted you to move into a new direction?***

I've always been an energetic, athletic person who enjoyed the outdoors and physical fitness. Even though I've had rheumatoid arthritis for thirty years, the disease didn't limit my activity. In my mid-fifties, I underwent hip surgery that failed and I lost my ability to walk. I had four more surgeries in three years to try restore my functionality. Most of that time I was on crutches and my functionality was significantly curtailed. It's almost certain that I will have to use a crutch or cane for the rest of my life. This physical limitation has impacted my ability to perform my job, which often requires me to be on my feet, and on the move. I'm also viewed differently by clients and potential clients. I have had more difficulty acquiring new clients since I've been on crutches. I've decided to explore other career options.

3. ***How do you see your career choice playing out in the future?***

   I love managing complex projects, and I'm good at it. I enjoy taking a concept, and putting all the pieces and people together to make it come to fruition. Thanks to years of experience, I can very quickly assimilate into a business culture and understand how a project fits into the broader function and purpose of an organization; and I have the broader perspective that comes with maturity.

   In the beginning of my career, I worked for a paycheck, and then I worked for career advancement; now I'm seeking a way to work for fulfillment. My goal is to work in project management or non-profit management. I'm seeking a company or organization whose mission is one I can support and contribute to in a positive way; who actively supports workplace diversity in all forms; and who is, in some form, contributing to a better world.

4. ***When do you anticipate actually retiring...or not working in some capacity?***

   I plan to continue working as long as I'm able.

5. ***What else would you like to share with other Baby Boomer women who may be contemplating an encore career?***

   Be your own loudest cheerleader. Create your own promotion plan that includes not just your strengths and experience, but also your passions, your values, and the world or community issues that are important to you. Don't waste time and energy on things that don't matter to you or on people to whom you don't matter. Surround yourself with people who are natural achievers, who are willing to share contacts and offer advice, and who inspire you. Embrace the unexpected opportunity.

From the interviews, you can see as baby boomer women, we're transforming and influencing many aspects of our community, going inward and taking time to reflect on what we want out of our lives for the future. We're searching for peace, solace, and direction for the rest of our days. We can finally be the women we've wanted to be and find our vocation of choice.

Dotsie Bregel in "Baby Boomer Women at Midlife" comments, "*We've had more choices than our mothers' generation and have lived and continue to navigate uncharted courses. We are pioneers in our own right. We're faithful, loving, and hard-working women who multi-task to survive. We continue to better ourselves so we can help those who need us. We come from various backgrounds carrying different baggage. We love our country, but we're probably not the rebels we once were. We're trying to be all that we can be.*"

We're at a crossroads, and many of us are choosing new paths to take, paths where we will learn, continue to grow, and serve our families and communities. We can't imagine retirement in its old definition of the word. We are exploring the opportunities of where our encore careers will take us.

**Informational Websites And Books To Explore:**

AARP: http://www.aarp.com

National Association of Baby Boomer Women: http://www.nabbw.com

Boomer Babes Rock: http://www.boomerbabesrock.com

Too Young To Retire: http://www.2young2retire.com

The Baby Boomers Surfing Center: www.boomernet.com

Merrill Lynch Investment Firm: http://www.ml.com

Harris Interactive®, Harris Interactive Inc. www.harrisinteractive.com

*Baby Boomer Women at Midlife* by Bregel, Dotsie. www.Boomernet.com, March, 2007

*Encore* by Freedman, Marc. New York: Public Affairs, 2007

# ABOUT THE AUTHOR

## Jan Felton

Jan Felton is President of **Attitudes *plus***, a private consulting firm that offers training opportunities to encourage participants to experience personal fulfillment and professional success by recognizing and pursuing their potential. She is certified by Development Dimensions International and the Professional Woman Network to offer workshops to develop skills in leadership, communication, diversity, and workforce development. Jan's 35 years as an experienced educator served students in both secondary and collegiate institutions. As a former high school principal, she gained valuable skills in leadership, team building, mentoring, and communication.

The Greater Cheyenne Chamber of Commerce recognized her as the 2002 ATHENA recipient leadership in her profession and the community and for her work to help other women realize and achieve their potential.

*Contact*
Jan Felton, President & Consultant
**Attitudes *plus***
710 West Dale Boulevard
Cheyenne, WY 82009
Phone: 307.635.2507
Fax: 307.635.2529
E-mail: j.felton@bresnan.net

TEN

# MENTORING: SHARING YOUR GIFTS WHILE LEARNING FROM OTHERS

**By Jan Felton**

"Life is like a box of chocolates," according to Forrest Gump's mama, and "you never know what you're gonna get." As Forrest's first mentor, Mama Gump provided a variety of opportunities for Forrest to learn from her wisdom; she cared for him, believed in him, and allowed him to be the person he needed to be in order to be happy and successful. He once said, "Mama always had a way of explaining things so I could understand them." She had the ability to help him believe in himself, and she let him experience life and learn from all those with whom he came in contact. Because of his mother's wisdom and encouragement, Forrest made the most of his life and shared his innocence, his love of life, and his gifts with others. He, too, became a mentor; he led by example and inspired others by being sincere and caring—that's what mentors do!

Those of us in the Baby Boomer generation are often referred to as "the sandwich generation" because we are currently the "middle generation." Many of us are fortunate enough to share our lives with important people who have influenced us in the past and with younger people who are part of our present and who will impact the future. The implication is sometimes that our generation is "caught in the middle" between our parents or others born before 1943 (Veterans or Traditionalists) and our children or younger relatives and co-workers born after 1960 (Gen X or Nexters). Rather than focus on the challenges of feeling "pressure" from above (parents or supervisors) and below (children or younger employees or co-workers), this chapter is designed to encourage you to consider the opportunities you have to create a "healthful sandwich" based on the relationships you build, and to make the best of whichever "chocolate" you get based on the choices you make.

**Learning From Others**

A mentor is defined in the *Merriam-Webster Collegiate Dictionary* as "a trusted counselor or guide." Forrest Gump was a Baby Boomer who was mentored and one who served as a mentor—he was the cream in the Oreo (sandwich) cookie and the meat, cheese, condiments, and veggies in your favorite hoagie. He made the most of each situation. He learned from Mama Gump, Captain Dan, and Bubba; then he shared with Jenny and their son, as well as others whose lives he touched throughout his journey. You have learned a great deal from mentors during your lifetime.

Take a few minutes to think about mentors in your life. On the lines below, list the first three names who come to mind and write words or phrases that describe each person:

| ***Mentor*** | ***Qualities & Characteristics*** |
|---|---|
| | |
| | |
| | |
| | |

Were these mentors "formal" mentors, a part of a structured program established by your company or firm, or teachers who were your mentors because of their chosen profession? Or, were they "informal" mentors, people who became part of your life because they were your parents or siblings, friends, or co-workers? If you were to have the time to think about all of the mentors you have had in your life, you probably could fill a journal because of the wisdom you have gained during your lifetime from individuals who have offered their guidance and touched your life. A mentoring relationship, whether formal or informal, is based on trust, mutual respect, knowledge, and willingness to share and encourage. As you discovered in the previous exercise, mentors have a distinct set of characteristics that impact their effectiveness in assisting others to grow and learn.

Although informal mentoring has been occurring in every company, many organizations have discovered that the establishment of a formal mentoring program is more effective to improve productivity and employee retention and advancement. Effective formal mentoring programs require the following:

1. Adequate time for meeting and planning
2. Appropriate mentor training that balances seeking and telling
3. Flexible structure that allows for a combination of mentor- and mentee-driven content for each session
4. Written contracts that provide guidelines for participation and identify desired outcomes for the mentoring partnership
5. Established timelines for the beginning and ending of the program and for completion of mentoring activities
6. Appropriate transitional plan (from formal mentoring to coaching or informal mentoring relationship)

An unknown author once said, "A lot of people have gone further than they thought they could because someone else thought they could," which is the reason for an effective mentoring program. Identifying the potential in someone, matching that person with the right mentor (based on personality, knowledge, and motivation), and providing the necessary resources are the responsibilities of a company that commits to bringing out the best in its employees. Baby Boomers are often called upon to serve as mentors because this generation possesses the knowledge that must be shared for organizations to continue to prosper when many Baby Boomers retire. They have learned from their predecessors (mentors) and are now being asked to share their expertise with those who will follow them (mentees). That's part of being a member of the "sandwich generation" at work.

What have you learned from your mentors—both formal and informal? Consider the mentors you listed previously. Record the skills and qualities that you have learned from them that have positively impacted your happiness and success in life and on the job:

| ***Skills*** | ***Qualities*** |
|---|---|
| | |
| | |
| | |
| | |

If you are in a position to impact the creation or improvement of a formal mentoring program at work, what will you do to ensure the quality of this program? Think about the value your mentors have added to your life—both personally and professionally.

An article in *Fast Company* by Fara Werner, "Inside Intel's Mentoring Movement," describes the "mentoring-with-a-difference" approach that Intel has implemented. Lory Lanesse, their mentor champion in New Mexico, is quoted:

"The great thing about mentoring is that it shifts easily to meet training needs, whether you are expanding your business or you are not hiring. When you are growing, it is great to help integrate people. When you are not, it can help people make the next leap in their careers."

Part of being a member of the "sandwich generation" in the workplace may require that you decide how the organization will continue to be successful once you retire. Entities that are concerned with developing a succession planning program would benefit from implementing a formal mentoring program as one of the primary components.

When you think about whether or not to add a formal mentoring program to the training opportunities for employees in your organization, you might find answering following questions to be helpful:

- Why does this organization need to create (or improve) a formal mentoring program?
- How will the organization/individuals benefit from this program?
- How will the organization fund the program?
- Who will lead this program?
- How will mentors be selected and trained?
- *How will the effectiveness of the program* ***be evaluated?***

What is the current role of mentoring in your organization? How can you be a positive force in the future of your organization as numerous Baby Boomers prepare to retire?

**Sharing Your Gifts**

Winston Churchill stated, "We make a living by what we get—we make a life by what we give." According to *Generations at Work* by Zemke, Raines, and Filipczak, Baby Boomers value optimism, team orientation, and personal growth; they are service-oriented, good at relationships, and driven; they enjoy working on teams and their leadership style is "collegial." This information indicates that Baby Boomers would make excellent mentors and coaches; therefore, they need to be encouraged to share their gifts.

You have already identified your mentors and the skills and characteristics you learned from them. How are you honoring them? Are you sharing these values and skills with others? **Identify three potential mentees and indicate their relationship to you (family, co-worker, friend).**

| ***Potential Mentees*** | ***Relationship*** |
|---|---|
| | |
| | |
| | |
| | |

In order to serve as a mentor and share your knowledge and expertise, it is imperative that you know yourself—your strengths, your preferred communication style, your personality, your core values. Take a few minutes to identify the traits you posses that will enhance a mentoring relationship; please circle all that apply to you:

| | | | | |
|---|---|---|---|---|
| *Accountable* | *Appreciative* | *Articulate* | *Caring* | *Concerned* |
| *Dependable* | *Dedicated* | *Direct* | *Enthusiastic* | *Flexible* |
| *Honest* | *Knowledgeable* | *Optimistic* | *Professional* | *Realistic* |
| *Reasonable* | *Responsible* | *Sincere* | *Tactful* | *Understanding* |
| | | | | |

Next, please circle all of the "hats" you are comfortable wearing as a mentor:

| | | | | |
|---|---|---|---|---|
| *Coach* | *Director* | *Facilitator* | *Guide* | *Learner* |
| *Listener* | *Motivator* | *Planner* | *Scheduler* | *Teacher* |
| *Trainer* | | | | |

Now, identify those characteristics that might challenge your ability to be an effective mentor; consider past situations in which you have had difficulty working with others. Then consider how you might address these areas of concern:

| ***Challenging Characteristics*** | ***Action To Improve*** |
|---|---|
| | |
| | |
| | |
| | |
| | |

Gandhi's famous quote, "Be the change you want to see in the world," describes the opportunity you have as a mentor. A sign posted above the door to a counselor's office states, "We teach people how to treat us." That, too, is mentoring. Your opportunities to impact positive change in your world are limitless. In addition to the individuals you listed previously as potential mentees, you are currently serving as a role model for anyone who observes your habits and behaviors and who communicates with you at home, on the job, or in the community.

Whether or not your organization has a formal mentoring program, you have numerous chances to serve as a mentor. You are surrounded by numerous people at home, in your community, and in the workplace, who could benefit from your willingness to share what you have learned about life and work. There are agencies that rely on volunteer mentors who are interested in helping improve the lives of others and to improve the quality of life in your local community; contact your local Chamber of Commerce or local churches for possibilities.

Consider the following quotes when deciding how much you have to offer to others:

*"The unselfish effort to bring cheer to others will be the beginning of a happier life for ourselves."* —Helen Keller

*"I've learned that people will forget what you said, people will forget what you did, but people will never forget how you made them feel."* —Maya Angelou

*"Children are likely to live up to what you believe of them."* —Lady Bird Johnson

*"What we have done for ourselves alone dies with us. What we have done for others and the world remains and is immortal."*—Albert Pine

*"Eat like an owl: take in everything and trust your innards to digest what's useful and discard what's not."* —Peter Elbow

*"Learning is finding out that you already know. Doing is demonstrating that you know it. Teaching is reminding others that they know just as well as you. You are all learners, doers, and teachers."* —Richard Bach

Each of these quotes provides "food for thought" as you determine how best to share your gifts. When you examined the knowledge and expertise that your mentors have given you, the first layer of your "sandwich" was put in place to serve as the foundation for future mentoring experiences. When you identified the skills, qualities, and characteristics you have to offer another, you added the "meat" to the sandwich. Now, consider the final layer: the knowledge and expertise you wish to offer to your current and future mentees. Previously, you listed three individuals who are potential mentees; list their names again, and identify the skills and knowledge you can offer that you believe will be of benefit to each of them as they pursue their personal or professional goals:

| ***Mentee*** | ***Gifts To Be Shared*** |
|---|---|
| | |
| | |
| | |
| | |
| | |

In addition to the gifts you have listed, consider the two most important ingredients that a good mentor must demonstrate to enhance the experience: active listening and honest feedback. Becoming an attentive listener means learning to ask open-ended questions that will encourage thought and developing rapport between the two of you, and to observe the non-verbal communication that is exhibited when these questions are answered. Providing honest feedback requires establishing mutual respect and trust that allows the two of you to communicate effectively, both when all is going well and when recommendations for improvement need to be discussed. Mentoring is a responsibility that requires an open-minded, non-judgmental approach to developing a working relationship between two individuals who are willing to work together to accomplish a common goal.

As you consider whether or not to serve as a mentor to someone who could benefit from knowing you and learning from you, begin by answering the following questions:

1. *Why do you want to be a mentor?*
2. *Who can you contact to begin the process of becoming a mentor?*
3. *How much time can you devote to mentoring?*
4. *Where will you seek training to prepare you to become a mentor?*
5. *How will you evaluate the effectiveness of the mentorship?*
6. *What do you need to know about other generations to be an effective mentor to someone younger or older than you?*
7. *How will you establish an appropriate mentoring relationship?*
    - *Planning the content of mentoring sessions*
    - *Developing rapport (mutual respect and trust)*
    - *Scheduling timelines and meeting locations*

Mentoring can be a very rewarding experience because both participants will learn from each other, and the opportunity of working together will have a positive influence on the present and the future of your company and your community. You are encouraged to treasure the gifts you have been given from individuals who have influenced the person you have become, and to honor those individuals by sharing your gifts with those who are looking to you for guidance, knowledge, and encouragement. "Life **is** like a box of chocolates"; however, regardless of the "chocolate" you get, a mentor who has experience in making good choices can enhance the possibility of helping others to choose wisely and of developing effective solutions to potentially difficult situations—to deal effectively with "whatever you get"! Mentoring is all about learning from others and sharing your gifts—creating a "healthful sandwich" for others and for yourself! What a difference you can make now! What an opportunity to impact someone else's life—and change the world—by creating the leaders of tomorrow!

**Reading Resources:**

*A Framework for Understanding Poverty* by Ruby K. Payne, PhD: ISBN1-929229-48-8

*Bridges Out of Poverty: Strategies for Professionals and Communities* by Ruby K. Payne, PhD, Philip E. DeVol, and Terie Dreussi Smith: IBSN 0-0647437-9-5

*Emotional Wellness for Women, Vol. II* edited by Linda Eastman

*Employing Generation WHY? Understanding, Managing, and Motivating Your Workforce* by Eric Chester: ISBN 0-9651447-7-1

*Generations at Work: Managing the Clash of Veterans, Boomers, Xers, and Nexters In Your Workplace* by Ron Zemke, Claire Raines and Bob Filipczak: ISBN 0-8144-0480-4

*How to Be Like Women of Influence* by Pat and Ruth Williams: ISBN 0-7573-0054-5

*Overcoming the Superwoman Syndrome* edited by Linda Eastman: ISBN 13: 978-0-9791153-6-3

*The Right Questions: Ten Essential Questions to Guide You to an Extraordinary Life* by Debbie Ford: ISBN 0-06-251784-8

*Well Done! The Power of Positive Relationships* by Ken Blanchard ISBN 0-7432-3538-X

*Women as Leaders: Strategies for Empowerment & Communication* edited by Linda Ellis Eastman: ISBN 13: 978-0-9799711-0-5

# ABOUT THE AUTHOR

## Karyn E. Taylor

Karyn E. Taylor is President and founder of The Whole Self Design Consulting Group, which is dedicated to inspiring and motivating growth in individuals and organizations through seminars, training, workshops, consulting, and coaching.

She is a member of the Professional Woman Network (PWN) and is a certified trainer in Diversity and Women's Issues, Professional Presentation Skills, and Career Coaching through the PWN.

Karyn's expertise in the areas of Diversity, Leadership, and Career and Success Coaching has given her the opportunity to empower and enrich the lives of others at work, at church and in her community. Ms. Taylor is a member of the Pittsburgh Human Resources Association, Toastmasters International; she is also a volunteer Victim/Offender Mediator with the Pittsburgh Mediation Center.

Ms. Taylor completed her Bachelors of Arts Degree in Legal Studies at the University of Pittsburgh and her Master of Arts Degree in Industrial and Labor Relations at Indiana University of Pennsylvania. She has an extensive background in Human Services, Human Resources and Training.

Karyn would like to thank her mother and mentor Dr. Elayne Arrington, for all of her support, guidance and inspiration. Linda Ellis Eastman, President of PWN, and Alicia Smith of Alicia Smith Consulting and Training, LLC are also Karyn Taylor's mentors. She acknowledges the contributions of Janice Myers and Aldine Coleman to this project.

*Contact:*
Karyn E. Taylor
The Nuin Center
5655 Bryant Street
Pittsburgh, PA 15206
www.nuincenter.com
(412) 235-1739
(888) 609-8992

ELEVEN

# THE AGE OF MASTERY

## By Karyn Elayne Taylor

Have you ever said to yourself, "I wish I had more time?" More time to spend with your family and friends, more time to relax and enjoy a good book, or more time to make your life dreams or aspirations come to fruition. Chances are you will have it. Research indicates that you may have up to thirty years worth of extra time.

Consider this **Great News:**

- The **extra** time seems to enter around age 50, and this **extra** time for most is not spent in old age. The three extra decades gained through longevity have really been added to the middle of our lives.
- A woman who reaches age 50 and remains free of cancer and heart disease can expect to see her ninety-second birthday.
- After your mid fifties, 70% of aging is controlled by your lifestyle: How actively you move around, whether you smoke or drink to excess, how well you sleep, how many close friends you keep in touch

with, and how engaged you remain in life, work, and community.

What will you do with this extra life, these extra years of longevity?

**Welcome to "Second Adulthood" and Second Acts!**

The term "Second Adulthood" was coined in 1995 by cultural observer and bestselling author of *New Passages,* Gail Sheehy. Ms. Sheehy refers to the period from ages 45-65 as the Age of Mastery, and the period from ages 65-85 and beyond as the Age of Integrity. Second Adulthood is midlife re-evaluation and transformation, rather than midlife crisis and chaos. The re-evaluation opens the door for reflection. You know you are entering this age as you begin to ask yourself, "Is this all there is?" And then you begin your personal journey to find and reflect new meaning in your life. Second Adulthood provides the chance to reshape your life. The Age of Mastery is defined by Levine as both a personal journey and a stage of maturity that is being defined as we live it an adult revolution. The larger question is, "What am I going to do with the rest of my life?" The answer can be found in three smaller questions: "What matters?" "What works?" and "What is next?" The key is to experience the power and the joy that comes from the answers.

Think about your life for a moment:

- Where are you in terms of Second Adulthood?

____________________________________________

____________________________________________

____________________________________________

- Are you on the "First Adulthood" side, ages 30-45? If yes, do you have any ideas or plans for getting a head start?

- What are your choices?

- Where do you want to go in your life?

- How do you get there?

- Who do you want to be with - Friends, family and coworkers?

- What changes in lifestyle do you need to make in order to stay healthy?

___

___

___

- What do you really want to do in your next adulthood?

___

___

___

**Your Second Act**

How many times have you said or thought, "If I only knew then what I know now, my decision or experience would have been different?" As you explore your possibilities for your second act:

1. Imagine the day you enter the Age of Mastery as the infancy to your new life.
2. You are armed with your years of rich personal experience and judgment. You are strong and you know who you are.
3. Whatever you are missing cannot be blamed on circumstance or other people. Whatever is missing or incomplete, it is you that left it out. You must begin to add these things now.

For the remainder of our time, let's briefly consider the following three points:

1. Living on purpose
2. Listening to your dreams
3. Listening to own needs

**Listening To Your Needs**

The great transition in the passage to second adulthood for women is to move from pleasing (the major survival characteristic of first adulthood, reflected in ages 30-45) to mastery. Mastery is a time that a woman is fully ready to speak with her own voice. At this stage and age, many of your family obligations may have faded. Now is the time that you may be able to fully listen to your needs. Questions for your consideration: Who do you need to forgive?

Who do you need to ask for forgiveness?
Who do you need to embrace?
What disappointments need to be let go?
Does your religious faith need to be restored or reconsidered?
How much personal time do you need, daily or weekly?

Please read the following poem:

***Comes The Dawn*** – *unknown*
(Alternate title – *After a While*)

*After a while, you learn the subtle difference*
*Between holding a hand and chaining a soul.*
*And you learn that love doesn't mean leaning*
*And company doesn't mean security.*
*And you begin to learn that kisses aren't contracts*

*And presents aren't promises.*
*After a while, you begin to accept your defeats*
*With your head up and your eyes ahead,*
*With the grace of a woman, not the grief of a child.*
*And you learn to build all your roads on today*
*Because tomorrow's ground is too uncertain for plans,*
*And futures have a way of falling down in mid-flight*

*After awhile, you learn that even sunshine burns,*
*If you get too much.*
*So, you plant your own garden and decorate your own soul,*
*Instead of waiting for someone else to bring you flowers.*
*And you learn you really can endure...*
*That you really do have worth.*
*And you learn and you learn...*
*With every goodbye comes the dawn.*

When I first read the poem, I immediately loved it. It spoke to me in a way that I had not known before. In a nutshell, it reminds me of my inner strength. Sure, other people and things can be extremely important to us. So often, so much is not within our control, and I have to respect that each person has to be free to make their own choices. Everyone has been let down by life situations and circumstances. Success comes in how we handle our difficulties. I have to plan my own life, build my own world, and share my world with those who can truly appreciate me. Otherwise, life is completely draining. I have had to learn to respect the power of goodbyes, whatever kinds they are.

- What are your reflections?

______________________________________________________________________

______________________________________________________________________

______________________________________________________________________

- Had you read the poem before?

______________________________________________________________________

- Were your reactions different this time around?

______________________________________________________________________

______________________________________________________________________

______________________________________________________________________

- What does it say about the source of happiness and fulfillment?

______________________________________________________________________

______________________________________________________________________

______________________________________________________________________

**Listening To Your Dreams**

This passage allows you to open yourself to new and more meaningful ways to be alive. Perhaps this is the time to get motivated, to stretch your independence. Return to school. Write that novel. Learn new skills. Start your business or your new career. Rediscover your adventurous creative side. A great deal of what we hear, read or talk about in terms of reinventing ourselves generally focuses on career. You may need or want to reinvent yourself within your personal relationships, including with yourself. Revitalize your relationships. This part can be terrifying and challenging. This can lead to many seen and unforeseen rewards, and most likely to a whole lot less regrets. Listen with your heart.

- Where is your creative expression?

______________________________________________

______________________________________________

______________________________________________

- What new hobbies will you pursue?

______________________________________________

______________________________________________

______________________________________________

- Are you happy with your work?

______________________________________________

______________________________________________

______________________________________________

- What will you do to continue to grow?

______________________________________________

______________________________________________

______________________________________________

## Mastery at Mid-Life

*"...Older and Wiser. Old enough to have life figured out; young enough to enjoy it."*—Dr. Elayne Arrington

*"The most delightful surprise in life is to suddenly recognize your own worth."*—Maxwell Maltz

*"Ah, mastery.... what a profoundly satisfying feeling when one finally gets on top of a new set of skills..... and then sees the light under the new door these skills can open, even as another door is closing."* —Gail Sheehy

## Living On Purpose

Living on purpose means thinking about your life, your dreams, and your vision. It means setting goals and making deliberate choices about the life you want to live. Yes, living on purpose and within your purpose means recognizing your talents and gifts and using them. Living on purpose means thinking about how you might want to give back to the world. It may mean leaving a job you have outgrown or ending a relationship that has faded or no longer meets your needs.

Living on purpose means to claim your vision. It may mean changing habits and altering some of your actions. To live on purpose, you must take steps that move you closer to your vision. Without action, dreams cannot be realized. Having a vision makes you live your life, instead of just going through the motions.

Living on purpose means that you must take time to recharge and nourish yourself. You must nourish yourself in **all** aspects of your life. Making time to live in the present and engaging in the moment will bring your actions more power. Living on purpose is hard work. Set your goals, large and small, and work step by step to achieve them. Your reward will be living the life you love. You already know you are worth it and you deserve it.

**Please Share You Reflections:**

- How are you living your purpose?

_____________________________________________________________________

_____________________________________________________________________

_____________________________________________________________________

- When have you NOT been living the life you love?

_____________________________________________________________________

- What are your main sources of happiness and fulfillment?

_____________________________________________________________________

_____________________________________________________________________

_____________________________________________________________________

- Are your sources of happiness consistent with your life's values?

_____________________________________________________________________

_____________________________________________________________________

_____________________________________________________________________

- In what ways do you make time for yourself and live in the present?

______________________________________________

______________________________________________

- Who do you know that is living life on purpose?

______________________________________________

______________________________________________

- What obstacles did this person have to overcome

______________________________________________

______________________________________________

**The Age of Mastery**

The Age of Mastery is a time of acceptance that you are getting older. You must go through a period of psychological and physical adjustment until you become comfortable with the changes that aging brings. Yes, you are older and smarter. You know what is possible, and sometimes you have to plan differently to accomplish the task.

The Age of Mastery is a wonderful time of personal transformation. It is the time when you remember that the gift of life entitles you to discover and nourish who you truly are. Failure becomes certain only in the not trying. Struggles are indeed a part of this age, but you have mastered life enough to know that you can and will 'make it through the rain'. The Age of Mastery is living the life you deserve. Customize your life so that you are living your life by design, rather than default. The Age of Mastery is in every sense mastering how you age. The words of my colleague and artist, Ruth Zachary, describe it eloquently. "One hopes to grow into the fullness of one's potential…using her own special gifts and insights, each stage deepening into the next." Make your extra time a time of progress, rather than decline. **Life is a verb! Listen to your needs! Listen to your dreams and live passionately on purpose!**

**References:**
*The Great News* – Parade Magazine December 2005, Gail Sheehy

*The Great Transition – New Passages-pg 172*

**Recommended Reading:**
*Passages* by Gail Sheehy

*New Passages: Mapping Your Life Across Time* by Gail Sheehy

*Inventing The Rest of Our Lives: Women in Second Adulthood* by Suzanne Brown Levine

*Notes:*

# ABOUT THE AUTHOR

## JUDY HARRIS

**Judy Harris** resides in Philadelphia, PA and wears many hats. She is the Human Resources Director at Frankford Foods and teaches Human Resources Management classes in the evening at the University of Phoenix. She is the President of Harris Training & Development (www.harristad.com) and works with executives, non-profit organizations, small businesses, and employees in the areas of: team building dynamics, career coaching and counseling, organizational development, business communications, and conflict resolutions. Judy believes that employees who work nights and on weekends deserve the same educational opportunities as employees working during the day. As a result, she is available for workshops and seminars after business hours and on weekends.

Judy recently launched Your Empowerment Network (www.YENetwork.org) a non-profit dedicated to empowering youth and women through education, information sharing, workshops, and networking events. She also started and organized the Philadelphia Chapter of NAFE (Natl. Assn. of Female Executives).

Judy received her Bachelor's Degree in Industrial Psychology from LaSalle University and her Master's Degree in Human Resources Management from Widener University. Judy Harris was previously employed by Rohm & Haas Company, a $6.5B specialty chemical company, and Albert Einstein Healthcare Network, one of the largest healthcare providers in Philadelphia, PA.

In addition to co-authoring "Emotional Wellness for Women, Vol. II, Judy is one of the co-authors of "Women's Survival Guide for Overcoming Obstacles, Transition and Change." Judy is in the process of writing her own book: "I Want You to Move" – a self-improvement book focusing on reaching your goals. She is certified in E-Commerce, Professional Coaching, Women's Issues, Empowerment, and Diversity, and a recent graduate of the Relationship Coaching Institute. Judy is an active member of several professional organizations:

| | |
|---|---|
| www.SHRM.org (Society of HR Mgmt)<br>Frankford-Northeast Rotary Club of Phila.<br>www.PALWV.org<br>(PA League of Women Voters)<br>www.NAFE.com<br>(Natl. Assn. for Female Execs)<br>www.leagueofblackwomen.org | www.NAWBO.org (Natlional Association of Women Bus. Owners)<br>www.Philacongressncbw.org<br>(Natl. Congress of Black Women<br>www.Prowoman.net (The Professional Woman Network<br>www.sqiralq.org (Children's Puppet Theatre) |

Judy serves on the National Branding Committee of www.NAAAHR.org (Natl. Assn. of African Americans in HR) and channels her volunteer energy in the community service sector. She volunteers her fundraising time with The National Alzheimer's Assn. and the American Cancer Society.

Judy says that she has never met a microphone that she didn't like. She is available for workshops, seminars, and motivational speaking on a local, national and international basis.

*Contact:*
Harris Training & Development
P. O. Box 27294
Philadelphia, PA 19118-0294
www.harristad.com
www.YENetwork.org
T: (215) 276-1010
F: (215) 276-1090

TWELVE

# RANDOM ACTS OF KINDNESS: 15 WAYS TO MAKE A DIFFERENCE

**By Judy Harris**

*"To the world you may be one person; but to one person... you may be the world!"*—Anonymous

There is always someone who needs our help, love, and attention. We can give that to someone effortlessly by MAKING A DIFFERENCE. There are hundreds of ways we can make a difference in someone else's lives, and it merely takes a little effort and energy. With careful planning, we can turn your spare time into quality time with someone who would welcome your caring and attention.

Let's face it; all of us cannot be Oprah Winfrey or Bill and Linda Gates – we just wish we could. We don't have to be wealthy philanthropists to make a difference to people and our communities. There are several cost-effective methods we can utilize to contribute to the well being of others.

We will begin this exercise by counting the letters in Make A Difference

| | | | | | | | | | | | | | | | | | | |
|---|---|---|---|---|---|---|---|---|---|---|---|---|---|---|---|---|---|---|
| M | A | K | E | | A | | D | I | F | F | E | R | E | N | C | E | **Total = 15** |

***This chapter will give you 15 WAYS TO MAKE A DIFFERENCE! Let's get started.***

**MENTOR A CHILD.** Mentoring programs can lead to several positive outcomes – especially when there is a one-on-one relationship with a caring adult.

**When adults mentor children, children may experience:**

1. Higher educational achievement
2. Improved self-esteem and self-awareness
3. Better relationships with friends and family
4. How to make wise choices
5. Decrease in drug and alcohol use

**What do mentors do?**

1. They offer a shoulder to lean on

2. Serve as role models

3. Give continuous guidance, leadership and coaching

4. Give emotional support and positive feedback

Mentors are dependable support systems in the lives of children.

**ANSWER CORRESPONDENCE FOR THE SICK and SHUT-IN.** When someone is ill, they often receive get-well cards, letters, and gifts from friends. Many times the person is unable to send a personal thank you note. When you answer mail and correspondence for him/her, your thoughtfulness shines. The visit to the home exudes warmth; the personal touch that you give can be just what the doctor ordered. Answering mail is a great way to communicate because it allows us to exchange ideas, discuss current events, and learn more about each other.

What other correspondence comes to mind that you can tackle for the sick and shut-in? I'll list a few and I'm sure you will be able to fill in the blanks.

1. Order items from a mail order catalog.

2. ______________________________

3. Write a thank-you note/send a thank you card.

4. ______________________________

5. Write checks for bills.

6. ______________________________

7. Make an entry into his/her journal.

8. ________________________________

**KEEP IN TOUCH WITH FAMILY MEMBERS WHO LIVE ALONE.** If you have family members who live alone, keeping in touch is very important. With today's active lifestyles, family members sometimes find themselves living alone – whether it is by choice, empty nest or unfortunately, due to a death in the family. Calling and visiting allows us to keep abreast of their health issues and emotional well-being. It definitely shows that we care about each other. I find that reminiscing about old times is quite rewarding and mentally stimulating. Did you know that when you keep in touch:

- It shows that we care.
- You touch their hearts.
- You share in the good and bad times.

**Heartwarming communication between families is priceless.**

**ESTABLISH TIME TO VOLUNTEER.** When we volunteer, we give back to our communities by helping individuals, groups, and our community. These websites have a plethora of information on volunteering:

1. www.servenet.org
2. www.volunteermatch.org
3. www.networkforgood.org
4. www.volunteer.gov

**Good things happen when we volunteer. We can:**

Make new friends.

Develop personal interests.

Develop new job skills.

Explore a new career.

Help others stay healthy.

Build a stronger community.

Help a friend or relative.

**Fill in the blanks for other reasons to volunteer: (answers at the end of the chapter)**

To learn leadership s__ i __ __s
To do our civic d__ __y
To gain r__ __ og__ __ __ __ o__
Feed the __ __ n __ __ y
To earn ac__ __ __m__ __ credit
To be part of a t__ __m

Right now, you may be the person who is able to help someone, but tomorrow you may be the receiver of someone volunteering their time.

**<u>ADOPT A SENIOR CITIZEN</u>.** There are several ways you can 'Adopt' a senior citizen. These are my top 10:

1. Reserve time to pray and read the Bible with them.
2. Visit and read to seniors.
3. Play card games or board games with a Senior Citizen
4. Surprise them with a gift certificate to a supermarket or to receive professional services.
5. Give them door-to-door transportation to/from doctors, supermarkets, and places of worship.
6. Take a senior citizen out to lunch or dinner.
7. Deliver healthy food, household products, and personal items regularly.
8. Go for a walk and talk with them.
9. Give them a hug and gift on their birthday and other holidays.
10. Telephone senior citizens on a regular basis to socialize and to find out if they need anything.

REMEMBER: It is the thought that counts.

What are your top FIVE?

1. ______________________________
2. ______________________________
3. ______________________________
4. ______________________________
5. ______________________________

**<u>DONATE TO A SHELTER FOR ABUSED WOMEN AND CHILDREN</u>.** Domestic violence victims in crisis who have just entered emergency shelter need everyday items that we all take for granted. Here are the basic items that a shelter has to provide for each person – so let's get out there and deliver items such as:

- new toothbrushes, toothpaste, hair brushes and combs, shampoo, and feminine hygiene items
- towels, washcloths, pillows, blankets, and sheets (usually twin size)
- new packs of socks or underwear; these are more appreciated than you can know.
- small alarm clocks
- panty hose, and bus passes; many women in shelters do not have cars.
- long distance phone cards. Re-establishing contact with lost family and friends can be an integral part of helping victims transition into survivors. www.aardvarc.org

***These websites cover various georgraphical areas that accept donations.***

http://www.safehorizon.org/page.php?page=sheltertour_door

http://www.sharingandcaringhands.org/index.htm

http://www.womenagainstabuse.org/programs.html

http://www.sunrisepasco.org/contactus.html

http://www.johnnieshouse.com/index.htm

www.aardvarc.org

**INVITE A REPRESENTATIVE FROM THE FIRE and POLICE DEPARTMENTS** to give a presentation. Fire and Police Department personnel have been trained in speaking with groups regarding safety and security. The Fire Dept Officer speaks on fire safety in and out of the home. Police speak on personal safety and identity theft. They value the opportunity to speak with community groups, schools, and professional and social organizations. Simply contact your local fire and police departments for additional information. You may videotape the presentations for later use or for someone who is unable to attend. It is important to the Police and Fire Departments to interact with the community and discuss issues or topics of concern to residents.

**WILL A BASKET WITH ITEMS FOR A HOMELESS SHELTER.**

***Items that are always needed:***

♦ toothpaste ♦ toothbrushes ♦ shampoo ♦ deodorant ♦
♦ combs ♦ soap ♦ mouthwash ♦ towels ♦ bed linens ♦

You can oftentimes pick these up at a discount store. You may pick up a few items while shopping in discount stores; I also look for the 50-75% off sale items. I save them until I have enough items to make a basket. I also save freebies that I collect from public events. Corporate sponsors usually give away items such as, t-shirts, baseball caps, pens, pencils, note-pads, lotion, soap, candy, books, key chains, water bottles, bottled water, snacks, lanyards, and neck wallets, that you can collect and give to shelters.

**FIND FUN WAYS TO GIVE BACK.** Giving back can be just as much fun as it is rewarding.

| THESE ARE GOOD, CLEAN, AND/OR SIMPLY-GREEN, FUN WAYS TO GIVE BACK? | |
|---|---|
| Team up with a group and participate in a walkathon for charity. | Become active with an eco-minded group and campaign to recycle. |
| Staff a visitor's center for your local park service for outdoor activities. | Keep your community cleaner and greener.<br>Keep America Beautiful (www.kab.org) |
| Reconnect with youth.<br>www.scouting.org<br>www.girlscouts.org/for_adults | Join the National Park Service. Help with ski or horse patrol, gardening; Lead a workshop. The possibilities are endless! www.nps.gov |

**ENHANCE THE LIFE OF A DISABLED PERSON.** *"Kindness is love's readiness to enhance the life of another person."* —Lewis B. Smedes. Do you have a friend, neighbor or acquaintance with alzheimers or that has a disability? The quality and value of their lives will be enhanced and much appreciated when we can help them with tasks that may be easy for us, but not for them. They would really appreciate it if we could assist them to a seat in church, and help them find a scripture in the Bible. As a caregiver, I have found it priceless to be the eyes and ears of a disabled person in their times of need. The need to communicate is invaluable. It is important to speak up on their behalf and listen to what they are saying, as well as sharing interests.

Sending holiday cards, birthday cards, or a card to say 'I am thinking about you' or 'I miss you' is heartwarming. Just as important is spiritual and physical support. The soft touch of our hands or a gentle massage to help them relax has an effect on our relationships. Children with physical or mental handicaps are thrilled when they receive a new toy.

*"If you stop to be kind, you must swerve often from your path."*
—Mary Webb

**READ TO A BLIND PERSON.** The Associated Services for the Blind (www.asb.org) has opportunities for readers to come in and read to the blind and visually impaired. You may also want to consider contacting the ASB regarding recording a "Book on Tape". I have a life-long friend, Richard Gross, who has glaucoma and is legally blind. He is employed by the ASB and I feel that I have made a difference in his life by helping him with reading, computers, and in any way that I can assist him.

**MAKE A DIFFERENCE in a visually impaired individual's life.**

Do you have a command of the English language?

Do you have office skills?

Do you have an interest in helping people?

Can you read correspondence and other print material?

**Answering 'YES' means you can MAKE A DIFFERENCE by...**

1. Recording print material.
2. Acting as a transcriber in the completion of printed forms, etc.

3. Proofreading typed documents.

4. Assisting, as needed, in editing material.

5. Contacting www.asb.org for information.

**ENCOURAGE OTHERS TO MAKE A DIFFERENCE.** Ms. Oprah Winfrey has made her entire career out of being a first class ENCOURAGER. Are you an ENCOURAGER? Raise your right hand and pledge to encourage your friends and family.

I ______________________________ pledge to encourage my friends, family, neighbors, and coworkers to make a difference. I will stand up and speak up regarding issues that are important to my community. I will encourage everyone to step out in all directions, influencing everyone they touch. I will do my best to try to encourage people, not only in their daily lives, but also in pursuing their dreams. **I AM AN ENCOURAGER**

**NETWORKING.** Listening, sharing, and supporting each other's ideas is the foundation of networking. By banding together, we are able to share experiences and help each other discover and pursue our goals.

*"Our nettlesome task is to discover how to organize our strength into compelling power."*
—Dr. Martin Luther King, Jr.

We can benefit from networking by attending events offered by educational, professional, and social organizations. Networking lends itself to:

1. Empowering others to meet their goals.
2. Learning something about other people's lives, interests, projects, and businesses.
3. Educating people about our products or services.
4. Finding opportunities to serve on a committee and become a part of the group.

**COORDINATE A BOOK DRIVE.** Both new and gently used books can be collected. This is a brief list of ideas for book collections. Check those that you plan to put into action.

____ Bring a collection box to a child's birthday party, classrooms at school, or to a place of worship.

____ Collect books at meetings or public events that you attend.

____ Collect books in common areas, such as food courts, cafeterias, places of business, etc.

Consider the tasks outlined below, and the scope of your book drive; then allow yourself enough time to complete the following steps:

1. Planning and organizing
2. Publicity
3. Collecting the books
4. Sorting the books
5. Delivering the books

**EDUCATE YOUR FAMILY.** Teach them how to make their homes safer and more comfortable. There are many simple changes we can make to our homes that can increase its comfort and safety.

- Install handrails on both sides of all steps (inside and outside).
- Secure all carpets and area rugs with double-sided tape.
- Install easy to grasp shaped handles for all drawers and cabinet doors.
- Use brighter bulbs in all settings.
- Install nightlights in all areas of night activity.
- Install lever handles for all doors.
- Place a bench near entrances for setting down purchases and resting.
- Install closet lights, as well as adjustable rods and shelves.
- Install rocker light switches; consider illuminated ones in select areas.

http://www.aarp.org/families/home_design/universaldesign/making_home_safe.html

*When we make a positive difference in others lives, it is our opportunity to improve the value of life for ourselves and others.* **May GOD BLESS YOU and YOUR FAMILY as you go forward with your RANDOM ACTS OF KINDNESS; explore additional methods to MAKE A DIFFERENCE.**

**Answers To Fill In The Blanks:**

Skills

Duty

Recognition

Hungry

Academic

Team

*Notes:*

# ABOUT THE AUTHOR

## Dr. Millicent Gray Lownes-Jackson

Dr. Millicent Gray Lownes-Jackson is a well-known entrepreneurial leadership authority. She is an entrepreneur, researcher, writer, business consultant, business trainer, university administrator and tenured university professor of business management. In addition to presently serving as the Associate Dean of Tennessee State University's College of Business, she is the President of *A Business of Your Own*, a business consulting firm focusing on supporting the entrepreneurial woman. Dr. Lownes-Jackson is also the Founder of The Interdenominational Services Organization of America, Inc. (ISOA), a non-profit economic development organization that has impacted the lives of more than 5,000 youth and women through entrepreneurial training and economic enlightenment.

Having been on the forefront in the area of entrepreneurial leadership training as well as social entrepreneurial leadership development, Dr. Lownes-Jackson has appeared and been featured in numerous stories including *Black Enterprise Magazine*, *Contempora Magazine*, the *Tennessee Tribune* and the *Urban Journal*. Her entrepreneurial endeavors have also been featured in an entrepreneurial training film produced by the International Association of Black Business Educators (IABBE). Dr. Lownes-Jackson's accomplishments and unwavering commitment to society have been acknowledged by numerous honors and awards.

Her educational background includes a Bachelor of Business Administration Degree from Fisk University. She also has a Master of Business Administration Degree, a Master of Management Degree, and a Doctor of Philosophy Degree, all of which were conferred by Vanderbilt University. Additionally, she has postdoctoral training in the field of Marketing.

Dr. Lownes-Jackson is the author of *Savvy Leadership: A Woman's Guide to 21st Century Entrepreneurial Leadership* and many other entrepreneurial leadership development publications including *Starting A Child Care Center*, *Starting A Flower and Gift Shop*, and *Starting A Craft Business.* Dr. Lownes-Jackson is also a certified professional business coach and is aggressively pursued for speaking and training engagements.

*Contact:*
Dr. Millicent Gray Lownes-Jackson
A Business of Your Own
P.O. Box 210662
Nashville, Tennessee 37221-0662
(615) 646-3708
E-mail: success@womaninbiz.com
Website: www.ABusinessofYourOwn.com

## THIRTEEN

# ENTREPRENEURSHIP: STARTING YOUR OWN BUSINESS

**By Dr. Millicent Gray Lownes-Jackson**

So, perhaps you're starting to think about retirement. Or, maybe you have already joined the growing number of retired baby boomers who have put in their time in the work world and have moved to the next phase of life. The question that may now be running through your mind is, NOW WHAT? You have knowledge and wisdom from many years of experience. You've always had a burning inner entrepreneurial flame that only had a chance to flicker while you were in the labor force, or while you were perhaps working at home raising children. Well, maybe now is the time to pour fuel on the flame and let your inner entrepreneurial passion explode. Maybe it's your time to really focus on starting a business of your own.

The entrepreneurial spirit is a driving force of the economic tapestry of America. In fact, new millennium entrepreneurs are thriving in many of the hottest business industries. What are these industries? These industries, identified by futurists, trade groups, and professional surveys, include, but are not limited to, technology and telecommunications, medical, child and elder care, business consulting, finance, transportation, tourism, the arts, and specialized niches such as natural food products. Also included are industries that seem to make life easier for an increasingly affluent generation of twenty-somethings and aging baby boomers. These flourishing industries are shaped by a world where boundaries are merely lines on a map. As we progress in the 21$^{st}$ Century, global business opportunities abound. Be it the former Soviet Union, South Africa, China, Afghanistan, or any other environment where we historically did not dare to even think about entrepreneurially, opportunities exist for the envisioned, aggressive, and savvy entrepreneur.

**What Does It Take To Be An Entrepreneur?**

Are you an individualist, an independent type person, an adventurer? Are you a risk taker? Do you dislike taking common orders and doing the same thing every day? Do you like the freedom of working independently? Do you like testing your own talents and reaping benefits directly from your personal efforts? Do you desire to use your ideas, abilities, ambitions, aspirations, and initiatives to the greatest degree? If you answer yes to most of these questions, then maybe you need to consider owning a business of your own.

Whether you are tired of your present work situation, tired of the routine, feel that you are in a rut, feel that your abilities go overlooked, simply desire a chance to make more money, or just have spare time on your hands, entrepreneurship may be the answer allowing you to realize many of your dreams.

Certain characteristics have been found to be common among successful individuals who have started businesses. Successful entrepreneurs tend to be decisive, yet versatile. They follow tasks through to completion, they are self-confident, they are persistent, they have knowledge of the field in which they start their business, they have a strong degree of drive and they are energetic. They are also creative and analytical thinkers, and have good human relations skills. AM I DESCRIBING YOU?

There is no question that all people are not qualified to be a business owner, nor is there a question that the person who wishes to establish a business must depend on his or her own qualifications, business knowledge and acumen, abilities, and personal qualities to make it as an entrepreneur.

You can learn management skills, you can learn how to handle people, you can obtain expertise, you can learn to be self-disciplined, and you can find financial resources. What is critical to consider is whether or not you have a strong enough desire to own a business of your own, along with assessing whether your personal life will allow you to devote as much as 24 hours a day, 7 days a week, to fulfilling your dream without negative interference from a spouse, family, or friends. You must have the guts to implement plans, and you must have unwavering determination and commitment to accept the challenge of business ownership with all its frustrations, pitfalls, tears, hard work, and long hours.

Not only do you need to assess your interests, talents, skills, and abilities, but you also need to determine if the business venture you are considering is a workable product or service that has a feasible chance to survive and be successful. You need to be sure that there is an actual need for the products or services you are considering offering and that you are not just merely trying to satisfy your own need to be in business. This process involves conducting in-depth research resulting in what is called a feasibility study. The findings from the feasibility study will be compiled and incorporated in your Business Plan, which is a must for any new or ongoing business.

Do you have what it takes to be an entrepreneur? Only you can answer this question after thorough soul searching, probing research, and an extensive personal inward assessment. This inward appraisal should also reveal what you really enjoy doing and your passion.

**Passion, Planning, and Perseverance...The Foundation for Entrepreneurship Success**

Passion, planning, and perseverance are three important components of everyday life and the cornerstones to building a successful small business. Small business ownership is the synthesis of an individual's personal characteristics, talents, and abilities. It is, in essence, an extension of one's self. While one can perhaps cite examples of businesses that have become successful that were not started out of an entrepreneur's passion, for truly enduring and enjoyable success, the business owner must offer a product, service, or concept that not only satisfies a consumer need, but also is their passion or love. After all, to be successful in business, you will have to live and breathe the business 24/7, and there is no sense of doing anything in life you don't love doing when you reach the age status of a baby boomer.

There is seldom the introduction of a totally new product or service. It is the business owner's job to make their passion better and ultimately more sought after than those of established competitors. This makes business ownership hard work, as it demands total commitment and perseverance. But, simply identifying a personal passion that fills the needs of the market is not enough to assure business success. Planning is the key to turning a passion into a profitable venture. After conducting in-depth research about the feasibility of the venture being considered, including a thorough assessment of the industry, research findings should serve as the basis for formulating a detailed plan for the business, commonly called the Business Plan.

**The Business Plan**

A business plan is crucial in the development of a business, as it forces the owner to think thoroughly about the venture, and ultimately serves as a comprehensive framework for the business. The business plan discusses in detail every aspect of the business, from location and the product to financial statements and marketing strategies. It includes both short-term and long-term goals for the business, as well as potential risks and problems.

A business plan is a report written by you about your venture at a particular point in time. Your business plan should describe your venture, what it is, who will be active in it, why you believe it will be successful, and how you intend to implement your plans. It should be a concise, readable, well-written document. It should anticipate setbacks as well as successes; and it should be dated because you will want to revise or rewrite it at different times during the evolution of your business. A business plan is crucial to the internal operations of the business, as it serves as a checklist and timetable for accomplishing stated objectives. Additionally, it is essential in attracting external resources, both financial and human.

A thorough business plan should include clear descriptions and evaluating remarks of the following components.

**The Business**

1. Detailed description of the business including name, location, business goals and objectives, industry information, economic trends, etc.
2. Description of the product (services and/or goods), potential of the product line, technology, and possible advances
3. Description of the marketing plan, including target market, marketing strategies, channels of distribution, market size and share, market potential, pricing strategy, and promotion
4. Assessment of the competition
5. Management, covering such areas as key personnel, names of accountants, lawyers, consultants, organizational structure, experience of key personnel, educational background and experience
6. Legal structure of the business
7. Personnel, position descriptions, labor trends, and compensation
8. Facilities and equipment
9. Sources of supply
10. Critical risks and problems
11. Economic trends
12. Strategies for the future

**Financial Data**

1. Capital equipment
2. Sources of funds
3. Balance sheet
4. Break-even analysis
5. Income projections or profit-loss statement
6. Pro forma cash flow
7. Uses of funds
8. Desired funding

**Supporting Documents**

1. Resumes of key personnel
2. Personal financial statements and credit reports
3. Letters of reference
4. Copies of leases
5. Legal documents and contracts
6. Vendor agreements
7. Copyrights
8. Patents

9. Drawings, photographs

10. Articles

11. Any additional pertinent information

Planning is an intricate endeavor that doesn't stop with the initial development of the business plan. It is a continuous, ongoing process that must take into consideration market shifts, economic trends and changes in the competitive environment. In other words, the visionary entrepreneur must strategically plan every aspect of their business.

Perseverance is the determination that keeps the successful entrepreneur forging ahead, regardless of the obstacles and setbacks encountered. Perseverance is that intangible element that separates the weak from the strong. You must continue relentlessly pursuing your vision until the victory of success is achieved. With the development of a business plan, you have a basic blueprint for operating your business. But the plan has to be implemented. You cannot achieve the vision of initiating and building a successful venture without strong leadership skills. After all, we are talking about leading your own business, your dream, along a road to success.

**Savvy Leadership For The Entrepreneurially Minded**

For the entrepreneurially minded who want to achieve their vision of success, savvy leadership skills may very well be the factor to determine competitive success in the global 21$^{st}$ century business environment.

The savvy entrepreneur knows the basics. They know they must have a well-formulated business plan that incorporates knowledge and information resulting from extensive research. They understand the critical need to develop, follow, and implement a realistic strategic plan. But, to propel a business to achieve competitive success, many don't understand how crucial it is to have strong leadership skills and to execute those skills with remarkable savvy. In other words, the entrepreneur needs to be a savvy leader.

And what do I mean by being a *Savvy Leader*? I mean taking the entrepreneurial helm with vision; having the ability to get others to see the vision; empowering and actuating others to help in achieving the vision; and leading decisively with sophistication and style. Whether you are simply leading a solo entrepreneurial venture along a path to your vision of success in the global business arena, or leading a team of talented individuals employed to assist you in realizing your dreams, being a savvy leader is vital.

What does the model for 21$^{st}$ Century entrepreneurial leadership encompass? It starts with an in-depth self-assessment of the entrepreneurial leader. The leader must know and be comfortable with who they are, and should assess themselves compared to qualities found to be common among successful leaders. These qualities include being a visionary, being trustworthy, having integrity, being consistent in behavior and in making decisions, having good judgement, having the persona of a leader, being resilient and adaptable, being knowledgeable, having courage, being decisive, being resilient, having the ability to influence others, and having the gift of discernment. The entrepreneurial leader must also have a clear, sharable vision and passionately detail the plan to bring the vision to fruition. They must also have the coveted ability to "get off of go." In other words, they must have the ability to execute plans. Additionally, they must know their leadership style, and know the style that works best in their operating environment.

The entrepreneurial leader must also understand the 21st century socio-economic environment, and must understand that the new millennium business environment has an operative backdrop of integrity, accountability, diversity, mutual respect, coaching, innovative thinking, resiliency, adaptability, continuous improvement, and assessment of outcomes. The savvy entrepreneurial leader also understands that along the road to success, their vision and plan may need to be altered due to changes in the operating environment.

After a thorough self-assessment, the savvy entrepreneurial leader next must focus on interpersonal relations. To survive the challenges of 21st century entrepreneurial leadership, the leader must thoroughly understand intricate group dynamics, the mystique of motivation, and the importance of getting along with people. Refinement of relationship skills, abilities to motivate others, communication skills, and the talent to develop a cohesive team desirous of pursuing the vision is critical. The entrepreneur must also know how to deal with difficult people and how to resolve conflict so as to encourage critical and creative thinking and positive action.

The final aspect of the model for 21st century entrepreneurial leadership directs attention to synergism. The savvy entrepreneurial leader must take the information revealed as a result of a thorough self-assessment, effectively utilize their knowledge and skills developed pertaining to interpersonal relations, and develop a business and organizational climate that encourages continuous strategic planning, assessment of goal attainment, continuous organizational improvement, and receptiveness to making organization changes, as necessary, to accomplish the vision and the strategic plan.

With an internationally focused and a technologically advanced business sector, along with a more culturally diverse workforce, it can no longer be business as usual in America. Changes are occurring on every front; and enthusiastically embracing and becoming knowledgeable in the critical aspects of 21st century entrepreneurial leadership will help those at the helm of entrepreneurial ventures to become savvy entrepreneurial leaders realizing their vision of success.

**Concluding Thoughts**

Now, no one said the entrepreneurial pursuit of happiness was easy. There are many challenges to consider, including the lack of a guaranteed paycheck, being out there on a limb with just a dream, working in isolation, difficulties in raising capital, burdensome paperwork, regulations, the business struggle in general, and not having enough business knowledge and experience, just to cite a few. On the other hand, the quest for entrepreneurship success is still very much a part of the American Dream. To many it offers independence, self-fulfillment, wealth, prestige, and a way of controlling one's own time and destiny. Entrepreneurship affords the opportunity to be your own boss, the ability to improve your economic status, the thrill of nurturing your dream into a viable business entity, the chance to reap direct benefits from your hard work, and the list goes on and on and is an individualized list for each entrepreneur.

So, you still think you want to start a business? There are many sources you can go to for additional information and support. As it certainly is beyond the limits of this chapter to provide all of the information necessary for starting a business, select resources are provided at the end of this chapter to assist you in acquiring the knowledge and skills necessary for your entrepreneurial pursuit of happiness.

You're never too old to dream. You're never too old to have an entrepreneurial vision. You must reach for the stars and only pause, for a brief rest, on the moon. Start with your passion; plan, plan, plan, and plan some more; and continue pursuing your entrepreneurial vision of success with unwavering determination, perseverance, and savvy leadership skills.

Support Sources for Entrepreneurially Minded Baby Boomers

A Business of Your Own
(615) 646-3708 • www.ABusinessofYourOwn.com

Minority Business Development Agency
(888) 324-1551 • www.mbda.gov

National Association for the Self-Employed
(800) 232-6273 • www.nase.org

NAWBO (National Association of Women Business Owners)
(800) 55-NAWBO • www.nawbo.org

National Business Incubation Association
(740) 593-4331 • www.nbia.org

SCORE
(800) 634-0245 • www.score.org

U.S. Small Business Administration and SBDCs
(800) 827-5722 • www.sbaonline.sba.gov

*Notes:*

# ABOUT THE AUTHOR

## ROSEMARY MEDEL

A City Planner for the last seventeen years in Southern California, Rosemary has worked for the cities of Huntington Beach, Cypress and Signal Hill. A Bachelor of Fine Arts degree with an emphasis in Environmental Design, California State University at Fullerton has prepared Ms. Medel for her current profession in Land Use Planning. She feels strongly about giving back to her community and has volunteered her Planning expertise to the community where she currently resides. Rosemary is a former Planning Commissioner for the City of La Habra where she assisted in guiding development during her three-year term. Currently, Rosemary is a Realtor, and is the owner and president of The Medel Group. Her firm is committed to training and preparing its clients facing risks with confidence, develop their professional image through improved public speaking and presentation skills. She is a co-author of *You're on Stage! Image, Etiquette, Branding & Style, Emotional Wellness for Women: Mind Body & Spirit, Survival Guide for Overcoming Obstacles, Transition & Change, Women as Leaders, Beyond the Body! Developing Inner Beauty,* and *Young Man's Guide for Personal Success.* She is slated to author the future book *The Baby Boomers Handbook for Women.*

Rosemary is a certified trainer in Woman's Issues and a certified Professional Coach and is an International Advisory Board member of the Professional Woman Network. She is also a member of both The Professional Woman Network International Speakers Bureau and the National Association of Female Executives. Rosemary is available for personal and professional coaching sessions.

Her most important role and accomplishment has been raising her two grown children Rosalie and Eli.

*Contact:*
Rosemary Medel
The Medel Group
P.O. Box 2204
La Habra, CA 90632-2204
rosemedel@juno.com
www.TheMedelGroup.com

## FOURTEEN

# SKINCARE, MAKEUP & LOOKING TERRIFIC AT ANY AGE

### By Rosemary Medel

Would you agree that beauty is more than skin deep? We as women are harsher on ourselves than any magazine, any fashion article or beauty book could ever be. As Baby Boomers, we grew up with the **SUPER MODEL!** Who could forget Beverly Johnson or Cheryl Tiggs on the cover of those fashion magazines we all purchased in the 1960's and 1970's? Come on; admit you purchased them. Our generation also embraced nutrition and exercise, unlike women have done before. No, we were not going to take a pill and take off 10 pounds. **WE** were going to run, dance or do aerobics until the pounds came off! We learned about eating healthy food. So after all these years, what have we learned from our quest to stay young and fit?

Well, I have created a **MUST DO** list in order to stay looking the best we can at any age, and more importantly, staying healthy into old age. Now before I share this list, I must share some information with you about myself, other than my biography on the previous page. What you do not know about me is that I am a licensed cosmetologist in the State of California. I received my license when I was 19 years old, and even after retiring as a hairstylist, I have retained a valid license to remind myself of the effort and determination it took to acquire my license, and of course to get discounts on hair products at the beauty supply store! At the writing of this book, I am 53 years old. On May 27, 2008 I will turn 54! Now come on, that's kind of getting up there. Good grief, next year I get a **SENIOR DISCOUNT**! I'm too young to be that old! But let me tell you, I do not look that old! So now I will share why I think I have managed to stay young minded and young looking. More importantly, I will give you all the information you need to start or continue to look and feel **YOUNGER!**

**Your Health And Your Spirit**

First, you must take care of your health. Staying healthy must always be your number one priority. Your skin, hair and eyes will reflect good health if you are taking care of yourself. Staying healthy also gives you a brighter outlook on life. You want to try more things when you feel strong and healthy. So, how do you get started if you have neglected your health or want to start taking care of yourself? To start with, a visit to your doctor's office to get examined and beginning an exercise program are some good choices.

Now, there is another choice for your health that I recently learned. It is call the Bio Energetic Synchronization Technique, B.E.S.T. This system of health care deals with the emotional cause of illness. It teaches you how to allow your body to heal itself as it is suppose to function, and how to align your subconscious emotions with your conscious emotions. Also, if dealing with prolonged stress, which can be physical, emotional or nutritional is an issue for you, the B.E.S.T. will help, as well. Dr. M. Ted Morter, Jr. wrote **Dynamic Health** to inform and teach us how to achieve optimal health! Simply, it restores balance in the body connecting mind, body and spirit. Sound good? In the words of the Morter System, "BEST principles acknowledge the concept of Interference we create in our conscious mind. This Interference caused imbalance in the autonomic nervous system to exhaustion of our organ systems over time." The reference section of this chapter will provide contact information.

You will also want to see your dentist. The health of your teeth relates to your over all health, as well. Improve your smile! Dentists can do wonders to improve a person's smile, which will give you more confidence. Now there are literally tons of information on vitamins, dentistry and healthy living available to you. What I hope to convey to you is that you need to get started taking good care of yourself! There is no excuse, given the access to all the information on the internet, local libraries and book stores. As a Baby Boomer, you are determined, multi-tasking woman who can achieve whatever your heart desires!

Let us work on the inside. Do not ignore your mental health and your spirit. For me, music is my heaven. Even if there are no words coming out of my mouth, there is always a song being played in my mind. Music is so wonderful for the soul and spirit. Did you know that music is one of the closest experience to getting in touch with your spirit? In fact, Dr. David Hawkins, renowned lecturer and expert on mental processes, stated at a recent seminar I attended, that the left brain deals with survival and the right brain deals with spirit. Music is so powerful that it evokes the emotion of tears. I agree with that statement. Let me give you an example. On Sunday mornings I love to have tea or coffee and play the Three Tenors. Sometimes I will just listen on the headphones to get the full impact of the music. Talk about evoking the spirit within! Have some quiet time just for yourself to get back to your spirit! Or walk in nature and enjoy all that God has created. Notice the birds singing, the sounds of everything awakening. Just enjoy being alive and be grateful for the moment.

I would also suggest that you read inspirational and self-improvement books. Books become our mentors and teachers. The first books towards building your library should be the entire Professional Woman Network (PWN) book library. The PWN library provides guidance, heart felt stories, advice and education for women, youth and the people who love them. At the end of this chapter I will provide a list of books to help rediscover YOU!

**Skincare: So Many Products!**

As with the generations before us, Baby Boomers have earned every line and wrinkle. While our generation has also made plastic surgeons rich over the years, we are starting to let the plastic Hollywood image go. We have come to realize that being in good health, good body weight, smart and spiritual creates the total beauty package. So let us talk about skin care. What is the first thing you must do for great skin? If you smoke, STOP! Nothing on the planet ages your skin faster than smoking. Not to mention those attractive lines around the mouth that it creates. Next, protect your skin if you are in the sun. Even we brown skinned girls have to protect our skin from excessive sun exposure. Again, there are lots of products to select from out in the market. Speak to a skin care professional so that your skin can be analyzed. So, how do you get started?

1. Wash your face each night to remove dirt from the environment.
2. Use a gentle cloth with tepid water and a mild cleanser to exfoliate the skin.
3. If you have really oily skin, a toner may help. But read the label so that it is not all alcohol, which will dry out your skin.
4. Drink plenty of water to flush toxins from your body and keep your skin hydrated.
5. Monitor the PH balance in your body. High acid equals bad skins causing breakouts.

So what do all the ingredients mean on the skin care product labels?

1. Alpha hydroxyl acid: A naturally occurring acid that helps loosen surface skin cells. It also helps to reduce the look of fine lines and minimize large pores.
2. Collagen: A natural protein found in the skin.
3. Glycolics: Helps gently remove dead skin cells to leave smooth skin.
4. Retinoids: Vitamin A derivative that stimulates collagen production.

**Makeup And Hair**

Let's face it, every once in a while we could all use some makeup! But whether wearing make is a special occasion thing or a part of your everyday routine, here are some helpful tips on selecting the products that are right for you. One of the best product line counters to have some makeup applied is the Bobbi Brown counter. They have great staff and they do not over-do the make application. Bobbi's makeup colors are fantastic for most skins colors. Her knowledgeable makeup artists are easy to talk to and are good teachers, as well. One makeup tip I learned from the experts is to define one part of the face at a time. If you choose a strong eye shadow color or really focus on the eyes, then soften the lip color to look nude, natural or just lip pencil and gloss. A must add to your library is **Bobbi Brown's Living Beauty**. This book is a great resource of information regarding skincare, makeup application at all ages, makeovers and aging beautifully. Details will be on the resource page at the end of this chapter.

Another popular line is M.A.C. (Makeup Art Cosmetics). They have stores in major malls across the country and Canada. Professional makeup artists use their line. Their claim to fame is their matte eye shadows, professional brushes and lipstick colors. Now I must warn you, if you want them to do your makeup, unless you specifically ask for a particular look, you will get the colors de jour! Oh yeah, you will be wearing whatever color palette is being promoted, regardless if it looks hideous on you. Unlike the Bobbi Brown counter, this line is geared to the younger consumer. Now once you know what you like, the line is great. I have been using their lip liners and lipsticks for years. And yes, I was a makeup promotion victim! GIRL I looked bad! I made the staff member take off the clown makeup and offered to do it myself, explaining that my intention was to purchase items from the more conservative categories. Yes, I embarrassed by daughter Rosalie who made the appointment for the makeup application. But I left a large tip as amends for being high maintenance.

Now talk about being high maintenance, my naturally curly hair is definitely high maintenance. I always believed God gave me this hair to keep me humble. Or he just had a great sense of humor! As I mentioned, I was a hairstylist for twelve years. My clients were mainly Caucasian men and women who all wanted a permanent like the one I got. It killed me to curl their straight hair. I know we all want what the other person has. But my favorite part of my business was cutting hair. To me, it was the most artistic and creative part, next to coloring hair. One of the best investments you can make on yourself is a good haircut. The tools that are used today to curl, flat iron (yes this is new to all my white sisters), and blow out your hair give you no excuse not to look your best. If you are not proficient with these tools, ask your stylist to teach you. If they refuse or give you an attitude, then find one who is more sympathetic. If you are looking for a good stylist, stop into a salon and observe who is creating a style you would like. Notice the creativeness of the hairstylist and their personality, observing to see which one you would feel comfortable talking to.

Most importantly, stay current with your look. Nothing ages you more than an outdated hairstyle. If you need to color your hair or would like to consider color, it will reduce the years off your appearance. However, remember that color is **HIGH MAINTENANCE!** Not to mention costly. But please **DO NOT** color your hair if you are not going to maintain the color. Grown out ROOTS are horrible. Again, this will set you potentially back $50 to $150 per month, plus tip, depending on what part of the country you live in. So now you have skin care expertise, makeup, and your hair is looking good. What next? Ahh, my favorite!

**Fashion**

What better way to express your self-image than through fashion. Being a native Southern California girl, I grew up in warm sunny weather. Our winter is rainy and with only occasional frost, so not many opportunities for coats, sweaters, and turtlenecks. But I absolutely love them all. Now, clothing is even more expensive than maintaining your hair. So what should you buy? Think of fashion and the purchasing of garments as an investment. Buy the best garment you can at the lowest price you can. Nordstroms has a discount store called the RACK. All the same designers, but much lower prices. Go there with enough time to browse for the perfect buy. Bloomingdales has great sales as well, so visit them, too.

Stick to basics and add color in a top or accessories. So, how can you tell if a garment is worth the money? Here is a professional secret; turn it inside out, and notice the stitching. Is it sewn with what is called a straight stitch and an over-lock? The over-lock is the S-shape stitching closing where two pieces of material meet. A well-made garment has both. So what if it is lined? How do you tell if it is a quality garment? Look at the finishing of the garment. Look at the buttons and top-stitching, which adds to the style, but also reinforces the garment. Look at the quality of the material. Now, when all else fails, we Southern California (So Cal) girls love jeans, heels, white tees and a stylish jacket. The final 'MUST HAVE' to complete your beauty makeover is Attitude!

**Attitude**

I would like you to start to notice people's appearance. Notice the total packet: hair, makeup and fashion. Notice if it seems to suit the personality they are projecting? Why this exercise? Because others are evaluating you, as well. You need to become the total package. Invest time and money to make the outside match the inside. If you are reading this book, you most likely have a good sense of self and are continuing to improve and reinvent yourself through self-improvement books. Beauty starts with attitude and confidence. Create the image you want to portray, and then do not think about it any further. The image you create will be your STYLE!

I believe a woman of style is confident, well-mannered, well read, considerate, compassionate, and world-minded. This woman takes nothing for granted and lives in gratitude every day. She knows that an education will get her a job, but self-improvement will make her a fortune.

In closing, I have dedicated this chapter to my beautiful daughter Rosalie Marisa Cetina. She is one of the most knowledgeable people I know when it comes to skin care and cosmetic lines. She is a true beauty inside and out. She worked at the table just coloring while I worked on my college art projects. I was always amazed that she could be so engaged in her projects and have such patience. Rosalie was born when I was 24 years of age, so we practically grew up together. More importantly, she has been my inspiration to develop to my full potential. How could I encourage and teach my daughter to reach her potential, or just to live in full happiness, if I did not have the courage to do the same. I am still a work in progress and have a long way to go. I love you Rosalie.

**Recommended Reading:**

Entire PWN Library (17 books)

*Living Beauty* by Bobbi Brown

*Stop Aging, Start Living* by Jeannette Graf, M.D.

*Don't Go To The Cosmetics Counter Without Me* by Paula Begoun

*Natural Healing* by Gary Null, Ph. D.

Power vs. Force by Dr. David R. Hawkins, M.D., Ph. D., Power vs. Force

The Eye Of The Eye by Dr. David R. Hawkins, M.D., Ph. D.

*You Staying Young* by Michael F. Roizen, M.D. and Mehmet C. Oz, M.D.

Morter Health Systems, www.morter.com

*Notes:*

## ABOUT THE AUTHOR

### Dr. Catherine R. Strecker

Catherine R. Strecker, Ph.D., is an Educational Consultant and President of Catherine Strecker Educational Strategies. Her client base includes school districts, businesses, clubs, non-profit organizations and individual groups. Her mission is to provide people an opportunity to engage in learning using their dominant intelligences and multiple ways of learning. She assesses people of all ages which provide the acknowledgement to their dominant intelligences and also strength in school or career.

Dr. Strecker holds a Bachelor of Science in Education, Master of Science in Reading and Education, and a Doctorate in Education. Her dissertation topic is: Assessing Multiple Intelligences In Elementary School-Students. She is a member of The Professional Women Network, the National Association for Female Executives, Business and Professional Women, Diocesan School Council Member and the Ellinwood Chamber of Commerce. She is married to Monty and have five children, Jacob, Nicklaus, Rachel, Rebecca, and Joanna, a daughter-n-law, Andrea, two grandchildren, Spencer, Adelynne, and a future daughter-n-law, Laura.

She is available for presentations, workshops, interviews, project design, and consultation on a local, national, and international basis.

Dr. Catherine Strecker would like to dedicate this chapter to her mother, Shirley R. Hunt for being a wonderful mother and role model.

*Contact:*
Catherine Strecker Educational Strategies
P.O. Box 93
17 North Main
Ellinwood, Kansas 67526
(620) 564-2510 Office
(620) 564-2620 Fax
crs@hbcomm.net
www.educationalstrategies.net

FIFTEEN

# LIFE IS AN ATTITUDE

## By Dr. Catherine R. Strecker

Life is given to us once. It is up to us to choose the attitude we will adopt in our approach. We have one chance to live life on the terms we select. What attitude is guiding yours?

I am of the "school of thought" that views life events as far less important than the attitude applied in facing them. Some people find a positive and content nature difficult to develop, even when things are going well. When good fortune "smiles on them," such individuals tend to downplay it, often with suspicious or superstitious fear. Conversely, when things go wrong, they almost take satisfaction in pronouncing, "See, I knew it was just a matter of time."

I would suggest to you that life lived in this way is a loss of a magnitude that will not be realized until life is nearly over. A focus on the positive side of any situation, coupled with an approach to life with openness, faith, joy, and gratitude, will replace such dread with an overwhelming sense of having lived a full, productive, and happy life. Life lived by these chosen terms can only attract positive events while deflecting the negative. This does not mean that bad things don't happen to good people, but it does mean that when they *do* happen, the impact can be minimized with a positive attitude. My friend, Ann Depperschmidt states, "Life is full of things we can't change. But we always have the power to change our attitude on how we view those things."

Also aptly put by author and speaker Zig Ziglar, "The way you see life will determine what you get out of it." Minister and author Charles "Chuck" Swindoll wrote the following meaningful passage on the importance of attitude that also provides a valuable perspective:

**ATTITUDES**

Words can never adequately convey the incredible impact of our attitude toward life. The longer I live, the more convinced I become that life is 10% what happens to us and 90% how we respond to it.

*I believe the single most significant decision I can make on a day-to-day basis is my choice of attitude. It is more important than my past, my education, my bankroll, my successes or failures, fame or pain, what other people think of me or say about me, my circumstances, or my position. Attitude keeps me going or cripples my progress. It alone fuels my fire or assaults my hope. When my attitudes are right, there's no barrier too high, no valley too deep, no dream too extreme, no challenge too great for me.*

*Strengthening Your Grip by* Charles R. Swindoll
(Used by permission of Insight for Living, Plano, TX 75026)

I consider myself a "bookworm," someone who can spend hours reading with a focus that completely "tunes out" my surroundings. When asked to contribute a chapter for this book on the topic of attitude, I approached the notion with enthusiasm and confidence. Yet days passed with minimal contribution to the project. Granted, hours were invested in researching and reading publications on the topic, but for some reason, the words I wanted just wouldn't flow onto the page. I could have halfheartedly regurgitated the thoughts of others or approached this opportunity with a "head-smart" attitude. My advice would have likely offered a textbook mentality, rather than the perspective from real and personal experience that I desired to deliver.

To me, what really matters are the real-life experiences that touch our inner soul, give us strength through the trials of life, and attract support from others who have lived through similar challenges. I seem to learn best from the experiences of others rather than theory. So rather than preach a theoretical formula, I would like to share with you the life benefits I have experienced by adopting a positive attitude.

As I began working on this chapter, my doctor discovered a lump in my breast. Suffice it to say, this was one of the scariest moments of my life. The mammogram was first, then a sonogram, as doctors worked to identify the lump. Anyone who has been through this knows the fear and confusion while waiting for the results with knowledge of the possible outcomes. One woman, Julie Boxberger, described the waiting as "feeling like you are in a fog," and she was right. This was exactly how I felt most of the time. It helped to talk with other women who were enduring the same experience or had done so in the past. Not only did I crave information, but I also needed to know I wasn't alone. Some of the stories had happy outcomes; others did not. However, most of the women who shared their experiences with me seemed to focus on maintaining a positive outlook, regardless of their prognosis. I decided to take the same approach. As I waited for the verdict, I relied upon my faith and support from my friends and family. I worked hard to nurture thoughts of abundant good health, and kept my mind occupied with work and projects such as this writing to you.

Suddenly, the proverbial light came on, like a spark inside my soul! I was so inspired by the many women who traveled this road before me, those who decided to live life with positive attitudes despite the prospects (or reality) of breast cancer, that I no longer needed the inspiration to write. The words lay directly in front of me. Women are truly amazing in their attitudes toward life. We can learn so much from one another's experiences.

While I awaited my test results, I journaled my thoughts:

*All of the "book knowledge", the "words of wisdom" I often give to others, I must now apply to me. Practice what you preach. Tell others how to live? How can I become a better person myself, and deal with life's attitude? I choose to be strong, to live this day, and to focus on the good things that are happening. To share with others my journey, and how God intervenes. How does He? Prayer, family, and friends are blessings in this journey of life. Find strength through adversity.*

During the seemingly endless waiting period, I kept my strength by praying, "God, I know you are in control today, and may *this* be the day I receive a miracle and restored health!" The Lord was the first person I thanked when the sonogram revealed a benign cyst with a probable cause of too much caffeine.

Another life experience requiring a positive attitude is childbirth. Are any of us *really* prepared for this, especially the first time around? You can read about it in books, talk to doctors and everyone you know who has been through it, but nothing really prepares you. It is truly one of those life events when attitude is the only thing within your control. When I was pregnant with my first child, my expectations included delivery on or very close to the "scheduled" date, as well as a "normal" delivery. Yet my son decided he would arrive several weeks ahead of schedule, and by cesarean birth. Was I ready for this to happen with suitcase packed and emotions prepared for surgery? Absolutely not! This was certainly not the picture-perfect childbirth experience I had envisioned, but rather than focus on what hadn't gone according to plan, I sought the positives. The easiest way to maintain this path was to keep my attention on what I just knew would be the most beautiful new baby in existence, and the gratitude I felt for his future presence in my life!

My second child was a planned cesarean birth with no surprises; well, at least not through the pregnancy. When the anesthesiologist placed the epidural, I was the "lucky" recipient of what is likely the worst nightmare shared among us all. The reality that I was not actually anesthetized was not discovered until I screamed in pain when the surgery began. Needless to say, the problem was rapidly rectified, only to then have my newborn son whisked away to intensive care immediately upon birth, where he remained for several weeks. Was this my "dream delivery"? No. Nor could I control or change the events as they happened; but I was able to choose how to cope with this life-threatening situation. I thanked God that my baby and I were alive, and spared myself the greater pain and discomfort of nurturing anger and prolonged fear over the incident. The attitude I chose allowed me to introduce my baby to the world on a positive, healthy note.

My third child, a daughter, was delivered without complications. Yet afterward, my doctor suggested no further childbirth attempts. While I understood the doctor's reasoning and caution, my attitude included an overwhelming trust in God to take care of my life. If I were meant to have more children, so be it. My fourth child was also delivered without complication. However, this time, the doctor plainly stated that I should have no future pregnancies. My fifth child, another daughter, was born on schedule, also with no problems. My experiences with childbirth have not been "ideal," and there were times I faced great risk. Yet my attitude, with each pregnancy and delivery, was to focus on my faith and my belief that life would manifest as God intended, and that He would ensure I was equipped to handle all that came my way. Choosing the road of faith and a positive attitude will see you successfully through many "rocky" journeys.

Approaching life with a positive attitude begins with widening your vision. When we have difficulty seeing the good in any situation, it's often because the scope of our vision is simply too narrow. Picture this: You are stranded on a deserted island, looking for a ship to come along and rescue you. You have a telescope with which you scan the horizon, searching in desperation for that rescue ship. You can't see one, and you despair, but your telescope is adjusted to one small portion of the horizon. Had you adjusted your view by just a fraction, you would have noticed the ship you so desperately needed sail by, just outside your limited range of vision. Sailing through life with a negative attitude is akin to using a telescope with a narrow field of vision. You are prevented from seeing the "big picture" and the blessings awaiting you just out of sight. When you expand the scope of your vision, you open yourself up to unlimited possibilities. As my friend, Sharon Schartz, advised, "Have a dream; pursue your passion." You will never know what could have happened if you don't try!

Believing that something good can come from any situation opens the full realm of possibilities for health, abundance, fellowship, fun, success, love, peace, and happiness. It is a phenomenon of life that we tend to receive whatever we focus our attention on, so doesn't it make sense to focus on the positive things in life? This could be the day a miracle manifests in your life—anything is possible! Sister Louise Hangeman reminds us to "continually explore and live new paradigms that foster transformation into all that is full human."

How can we maintain a positive attitude about life when we are surrounded by others who are negative? This is always a challenge, especially if you're someone who gives great credence to the opinions of others. It's not easy to disregard what people think of our decisions or of us, especially if they're loved ones or others we respect. All are entitled to their opinions, and approval of us or our choices is not a prerequisite. The difficulty we have, as human beings, is our need for that approval, which causes us to stumble more often than any other obstacle. The key here is that what *you* believe has a far greater impact on your life than the beliefs of others. While listening to the opinions of others is a natural reaction (After all, it never hurts to reflect upon all sides of an issue!), it's what *you* believe—and how *you* act on what you believe—that will impact *your* life. If you live your life by the opinions or advice of others, choosing only what makes others happy before yourself, you are indeed living a life that is not your own. It can feel "easier" to allow others to make decisions for us, but the feeling is false because nothing is ever easy when we're not living authentic lives. Abdicating responsibility for our own choices will ultimately catch up to us in adverse outcomes out of our control. Never substitute your own good judgment for the judgment to others.

When you are confronted with a big decision, or facing a personal or professional challenge, and those around you can't or won't be supportive and positive, "step back" from those relationships to distance yourself from the negativity. I am not suggesting a need to eliminate such people from your life, but temporarily minimizing the nature and amount of contact during a stressful period will help you to deal with the situation at hand in a more positive fashion. For instance, when considering a major life change that may be positive for you, while unwelcome by others, delaying discussion of the potential change with these individuals until you have decided what is best for you will allow you to progress through the process in a more positive manner. Inviting negativity from those with their own agendas will not introduce constructive feedback. One practical scenario might be receiving a diagnosis of a serious health problem. You are committed to approaching it with the most positive attitude, but individuals close to you are focused on their own fears of what "might" happen and can offer no positive support. They are entitled to their personal fears, but their perspectives will not contribute to your own commitment toward a more positive perspective. Spending time with those who *can* provide you with the type of support you need will keep your attitude on your chosen path.

It is important to surround yourself with people able and willing to support you unconditionally, those who will cheer you on without consideration to any personal agenda of their own. Look around you. Do you spend time with people who tend to be positive or negative about life events? Perhaps it's time to seek new friends with an outlook on life that matches your own. When a "friend" cannot be happy for you when you are doing something good for yourself, or cannot provide the type of support you need when things get tough, such a friendship must be reconsidered. You have the ability to choose your friends as well as your attitude. Choose wisely. In the perfect words of my friend, Linda Henderson, "Don't let others write your life story for you. Take pen in hand, take control, and write your life story the way you want to live it."

I've met people who seem to wear a negative, skeptical attitude like a "badge of honor." They're proud of what they call their "street smarts," their sarcastic or even paranoid views of the world, and even their own negativity. They live convinced of their need for that type of attitude to "succeed" in life, fearful that, without it, someone will come along and take advantage of them. This approach to life may reap certain types of success, but true happiness and an enjoyment of life are typically not among them. Choosing a positive attitude also does not equate to progressing through life with blinders on, ignoring the fact that pain and suffering exist in the world and that, at times, we are on the receiving end.

Staying positive doesn't mean a "Pollyanna" approach to life, nor does it mean "burying your head in the sand," avoiding reality. A positive nature refers to designing and creating the life you ultimately want to live, intentionally constructing a specific quality of life for yourself and those you love. It is living consciously rather than unconsciously, with an understanding that your attitude really does make a difference. When you begin to realize that your *attitude* about life actually *shapes* your life, priorities become clear. At the end of the day, it is your attitude toward life that is paramount because, simply put, life *is* an attitude. My fiend and colleague Alicia Fricke says it all with these words, life is a whole easier if you have the right attitude. The choice is yours.

The completion of this chapter entails my wonderful mother's tidbits of wisdom that she continues to formulate on her life's journey! Mother's continuing journey consists of 56 years of marriage at the age of 16 years old. She completed her general education degree and continued her education by taking several college classes. For twenty-five years mother's occupation involved being a waitress and proceeding as a warranty clerk.

**Life Lessons** by Shirley Hunt

1. Believe in God.
2. Believe in family life.
3. Believe in education.
4. Make lemonade out of lemons.
5. Hobbies can relieve stress.
6. Never repeat gossip.
7. Follow the golden rule.
8. Be kind to everyone as one could be an angel.
9. Be strong.
10. Anger doesn't accomplish anything.

Thanks to Jill Eastwood and Lisa Taylor Huff for their contributions to this chapter which is dedicated to my mother Shirley Hunt.

*Notes:*

## ABOUT THE AUTHOR

### TREIVOR BRANCH

This chapter is dedicated to my mother Mary Branch for her continued support, positive spirit, and exemplary approach to *dealing with stress and anxiety.*

Treivor Branch is the President and Founder of *Success Her Way,* an international coaching and training network for women. Ms. Branch founded *Success Her Way* based on her passion to help women reach their full potential and improve their quality of life by transforming challenges into opportunities for success. She conducts training focused on life skills and self-empowerment which have been presented throughout the United States and abroad. Through her interactive training programs as well as individual and group coaching sessions Ms. Branch provides strategies to develop a life plan, overcome obstacles and achieve goals. Ms. Branch has a warm inviting demeanor which helps her get to the heart of the issues her clients face.

Ms. Branch has over 12 years of experience in the field of human resources management with specializations in employee relations, staffing, global deployment, and training and development. She graduated cum laude with a Bachelor's in Business Administration and is currently pursuing her Master's in Psychology. Ms. Branch is a certified professional development trainer specializing in women's issues, diversity, and conflict resolution. She is also a certified life coach, conflict management and human resources consultant.

**Professional Affiliations**

The American Society for Training & Development (ASTD)
The International Coach Federation (ICF)
The National Association for Female Executives (NAFE)
The Professional Woman Network (PWN)
The Society for Human Resource Management (SHRM)

*Contact:*
Treivor Branch
Success Her Way
P.O. Box 3685
Milford, CT 06460
Phone: 203-927-0179
Email: tbranch@successherway.com
Website: www.successherway.com

SIXTEEN

# WIRED! HOW TO DEAL WITH STRESS & ANXIETY

**By Treivor Branch**

*"Janice, the client has accelerated the closing date. We need you to work late this week to bring this project in on schedule."*

*"Mom, I have my recital in two days and you haven't finished my outfit."*

*"Honey, I'm having my boss over for dinner tomorrow night and we need to impress. I want this promotion."*

*"Darling it's your mother, I haven't heard from you in weeks. Is everything okay? I'm flying in tomorrow to spend the week with you."*

Janice is officially WIRED! Likely you can empathize with Janice. Have you ever had the feeling that your hair is sticking straight up and your eyes are popping out of your head like you've just experienced an electric shock? If so, then you are all too familiar with the effects of stress and anxiety. Daily living in today's society provides us with no shortage of contributors to stress and anxiety. In addition, being a member of the "sandwich generation" provides a direct connection to stress and anxiety.

**Attitude Adjustment**

We are not able to eliminate stress and anxiety from our lives because any life event, positive or negative, can be a contributor. However, the ways in which we deal with stress and anxiety make all the difference. Start by adjusting your attitude about stress and anxiety. Not all stress and anxiety are bad; in fact, they are a necessary part of life and we should welcome them. Yes that's right, roll out the welcome mat! A positive attitude towards stress and anxiety prompts us to action. Let's first consider some of the positive effects.

**Positive Effects of Stress & Anxiety**

Stress is your body's response to stressors; events or activities that may cause stress in your life. How can these be positive? Consider this, have you ever been asked to host a dinner party or to contribute a meal for a dinner party? If so, then you've likely experienced the increased pulse rate, pounding heart, and racing thoughts about what to prepare - all before you've even agreed to host the dinner party or contribute the meal! Your body naturally responds in this manner because this is an event that requires you to act. You want to make sure you have the time to make a good meal and, make sure you have enough of it to feed all in attendance.

Anxiety is the feeling of worry, irritability, or nervousness. Anxiety is positive when it gives us that push we need to get things done, such as caring for our loved ones. For instance, Janice's anxiety about properly caring for her family moves her to take steps the night before to make sure her family has everything they need to start their day on time. She prepares for the next morning by ironing the suits she and her husband will wear to work and the clothes her children will wear to school. She also prepares the lunches and makes sure she has everything in place to get them and herself out on time the next morning.

Also consider Caroline who is suddenly faced with the decision of choosing an assisted living facility for her elderly mom. Anxiety prompts her to visit and thoroughly research several facilities before making a decision. She wants to make sure her mom receives the best care and is in a comfortable safe environment. She also wants to make sure it is close by so that she can visit regularly.

These are just some of the positive effects of stress and anxiety. Use these examples as your guide to identify some of the positive effects of stress and anxiety in your life.

________________________________________

________________________________________

________________________________________

________________________________________

**Negative Effects of Stress & Anxiety**

As with any good thing, too much of it can be hazardous to our health. The same is true of stress and anxiety. We need some stress and anxiety in our life, but prolonged exposure can be hazardous. If you think hard enough you can fill a book with the negative contributors to stress and anxiety (e.g. health problems, financial concerns, toxic relationships, and environmental pollutants). Prolonged stress and anxiety can have negative effects on our body, our thoughts, and our behavior. Consider some of the negative effects of prolonged stress and anxiety. Check off any you may have experienced recently*:

**Physical Effects:**

- ☐ Headache
- ☐ Chest pain
- ☐ Shortness of breath
- ☐ Increased sweating
- ☐ Muscle aches
- ☐ Teeth grinding
- ☐ Digestive problems
- ☐ Trouble sleeping

**Mental Effects:**

- ☐ Irritability
- ☐ Anger
- ☐ Insecurity
- ☐ Guilt

☐ Forgetfulness

☐ Lack of concentration

**Behavioral Effects:**

☐ Mood swings

☐ Depression

☐ Eating disorders (over or under eating)

☐ Isolation (withdrawal from association)

☐ Increased smoking or alcohol consumption

☐ Angry and violent outbursts

**Take Inventory**

Consider the contributors (stressors) to prolonged stress and anxiety in your life and how often as well as how long you experience any of the effects:

1. What is the Stressor? (e.g. marriage, divorce, new job, retirement, death in family)

2. Is the stressor considered a positive or negative event in your life? (+/-)

3. When did the stressor occur? (e.g. last week, last month, last year)

4. Are you still exposed to the stressor? If so, how often? (e.g. daily, weekly)

5. What is the effect of the stressor? (e.g. specific physical, mental, or behavioral effect)

6. What is the frequency of the effect? (e.g. daily, weekly, monthly)

7. What is the duration of the effect? (e.g. 30 minutes, 1 hour or more)

8. Did you experience this effect prior to the stressor occurring?

**If you have extended periods of stress and anxiety and are frequently experiencing any of the effects noted in the previous section, consult your doctor.*

***Take Action***

There are some stressors in our life that we can control and others that we cannot. However, the key to dealing with stress and anxiety is to be proactive and take action before they control our life. Consider some simple ways to be proactive in dealing with stress and anxiety, regardless of whether the stressor is within or beyond our control:

***Get Your Energy Flowing***

Exercise regularly to help reduce stress and keep the heart healthy and strong. Experts indicate aerobic exercises at least 3-4 days a week for 30 minutes per day can condition strengthen the heart (e.g. brisk walking, dancing, swimming, bike riding).

In addition, deep breathing is a great way to ease the effects of stress and anxiety. Take 3 to 5 slow deep breaths with a slight pause between each, breathing in through the nose and slowly out through the mouth with pursed lips. This will assist in lowering the heart rate and calming nervousness.

***Don't Short Circuit***

Keep a positive attitude and don't let anxiety or its effects take control of your thoughts, emotions and behavior. Angry outbursts only contribute to the effects of stress and anxiety. Instead remain calm and focused.

***Connect To The Power Of Prayer***

Close your eyes and say a quick prayer asking God for help in dealing with an event that causes stress and anxiety. God gives us the power to deal with events that may be more than we can handle on our own.

***Tap Into Your Network***

Find support in a family member, friend, coach, or mentor who will listen and allow you to talk about your concerns. If necessary, seek the support of a professional, particularly if you experience prolonged effects of stress and anxiety.

In addition, you can find great relief from stress and anxiety by delegating as many daily tasks as is reasonable. Tap into your network for support in handling some of these tasks (e.g. assignments at work, babysitting, housecleaning).

***Get Unplugged***

Create quiet time for yourself; this can include as little as 10 to 15 minutes of solitude and complete relaxation. Find a place where you can be by yourself and turn off any distracting devices (e.g. phone, computer, television). This is complete and total YOU time. Use this quiet time to meditate, read a book, journal or simply dream!

**The Plan**

Let's consider how Janice, mentioned earlier, dealt with the events contributing to her stress and anxiety. The first thing she did was create a moment of silence. She stood still, closed her eyes, calmed her thoughts, and took a deep breath. She then said a prayer, as simple as, "Dear God, help me." Next, she developed an action plan to tackle her stressors one by one. Janice's plan looked something like this:

- **Stressor 1: Assignment at work with a tight deadline**

  Janice places a call to inform her boss she will require an assistant to help her with research so that she can meet the accelerated deadline. Most of all, she informs the boss of the one night this week in which she cannot work late because she is looking forward to being present at her daughter's recital.

- **Stressor 2: Finishing the outfit for her daughter's recital**

  Since her mom will be visiting this week, Janice will ask her to finish working on the outfit with her daughter. She hasn't seen her granddaughter in a while and this will allow them to spend some quality time together.

- **Stressor 3: Hosting a dinner party for her husband's boss**

  Hire a cook to prepare the meal for her husband's boss; this individual will also decorate for the occasion. This will allow Janice to be relaxed and prepared to be a gracious host.

- **Stressor 4: Mom hasn't heard from Janice in weeks and is concerned.**

  The last thing Janice wants to do is cause her mom unnecessary worry. When mom arrives, she lets her know she will call her at least once a week to keep in touch. Since Janice has also been concerned with her mom's well-being, she discusses with her mom a plan to move her to the same city as Janice and the family so that they may better support each other. Keeping in touch and having mom closer to home will also alleviate some of Janice's stress in ways only mothers know how.

**The Reward**

After a successful dinner with her husband's boss and his wife the night before, Janice is excited about her daughter's recital. On the day of the recital, Janice finishes up her day's work on the project and heads directly to the school, arriving in time to enjoy her daughter's first recital. Afterwards, she gets home and is surprised to find a hot bath filled with rose petals, surrounded by candles, and a note that reads, "*Sometimes you have to stop and smell the roses. Love Mom, Hubby, and Jenny.*"

The stress and anxiety we experience in life pales in comparison to the rewards we can experience when we adjust our attitudes and take a few simple steps to reduce its effects.

**References:**

Mayo Clinic. Stress Symptoms: Effects on your body, feelings and behavior. Retrieved April 2008 from: http://www.mayoclinic.com/health/stress-symptoms/SR00008_D.

American Heart Association. Ten Questions A Woman Should Ask Her Healthcare Provider. (7. What kind of physical activity is right for me?). Retrieved April 2008 from – http://www.americanheart.org/presenter.jhtml?identifier=2759

**Online Resources:**

American Heart Association – http://www.americanheart.org

American Psychological Association – http://www.apahelpcenter.org

Mayo Clinic – http://www.mayoclinic.com

National Women's Health Resource Center – http://www.healthywomen.org

US National Library of Medicine – http://www.nlm.nih.gov

*Notes:*

## ABOUT THE AUTHOR

### LAURA KELLEY

Ms. Laura Kelley, President and CEO of **A One Coaching** is a Certified Coach specializing in Life Skills, Transition, Recovery, Career and Wellness Coaching.

Ms. Kelley is an expert in the areas of consulting, office, retail and marketing management with over thirty years experience. She is an invaluable "listener" and has conducted numerous self-help groups.

Through individual coaching, seminars and workshops A One Coaching encourages client-generated strategies and solutions which help clients produce extraordinary results in many areas of their lives. A One Coaching aims to "*Help you move your life forward*".

Laura has lived and worked on Cape Cod, MA. and in the United States Virgin Islands where she continues to empower women who are ready for a new direction! She now resides in Delray Beach, Florida and she is available for personal and recovery coaching.

Ms. Kelley is a member of The Professional Woman Network, The International Coach Federation, Recovery Coaches International and The National Association of Female Executives. She holds certificates in Disaster Mental Health Intervention, Stress Reduction and Meditation, and is a Certified Wellness Trainer involving self-esteem and holistic wellness.

**Expertise:**

- Life Coaching
- Recovery Coaching
- Personal and Professional Development

**Seminars and topics offered:**

- Stress Management
- Career and Success Management
- Women's Issues and Empowerment
- Life Skills and Balance
- Emotional Wellness
- Post 12 Step Development

*Contact:*
A One Coaching
1720 NW 21ST Court
Delray Beach, Florida 33445
Tel: 561-577-3083 / 800-995-0706
FAX 561-276-6061
Email: aonecoaching@yahoo.com
Web: www.aonecoaching.com

## SEVENTEEN

# JOURNEY TO SUCCESS: ONE WOMAN'S PATH

**By Laura Kelley**

Everyone has talents. Some come naturally; others are acquired through learning and experience. Developing awareness of these talents and applying them assure you a journey to personal success. As women, we are so busy serving others that we minimize or ignore our abilities and miss the opportunities to step out into enjoyable and fulfilling careers.

Have you watched other women move forward into successful careers and wondered why you can't find a direction? The good news is that you can accomplish purpose and direction when least expected!

I am a "first wave" Baby Boomer raised in a rural New England community during the 50's. My role models were the stay-at-home Moms who set firm guidelines for the role of women. These examples were embedded into my belief system and I didn't trust that I was capable of becoming the new 60's woman who voiced her beliefs and was career-bound.

The sixties began a revolutionary change in the role women played at home and in society. During the next several years, I was employed in diverse professions and surprising patterns began to appear. Each job I held, from retail to restaurant to hospitality, resulted in promotions to managerial positions.

I married and spent the next two decades becoming "super" mom and wife. This was a challenging lifestyle at which I was determined to succeed. During this time, I began designing and decorating cakes for family events, which led to a cake and gourmet dessert business. Simultaneously, I became a self-taught office manager and bookkeeper for my husband's company, which later led to a successful career in office management. I sold crafts, which I had considered only a hobby (needlepoint, jewelry, knitting, rug braiding, etc.), and I started a housecleaning company when hearing women discuss the need to find a trustworthy service. During this time, I could not see what I was accomplishing nor did I have any idea as to where this would take me.

As the seventies became the eighties, my children grew into adulthood. I became a single woman and also experienced the empty nest syndrome. Fear and confusion consumed me as I tried to determine the direction of my new life and how to become self-supporting. Little did I know that I had set in motion a direction of success that would utilize the talents and strengths that I had minimized and considered only daily routines. A friend suggested that I write a list of all that I had done in my life so that I could actually view my accomplishments.

Listing your personal talents reveals the secret to your future life and business success. Now is the time to start! Give ample time and consideration to this process. You are important.

**Exercise 1: Identify Your Talents**
Write a list (no matter how unimportant it may seem) of your:

1. **Artistic abilities** i.e. crafts, cooking, sewing, pottery, needlepoint
2. **Household decorating** i.e. painting, wallpapering, refinishing furniture, draperies, upholstering
3. **Personal interests** i.e. reading, sports, apparel, gardening
4. **Community interests/accomplishments** i.e. clubs, organizations and positions held, fundraisers, political and volunteer events
5. **Your personality** i.e. calm in chaos, handle crisis well, composed, patient, helper, problem solver
6. **Business accomplishments** i.e. jobs, positions, responsibilities

These categories may be the tip of the iceberg for you. Add as many as you want.

**Exercise 2: Expand On Your Information**
Ask three (3) people who know you well, to complete this same list ***about*** you. (They can be friends, your boss, your significant other – anyone you choose.) How we perceive ourselves can be very different from how others perceive us.

1. Discuss the lists with someone whose opinion you respect and who empowers you to move forward.
2. Write a daily gratitude list including one of these talents.
3. Speak your talents aloud to yourself. Call this "self-talk".
4. Do this for 21 days. A new habit can be formed, or an old habit broken in 21 days.

If allowing people into your life has been difficult, now is the time to work on trusting others. There are many ways to overcome this problem, such as reading books on the subject of trust and intimacy, as well as counseling. The key to your moving forward is a trusted confidant. They can be called mentor, best friend, Mom, coach etc. She/he need only be someone you trust and who encourages you to be the very best that you can be. Through this process you will discover your personal strengths, learn to establish goals, and be encouraged to move forward.

Throughout your growing process, focus on becoming an ***attentive listener***. When one hears, one perceives sound/words but doesn't pay attention to them. When one listens, one is alert and gives thoughtful consideration to what is being said.

*I did not listen to the words "I need a cake for my child's birthday" or "I wish I could find someone to clean my house" or "I need someone to do my bookkeeping" until my close friends would nudge me and say, "You can do that!" When my neighbor urged me to get my Real Estate license, I walked through my fear and took the test! I had considered the suggestions and moved forward.*

While practicing your gratitude list and "self-talk", continue to gather more information about yourself.

**Exercise 3: Clarify Your Direction**

On a separate piece of paper, complete the following:

1. Define what you mean by "success".
2. Examine your list of talents and accomplishments.
3. Make a list of *everything* you might want to do.
4. Determine what areas you want to focus on.
5. Research your interests.
6. Ask for help.
7. Set goals.
8. Discuss your ideas with your mentor or coach for clarification.

You may make the wonderful discovery that you have more than one interest you would like to pursue, and that your definition of success has taken on a new meaning. Personal success is not defined by fame and fortune (although it is nice!). It is self-worth, willingness to try, persistence, and belief in self that is needed. Choosing to no longer allow fear and worry to control you leads to unimaginable opportunities and new directions. A positive attitude attracts positive results, so don't be surprised when doors open and opportunities arise.

*After several years in Real Estate, I was invited to the Virgin Islands to visit a friend. On a whim, I applied for a job and was hired. As I loved the Caribbean, I accepted and became Retail Manager for Vogue Boutique. Remaining positive and open-minded, I was promoted to Marketing Manager for the wholesale perfume division of the same corporation. This was a field I had never considered.*

From your previous lists, you have done the homework necessary to start the process of prioritizing the goals that you would like to achieve. You have identified (on paper) your accomplishments, strengths and interests. It is now time to evaluate your **attitude**, **awareness** and **action.** This is vital to moving forward. This will be accomplished by completing the following exercise.

**Exercise 4: Keys to Success**

Rate yourself 1-10 with 10 being best. Explain how you are applying it to life today.

1. Remain open-minded ________________________________
2. Accept challenge when opportunities appear __________________
3. Avoid negative people ________________________________
4. Acknowledge your strengths ____________________________
5. Realize that change really means opportunity ________________
6. Have and use a support system __________________________

7. Encourage and compliment others and expect the same in return _______
8. Read inspirational books_______________________________
9. Take deep breaths, pray and step into the unknown ____________
10. Eat right ____________________________________
11. Balance and nourish mind/soul/body _________________
12. Use positive affirmations _______________________
13. Ask pertinent questions________________________
14. Prioritize ___________________________________
15. Learn from your mistakes ______________________
16. Make decisions _______________________________
17. Practice determination _________________________
18. Be patient ___________________________________
19. Enjoy what you are doing ______________________

Evaluate your new direction. Be certain that it does not oppose your principals (a rule of personal conduct) or your ethical standards (conforming to accepted professional standards or personal values or philosophy). Turmoil and discomfort may indicate compromising your beliefs.

Pay attention to your guidance system, better known as "your first reaction", "intuitive thought", or your "gut feeling". If you find yourself questioning an associate or a decision, allow yourself time, gather your information, and consult with others.

*At each turning point in my life, when I have used these formulas, the doors then opened to new and very different careers. Throughout my life I have been the Manager of a restaurant and a department store; a boutique Retail Manager, a Marketing Consultant, a Marketing Manager, Assistant to the President of a corporation, a Real Estate Broker and an Office Manager. I have also owned my own businesses and traveled extensively for business and trainings. In my relocation to South Florida,*

*I became the director of a recovery center where I worked with individuals and groups on personal, spiritual and career issues. Remaining open to new possibilities and being aware of how one position leads to another, I am now a Life Coach who employs the information that I have gathered through my journey.*

As you continue on your journey, attend trainings and gather and expand your resources. Join organizations and network. Exposure to new ideas and information will help you improve your profession. As you participate in events, you discover the importance of not only receiving, but also giving. Become a mentor. Remember, there is enough to go around. Help someone else!

Through this process, you have the opportunity to discover who you are and what you are capable of doing. Everything that you have done and learned in your lifetime, no matter how long or short that may be, becomes a valuable tool. You will find, if you look, that you will use every talent you have been given and acquired in your life's journey. All the jobs you have had, the difficulties you have encountered and survived, the lessons you have learned, the friendships you have made, your family relationships, and the changing eras have contributed to who you were and who you are today.

*Every segment of my life has been exciting because I consider it so. Life is in one's attitudes. My greatest lesson is that my seemingly "common" talents have blossomed into extraordinary successes. Success is always present. Our ability to see it is not. Discovering and applying talents and abilities takes time. While the exercises I have listed may seem tedious, they are crucial to discovering who you are and what you would like to become or improve. I have found patience and persistence vital on my journey.*

There is one more area to consider that will bring this process to a productive conclusion – **acceptance**! Do you believe that you accept yourself but inwardly squirm when you are complimented? Do you minimize or give credit to others when your achievement is noticed? Do you brag and take all the credit? A balance of modesty and humility coupled with acknowledging your accomplishments defines a successful person. It sounds nice, and simple, but not always easy to attain. To get a realistic view of yourself, write your biography.

**Exercise: Write Your Biography**

Use books to view how others have written theirs. Keep your biography brief, yet interesting. Tell a little about yourself, where you are from, list your education and trainings (be selective if this is lengthy), describe what you do and what you offer. You may rewrite this several times. Have friends, colleagues or teachers edit it for you. You may wonder who this person is as you read the finished product. Using this process, you will begin to accept your successful self!

Do you now see the capable, talented woman you are? Can you envision the woman you can become? Enjoy your journey and become a "booming" success!

The following is an overall exercise on maintaining and improving your life and career. Evaluate yourself on a monthly basis to determine your present position on your successful journey.

### 15 Tools For Success

I am on my successful journey:

1. **If I** ask for help

2. **If I** look for the best in every person, situation, and thing

3. **If I** refrain from personal criticism

4. **If I** write a daily gratitude list and include one of my qualities
5. **If I** acknowledge my accomplishments
6. **If I** list my goals – realistic or not
7. **If I** identify my self-defeating thoughts
8. **If I** practice positive affirmations
9. **If I** remain open to change
10. **If I** devote a set amount of time to daily prayer and meditation
11. **If I** ask probing questions
12. **If I** become an attentive listener
13. **If I** read books on diverse subjects
14. **If I** keep balance in my life – physical/mental/spiritual
15. **If I** commit to being of service to others (mentor someone – get out of "self")

**Meaningful Statements:**

1. Don't be judgmental, but use good judgment.
2. If you want what you have never had, you have to do what you have never done.
3. People may doubt what you say, but they will always believe what you do.

I honor the following people who have impacted my journey:

My Mom and Dad, my life partner Trey, my precious daughter Kim, my dear friend Judy, my lifelong friends Sally and Nancy, and my mentors Frank and Chantal Machover.

**Recommended Reading:**

*Becoming the Professional Woman* by The Professional Woman Network

*Power Through Constructive Thinking* by Emmet Fox

*Think and Grow Rich* by Napoleon Hill

*The Law of Attraction* by Esther and Jerry Hicks

*The Top Ten Mistakes Leaders Make* by Hans Finzel

*The Prayer of Jabez* by Bruce Wilkinson

*Blink* by Malcolm Gladwell

*Who Moved My Cheese* by Spencer Johnson, M.D.

*Notes:*

# ABOUT THE AUTHOR

## DANETTE BOONE

Danette Boone is the Founder and Chief Executive Officer of D. Boone & Associates. D. Boone & Associates is a consulting organization that focuses on providing educational training and development on Women's Wellness and Eldercare.

As the Principal Consultant, Ms. Boone is a certified trainer on women's wellness topics that focus on the mind, body and spirit connection. These sessions have been created to empower women of all ages regarding emotional, mental and spiritual health. Her current workshop series includes topics such as: the Superwoman Syndrome, Living a Spiritual Life On Purpose, Building Sisterhood, Women's Health and Giving Yourself the Gift of Love. She is currently creating a seminar series that focuses on care giving with a special emphasis on eldercare.

Ms. Boone is a member of The Professional Woman Network which is an international training and consulting organization that focuses on empowering business women. Other memberships include the National Association for Female Executives and Delta Sigma Theta Sorority, Inc.

With an extensive twenty year background in management, finance as well as sales, Ms. Boone has a Bachelors degree in Business Administration with a concentration on Management, and a Masters degree in Human Resource Management. She is currently completing a degree in Accounting. Ms. Boone is also a licensed Realtor.

Ms. Boone is available to facilitate workshops and seminars for churches and women's groups, as well as implement trainings for nursing home staff and other facilities that cater primarily to the elderly. She is also available for keynote speaking.

The mission of D. Boone and Associates is to educate, inspire and empower through imparting knowledge, for Knowledge IS Power. Ms. Boone's sole purpose and passion is helping others reach their next level. She believes that everyone has a purpose in this life, and that to know your PURPOSE you must begin to live ON PURPOSE!

*Contact:*
Danette Boone
D. Boone & Associates
P.O. Box 6928
Largo, MD 20792
Phone: 301-509-1074
Email: booneconsult@gmail.com

## EIGHTEEN

# ESTATE PLANNING TIPS FOR BABY BOOMERS

**By Danette Boone**

Wills, trusts, advance directives, power of attorney… What are they? What do these terms mean? What, if anything, do they mean to you? Should they mean something to you? These documents are, in fact, very important. They should mean a lot to you. These are just a few of the documents that just about every adult should have in place. They are pieces of a much bigger puzzle…Estate Planning.

In October 2007, we witnessed the first Baby Boomer at retirement age file for Social Security benefits. Baby Boomers…that generation of approximately 80 million Americans born from 1946 to 1964, when birth rates rose sharply. They grew up during one of the most prosperous and sustained economic growth periods in this country's history. Baby

Boomers...that powerful generation that plays by its own rules. That largely educated, economically sound, comfortable with technology, individualistic generation. They are also the generation that has enjoyed a considerably higher standard of living than any previous one.

As Baby Boomers age, they will, of course face normal emotional and physical transitions. They will also face some unusual financial, familial and medical concerns. Baby Boomers will begin to face some of the standard chronic health problems and begin to face their own mortality.

Baby Boomers are being referred to as the Sandwich Generation. They often find themselves caught between two generations, struggling to raise their children while caring for an aging loved one. In addition, in most cases, they are also trying to plan for their retirement.

Planning for retirement is a process that requires focus, discipline and commitment. With so much to deal with on a daily basis financially, emotionally, psychologically and possibly medically/physically, it's perfectly understandable that many people have difficulty focusing on the future.

What about you? Are you prepared? Is your plan in place?

**What Is Estate Planning?**

Most of us are familiar with the term "**estate planning**", however many of us do not have an in-depth understanding of what an estate plan is. For those of us who do, many of us haven't taken the necessary steps to implement an estate plan. Estate planning is one of the most important steps you can take to make sure that your property and healthcare wishes are honored, and that your loved ones are provided for in your absence.

Your **estate** consists of all property owned by you at the time of your death, including real estate, bank accounts, stocks and other securities, life insurance policies, and personal property such as automobiles, jewelry and artwork. Estate planning covers all aspects of deciding how your estate will be handled after you pass away. Often overlooked, a comprehensive estate plan can resolve a number of legal questions that could arise when you pass away, including questions regarding funeral arrangements, property ownership and distribution, as well as the state of your financial affairs.

Understanding estate planning options can be a complex undertaking. The information provided in this chapter is to be used as a guide. It is for informational purposes only. It is advised that you seek the assistance of an experienced estate planning attorney to guide you through the estate planning process.

Regardless of your age, or the size and complexity of your estate, an estate plan can accomplish many things, ten of which are listed below.

**10 Things Estate Planning Can Do For You**

- ☐ Provide for your immediate family.
- ☐ Provide for other relatives who need help and guidance.
- ☐ Get your property to your beneficiaries quickly.
- ☐ Plan for incapacity.
- ☐ Minimize expenses.
- ☐ Choose executors/trustees for your estate.

☐ Ease the strain on your family.

☐ Help a favorite cause.

☐ Reduce taxes on your estate.

☐ Make sure your business goes on smoothly.

**Review the list above. Now, put an asterisk next to each number that indicates what an estate plan would do for you. My guess is that you will have not less than three asterisks.**

Despite the advantages of having a will in place, it is estimated that at least 70 percent of Americans do not have valid wills. While it is difficult to contemplate mortality, many people have great peace of mind when their affairs are in order. Are you and your family prepared for when the time comes? Will you and your family be ready?

### Documents Needed For Estate Planning

You will find below a list of documents that should be included in your estate plan...

### Wills

Wills are the most common way for people to state their preferences about how their estates should be handled after their deaths. A well written will allows people to express their deepest sentiment towards their loved ones. It also eases the transition for survivors by transferring property quickly and avoiding many tax burdens.

Formal requirements for wills vary from state to state. Generally, the **testator** (the person making the will) must be an adult of sound mind, meaning that the testator must be able to understand the full meaning of the document. Wills must be written, but a better more enforceable option is to use a typed document. The testator must be able to sign his or her own will. If unable to sign, the testator must direct another person to sign the will in the presence of witnesses, and the signature must be notarized. A valid will remains in force until revoked or superseded by a subsequent valid will. Some changes may be made by **codicil** (amendment) without requiring a complete rewrite.

A will usually appoints an **executor** (personal representative) to ensure that the specific wishes of the testator are adhered to after he or she passes on. This person may or may not be a relative of the testator.

If a person dies without a will and did not make alternative arrangements to distribute property, survivors may face a complicated, expensive and time-consuming legal process. Dying without a will leaves an estate **intestate**, which means that any property that the person possessed passes by what is called **intestate succession** to heirs according to state law. In other words, if you don't have a will when you die, the state will make one for you.

The purpose of intestate succession statutes is to distribute the decedent's wealth in a manner that closely represents how the average person would have designed his or her estate plan, had that person had a will. This default, however, can differ dramatically from what a person really wanted. Even when it is known what the person's final wishes were, no exceptions are made where no valid will exists. Nor are there any exceptions made based on need or special circumstances.

There are several different kinds of wills. Do your research and talk with an attorney to determine which is most suitable for you and your family.

**Trusts**

Trusts are estate planning tools that can replace or supplement wills. Trusts can also help manage property during life. A trust manages the distribution of a person's property by transferring its benefits and obligations to different people. There are many reasons to create a trust, making this property distribution technique a popular choice for many people when creating an estate plan.

The basics of trust creation are fairly simple. To create a trust, the property **grantor** (owner) transfers legal ownership to a **trustee** (person or institution) to manage that property for the benefit of the **beneficiary** (another person). Trusts fall into two broad categories, **testamentary trusts** and **living trusts**.

A **testamentary trust** transfers property into the trust only after the death of the grantor. Because a trust allows the grantor to specify conditions for receipt of benefits, as well as to spread payment of benefits over a period of time instead of making a single gift, many people prefer to include a trust in their wills to reinforce their preferences and goals after death.

A **living trust** starts during the life of the grantor, but may be designed to continue after his or her death. This type of trust may help avoid probate if all assets subject to probate are transferred into the trust prior to death. A living trust may be "**revocable**" or "**irrevocable**". With a revocable trust, the grantor can change or revoke the terms of the trust any time after the trust is created. Conversely, the grantor of an irrevocable trust permanently relinquishes the right to make changes after the trust commences. A revocable trust typically acts as a supplement to a will, or as a way to name a person to manage the grantor's affairs should he or she become incapacitated. Even a revocable living trust usually specifies that it is irrevocable at the death of the grantor.

A living trust has both advantages and disadvantages, so again, do your research and consult with an experienced estate planning attorney.

**Are you unsure if creating a trust is the right thing to do for you and your family? Listed below are a few reasons why you might want to consider creating a trust.**

**Parents With Young Children** – If you have young children and want to ensure they have a good education and will have enough assets if anything were to happen to you, perhaps you should consider setting up a trust.

**Beneficiaries Who Need Help** – Trusts are popular among people with beneficiaries who aren't able to manage property well. This includes elderly beneficiaries with special needs, or a relative who may be irresponsible with money.

**People Who Own Property That Is Hard To Divide** – Trusts help transfer property that's not easy to divide evenly among several beneficiaries.

**People Concerned About Estate Taxes** – Trusts are very useful to people with substantial assets, because they can help avoid or reduce estate taxes.

### Guardianship

Application for **guardianship** can be made through the courts in the event that a person is no longer able to make decisions and there has been no advance planning. The court decides whether the person applying is the best choice to be guardian. If there is no suitable person to act as guardian, the court appoints an agency, or person. Guardians have decision-making power over healthcare, finances, and other care matters.

**Advance Directive**

An **advance directive** is a healthcare term to help family members and healthcare providers with decisions about care if a person is unable to make decisions for him/herself. It covers both **living wills** and **healthcare power of attorney**. Although advance directives focus on healthcare and not transfer of property, most people who have an estate plan have a properly recorded advance directive.

**Living wills** usually become necessary when people are no longer able to speak for themselves. While you are still healthy and able to make decisions, you can instruct your doctor to withhold or remove life support treatments if you become seriously ill or injured, with no hope of recovering. Living wills must be in writing in most states.

There are three basic forms of **power of attorney**.

**Healthcare power of attorney** allows you, while you are still healthy, to choose someone you trust to make healthcare decisions for you. You will always have the final say in decisions, as long as you are able to do so. However, once you become unable to make decisions, your **agent** (person given power of attorney) will then make the decisions. This gives broader power than a living will, which only covers life-support treatment. Your agent will act as your advocate to make sure your wishes are followed for all treatments when you are unable to do this for yourself.

**Financial power of attorney** allows your agent to make financial decisions on your behalf, such as bill paying. You choose which decisions your agent is allowed to make on your behalf.

**Durable power of attorney** allows you to choose an agent to make all decisions, if you are unable to make decisions on your own. A doctor or court system must decide if you are unable to make decisions. Some states allow the person granted power of attorney to assume durable power of attorney, even if you have not specifically requested it. This must be done through an attorney.

### Personal Affairs Record Book

A **personal affairs record book** is intended to assist you in organizing your personal and financial papers. By completing this booklet, you will help ensure that your loved ones do not encounter difficulty when settling your estate and tending to your final wishes. The booklet is typically divided into five sections: 1) personal and family information, 2) employment, 3) assets, 4) liabilities and 5) other information.

### Keeping Your Documents Secure

Because the documents discussed in this chapter text are very important, it should go without saying that they need to be stored in a secured place. They all should be stored together with other important family papers, (i.e. passport, mortgage, birth certificate, etc.). Most people store their important papers in a safe deposit box at their bank, or at their lawyer's office. Be sure to let your agent, personal representative and/or nearest relative know exactly where these documents are stored, in the event they are needed.

Because the primary purpose of this chapter text was to serve as a catalyst in assisting you with the start the estate planning process, the focus was on the very basics of estate planning. You should and must research what exactly works for you. Again, it is highly recommended that you seek an experienced estate planning attorney once you've done some of your own research.

Estate planning not only preserves wealth for succeeding generations, it also gives you satisfaction and peace of mind. Won't you start your plan today?

**Estate Planning Quiz**

Match the correct letter with the corresponding description:

a) Beneficiary b) Executor c) Guardian d) Intestate e) Trust Estate
g) Grantor h) Healthcare Power of Attorney i) Probate j) Will

____ The person who transfers assets to another, usually into a trust
____ The term used when a person dies without a will
____ The person who receives funds, property or other benefits from a will
____ An individual's property and assets, including real estate, bank accounts and personal property
____ The document which designates a person to make healthcare decisions, in the event that the individual is unable to do so
____ A written document providing that property be held by one for the benefit of another
____ A document that directs how property shall be distributed upon a person's death
____ A process whereby a court reviews a will to make sure that it is authentic_
____ An individual with the legal authority to care for another
____ A person named in a will who is authorized to manage the estate of the deceased person.

The answers are found within the text of this chapter.

Don't wait until tomorrow for what must be done today. Protect that which you have worked so hard to attain. See an attorney NOW to draft an estate plan for you. Leave your legacy protected.

*Notes:*

# ABOUT THE AUTHOR

## Bonita F. Basara

Bonita (Bonnie) Basara is a mentor, trainer and coach. She has held a variety of positions in the customer related fields over the past twenty-five years.

Ms. Basara received a Bachelor of Arts Degree in Management and Marketing from Saint Martin's University at the age of 52. After a brief break of a few years she obtained her Master of Science Degree in Human Resources, and simultaneously a Certificate in Organizational Leadership from Chapman University at 56 years of age.

Bonnie is a member of Altrusa International of Olympia which serves the community needs and challenges; by working locally as caring, concerned individuals making handmade chemo caps for cancer patients; collecting children's books for the local food bank; stuffing diaper bags with books and materials to encourage reading to newborn babies for the local hospital; providing deserving high school students over $9,000 in awards and scholarships per year; and working together as a powerful association of clubs and districts. In addition, she is a member of American Association of University Women (AAUW) and the National Association of Female Executives (NAFE), and The Professional Woman Network (PWN).

Her passion is assisting others to recognize their true potential and truly believe that education is never too late. Her plans for the future are to expand and develop her own coaching business "Excel in Life." She is focusing on women's issues such as: Diversity, Self-Esteem, Women's Wellness, Customer Service and Financial Independence. Bonita is available as a keynote speaker for personal and professional coaching sessions.

*Contact:*
Bonnie Basara
Telephone : (360)556.0474
Email: bonitabasara@yahoo.com
www.excelinlife.net

## NINETEEN

# EDUCATION: IT'S NEVER TOO LATE

### By Bonnie Basara

I don't know about you, but when I was in school my grades were either average or mediocre, and being a child, I didn't realize how important they were. But due to my substandard grades at the time, education just didn't mean anything to me. In the immediate postwar era, I can't remember if any of my teachers really cared or not about how I was doing, for I don't recall any talks with any teacher or counselor. I really struggled in school from elementary through high school. My parents couldn't help me with my homework because my father had only an eighth grade education, and since mother's father passed away when she was a young child, my mother dropped out before fifth grade to help with the housework while my grandmother worked. Yet through all this, my parents were very supportive and encouraging, all the while telling me I could be anything I wanted to be.

My fifth grade teacher, Mrs. Keen, inspired me to take an interest in wanting to become a teacher. She was newly out of college, so she was a lot younger than any of the other teachers. She was always willing to listen to me and would encourage me in whatever it was I was doing. She is the only teacher I look back on with fondness. Just being around her really made me feel that I could pursue a career in education. Yet, I had a rude awakening.

When I was in my junior year of school, I applied to the nearest local college that had a teaching program, but wasn't accepted. So I did the next best thing, I got a job as a file clerk in an insurance company. I worked there for two years and then had a series of other odd jobs in sales, customer service, and even worked in the unemployment office as an interviewer.

My dad worked as a mechanic, both on cars and repairing production lines. My mom was a waitress and a sales clerk. At the age of 50, my father decided he needed to do more with his life and family, so he took a correspondence course for his real estate license, passing all of his tests at ninety percent or above. Being inspired by my father's determination while I was doing all of these other jobs, I also took a correspondence course to learn to be an airline reservationist. However, I found out later I should have applied to the airlines directly. In between all of this, I met the man of my dreams, Brian.

He enlisted in the Air Force to serve his country. When he came home from basic training, he presented me with an engagement ring. We dated a few years and were planning on getting married, but he got orders to go to Vietnam. I was working as a customer service clerk for a retail store and read in our newspaper our local community college was offering this new dental assistant program. I decided to apply and would be able to complete the program while he was away. I thought that after we got married I could have a career in the dental profession. I was accepted in the program and started my studies. Upon completion of my studies, I was offered a job as a dental assistant for an orthodontist and worked several months for him until Brian came home from Vietnam. When he decided to re-enlist and stay in the Air Force, we decided to get married a year later.

I thought I could work as a dental assistant on the air base. Boy, was I wrong. They said I could volunteer because they didn't hire civilians for these positions, but instead had airmen perform the duties. So, I finally found a job with a bank as a vault teller, which included answering phones, as well. I worked there only a few months when I found out I was going to have a baby; we had been married for two and half years by that point. In the meantime, my husband got orders to transfer to Langley, Virginia, so we packed up our belongings and moved.

My career life was put on hold and I became a mother of two boys in two years. We lived in Virginia for five years, and then we got orders for Germany. We were there for three years and later assigned to New Mexico.

By this time the boys were nine and seven, so I decided I could get a part-time job and took a job as a bank teller working part-time for two years before I decided to take some banking classes. Eventually, I was hired full-time in the bookkeeping department. But as luck would have it, the bank was taken over by a larger bank and I had to go back to being a teller. I felt I wasn't getting anywhere with my job, and there were a lot of inner office politics going on concerning assigned duties and I felt I was being treated unfairly, so I decided I needed to do more with my life and tendered my resignation.

Even though by this time I was nearly 40 years old, I started to look into going back to school to get some type of degree. I went to the local community college to get information on what type of programs they offered and started to think maybe I could be a computer programmer.

The school required I take a placement test, since I been out of school for more than 20 years. I found that I needed to take brush-up classes in reading comprehension and basic math, so I registered to take these classes in the spring quarter of 1987 at age 40.

I figured that I would get a part-time job while going to school, and was luckily hired by the local power company as a Customer Service Clerk. My past experience as a bank teller helped me get the job. I was supposed to work, as they call it, on a casual basis, but I ended up working full-time. When I was offered a permanent full-time position, I decided to accept it. I felt being with a utility company would offer the stability of long-term employment and that I could work there for the next 25 years, getting a good retirement pension when it was all said and done. At the time, the office was considered a Customer Information Center, so there were about 25 employees in my office holding various customer service positions. I asked the other women what was required to advance in the office and the response was that a new criterion was put in place that you had to have two quarters of college accounting. So, I decided when I was done with the spring and summer classes I would take accounting I as my first *real* class for the fall quarter.

After I completed the two accounting classes, I also took payroll accounting, but decided I didn't want to be an accountant or CPA. I re-evaluated my options and decided if the company I worked for required two quarters of accounting, then I should fulfill the next level of eligibility for advancement beyond that, as well. So, I decided I would work toward an associate's degree. But that was easier said than done.

I now had a full time job and two boys to bring up, because my husband was still in the military and would work anywhere from 8 to

16 hours a day. I had to be there for the kids and run the home. My choice was to take one class per semester and break for the summer to be home for them. It took me a full nine years to complete my associates degree, but I had such a feeling of accomplishment when I walked down that graduation aisle in May of 1997 to receive my diploma, I felt like shouting for joy. While I was doing all this, I had a few co-workers who thought I was nuts for putting myself through the agony of writing papers and studying for exams. I told them it was worth it to me. Even my husband was voicing his opinion on why I was putting myself through so much torture to get a degree. I told him I felt a huge sense of accomplishment whenever I completed a class, and even if I got a "C", I knew I did my best. I felt that knowledge could never be taken away from me. In addition to going to school and working, I was also teaching religious education classes once a week since 1983. By this time, my brothers and sister were starting to call me a professional student.

In 1987, the director of the program asked me to start a new program for children who wanted to join the catholic faith, but were never baptized as infants or received their Holy Communion in the normal time-line. I was given the authority to choose the curriculum for the program, as long as it followed the guidelines of the church. In my classes I had an age range from nine to 18 year olds and class sizes from one to 35. I get such a sense of faith fulfillment in my class preparation and participation from the youths, that it is awe-inspiring.

A few months later, I was talking to a counselor about where I was going in my life, and she asked me what I wanted to do for myself. I answered that I would like to have a bachelor's degree in business. She asked the question of what was stopping me, and I thought a few moments about it. Ultimately, I couldn't come up with anything. I then started to look around my community to see about applying to a four-year college.

Here in Washington State, I live close to McChord Air Force Base and Fort Lewis, both of which have extended learning facilities. I decided to apply to Saint Martin's University, as their main campus is also close by. I started my classes in August of 1997 and graduated May of 1999 with a dual degree in Management and Marketing, and a grade point average (GPA) of 3.54. The most poignant moment of my graduation was that my mother and older sister made the trip out from New Jersey, especially since my mother passed away only a few months later in October.

I took a break from studies for about a year and a half, and then decided to go for a master's degree in Human Resources. So again, I evaluated the colleges on the two bases and decided to enroll with Chapman University. The one thing I remember, looking back at that time, is when I told my husband Brian I was considering going back to school, and he asked how old I was. I looked at him and said I was 54. He then asked how long this would take and how old I would be when I got done. I said it would probably take two to three years, depending on how many classes I took, and I would be either 56 or 57. He wasn't too enthusiastic about it, but I would be that age whether I did it or not. Naturally, I went ahead and decided to do it. I enrolled with Chapman and graduated with a Master of Science degree in Human Resources, plus a certificate in Organizational Leadership, with a GPA of 3.55 in December 2003.

I felt I was too comfortable and complacent about working for the utility company anymore, so I retired in March, 2006, because deep down what I really wanted to do was coach and inspire other women to go for their dreams. I came across an advertisement in NAFE magazine on coaching seminars from an organization called The Professional Woman Network, and I made the call to Linda Eastman and talked to her about her program. I enrolled in her coaching class for July 2007. When I met her, I was so humble and surprised when she offered me the opportunity to write this article. It's so gratifying to help and inspire others. I am going back again in July for another seminar, since you can never learn too much.

This past September I got the bug again, and this time it was a class to do tax preparations for H & R Block. Naturally, I'm never finished. I ended up taking the second level of tax preparation classes, and I also enrolled to obtain my financial license. Ultimately, I'd like to incorporate all of this into my coaching business, which is in the early stages of development. I feel I will always look for something I can learn. I know I'm not that unique, so I did some research and found other people out there that feel the same way as I do. I selected a few articles to show age doesn't matter.

**Case History #1: Madonna (Disabled)**

In an article from *Contact*, a woman named Madonna had a learning disability that prevented her from doing well in school. In fact, she had to drop out of school three times by the time she got to eighth grade. She said she was totally frustrated when seeing her friends going on to high school and even universities. She felt that there was something wrong with her. Why couldn't she move on with her life? After she quit school, Madonna worked in a convenience store at a minimum wage, which weighed heavily on her mind. She often felt she could do better, if only she could improve her ability to read. She finally enrolled in an Adult Basic Education class and graduated in 1992, but her reading ability remained at a sixth grade level. Her situation changed for the better in the fall of 2000 when, at 35, she began the Spell Read Phonological Auditory Training (P.A.T.) program, with assistance from Human Resources Development Canada. Now, Madonna is in a pre-Social Work degree at Memorial University, and is truly appreciative of having been sponsored by HRDC in the Spell Read program. A single mother since the age of 21, Madonna says her motivation to get ahead came from her two children. She felt if she didn't do anything for her future, neither would her children have a future. Madonna admits that the road to knowledge so far hasn't been an easy one. Madonna points out that her learning disability was known when she was in fourth grade. The professional who evaluated her said she was amazed she had gotten as far as she did. She never saw that person again. Despite delays earlier encountered on the road to learning, Madonna's commitment to education demonstrated her determination to achieve a goal that once seemed impossible.

**Case History #2: Joan (Changing Careers In Mid-Life)**

My next article was found on the internet at boston.com. Joan realized she needed a change. For 15 years, she was a co-owner of a jewelry manufacturing business. China was providing stiff competition and affecting her company's bottom line. In her late 40's, she knew she needed to make a career move and quickly. Her challenge was to go into a field that would stay lucrative until retirement. That is when she learned about the Accelerated (ACCEL) Bachelor's Degree Nursing Program at Curry College. Even though Joan spent most of her life in manufacturing, she had a bachelor's degree in public health and experience as a health educator at the American Lung Association.

She wanted to work directly with people, so the idea of nursing as a career offered her a lot of opportunities. While she was researching the job market, which is experiencing a shortage in both registered nurses and instructors, she came across a newspaper advertisement for Curry's ACCEL program. What appealed to her was she could earn her bachelor's degree in about two years. She already had an undergraduate degree in public health, so she had most of the science prerequisites. In January 2004, Joan enrolled in Curry's first class of students in the ACCEL program. There was a joint initiative of the school's Division of Nursing and the Division of Continuing Education and Graduate Studies. Graduates of the program were eligible to take the national licensing exam. They also included special classes to help prepare the students to take the exams. Joan graduated in May 2005 and was qualified and passed the boards in July, at which time she became a registered nurse at Sturdy Memorial Hospital in Attleboro. Now, Joan is aiming to earn her master's degree and become a college nursing instructor. So, Joan started a promising career at the age of 50.

**Case History #3: Ralph (77-Year-Old Law School Student)**

In the University of Buffalo Reporter magazine May 2006, a University of Buffalo law graduate received his bachelor's degree at age 77 with a doctor's hood. At the time Ralph was going to UB Law School in 1953, it wasn't mandatory to have an undergraduate degree for admission to law school. After he graduated from high school, he studied math at UB, but opted to enter law school before receiving his bachelor's degree. Once receiving his law degree, he pursued a master's degree and taught as an associate in the School of Law at Northwestern University. The Korean War changed his career direction and he served three years in the Army Judge Advocate General Corps. In 1957, Ralph returned to Buffalo and embarked upon a distinguished career in the community. Despite of all his accomplishments in the legal field, he never got over the fact he didn't have a bachelor's degree. Throughout your life, there are always forms you have to fill out and this always reminded him of that fact. He contacted UB to look into his academic records and found he had enough math credits on his transcript from the 50's to earn his bachelor's degree with no additional coursework. Ralph felt it was important to him to participate in the commencement ceremony. Even if, in this case, it took more than 50 years to officially wear the "cap."

**Case History #4: Tomasina (87-Year-Old High School Student)**

From the *New Castle News*, in the class of 2006, a woman, 87, proves it's never too late to earn a high school diploma. Tomasina, after more than 70 years, decided it was time for her to complete her secondary education. She quit school at the end of ninth grade and later regretted it. She wanted to go back to school, but marriage, children, work and grandchildren pre-empted that desire for more than 70 years. One day she decided she put it off long enough. Tomasina received her General Educational Development (GED) diploma May 2006 from the Pennsylvania Department of Education, after 16 months of isolation from social and family activities so she could study. "I wanted to do this for myself, for my children, my grandchildren, and for a lot of students who drop out, to say it's never too late," she said. Tomasina attended New Castle High School during the depression. She was one of six children and money was tight, so they couldn't afford any luxuries like nylon stockings and high heels. She got a housecleaning job, then a job at a china shop. In 1945, she got married and worked at a supermarket while she and her husband Paul raised their children. Paul was a teacher, but Tomasina wasn't ready to take on the studying to get her diploma. In 2005, she finally decided it was time. She attended classes daily at Team PA Career Link and the Learning Center. She was the oldest student by at least 50 years. After going to school for eight hours, she would come home to study. She did all this without telling her family. Finally, in May 2006, she invited her family over to announce her accomplishment.

**Case History #5: Janet (108-Year-Old Computer Student)**

In my research, as reported by *The Guardian* newspaper, the oldest student so far has been Janet, from Rotherham in Yorkshire, who at the age of 108 has just completed a six-week course in basic computing for the over 55's at her care home. She learned how to send an email. It sounds like a small accomplishment, but to put it in perspective, she was almost 40 years old when WWII broke out.

No matter how old you are or how long it's been since you have gone to school, it's never too late for you to get out there and educate yourself, even if it's non-academic. Pursuits like learning to play an instrument or developing your skills in some craft are just as noble. Don't let doubts, worries, or others talk you out of heading back to school or pursuing your desires to learn something new. Maybe you dream of owning your own business or of becoming an attorney, a real estate broker, a computer scientist, an interior designer, an artist, or a writer. To pursue a career in any one of these fields, it takes time and often requires going back to school for several years or more. It's funny that I hear time and time again people say, "I would go back to school, but I'll be too old when I finish." I say, "You'll be that age anyway." Education has proven to be the best route towards personal success. It takes one step at a time to accomplish your goals, and the first step is acknowledging your desire to learn.

*Notes:*

# ABOUT THE AUTHOR

## THERESA DOZIER-DANIEL

Theresa Dozier-Daniel is president and founder of Kingdom Ambassador Outreach Ministries/Women of Essence, a training and personal enhancement company. She specializes in the areas of empowering individuals to fulfill God's original plan and purpose for their lives. Theresa's focuses on personal growth through gaining confidence in one own abilities. Learning how to view you through the word of God, Her motto is "I can do all things through God that gives me strength".

Her own story is one of how a person can overcome great difficulties in life to become a survivor.

She has served various faith-based organizations, hospitals, social-services agencies, through facilitation, keynote presentations, workshops, training, consulting, conferences, women retreats, , and other special events. Theresa has facilitated workshops on life skills, self-esteem, cultural diversity, conflict resolution, chemical dependency/alcohol tobacco and gender specific issues.

She is an ordained minister, author, counselor and senior adjunct professor at Burlington County College. Theresa has over twenty-five years of professional experiences dealing with the social ills of our society mental health, addiction, criminal justice and domestic violence.

Theresa holds certifications and professional membership in the following organizations:

- Board Certified Professional Christian Counselor American Association of Christian Counselors
- National Association of Forensic Counselors
- The American College of Certified Forensic Counselors
- Masters of Addiction Counselor
- Domestic Violence Counselor
- National Assoc of Female Executive
- Delta Sigma Theta Sorority

Theresa holds a Master of Science degree in Counseling and a Bachelor of Arts degree in Psychology.

She is an advocate for women and children's rights. Theresa has a strong desire to bring women together where topics and relevant issues is discussed and knowledge is shared to address needs that are of importance to them such as health/wellness, economic advancement of women, women in business, advancement in education, violence, and justice…

Theresa Dozier-Daniel is the Author of ***The Hidden Hand of God.***

*Contact*
Women of Essence
P.O. Box 2462
Cinnamison, NJ.08077
(609) 280-2866
Tdozierdaniel@verizon.net

## TWENTY

# SELF-ACCEPTANCE

## By Theresa Dozier-Daniel

Self-acceptance is being in total agreement with yourself, to the point where you appreciate, validate, accept and support who you are at the core of your being. It is the foundation upon which you stand, the vantage from which you address the world around you. It is loving and being content with who you are, as well as how you value yourself as a person. It is the sentimental worth and importance that you place upon **"You".** For those who are Baby Boomers, it is all about accepting yourself at every age and every stage of life!

Many studies have shown that the higher a person's self-acceptance is, the higher their self-esteem is. It is your willingness to love yourself and your body unconditionally, even though there are things that you would like to change. You have accepted the fact that you will never become perfect, and therefore you have made the decision to stop being self-critical. Now you are *a person that lives life from the inside out. You have become a* ***more authentic person.*** *You have made a quality decision* not to measure you value as a person mathematically. (Waist, bust, and hips, etc.)

How you feel about yourself or value yourself is self-esteem. It is your **perception** of how you are doing in the world and how you **see** yourself as the **unique** person that you are, through the lens in which you filter the light of your soul. Your self-esteem may go up or down, depending upon what is happening to you at a given moment. For instance, if you get an "A" on an exam, you will feel great, but if you fail the exam, you feel terrible. **Self-esteem is changeable**.

Self-worth differs from self-esteem**. Self-worth is what you are born with**. As one of the creations of the universe, you are worthwhile and have value, which cannot be taken from you. You can't lose it, but you can **lose sight of it.** You can forget your value as a person.

There is a scripture in the Bible that states, "You were fearfully and wonderfully made," (Ps: 139:14), which can be rephrased as, "You're an awesome wonder that is fashion, designed and created for the **leading lady position and executive director** of your own show." You may ask, what show? **(This is your life show!)** Each of us has been created with a purpose and endowed with gifts and talents to give rise to greatness in our lives.

The show has already started, whether you or ready or not. It is time for you to **step forward to the forefront and lead.** You will get only one opportunity to make a lasting impression. In life, there are no dress rehearsals. You and only you are responsible for how your performance turns out. It is about accepting full responsibility for your life. When you take charge of your life, you will feel terrific about yourself and your level of self-acceptance and self-esteem will soar.

The curtain call occurs at the end of your performance. This is when you return to the stage to be recognized by the audience for your performance. Write your script for how you want to be remembered. Consider the curtain call to be the end of your life. All of your family/

friends and some of your enemies will be there to celebrate your life, one way or another. So be audacious and give them some powerful mementos to remember you by. Be a history maker and a world changer. Change the world and the lives of people around you.

I am not endorsing an individual to be self-centered, selfish, narcissistic and vain. I am encouraging a person to understand how priceless they are as a human being. It is okay to validate oneself, and have self-love, which is the greatest love of all.

Whitney Houston's mega-hit, **"The Greatest Love of All", symbolizes this core belief**. Many of you may be familiar with this song, and may even have hummed along with it. But, how many of you have fully embraced the meaning? There is a powerful message in this song, and it radiated that the greatest love of all is **within you,** and that it is not impossible to achieve. As we learn how to love ourselves, we discover that this really is the greatest love of all. This message indicates that learning is a process of growth and development, and it will require some work on our part. Process is a series of actions that are directed toward a specific thing. Process is a progression, a forward movement, or an advancement toward something, (loving oneself). The method that one may use to fulfill this self-fulfilling prophecy can be involved, because it will require some changing of one's negative thought process, which produces something we call self-talk. Self-talk or mental talking is thoughts that an individual says to themselves that can be unconstructive, pessimistic, unenthusiastic, downbeat conversation, and can be very negative.

**A Serious Question to Consider!**

"Who is the most important person in your life?" Most of us would list our spouse, our children, our parents, etc. Why? Because we feel that they need us, and we can place ourselves on the back burner. There is a universal spiritual principle that helps us to re-focus our sense of worth as a person, so embrace this code for your life. "Love your neighbor as yourself," is the Christian version, but this belief is found in all major religions. When you love your neighbor as yourself, who do you begin with? Who do you adore and value first? Let examine this closely. Is it your neighbor or yourself? Most people believe that love begins with the other person first (their neighbor), so they focus on their neighbor wholly, to the point that they neglect themselves.

They give and give to others until they give out and then collapse into exhaustion. Once you are in a state of exhaustion, you cannot help yourself or anyone else. Many of us were trained that the focal point should be on the other person and not on ourselves. Many of us learn this as a child. We were told not to brag or be selfish. During our teenage years, (a critical time during our development), we long to be accepted by our peers, so we minimize our accomplishments to avoid appearing vain. Now, as adults, we have leaned how to put on a facade and mask our true feelings. That is called false humility to avoid looking prideful. Unconsciously, our motives of operation display that we do not like ourselves and believe that we do not deserve the best things of life, because of the lies that we were told. Why? Because most of us were raised by folks who had negative self-worth, themselves.

### Losing Value of Self

**The reality is that loving anyone begins with you**. The attributes of love, self-worth and self-esteem flow from the inside of a person to all those around them. Self-love, respect and value must first be a part of me, before I can love, respect and value others. I must acknowledge my own self-worth as a person, and learn how to take care of me so that

I *can* love and help my fellow man. This thinking does not make you selfish. It makes you a responsible person.

Acceptance exists at the core of our being. Self-acceptance begins in infancy, with the influence of our parents, caregivers, older siblings, and other important people in our lives. During our formative years of development, we yearn for love, support and acceptance. We need it to grow and develop, just as we need food for our physical bodies. There is nothing more damaging than for love and care for the developing and emerging of someone's personality to be withheld from a child by someone they consider to be important. In order for a child to develop into an emotionally healthy adult, here lies the basis of its foundation. Our own level of self-acceptance is determined by how well we feel accepted by important people in our lives.

In our materialistic society today, we place value on everything we own, our homes, automobiles, jewelry, handbags, but do we value ourselves? It saddens me that some people are probably going to answer no to this question. This is a heartbreak, a misfortune in all of the abundance of things that we have.

Webster dictionary defines the word value as worth in usefulness or importance to the possessor. It defines importance as significance**. So value equates significance**. Most people feel insignificant; I see it every day in my interaction with people. Our value system was established during childhood. If you watch a young child, they are not concerned with how they appear to others. They are not concern about appearing selfish; they will ask continuously for what they want. But in our attempts to teach them how to be generous and unselfish, we sometimes make them feel guilty or even ashamed for trying to stay true to their own needs. Now we can begin to see how we have influenced their values, self-respect, and the principles by which they judge themselves.

As we grow, our negative self-respect is expanded upon by people we admire, and by companies marketing products, according to them, we will not be complete without, like face creams, shampoos, diets, make-up, etc… As adults, we often choose to do things for others that we really don't want to do because we fear being judged by others as selfish or uncaring. When we act out of duty or obligation, that leaves us feeling anger and resentful inside, and these feelings get buried inside of us.

Finally one day, we become aware that we have given up our power and feel detached from ourselves. Sometimes we no longer feel anything; our emotions are frozen.

We have often given up our power to our family members, friends, spouses, children, supervisors, and co-workers, who unfortunately control us most of the time and take advantage of us. These are the people that will send us negative messages about our dreams and visions, if we try to break away from their power and influence over our lives and step into something different. We are consistently being eaten away at inch by inch, making us feel more detached from ourselves, lost and **devalued as a human.**

Some of us have given up our power to the medical doctors, who because of time constraints and education, sometimes no longer treat the whole person, physically, emotionally and spiritually. We must learn that we are **not defined by a diagnosis that has been given.** (Hypertension, diabetics, depression, bi-polar arthritis, heart disease…)

Self-Respect = a blend of internal confidence + our external triumph over negative self-talk + showing kindness to oneself.

- We must remember - It is your life and NO ONE else is responsible for how it turns out!
- Every human has value. We were created for a reason and a purpose. We wouldn't be here otherwise.
- It is important to accept ourselves as we are, with all of our faults and positive attributes.
- Remember, your belief system was shaped by your parents, culture, peer expectations, and by your need to feel loved, to belong, and to feel safe and good about yourself.
- It is not selfish to place yourself number one on your list. It is an indication of you accepting and valuing yourself. Remember what they say on the airplane – put your mask on first before helping others, even your little child. There must be something to this placing you first on the scheme of things.
- Acceptance is a skill that takes time to acquire and improve upon; it is at the core of your value system.
- Treat yourself as you want someone else to treat you. When you are kind to yourself, others will take notice. You will find that others will respect you more for valuing yourself because people tend to treat you as well as you treat yourself.
- Loving self-talk can wash away the sediment of hurt and rejection that may have covered your innate self-acceptance for years.
- Forgive yourself by letting go of any past incident that made you feel unloved, or unwanted.

- When you fully believe in yourself, and place value on yourself, an attack on your person becomes unacceptable. You will stand up for yourself, and show the world that a transformation has taken place, inside of you. You not only believe the message of the song, but you are living proof that the greatest love of all is in "You".
- You'll feel determined, strong and have clear purpose in mind. For you are a world-changers and a history maker. You are infiltrating all of the systems of the world. **You are on your way to make it happen...**

**Self-Absorbed**

Those that we label as narcissistic, vain, and self-important really do not accepted themselves. It has been my experience that those that are loud, overbearing, and go out of their way to display their "importance" are actually covering up a great deal of inferiority, self-doubt, incompetence, and fear. When a person feels a sense of inner acceptance and self-worth, there is no need for approval from others to define who they are. When asked the question am I a worthy/valuable person, you can answer in your own voice with a resounding "Yes!"

**There Are Two Major Considerations For Accepting Yourself:**

1. Self-acceptance is a choice. The choice is yours, and only you can make that decision.
2. Awareness – When you become conscious that you have a problem, you have to solve it.

**Questions To Reflect Upon:**

- What do you value most? Does your life reflect what you value most?
- Are you living by someone else's values or yours?
- Where do you place yourself on your list of priorities?
- Are you waiting for someone else to make you number one?
- Isn't it time to change your bag that you have being carrying around? (Is it filled with pain, shame, unforgiveness, guilt, resentment, or fear?)
- Take a look at your ongoing, negative commentary inside your mind that undermines your self-worth. (Examine your self-talk, that critical inner voice.)

**Quotes:**

*"A man cannot be comfortable without his own approval."*
—Mark Twain

*"Until you value yourself, you won't value your time. Until you value your time, you will not do anything with it."* —M. Scott Peck

*"To increase your level of self-acceptance,*
*think of your unique talents and abilities."* —Brian Tracy

*"The most terrifying thing is to accept oneself completely."*
—Carl Gustav Jung

*"The fruit of self-understanding is self-acceptance. The fruit of self-acceptance is self-love. The fruit of self-love is love for the world. The fruit of love for the world is service to the world. The fruit of service to the world is peace."* —Russell Rowe

*Notes:*

# ABOUT THE AUTHOR

**SUSIE MATHEWS**

Susie Mathews is the Founder and President of Winning Directions, a training and consulting organization that specializes in helping individuals and organizations understand that working with *passion* = performance. She conducts workshops and seminars that teach strategies for lifelong personal and professional success. Susie shares insights on how to actively achieve what you desire and transform your dream life into reality.

For ten years Susie has helped guide thousands of individuals who wanted to change the direction of their professional career. She's been able to identify the foundation of an individual's success. Do what you love, believe in it with every fiber of your being and give your gifts to those who need it. Through her workshops, seminars and one-on-one coaching she helps her clients bring out the power and strength of their full potential

Susie Matthews is a co-author of the best selling book, *Wake Up and Live the Life You Love... Seizing Your Success.* She was recently featured in the Chicago Tribune as a leading authority in career strategic planning. And her new book, *Cash In on the Passion Do What You Love... Love What You Do,* is now available.

*Contact:*
Winning Directions
www.Cashinonthepassion.com
Susie@Winning-directions.com
10936 N. Port Washington Rd. # 120
Mequon, WI 53092
(262)243-1201

TWENTY-ONE

# LIVE LIFE WITH PASSION: EMOTIONALLY, PHYSICALLY, SPIRITUALLY AND... FINANCIALLY

**By Susie Matthews**

I believe that each of us has been put on this Earth for a purpose. For instance:

1. During the American Civil War, Harriet Tubman was *supposed* to help free slaves in the south and bring them up north through the Underground Railroad.

2. In India, Mother Theresa was *destined* to help feed the starving children.

3. Carol was *born* to work with animals, and might say something like, "I love the research that I do with the dolphins."

4. Sarah just *comes alive* when she's taking a tour group down the Colorado River in the Grand Canyon. It would not be uncommon to hear her say, "I'm just in awe of this place, and I love to share it with people."

5. Me? I was born to gab—and to *help* people believe in themselves and to find the passion within.

Not only do I believe that we all have a purpose, but I also know deep inside that each of us has a niche that contributes to our purpose and a sense of inner fulfillment. This sensation is what I declare *Living Your Life with Passion.*

In my seminars, I share with my audiences that they're not going to find that niche without a good hard look in here, tapping my chest, pointing to my heart. When you are doing what is in your heart, you are giving with your heart. And when you're giving with your heart, you are giving to the world your gifts, your God-given, self-developed talents.

So why are there so many people living less-than-fulfilling lives? Because, for the most part, they do not take the time to investigate their history, their life experiences that we hold closest to our heart. To change this direction, it is my desire to teach you to honor those treasured experiences by actively incorporating them into your life, then finally appreciating the wonderful impact this has had on your life. I'm quite confident you have heard the phase, "Life is Good." The feeling of joy and satisfaction which comes as a direct reaction to this process is the sensation that life is, indeed, Good. This process develops into a confidence that is hard to stop.

*"Success is not the key to happiness. Happiness is the key to success."*
—Albert Schweitzer

By not searching deeply within to discover our distinct capabilities and capacities and utilizing them, we let the outside world direct and dictate to us. We find ourselves conforming to the surroundings and influences imposed on us by others, which may or may not be the right place to invest our efforts. We begin acting out whatever behavior someone else wants, not what we may want for ourselves.

There's a reason you picked up this book. Now is the time to evaluate the most precious commodity you possess: the potential of your well-defined self. You, too can discover, uncover and put to use your skills, unique talents and abilities, the very things that bring great joy into your life.

But, how do you know what you need to achieve a life you would dream of? The good news is that you already possess everything you need to begin pursuing and acquiring your desired future. You see, the life you have lived is already full of clues that will reveal to you what path you should follow, what course you should plot. You just have to do a little investigative work to help bring them to light . . . and life. Everything you've ever done—and just as important, what you have chosen not to do—over your lifetime reads like a blueprint for your success. I suggest you simply realize the tremendous value of these collective experiences.

I believe that if you inspect your past closely enough, you will discover the path to a destiny you will relish.

The way I look at it, revealing your gifts to yourself is the most critical component to living your life with the passion and zest you deserve. For you to have the type of success we are talking about, you need to understand that you have to LOVE whatever it is that you *choose* to do. At this point, you might be asking me, "Susie, how can I know what I would love to do when I haven't done it yet? Aren't we looking at the future?" Well, yes, but I'd like for you to understand how important it is to see how your future is directly related to your past. What you choose to do as your life unfolds needs to be based on the fact that you use your unique skills that you LOVE to use. It follows, then, that you will love what you do. When you are doing what you truly love, every day, you are living your passion. You are following your heart and living the life you've always dreamed of.

The first step on this journey is looking deeply and honestly at yourself. What are your unique skills? What are your unique abilities? I want you to think about and answer this question: Do you believe that you are unique? What is it that distinguishes you from the other six billion people on this planet? Give yourself a few minutes to really think about it. On the following page, make a list of everything that makes you unique.

*What makes you unique?*

**Write Down Everything You Believe Makes You Unique.**

______________________________

______________________________

______________________________

______________________________

______________________________

Let's look at your responses. Did you say something like, "I'm very personable," or "I'm honest," or "I work hard," or "I enjoy working with people"? This is where many people searching for their futures go wrong.

"Wrong? That's not wrong," you might say to me, with your feathers ruffled a bit, "I am all of those things. What do you mean . . . wrong?"

What I mean is, when you wrote those words, were you saying that these things are uniquely yours? Were you saying that you are the only person on the planet who is honest? That you—and only you—work hard? And perhaps you're the only one who gets to enjoy working with other people?

I don't doubt that you have all of the characteristics in your response, but that's not what I'm asking you for here. I want you to change your vision of yourself, to begin to think about the collection of things that make you unique, distinctly different from anyone else.

Would you agree that the universe will never see and enjoy another person or being who is like you ever again for eternity? Would you agree that you are uniquely set apart from all the rest? You have wondrous and countless things to offer the world every day. You express yourself in a manner no one could ever duplicate. You are one-of-a-kind who will never come again. Start looking at yourself with loving respect, a great deal of compassion, and adoration. Give yourself the kind of unconditional love that you deserve.

I want you to understand you have uniqueness, a greatness that only YOU possess. By understanding your greatness, you can begin to extend and multiply that greatness in everything you do, in everything you think, in everything you say, to everyone you meet. When you are doing what it is you love, then you are giving to the world what you are great at! Once you truly understand and believe that, "Before you love what you do, you have to love who you are," we can move forward.

Like a rare, valuable jewel, it's critical to identify the facets that uniquely set you apart from everyone else on the planet. It may appear hard at first, but once you get rolling, you'll see how easy it really is. Because who, better than you, knows everything about the topic that we are going to explore. And that topic is, of course, YOU!

To help you get a better understanding of what I'm aiming for here, let me give you an example of what I believe, and what I know, makes me, Susie Mathews, unique:

I know I am able to be in front of hundreds and energize people when I talk to them. I know I am able to teach complex concepts in an easy-to-understand and entertaining manner. I know I am able to persuade people to take action because they know it comes from my heart and I have their best interest in mind.

The purpose of the next exercise is for you to able to generate statements like these for yourself. I want you to begin to develop a mind-set that echoes, loud and clear: "There is nobody that can even come close to doing or being what I am or can do." How do we get to this point? We begin by understanding the power of our unique strengths. We do that by looking at the thing we love to do. Like a gemologist refines and polishes the gem, you, too, will have a chance to keep adding to your luster and individual appeal in your own "I AM" statement later.

### *What You Do is Based on What You Value: The Jewels of Your Life*

**Exercise: Million-Dollar Dream**

If you were given a million dollars today, write down what you would want to do with it. Here is an example of what I would say:

*I would plan a two-week cruse to Alaska, and I would take my entire family. I would buy a new Blue BMW M3 convertible. I would then pay off all my bills, and I would put half of what's left in secure investments that would help my company grow. I would buy some land in an upward-growing community. Then I would take a month and travel to Tahiti, then go to Australia and New Zealand on my way back. I would probably travel to a few more wonderful places, if there were some money left.*

**Now It's Your Turn.**

_______________________________________________________________________________

_______________________________________________________________________________

_______________________________________________________________________________

_______________________________________________________________________________

_______________________________________________________________________________

_______________________________________________________________________________

_______________________________________________________________________________

_______________________________________________________________________________

_______________________________________________________________________________

_______________________________________________________________________________

What does this exercise tell you about yourself?

You put a value on things. Based upon your personality, you value things differently than others. What you value is going to be different from what I, or anyone else, values.

What does that mean, value? It tells you how important something is to you in your life.

Let's look at some of things we value. I'll start . . .

1. My family
2. Hugs: energy
3. Helping people
4. Travel
5. My cats . . . don't laugh
6. Driving in the country . . . OK, it's more fun if I'm going fast and I have the convertible top down.

**What Do You Value?**

________________________________________

________________________________________

________________________________________

________________________________________

________________________________________

There is something here I want you to see. Your behavior is based upon your values.

How much you value something equals how important it is to you.

Important => priority

Priority => choice

Choice => behavior

If something is important to you, then you know why you will act on it, and it becomes a priority. If you don't know why something is important to you, then you are more likely to be vague and indifferent. It's helpful if you know what your priorities or your values are when it comes time to make those decisions that can or will change your life. Clearly, some of these choices are BIGGIES.

Let me give you an example of how this can work. A great example is peer pressure. Everybody is faced with peer pressure at some point in his or her life, and young adults have to deal with an unfair battery of peer pressure. But, they haven't had enough life experiences to know really how to arm themselves against this constant borage. If they don't know what their values are, they might get dragged into something they don't want. It may get them on a path they don't want to walk down at all. Take for example, smoking. Do you really think people start smoking for the taste or the sensation of the smoke choking their lungs? But, if they can arm themselves with reasons, good reasons, as to why they don't even want to try smoking, it might help them make a decision. For example, it they have experienced the heartache of watching a loved one die due to lung cancer, it might make saying no to their first cigarette much easier. If they can't express why they don't want something, they might collapse—fall prey to the pressure. Do yourself a favor: think about what's important to you. Try to understand why it's important so you can arm yourself and then take action.

Let's bring this back to the topic at hand. What do you gain by knowing what your values are when it comes to living with passion? We've already established that when you value something, it is important to you. It has meaning and purpose ***to you***. Not Joe, not Sally, not your parents, not me, and not Mr. Brown, but to you. You need to know what your values are when it comes to making choices about who you are, what you want to be, and how you want to spend you life.

Your behavior will be based upon what's important to you. If you don't find out what is important to you when it comes to going after your dream, then you will find yourself floating around not going after anything. If you don't go after what you want, you will spend a lifetime going after what someone else wants you to do . . . *for their benefit and their profit.* Do you think it really matters to them what you choose for your day-to-day life?

**Exercise:**

Think back to the times when you were your happiest. What events in your life have given you a wonderful sense of fulfillment? Let your fondest recollections come to the surface. First, look at activities or situations that have brought you great joy and that you truly love doing. Ask yourself questions like:

I seem to be at my best when ________________________

The type of environment I appear to thrive in is

____________________________________________________________

When I'm involved with this activity I could spend hours at

____________________________________________________________

Make a list of at least ten different events in your life that bring you joy, and be as specific about the situation as you can.

____________________________________________________________

____________________________________________________________

____________________________________________________________

____________________________________________________________

____________________________________________________________

____________________________________________________________

**Creating Your "I AM" Statement**

I AM = ***I***nventory your ***A***chievements ***M***odel.

I would like you to craft an "I AM" statement based upon your achievements.

Once you know who and what you are, bringing those descriptions to the forefront, both for yourself and people you meet or work with, you will exude confidence and get closer to living the life you've always dreamed about. You know what makes you unique, your skills, talents and personality. Now continuously acting with these elements in mind and folding these rich attributes into your day-to-day actions will put you into the driver's seat for the rest of your life.

Congratulations are definitely in order! You have created your very own, unique, special list of achievements, accomplishments, and successes. In your hands you are holding concrete evidence of what you do naturally and you do well. These are your gifts that are meant to be shared with the world, which will, in turn, reap you a rainbow of rewards.

# ABOUT THE AUTHOR

## Hope Hatfield

Hope Hatfield is the president, CEO and founder of Hatfield Consulting, Inc, which provides training and consulting in the areas of business and technology.

In the past 20 years, Hope has owned and operated several successful businesses in the fields of Business, Training, and Technology. She spent most of those years providing training and enabling entrepreneurs and businesses gain the technology and confidence to grow into successful enterprises. Because of this experience and her desire to help others, Hope's path and direction has expanded to assisting others achieve similar success in the business world. She has a particular passion for helping women become successful entrepreneurs and is a Certified Women's Business Trainer.

In addition to running Hatfield Consulting, and raising her son, Hope teaches college classes, speaks to local businesses, women's groups, run workshops, and gives seminars on various business, technology and professional skills topics. In her spare time Hope is a freelance author and editor. Many of her writings and published articles include topics on women's issues, entrepreneurial issues, business issues and technology techniques.

Hope is a fun and engaging speaker who enjoys helping others. In her teaching and speaking mode, she has the skills to motivate her audience to participate and interact with her presentations. She is an experienced Business Coach, Marketing Consultant, Public Speaker and a certified eBay Trainer. She is also a Certified Branding & Image Consultant and knows how to impart Leadership and Empowerment skills, particularly to women. She holds a black belt in Taekwondo and regularly participates in mini marathons.

Hope has a MPA in Public Administration, a BS in Computer Technology, and is currently working on her MBA.

*Contact*
Hatfield Consulting
11 Apple Tree Circle
Fishers, IN. 46038
(317) 517-0510
hope@hatfieldconsulting.com

TWENTY-TWO

# LEADERSHIP: BEING THE LEADER OF YOUR PACK

**By Hope Hatfield**

*"Leaders do not command excellence, they build excellence."*
—Author Unknown

**What Is Leadership and What Makes a Good Leader?**

Leadership can be defined as "the process of directing the behavior of others toward the accomplishment of some common objectives." Leadership can take different forms: a CEO of a Fortune 500 company, a single mother, or a president of a volunteer organization. The skills it takes to be the leader of a Fortune 500 company are similar to the skills it takes to be the leader of your family.

**Exercise:**

**Take a couple minutes and write down all the places where you are in a leadership role.**

________________________________________________________

________________________________________________________

________________________________________________________

________________________________________________________

________________________________________________________

## Qualities of Good Leaders

Being a good leader is not an easy task. Each of us has the basic abilities to lead. Leadership styles are different depending on your personality and the people/organization you are leading. However, there are qualities and traits that successful leaders have in common. Personally, when I think of all the people I know who are great leaders, they all share a lot of the same traits—hard working, honesty, a great visionary, confident.

Some of the traits of good leaders are:

- **Honesty**
- **Self-Confidence (not to be confused with arrogance)**
- **Visionary – being able to see the big picture**
- **Assertiveness – knowing when to take charge and knowing when to let others lead**
- **Good Listener – being able to listen to what your followers are saying**

- **Strong Interpersonal Skills – being able to effectively communicate**
- **Flexibility** – being able to stay the course, but adapt as necessary

A good leader will surround themselves with good, competent support people who also believe in their vision. A good leader will also be the first to admit when they need help or have made a mistake.

**Why Women Make Good Leaders**

Traditionally, in corporate America men have held the majority of the top leadership roles. Also, in many cultures it is the man who is the head of the family. Men naturally have some good leadership qualities, but women also have leadership qualities that are often overlooked.

Women are natural multi-taskers. Think about a day in the life of a working mother: she gets up in the morning, feeds the pets, cooks breakfast for the family, makes the children's lunches, checks the homework, gets the kids out of bed and ready for school, puts a load of laundry in the washer, gets herself ready for work, puts the kids on the bus, cleans up the mess from breakfast, gets out the door for work. After work she races home to get the kids off the bus, makes sure the kids do their homework, feed the pets, finishes dinner, throws the clothes in the dryer, cleans up dishes after dinner, gets everyone ready for bed, and gets ready to start another day.

Maybe, your life isn't as hectic as that, or maybe it's worse. Either way women, as a woman you are naturally good at handling several things at once. There are other reasons why women make good leaders:

1. They are compassionate and helpful.
2. They are good listeners.

3. They are good at communication.
4. They are empathic and value relationships.
5. They have insight and intuition.
6. They can look at issues from many different angles.
7. They use maternal instincts to take charge, when necessary.

**Exercise:**
Make a List of All of Your Leadership Traits.

__________________________________________________________________

__________________________________________________________________

__________________________________________________________________

__________________________________________________________________

__________________________________________________________________

__________________________________________________________________

__________________________________________________________________

__________________________________________________________________

__________________________________________________________________

**Age and Experience Are Essential for Leaders.**

Do you know that a person can't become the President of the U.S. until they are at least 35? The majority of Fortune 500 CEO's have gray hair/no hair. Why is that? With age brings wisdom and experience that can't be taught in a classroom or seminar. Leadership is situational and requires people to rely on past experience to make the best decisions. Many times experience is the best teacher. That isn't to say that eduction is a waste of time, because education is valuable. But, there are things that age brings—wisdom, experience, patience and confidence—that can't be replaced. This is especially true for women. Most women don't become fully confident until after their mid-30's.

**Don't Keep Chasing Your Tail.**

As a leader, it is important to have a clear vision for your organization or group. If you are going to lead, you need to make sure you know where you are leading your followers. It is also important to share your vision and the path with everyone else. They need to know where you are leading them. It is important to make sure that you are not chasing your tail...have you every watched a dog chase his tail? While it is amusing to watch, it is something that a leader should never do. As a leader, it is important to make sure you are not running around in circles and there is a clear path to your vision.

**Failure, Confidence and Self-Sabotage**

Three critical pieces to good leadership is knowing how to handle failure, displaying confidence, and avoiding self-sabotage. Don't be afraid to abandon a failing strategy if it will not help you to achieve your goals. You must also be able to learn from your successes, as well as your failures. Use what works and get rid of what doesn't. Don't dwell on your mistakes. Learn from your failures and try not to repeat them. There is no room for fear of failure. A leader who is afraid to fail will never be a good leader

To be great leader you need to have and to display confidence. No one is willing to following a leader that doesn't have self-confidence. Sometimes, it's difficult to have confidence in yourself. You need to take a good look at yourself and know that you are capable of being a good leader. Surround yourself with people who support and believe in you and your abilities.

One of the biggest stumbling blocks women have is self-sabotage. Women can be their own worst enemies. Women will often use negative "self talk" to destroy their own self-image and confidence. Another way women sabotage themselves is in the standards they establish for themselves. They will compare themselves with great leaders and set goals so high they can't be reached. The last way women often self-sabotage is by surrounding themselves with "confidence suckers" ... you know these type of people. They are the ones that tell you that you can't do it, or that you are not qualified, etc. Try to avoid these people, if at all possible.

**Exercise:**
**List All of The Ways That You Sabotage Yourself.**

______________________________________________

______________________________________________

______________________________________________

______________________________________________

______________________________________________

______________________________________________

______________________________________________

______________________________________________

______________________________________________

**NOW STOP DOING ALL OF THEM!!!!**

### How to Develop Leadership Qualities and Become a Better Leader

Effective leaders recognize that there is always more they need to learn. Becoming a great leader is the eternal process of learning more and doing better. You should be open to new ideas, insights, and revelations that can lead to better ways of accomplishing your goals. This is a continuous learning and growing process.

There are four steps to develop leadership qualities and become a better leader:

1. Model other leaders.
2. Improve your inner self.
3. Recognize what skills can be translated into leadership.
4. Practice! Practice! Practice!

The first way to develop better leadership skills is to model other leaders. You need to be careful, as you don't want to change your personality or leadership style to match theirs. What you are looking to do is to mirror the leadership traits that they have that make them good leaders. For example, if you have a boss that is a great leader, then try to identify what makes them a good leader. What traits do they have, how to they handle crisis, how do they interact with other people? Then start to mirror some of these traits in you own leadership roles.

**Exercise:**
**List Some Great Leaders and Traits You Can Mirror.**

| **Leader** | **Trait** | **How I can incorporate this into my daily life?** |
|---|---|---|
| | | |
| | | |
| | | |
| | | |
| | | |
| | | |

The second way to become a better leader is to work on your inner self. This is highly individualized and each person has their own list of things to work on. Some women need to work on self-confidence, some women need work on assertiveness, and some women need to improve their communication skills. Try to do a personal leadership assessment of yourself. You might want to ask a close friend help you with it. Make a list of inner self things (confidence, communication skills, listening skills) and, take one or two and start working on making it better.

The third way to be a better leader is to recognize what non-leadership skills you have that can be translated into leadership skills. Mothering may be the best place to practice and learn leadership. Women who are busy juggling kids' sports schedules and doctors' appointments are good at multi-tasking. Women who handle the hurdle the politics and scheduling of play dates are good collaborators. Women who have multiple children become very good at conflict resolution.

The fourth way to be a better leader is to practice, practice, and practice. You need to practice developing leadership skills, self-improvement and mirroring other great leaders. Step into leadership roles without fear.

**Conclusion**

Becoming a great leader isn't difficult, but it does take time, practice and change. Women are natural leaders and we are forced into leadership roles everyday as the primary caretakers of our families (children, spouse, elderly parents, pets). The key to becoming a great leader is to not be afraid to step into the position with confidence, vision and a willingness to fail.

**Exercise:**
**As a Summary of This Chapter, Think About and Answer the Following Questions:**

1. How do you define leadership?

___________________________________________

___________________________________________

___________________________________________

2. Who are the leaders you admire?

___________________________________________

___________________________________________

___________________________________________

3. Why do you admire them?

___________________________________________

___________________________________________

___________________________________________

4. Do you believe that a woman can be as good a leader as a man? Why or why not?

___________________________________________

___________________________________________

___________________________________________

5. What aspects of a woman's life do you feel develop her leadership potential?

___________________________________________

___________________________________________

___________________________________________

6. Does your workplace encourage women to develop their leadership skills? If so, how?

7. What forms of support would you like to see in your workplace/organization to help women develop leadership skills?

8. Do you feel that women in a work and personal setting help each other become leaders?

9. In what area of your life do you see yourself as a leader?

10. In what area of your life would you like to become a leader?

11. What is your vision as a leader?

12. What forms of support do you need to make this possible?

______________________________________________

______________________________________________

______________________________________________

I wish you wonderful success on your journey to becoming a dynamic and impactful leader. Surround yourself with people who believe in you.

## ABOUT THE AUTHOR

### PAULINE M. LEE

Pauline M. Lee is Chief Executive Officer of Etiquette Works, Inc. She is an expert in international protocol, business etiquette, and young adult/youth manners. She has extensive knowledge and experience in management, leadership skills, customer service, public speaking skills, and women's issues. She is known for her seminars, keynote presentations, professional and personal development seminars. Ms. Lee is committed to helping individuals acquire the polish, productivity, and professionalism necessary to thrive and excel in this ever-changing, high technology, global economy. Pauline provides her listeners with interactive training and the tools needed to remove the business etiquette obstacles and minimize the challenges that make doing business a pain rather than a pleasure.

Ms. Lee is certified as an International Protocol and Business Etiquette Coach by the Protocol School of Washington; is a Certified Seminar Leader (CSL); has a Masters Degree in Public Administration and a Bachelor of Science Degree in Business Administration. Ms. Lee is a member of the National Speakers Association (NSA), Toastmasters International (ATM-G), National Association of Female Executives (NAFE), and the Association of Image Consultants International (AICI).

Pauline is an informative, energetic, and humorous presenter. It is her desire that all people exhibit confidence, project intelligence, speak clearly, concisely and eloquently while achieving the greatness they deserve. She is dedicated to providing workshops and seminars that will increase self-esteem, personal empowerment, leadership and overall confidence in the dining room, classroom and the Boardroom.

*Contact:*
ETIQUETTE WORKS, INC.
6709 LaTijera Boulevard #550
Los Angeles, California 90045
(323) 253-1908
www.etiquetteworks.org
etiquetteworks@sbcglobal.net
www.protrain.net

TWENTY-THREE

# NEVER STOP REACHING! THE BEST IS YET TO COME

**By Pauline Lee**

"Gearing up for the second act!" "Hey, fifty is the new thirty!" "Retirement." These are all statements related to the "Baby Boomer" generation. You have been taught that the possibilities in life are endless, and there is a new definition for the "R" word. Retirement—what does that mean? Rather than sitting at home, the new trend is to reposition yourself, reinvent yourself, see the world and live your life to the fullest. Retirement means doing the things you have always wanted to do. While the baby boomer generation is not all alike due to different cultural reference points, they all have one thing in common -- it is a craving of self-fulfillment and self-actualization. Through this period of time called life there have been births and deaths, weddings and divorce, corporate downsizings, natural disasters, economic recession, financial hardships, and medical breakthroughs. Life has had its joys and sorrows; its ups and downs; its trials and tribulations. In the midst of it all, you have learned to ***Never Stop Reaching*** for peace of mind, financial security, perfect health, fulfilling jobs, and meaningful relationships. You name it and the baby boomer generation has tried it. Although you have reached another milestone in life, this is no time for stopping. The ability to fulfill your retirement dreams is primarily based on preparing and budgeting for them. You need to develop an action plan. You need to develop a list; then transform the ideas into reality.

The great motivational speaker Brian Tracy says, "It doesn't matter where you are coming from. All that matters is where you are going." Wherever you are on life's journey, it is extremely important that you ***Never Stop Reaching***. Theoretically, retirement could be viewed as a time to stop. The reality is, however, that this is a time to begin. There may be times when you have been knocked down, but as long as you can look up--you can get up. The challenge with many plans in life is that they are based on the way things are now. To achieve your dreams and goals, you must focus on what you want, not on what you have. Eight principles to help you continue achieving your dreams and desires are as follows:

1. **DARE – Dare to Change**.

   ***"It takes a lot of courage to release the familiar and seemingly secure, to embrace the new. But there is no real security in what is no longer meaningful. There is more security in the adventurous and exciting, for in movement there is life, and in change there is power."*** **—Alan Cohen**

As you travel along life's road map, you will find that change is inevitable. Life changes, dreams change, opportunities change, relationships change, and your goals change. It is never too late to try something new. It is never too late to change your old way of thinking. Dare to make a difference in the lives of others. Dare to dream. Dare to take risks. Have courage to stand up for what you desire to do. What ordinary thing can you do in an extraordinary way? Develop courage for living. As a child, most of us had the experience of learning to ride a bicycle. Remember the first time you tried to balance yourself? You wobbled and perhaps fell several times because you were not able to coordinate balancing and peddling at the same time. In spite of falling, you got back up and tried it again. Perhaps you tried again because your parents insisted or your siblings challenged you, but you didn't give up. Eventually you learned to ride a bicycle. So it is in life, you must keep trying. If you want to make a meaningful change in your life, acknowledge what it is that needs changing and implement a measurable strategy to begin making the change. Change your attitude. Change your way of thinking about life.

One way to start this process is by changing your vocabulary. Here are a few suggestions:

| **Eliminate These Words** | **Replace with These Words** |
|---|---|
| 1. I can't | 1. I can |
| 2. If | 2. I will |
| 3. Maybe | 3. Absolutely |

| | |
|---|---|
| 4. I don't think | 4. I know |
| 5. I don't have the time | 5. I will make the time |
| 6. I don't believe | 6. I do believe |
| 7. Doubt | 7. Expect the best |
| 8. I am afraid of | 8. I am confident |
| 9. (less) I | 9. (more) You |
| 10 It's impossible | 10. All things are possible |

**2. DESIRE – How Badly Do You Want It?**

***"A quitter never wins and a winner never quits."*** **—Napoleon Hill**

Your desire for change must be greater than all the challenges that stand in your way. How badly do you want it? What sacrifices are you willing to make to attain it? Now is the time to live life in the manner you intended to live. You can never give up on your dreams. You can never give up on fulfilling that burning desire to achieve the greatness you deserve. You can never give up on the life you envisioned. You have everything you need to achieve your dreams. You have been empowered to succeed. Reprogram your mind to know that you can achieve whatever you want, you can have what you want, and you can live the life you desire. Believe in yourself. Expect only the best. Embrace your high self-esteem, self-confidence, and determination, along with ambition. Know that you can. All of these qualities begin with the way you think of yourself. Think of the life you desire. Think of all the details of that life. Focus on those things. Identify your priorities. What do you think about first and foremost? Whatever you think about and desire, you will achieve.

3. **DISCOVER – Know Who You Are and Whose You Are.**

***"There is one quality which one must possess to win, and that is definiteness of purpose, the knowledge of what one wants, and a burning desire to possess it."*** **—Napoleon Hill**

Discover who you are and what you want. Discover your purpose in life. Find something you are passionate about. In the book the *Purpose Driven Life* by Rick Warren, there are five benefits of living a purpose-driven life. They are:

a. **Knowing your purpose gives meaning to your life**. When life has meaning, you can bear almost anything.

b. **Knowing your purpose simplifies your life**. It defines what you do and what you don't do. Your purpose becomes the standard you use to evaluate which activities in life are important and which are not.

c. **Knowing your purpose focuses your life**. Your energy and effort are concentrated on what is important. You become effective by being selective.

d. **Knowing your purpose motivates your life**. Life is energized when there is a clear purpose.

e. **Knowing your purpose prepares you for eternity**. Leaving a legacy is not enough. You must leave an eternal legacy of using your gifts, talents opportunities, energy, and relationships.

Perhaps you have not had the opportunity to focus on your purpose because you were concerned with the nurturing and caring of others. Now is your time. Learn something new. Learning is a continuing, never-ending process. Invest in yourself and keep learning. Take a gourmet cooking class. Take a dance class. Learn to sew. Take a computer class. Take an art class. Learn a foreign language. Read, read, and read. Life is full of opportunities. **Discover** what you want and don't let anyone talk you out of living your dreams.

4. **<u>DETERMINATION</u> – Don't Look Back.**

***"If you can't fly, then run. If you can't run, then walk. If you can't walk, then crawl. But whatever you do, keep moving."***
**—Dr. Martin Luther King, Jr.**

Once you discover your purpose in life, you must commit to pursuing it, no matter what. This requires determination, commitment, and perseverance because something or someone is sure to come along to distract you from what you have defined as your purpose. Forget about the past. Forget about past failures, past hurts, past rejection. Let the past be the past. If you focus on what you left behind, you will never be able to look ahead. Have you ever asked yourself, "Why is it that people are ahead of me in life? I feel I have as much talent and am equally as smart?" It is because they began the race and they endured to the end. The one thing they do is to persevere. Remain determined to stay the course, no matter what obstacles come your way.

5. **<u>DECIDE</u> – Take Responsibility For Your Life.**

***"You must take personal responsibility. You cannot change the circumstances, the seasons, or the wind, but you can change yourself." —*Jim Rohn**

Take responsibility for your life – you cannot hold anyone responsible for your success or failure. You must stop waiting for somebody to help you change. Make a conscious decision to do what needs to be done in order to change. The first steps begin with the words we speak. Decisions are based on your memories of past failures or successes and your faith in possibilities of the unseen. The acceptance of complete responsibility for your life means that you refuse to make excuses or to blame others for anything in your life that you are not satisfied with. Stop complaining about your situation and about what has happened in the past. You should eliminate the "what if's" and focus instead on what you really want and where you are going. If you are not happy with any part of your life, DECIDE to get busy changing it. If something goes wrong, accept responsibility and begin looking for a solution. If you are not happy with your current financial situation, accept responsibility and DECIDE to do those things that are necessary for you to increase your wealth. (Get a part time job, start your own business, DECIDE to save, cut back on eating out, stop using credit cards, etc.) If you are unhappy with your weight, DECIDE to accept responsibility and begin exercising and eating properly. If you are not happy with the amount of time you are spending with your family, accept responsibility and DECIDE to designate specific time as family time. Begin to do something about it now.

6. **DESTINY – Control Your Destiny.**

***"If you doubt you can accomplish something, then you can't accomplish it. You have to have confidence in your ability, and then be tough enough to follow through."*** **—Rosalyn Carter**

***"It's choice - not chance - that determines your destiny."***
**—Jean Nidetch**

Do you have trouble staying focused on a goal? Do you start something and get distracted? It is not our circumstances, our spouse, our finances, or our family background that determines our destiny. It is the decisions we make in life. The old adage is true, "If you fail to plan, then you plan to fail." When we take a road trip, we take the time to get a map and strategically plan where we are going and how we are to get there. Isn't our life equally as important? At this stage many have not done so, but it is not too late. The key is to start right where you are. Take immediate action. Set specific goals. Set measurable goals. Set realistic goals. Set a time period to achieve your goals. Establish a budget for your "list" of things to do. See a financial planner. Decisions determine your destiny.

7. **DO – Do Your Part.**

***"If it is to be, it is up to me."*** **—William Johnson**

My mother often reminded me of this saying. Take action now, time is passing. Are you waiting for things to get better before moving ahead? If you are waiting for things to be perfect, nothing will ever get done. Start right where you are and implement the first step to change — your way of thinking. You must bloom right where you are planted; do what you can where you are, with what you already have. Stop making excuses. Eliminate the "If I coulda, woulda, shoulda" phrases. "If I would have invested sooner." "If I could get a better job." "I should have gone to college." "If only……." You must change your "if only" into an "I will." "I will get out of credit card debt." "I will create and nurture my relationships." "I will eat properly." In order to be who you want to be, you must do what you need to do, to have what you would like to have. Action is better than agony.

8. **DREAM – Dream Big Dreams.**

***"I will! I am! I can! I will actualize my dream. I will press ahead. I will settle down and see it through. I will solve the problems. I will pay the price. I will never walk away from my dream until I see my dream walk away: Alert! Alive! Achieved!"***
**—Robert Schuller**

See yourself as you want to be. Picture the outcomes you want in life as if they have already happened. Use visualization to get you closer to your dream. Close your eyes and project yourself one year into the future. Envision your ideal life situation and that you've reached a stage that you consider successful. See yourself as though you have achieved your dreams. If this level of success were your reality, how would you act? How would you carry yourself? What would your life look like? How would you interact with others? How would you contribute to the lives of others? How happy would you be? Who would be in your circle of friends? How would you feel? Now that your have visualized your success, how does this vision compare to the way you act, feel and carry yourself now?

Know that you already have everything you need to achieve this level of success. If there is a difference in how you act, feel, or carry yourself now, look inward and realize that you are made of the same DNA as every successful person. Embrace your dreams. Take the feeling of success you experience in the visualization and bring it to the present. Walk into your destiny and start having that sense of success. Carry yourself as though it has already happened. Begin to focus on being the type of successful person you know you are destined to be.

Creating change at this juncture in life may be challenging, but your life lessons have prepared you for the change. Change is inevitable. In spite of illness, the death of parents, siblings, and friends, reorganization at work, empty nest syndrome, and financial challenges, each of these principles is an integral part of life. Everything you have.... everything you are.... everything you see and hear at this point in your life is the sum total of what you have thought, believed, and acted on (or not acted on) up to this moment. The new journey has started and you have the opportunity to chart a new course. Every day is an opportunity for a new beginning. Learn from life's lessons and the character you have developed. Start right where you are. Dare to make a change, control your thoughts, focus on the right things in the right way, and stay with something long enough to get results. The wisdom you have gained and your positive attitude will carry you through. Enjoy the journey. Remember---

## ***Never Stop Reaching! The Best Is Yet To Come!!***

**Reading Resources:**

*Women and Money* by Suze Orman

*Reposition Yourself* by T.D. Jakes

*What's Really Holding You Back?* by Valorie Burton

*Reallionnaire* by Farrah Gray

*You're Fifty—Now What* by Charles Schwab

*Purpose Driven Life* by Rick Warren

## ABOUT THE AUTHOR

### VERDONDA ALEXANDER WRIGHT

Verdonda A. Wright is a native of Norfolk, VA and President of Family Empowerment Solutions, an organization specializing in personal development workshops and professional training seminars. She graduated magna cum laude from Norfolk State University with a Bachelor's degree in Consumer Services and Family Studies Education. She has taught in both middle and high schools and is a certified secondary culinary educator and safety and sanitation instructor and currently teaches culinary arts at Phoebus High School in Hampton, VA. She loves working with teenagers and sponsors one school club, Family Career and Community Leaders of America (FCCLA) and also sponsors the Class of 2007. As a teacher, she is proudest of the nomination by her students for five consecutive years of Who's Who Among American High School Teachers.

She is passionate about the family, women's issues, and parenting. She has presented at numerous workshops and conferences at churches, college campuses, and school divisions. Verdonda and her husband Timothy are certified to conduct interactive marriage enrichment classes through Family Dynamic, Inc. Workshop topics include "Me, Myself & I," "Building Resiliency in Children," "Women: Stepping Into Excellence," "Know Your Ministry Gift," "The Phenomenal Family," "Temple Care," "Professional Etiqutte and Protocool," "The Balancing Act: Family & Career," and "Aging with Dignity and Grace."

Professional affiliations include American Association of Family and Consumer Sciences; Virginia Association of Teachers of Family and Consumer Sciences, Associations for Supervision and Curriculum Development, National Restaurant Association; National Council on Family Relations and The Professional Woman Network.

Wright, a licensed evangelist, serves as Director of Womens' Ministries and Christian Education at Victorious Living Ministries COGIC, where her husband is pastor. She married Elder TImothy E. Wright in 1979 and three children were added to this family by birth and one by marriage, Kimberly and her husband Bob, Dedra, and Timothy. Verdonda is the proud "Mema" to two beautiful grandchildren, Xavier and Brianna.

*Contact:*
Family Empowerment Solutions
4221 Pleasant Valley Road
Suite 125 #123
Virginia Beach, VA 23464
(757) 343-5070
www.protrain.net
www.missiontransition.org
vwright@missiontransition.org

## TWENTY-FOUR

# 15 KEYS TO HEALTHIER LIVING

**By Verdonda Wright**

78 million Baby Boomers were born between 1946 and 1964. We possess unique beliefs, one generation removed from the Great Depression, which causes us to be more optimistic economically than our parents. We are better educated as a whole and have become quite comfortable with technology and the use of personal computers. Our lifestyle is hectic, our time is poorly managed, and we seek conveniences in many areas of our everyday life. We are a generation of spenders, rather than savers. We spend our money (cash or credit) in drugstores, restaurants, bookstores, jewelry stores, technology stores, and for travel, luxuries, our aging parents, our adult children, and our grandchildren. We Baby Boomers are characterized by our strong work ethic, embracing informality, questioning, and enthusiasm for causes. Our attitudes embody the attitudes of "working your way to the top", and the importance of job status and position, if a relationship

makes you unhappy, end it, and live your life around your work. Baby Boomers are working longer and retiring later, while our consumption and lifestyle have a top priority. Baby Boomers are the wealthiest of the generations. Many of us live alone and would have it no other way – we love our independence.

The first Baby Boomers started turning fifty in 1996. There's something magical about turning fifty! Your attitude changes by leaps and bounds; it just morphs. Things that you used to be very careful about just don't seem as important anymore. So what if it is after Labor Day; if you want to wear the straw hat, you can!

**Some Boomer Life Lessons For The Second Half Of Life Include:**

1. Learn to delegate.
2. Release the need to be in control.
3. Eat less.
4. Stop dieting.
5. Eliminate hydrogenated oils and food additives from your diet.
6. Cultivate a simple lifestyle.
7. Embrace patience.
8. Spend time alone with your thoughts, dreams and God.
9. You will never have it ALL, so stop fretting about it.
10. Faster and easier are not always better.

11. Don't settle for a good thing and miss out on the BEST thing.
12. Be real, reject pretense.
13. Relish silence.
14. Getting professional counseling when needed is a good thing.
15. Everything cannot be done today.
16. Aspire to be debt free.
17. Just because the phone is ringing, doesn't mean you have to answer it.
18. Cook meals for more than one day at a time. Yes, cook.
19. This, too, shall pass.
20. Cultivate a life of gratitude.
21. Season your words with grace.
22. Know what is essential in your life, and what is not.
23. Learn to laugh at yourself.
24. Disappointment is inevitable; misery is a choice.
25. Live a healthier lifestyle.

**Healthy Living**

Many Baby Boomer women have learned from experience that living a healthy life is critical to mental, emotional, and physical well-being. So, what is "healthy living"?

Healthy living is embracing wellness in all of its forms. Wellness is more than eating fresh fruit; it is a lifestyle. Women who embrace wellness understand that good health is more important than good times. Because we desire to minimize future health challenges, we should refuse to ignore or deny health risks currently facing us. Wellness covers the five dimensions of who we are: physically, spiritually, emotionally, socially and intellectually.

**The 15 Keys to Healthy Living:**

1. **The Balancing Act: The Choice is Yours - Family and Work**

   There is an old adage that says, "When you get to the end of your life, the type of car you drove, the size of your house and the corner office with the view will not be the pressing items on your mind. Time missed with family and loved ones will be." As we continue to work and change careers after retirement, keep in mind what's truly important. Things are temporal, but people are not.

2. **The Slow Food Movement: Taking It Back Home**

   It is no secret that fast food is killing us fast. Now is the time to take dining back to the dining room table in your house. There is truly a "slow food movement" growing quickly. We are the generation that learned to cook. We took home economics. Revisit those skills. Get a good cookbook. Pair up with a friend. Start a cooking club at church or your community center. There is surely a correlation between obesity and eating out of a greasy bag 5-7 days a week. There is an enormous amount of money spent paying for food that isn't even "real food". The amount of time needed to shop and cook is usually the complaint, but it is an investment that will benefit our overall health and well worth the sacrifice.

3. **Slow Down: Rest – Recess – Relaxation**

   Baby Boomers are hard workers. Rest is not always on our regular agenda. But, in the words of my grandmother when she was 90 years old, "If I don't do it now, when will I do it?" Whatever happened to recess? That's a routine we need to return to as adults. Taking time off to rest, play, or do absolutely nothing would be what the doctor ordered, with a bill. For it is with rest and play that the refreshing comes. That's when rejuvenation takes place. That's when we can dream and reflect.

4. **Enough! Managing Toxic Relationships**

   Those relationships can be in many forms: friendships, siblings, parents, children, partners, colleagues and supervisors. The key is to know your role. Siblings, for the most part, don't have any authority over one another. It can become bitter when one tries to. If it is a relationship important enough for you to care about, try writing down the behaviors that bother you about the specific person(s). Study those things, but be mindful of the role you play in the chaos.

5. **Temple Care: Decorating The Titanic**

   It does not make much sense to talk about decorating the Titanic knowing it's fatal end. It also does not make much sense to put all of our attention on beautifying and adorning the outside of our bodies while giving little care to the inside. We need to care for ourselves physically, mentally, spiritually and emotionally.

**6. Stress Less: Keep the Main Thing The Main Thing.**

Stress manifests itself in us mentally, socially and physically. We may experience exhaustion, anxiety, mood swings, sleeplessness, headaches, crying, or loss of appetite. We may feel frustrated or apathetic, disorganized or forgetful. Stress, however, is a part of everyday life. Although it can be managed, it can't be avoided. One of the most important strategies for managing stress is to take care of your body. Talking with a confidant helps to avoid the abuse of over-the-counter drugs and alcohol. Sometimes it's therapeutic to just have a good old-fashioned cry. Above all, connect with others – don't go it alone.

**7. Boundaries: Guard Your Gates.**

As we age, we still need to guard the sacred gates — our ears, eyes and mouth. These are the avenues to our inner self. Be mindful about what you let inside. Set some limits concerning your entertainment. Don't listen to just anything, read just anything, or ingest just anything. What we allow in does make a difference. Our attitudes change, our health changes, our dreams can even become deferred. Guard your gates. We are more sensitive to the quality of gasoline we put in our cars than the quality of "stuff" we take into our minds and bodies. All that goes in, in time, will have an outward manifestation.

**8. Get To Stepping: Exercise**

There is no age limit on the ability to look good and feel better. Find the activity that works for you and "work it". Whether it is walking or aerobics, move. Studies have shown that regular exercise wards off many maladies that go along with aging, such as diabetes, obesity, stress, heart disease and osteoporosis. Putting make-up and the latest fashions on a body that is neglected doesn't make much long-term sense. According to the American Heart Association, cardiovascular disease kills about one woman a minute. 64% of women who die suddenly of heart disease have no previous symptoms. Start easy, start slow, but please start.

**9. Social / Emotional Graces**

There is no excuse for bad manners, and few things are more distasteful than a crabby old lady. Become comfortable experiencing the full range of human emotions, but keep a reign on lashing out with abrasive words and attitudes. Instead, aspire to become even-tempered, particularly when turmoil is rampart. This stage in life is a prime time to nurture and mentor someone younger than yourself, but becomes difficult when no one wants to be around you. Season your words and actions with grace.

**10. Primary Focus: Personal Mission Statement**

This is a wonderful time in life to draft a personal mission statement if you haven't already done so. This portion of your life can definitely be exciting, as well as fulfilling. Discover or rediscover your passion. Commit to a cause larger than yourself. Become civic-minded by getting involved in community affairs. Continue learning; keep your brain active. Become an expert on something of interest to you. Read, take classes, attend workshops, and network with others with similar interests.

**11. First, Seek The Kingdom of God.**

Have a clear sense of purpose and direction, which can only come from God. We frustrate ourselves when we try to fill a role that is not ours to fill. We frustrate others when we try to make them fill roles that are not theirs to fill. It would be great if we only knew our assignment and stuck to that until completion. We should put effort in perfecting the gifts that we have. We would affect change in the lives of those who come in contact with us. The Word of God gives us instructions for living a victorious life. Just like the toys we try to put together at Christmas without reading the directions, not taking the time to read first is a waste of time and causes unnecessary frustration. Read the directions and you'll be surprised how much smoother your journey will be.

**12. Acknowledge Unhealthy Habits as Destructive.**

Come on ladies, bad habits wreak havoc on our lives and those we care about. Commit to shedding the habits that bring us down and destroy our health, relationships, and dreams. Whether the habit is smoking, drinking, drug use, overeating, abusive behavior to self or others, or working too much...... you need a plan to stop. I've learned the hard way that denial doesn't make your blood pressure go down. Identify the problem and address it.

**13. Sign Everything You Do With Excellence.**

We all heard it growing up. Let's hear it again. *If it's worth doing, it's worth doing well.* It can be as simple as a peanut butter sandwich, but prepare it with class. Nurture a reputation for doing things well, very well. Live above the level of mediocrity. Don't settle for reaching the bar, become the bar.

**14. Laughter Is Medicinal.**

Laugh long and laugh often – daily. There is no substitute for a good laugh from deep within. My cousin Carolyn has the ability to make me laugh every time we talk. Whether it's reminiscing over childhood times or the calamities of getting older, we find something to laugh about. Know someone you can call for a good, clean laugh. It will work wonders for your spirit and your blood pressure.

**15. Remember, We Are Mortal and In Time, Death Will Prevail.**

Health, retirement and death are topics of great avoidance in our generation. It is reported that 10 million Baby Boomers will develop Alzheimer's disease in their lifetime, and heart disease continues to be the leading cause of death in men and women. Trust me! Ignoring these realities of life will not make them nonexistent. In all you do, remember, you will not live forever. There are people who act as though they will. We should be forward thinking, optimistic and positive, but prepare for the inevitable. Prepare your family, prepare close friends, and prepare yourself.

# ABOUT THE AUTHOR

## LINDA FARR

Linda Farr is founder and sole proprietor of A Spark Within Coaching. As a mid-life transition and business coach, she specializes in empowering others to clarify the truths, beliefs and attitudes that direct their lives, leading to increased self-satisfaction and success both on a personal and a professional level.

Ms. Farr completed two years of training with The Coaches Training Institute, a premier global training school for life coaches and is a member of the International Coach Federation Her expertise is also based on the culmination of a variety of life experiences. After earning her bachelor's degree in Education from Northern Illinois University and teaching in an academic setting for eight years, she followed the entrepreneurial call and opened several floor covering and furniture businesses that flourished for 25 years. During that time, she embraced marriage and motherhood, obtained her private pilot's license, owned and managed several real estate ventures, and took time to enjoy a horse, dogs, oil painting and travel. She also enjoys being a member of The Professional Woman Network.

Ms. Farr shares her experiences and insights with others supporting and guiding them through important life decisions. She specializes in:

- Mid-Life Coaching. This age brings different experiences and decisions. She leads clients in examining and resolving their issues.
- Business Coaching. Her business programs include Illuminating Marketing, Mastermind Brainstorming Sessions, consulting and development.
- Writing. She develops programs and activities for coaches and trainers, and produces workshops for educational and speaking events.

Ms. Farr is available for one-on-one and group coaching, in person and via phone.

*Contact*
Linda Farr
A Spark Within Coaching
W332 S450 Government Hill
Delafield, WI 53018
(414) 315-2021
sparkcoaching@wi.rr.com
www.asparkwithincoaching.com

## TWENTY-FIVE

# LESSONS FROM ENLIGHTENED MOTHERS

**By Linda Farr**

You have had your children – maybe even grandchildren. You have lived through many experiences – love, losing love, schooling, employment, traveling, and much more. You know a lot more now than you did during your child rearing times. This system of having kids early – *THEN* increasing your knowledge from life experiences doesn't always make sense, but it is the way things have been. So, if you were to have your children today, what advice would you NOW know to offer them because you now understand life differently?

This chapter offers an opportunity to reconsider some of the less enlightened 'mother messages' you may have given or even received yourself. As you take a moment to review these memories, you open up an opportunity to rewrite these experiences with a new outlook. This can be a powerful process. It is not about adding guilt or fantasizing. It's about healing as you replay some of the memories you had as a child or as a parent. It is powerful to rewrite the messages you sent because you also sent them to yourself. These new messages can then become the new way you talk to yourself and others. You may still be listening to some of the old lessons, and they are draining your energy. Would you still wear your bellbottoms and that midriff top, or is it time to change?

Baby-Boomers have always been a unique group of women. The world was seen through the eyeglasses of the 50, 60 & 70's – sometimes rose-tinted, not always in focus, but always as a reflection of this special time period. You brought new ideas and new ways of living. You often were just experimenting, but the intention was on improving the world. It is worthwhile to look at some of the lessons you may have offered, and to question, "Would that be true for me, NOW?" If not, take this opportunity to reconsider what you do believe, and what messages would you want to teach.

The following guide consists of simple THEN & NOW scenarios. 'THEN' describes a situation that could have occurred in the past. 'NOW' offers an alternative response based upon more positive perspectives and new insights. You are given the opportunity to record your own reflections in order to convert former behaviors into better feeling alternatives.

**I. Survivor-Mom Gets Lost**

**THEN** – Baby Boomer women were often brought up to be caregivers to spouse, kids, house, job, and extended family. These responsibilities were taken on to avoid confrontation, be 'nice', and ease another's difficulty. There may not have been enough attention paid to self-care, personal goals, or receiving respect and cooperation from others.

**NOW** – Imagine a new reality TV show. Families compete for a million dollars by trying to become the most outstanding, efficient and organized model of family life. The catch is that the show organizers will send all the moms on a month long vacation at some fancy spa resort. Of course, families enroll in vast numbers because no one thinks that their mom's job is really that demanding. Let the drama begin.

Your job is to record the tasks that you perform each week. This will be a longer list than my editor has provided room for, so bring out the notebook. Divide the sheet into two columns. The left is your TASK LIST. On the right, record who could step in and most effectively handle each task. You know the players and you are doing them a favor to prepare. REMEMBER THE MILLION DOLLARS.

| TAST LIST | NEW TASK PERFORMER |
|---|---|
| | |
| | |
| | |

Of course the real purpose is for you to REALIZE just how much you do. Are you feeling overwhelmed, satisfied, or irritated by your list? Are there tasks that could be assumed by another family member? Remember that children learn by doing and that when you are gone (to the spa) they could have benefited from the practice.

**II. Bedtime Cuddles**

**THEN** – When your child became afraid at bedtime, you may have offered the favorite stuffed animal. It was furry, soft and a habitual pleaser. You sat by your child on the bed, listening to her story or just taking time to comfort and be present. There would be a hug, and gradually she fell off to sleep. This experience offered her security, from the outside. A hug and a soft ever-present friend provided loving bases from which to build her confidence in the world.

**NOW** – The adult task is to build this security from – WITHIN. Can you help your older child envision a larger power coming to her support? This could be as God, an angel, or inner voice. Have her imagine strong, unconditional loving arms encircling her (or soft and fuzzy ones). As she breathes in, a secure feeling of aliveness and trust fills her lungs and body. She pictures the breath linking her to a higher power – her god within. It is much more dependable than a stuffed animal that got lost sometimes. She will learn that whenever she asks, whether is it a gentle request or an angry hopeless shout, a response ALWAYS comes.

**What larger power offers you support and peace? Describe your connection and how it nourishes you and can empower your children, as well.**

__________________________________________________

__________________________________________________

__________________________________________________

### III. Increasing Possibilities

**THEN** – When graduating from high school, many early Boomer women were directed into a limited number of occupations, such as nursing, office work, mothering or teaching. Women weren't encouraged to enter into other careers and often were met with resistance. Many parents weren't aware of the opportunities that college could offer. Women in their 20's were expected to marry, stay at home and raise a family.

**Record your expectations and experiences of those years.**

______________________________________________

______________________________________________

______________________________________________

**NOW** – Thank those women who went before you and had the courage and intelligence to enter into new fields and follow their passions. They followed personal ambitions, mixed family with school or employment, or returned to school. They pushed the boundaries, opened new doors, and overcame their fears. How can you inspire your children and yourself to follow personal goals, continue learning, and keep passion alive?

Here is one exercise you can use to strengthen and increase self-confidence. Stand in front of a mirror. Look into your eyes. Say, "I am loving and lovable. I deserve to attract good things into my life." Really mean the words. You may not believe them in the beginning, but just do it. The belief will come, along with self-satisfaction and confidence.

**Record your experiences with this activity as you practice daily.**

______________________________________________

______________________________________________

______________________________________________

**IV. The Dog Whisperer**

**THEN** – "Don't slouch. Sit up straight. Stick your chest out, keep your head up high." Mothers admonished their children. These postures were indications of insecurity in their kids and were difficult to watch. Mothers nagged as a possible solution, but often without a helpful explanation. Maybe, if it were said just one more time, it would be heard.

**NOW** – You can learn from the television show 'The Dog Whisperer'. Through his work with dogs, Cesar Millan knows that a confident relationship is due to the training of the owners. Most of the dog's behavior is in response to the emotions of the owners. When the owners are confident, so is their dog; when the owner is afraid, the dog becomes aggressive or nervous.

In one session, Cesar was taking a fearful woman through an enclosure of PIT BULLS. She shook, looked down, and was ready to run. He said something like, "Stop! Own your space! You are the RULER OF WHERE YOU WALK! Your space extends three feet around you. When you walk through the enclosure, focus only on your destination. Walk calmly towards it. Head up, with confidence!"

This woman transformed in front of my eyes. She stood taller, slowed down her racing emotions, and supported by Cesar's image of herself, she strode empowered through ten to fifteen curious pit bulls. Not a growl. She didn't give energy to her past story of 'pit bulls rip people apart'. She believed the new story of I am the RULER OF ALL IN MY SPACE.

This attitude transformation can work in your encounters with animals, other people, and especially with children.

**List some of the fears you have**.

________________________________________________

________________________________________________

________________________________________________

Now stand up – tall. Become the RULER OF YOUR SPACE. Look out over your room or life situation. Image one of your fears as some not too scary little dogs (always set yourself up for success). Picture yourself walking confidently through the pack. As you approach, picture the dogs (your fears) just backing away. Ramp up this vision and repeat until you have dispelled your list of full-blown 'pit bull' fears.

Then play this game with your children. Let them watch your composed strut, then encourage them to walk through their own pack. They will learn much by imitating and playing with new attitudes versus listening to nagging. **Record your experience.**

________________________________________________________

________________________________________________________

________________________________________________________

**V. Super Moms**

**THEN** – "I raised two children, ran the home, worked outside of it, and embraced a marriage. Much of my mothering was like a blur. I tried to do my best, but I often was overwhelmed."

The following is a possible scenario.

A young child calls from her bed, the nightly tasks are performed and she is ready for a story. The stressed mom enters, sits at the bedside, and drones through a short book. A kiss and mom is gone. Did the child get a connection with the mom who read the story? Does she unconsciously feel that something is missing? Is she just an unseen, small, unimportant person?

**NOW** – Mom sees herself as a woman with many tasks to perform. But now, she also knows she is an empowered and centered being with a lot to get done. She pauses, takes a breath, and connects to her spirit, her best self. It is this woman that sits with her child. Knowing her own empowerment, she is able to see this same growing light in her child.

This is the true expression of love, seeing the greatness in the eyes of another. Both come away feeling seen and appreciated. Mom can then continue her tasks from an empowered state, and the child sleeps easy and confidently.

**Record the loving messages, spoken or not, that you would like to send to your child. You may then tell, write or send it through loving eye contact.**

___

___

___

*"The most difficult times are those we give ourselves."*
— Pema Chodron from *When Things Fall_Apart.*

**THEN** – A. "If you aren't nice, you will end up alone."
B. "You won't look like Barbie when you grow up."
C. "Money is hard to deal with."
D. "You have failed before, you will fail again."

From childhood on you have heard or imagined hearing hurtful statements from parents, family, peers, and media that were consciously or unconsciously assumed as truthful. Theses messages got locked into your memory, adversely affecting self-image and behavior. Chodron's quote points out that continuing to act from these negative beliefs into adulthood can bring much pain into our lives and be debilitating.

**Record below the negative thoughts that you often catch running through your mind:**

___

___

______________________________________________________________

______________________________________________________________

**NOW** – There are many processes available to rewrite these old stories into scripts that allow you to come out as heroine or as a positive player. What is the logic of continuing to see the world through the eyes of a 9 or 19 year old? Would you want your 9 year old to drive your car? Suffering from worry, fear, or guilt messages from the past cannot solve today's problems, and serves no helpful purpose. Only when you focus and become aware of the negative thoughts rushing through your mind are you able to see them differently and make changes. You recorded these thoughts, not to give them more of your attention, but to transform them into more positive statements that will allow you to feel better. Through your improved feelings about yourself, you release the control these thoughts are having on your life. This process seems simple, but it is very powerful.

**Now, rewrite your negative thoughts into supportive statements you wished you had heard. Following are some examples:**

A. "People will like you for who you are. You will attract a lot of friends."

B. "You have your own beautiful body just the way it is. Each person is born with special gifts, strengths, weaknesses, and passions. Celebrate your uniqueness."

C. "There are skills to study when dealing with money. You can learn them easily because you are smart. Then your money will help you to feel abundant."

D. "When you fail, you have a big opportunity to learn how to succeed the next time. If you don't risk trying something, you will never improve. Failure is part of life."

Congratulations.

### VI. Mother Blame

THEN – Have you ever caught yourself blaming your mother for your life not turning out the way you hoped? Complete this sentence. "If my mom would have been a different mom, I would have:

**NOW** – Especially if you have your own children, you know that parenting was hard work and the preparation wasn't as good as it could have been. So the new adage is, "I know my mom wasn't perfect, but she did the best she knew how." By releasing the blaming, you actually let go of the judgment and resistance that has been keeping you stuck and not achieving your goals. It seems contradictory, but if you blame another, you prevent yourself from taking charge of your life and obtaining the things you want. The new responsibility can be scary, but it is also empowering, as you realize you are really the only one in your head making your decisions.

**Refer to your list above. Now, record how YOU can take charge and make these desires a reality for yourself.**

May this chapter serve as a wake-up call for healing old hurts that were self or mother inflicted.

It's time now to release them as a lead weight that you may have been dragging around for 10 to 40 years or more. Scientists have now discovered that fetal cells stay in the mother for 27 years. It is possible that your children's stuff has been in your basement for maybe even longer. This is a long, long-term relationship. You want it to be great. So do your children. So forgive yourself and them, and look to the present day (or in the mirror) and know that you have the bond you desire, and that it continues to grow and improve. NOW imagine taking the hands of Mother and/or Child and share this prayer from Christine Northrup, MD during her PBS special.

*"We are willing to support the highest and best for each of us. We honor and respect each other, and without undue sacrifice we are willing to forgive the pain that we unwittingly caused each other. We honor each other as the profound teachers we are for each other. We know that Grandmother Earth wisdom is available to us when our own mothers are no longer available to us. We hope that Mother-Daughter relationships of the future will be so steadfast and supportive that when someone says, 'You are becoming your mother,' the reply will be, 'yes, I know', and the daughter will beam with pride."*

# ABOUT THE AUTHOR

## DARCY L. JONES

Darcy L. Jones, Financial Advisor and Financial Planning Specialist with Smith Barney, has been guiding clients towards financial success for over ten years. Darcy's financial planning practice is focused on working with clients in transition moving towards retirement, small businesses and non-profit organizations/foundations. She is well versed in all areas of wealth management including equity and fixed income investing, estate planning, insurance strategies, and business strategies with a special focus on retirement planning. Darcy works with a diverse client base and continues to bring on new clients by referral.

She holds a Bachelors Degree in Business Administration from the University of California, Riverside, where she graduated with honors. She continues to seek higher education and improve her skill level, and is currently working on completing her Certified Financial Planning designation.

Darcy is continually feeding her entrepreneurial spirit with different projects. She partnered with a friend to develop The Wino Club, a wine tasting game that is now being sold on the internet and in stores. She is also co-host of Only2Degrees.com, a talk radio show that airs via the internet and iTunes. She acts as a keynote speaker for organizations and conducts educational and financial seminars.

Giving back is a top priority for Darcy and she is committed to serving her community and the world through several different organizations. Taking on leadership roles with Rotary International: Temecula Noon Club, Murrieta Chamber of Commerce, Professional Women's Roundtable, and Michelle's Place allows her to give back through mentoring and education. She enjoys outdoor activities, traveling, and friends, and currently lives in the Temecula Valley with her husband, Steve, and Jack Russell Terrier, Cannon.

Darcy would like to extend a special thank you to Heather Vinton for providing the illustrations.

*Contact:*
Darcy L. Jones
Smith Barney
One Ridgegate Dr., Ste 245
Temecula, CA 92590
(951) 506.8081
Darcy.L.Jones@smithbarney.com

## TWENTY-SIX

# BUILDING A RELATIONSHIP WITH YOUR MONEY

**By Darcy Jones**

*The beginning of knowledge is the discovery of something we do not understand."*
—Frank Herbert, US science fiction novelist (1920 - 1986)

When you begin to talk about your relationship with money, do your hands get cold and clammy? Does your stomach start feeling a little sick? Or does your heart start racing and you feel like you can't wait to get started? The question is not if you do or do not have any money, but how stable your *relationship* is with your money. A better question might be, "Do you have ANY relationship with your money at all?" Do you spend your money with reckless abandon like a blind date that you can't get rid of fast enough? Steady you have a steady relationship, but you're just not sure what your future together looks like. Or is it like wedded bliss and you are comfortable and secure knowing where every penny goes?

We all have some sort of relationship with money. Obviously, some relationships are tougher than others. Most people have to work really hard to make a relationship successful. Others don't, and it is perfect from the beginning. Almost everyone has had one relationship in their life that was just perfect; they didn't fight, never had issues or struggles, and every discussion was solved without anxiety or fear. Would you like to feel this way about your relationship with your money? Maybe it's not the way you feel at this moment; instead, you may have to work at developing a relationship with your money.

1. Do you worry that you don't have enough money?

2. Are you wondering how you will prepare for retirement?

3. Do you let your spouse/partner do all the "dirty" work with money while you live in blissful ignorance?

If you answered 'Yes' to any of these questions, then it's time to start getting a little friendlier with your cash!

While I was growing up, my family did not talk openly about money or about our financial situation. Now, I don't know if this lack of communication was because there wasn't any money to talk about, or if my parents just didn't want my brother and me to know that we were broke. I vaguely remember my mom sitting down at the kitchen table to pay bills, and every once in a while there would be a heated argument with my dad over some money matter. But that's about it. My dad was in the car business. My mom was (and still is) an x-ray technician. Both of my parents worked really hard. Or at least it seemed that way to me, since they both worked long and crazy hours. As far as an allowance for me, I don't really recall getting a set amount. They just handed over a few bucks here and there to cover lunch, gas and school/ sports supplies.

My parents had very different money habits. Dad gave me money at the beginning of the week. Mom doled it out as needed. My dad was a justifier. My mom was a compromiser. Dad said, "I bought that because…" Mom said, "If we don't do this, then we can afford to do that." One of my favorite memories of my mom in her typical money compromiser fashion was that she would tell my brother and me that if we brought our lunch to school, rather than bought it, we could afford lift tickets to go skiing on the weekend. What kid wouldn't want to do that? We ate a lot of peanut butter and jelly sandwiches!

The type of money habits you have today is most likely a product of how your parents handled money in front of you. As you read and reflect on your habits, you will likely see how your parents influenced your decisions about money. Most likely, each of your parents is in a different category. Because of this, you may be a combination of any and/or all three of the following money types. Taking time for some self-reflection to learn what your financial habits are will help you use the tools you need and leave a legacy of wealth, rather than debt.

*"I'm living so far beyond my income that we may almost be said to be living apart."*—e e cummings US poet (1894 - 1962)

### The Blind Date

Okay, so your best friend set you up on a blind date. You are excited! You go out and buy a new dress and shoes to match. You see a purse that matches the shoes perfectly. As long as you're at the mall, you might as well get that matching lipstick. Oh, and don't forget the new perfume, as your other brand reminds you of your ex. Don't forget the new underwear and bra! You have now spent more time with your money getting ready for one date with a person you don't even know than you have spent thinking about your finances in the last month. Not only that, but you are probably putting all these purchases on your credit card without a second thought.

1. Do you have your head in the proverbial sand when it comes to your finances?

2. Are you digging a hole and getting further and further into debt each month?

3. Do you wonder where your paychecks go every month because the money is gone before the bills are?

4. Is your credit card your best friend?

Here are a few common ways of dealing with money that are not, I repeat, <u>**NOT**</u> good strategies:

1. **Hope:** "I *hope* I have enough to pay the bills."

2. **Denial:** "I can afford that new BMW. If the neighbors can, I can, too!"

**3. Displacement:** " I don't need to know; my husband will take care of me."

Believe me, I do encourage hope and prayer, but it does not negate planning.

**List 5 Ways You Can Improve Your Spending Habits.**

1. ______________________________
2. ______________________________
3. ______________________________
4. ______________________________
5. ______________________________

Now, come on. These don't have to be hard. Could you cut out a Starbucks run once a day, or how about staying home for dinner one or two extra nights a month? These are the expenditures that are not even thought about through the month. You should see my husband's Starbucks bill! I'm sure I have a vice or two myself, but I can't think of one right now.....sound familiar?

*"54% of women are more likely to accumulate 30 pairs of shoes before accumulating $30,000 in savings."*—Oppenheimer Funds Survey 2001

**Going Steady**

You and your honey have been getting along for a while now and you think everything is going great. But you're not quite comfortable enough to tackle the really tough subjects. You get along fine and have a lot in common, but actually you're in the blissful ignorance stage. You can't ask too many questions or he may think you're being too clingy or needy. Everything seems to be humming along and you are meeting your financial obligations every month. But if you start asking too many questions, it is going to get very complicated. No sense in rocking the boat. It's too soon to be talking about marriage, kids, retirement, and God forbid you bring up the M word (money). Is this how you feel about your money?

Money is and always has been a taboo subject. It's the biggest reason for splitting up. You are afraid that everyone else is doing better than you and you will look stupid or incompetent. You are embarrassed when you get in over your head, and feel like you are drowning in debt. You have trouble dealing with any of the number stuff, such as investing, budgeting, and paying bills. It all seems so foreign.

1. Can you change your ways and give yourself a chance at financial success?
2. Are you setting a good example for your children's spending habits?
3. Have you ever built a budget for the family?
4. Are you planning for retirement?

You have to acknowledge your financial challenges and learn to make small changes for a big difference, such as the $50 per month you begin putting away for little Sally's education. This requires planning and new money habits.

**List 5 Ways That You Can Learn About Your Financial Standing (good or bad!)**

1. ______________________________

2. ______________________________

3. ______________________________

4. ______________________________

5. ______________________________

Once again, this is not a trick question. These answers may be as simple as logging on to the computer to balance your checkbook, or spending the first day of each month paying the bills.

*"Live as if you were to die tomorrow.*
*Learn as if you were to live forever."* —M Gandhi

**Happily Married**

You've been together a long time and have a harmonious relationship. You enjoy the same hobbies and love to vacation together. The children are grown, out of the house and financially stable. There isn't a conversation topic that is taboo, nothing that is left unsaid. It hasn't always been easy. Sometimes it seemed that there wasn't enough money to go around, but you made it through the tough times. You have a plan and it is executed consistently, moving you successfully towards retirement. These are what they call the Golden Years.

1. Have you shared your finances with family members that may have to help you someday?

2. Is your personal paperwork in order and easy to find if necessary?

3. Do you know if you have enough money to retire?

4, Will you continue working into retirement?

You have a healthy relationship with money. It took a lot of hard word. You really love being financially stable and you have watched your money add up over the years. You know where your money is and where it's going. You know how much you make and how much you spend. You and your husband have discussed your financial future. Your money is working for you now, so you don't have to work as hard.

**List 5 Ways You To Improve Your Financial And Emotional Success.**

1. ______________________________

2. ______________________________

3. ______________________________

4. ______________________________

5. ______________________________

These answers might include giving back to a charity, mentoring someone else with money questions, or doing some insurance planning for your family. Maybe you need to get all your financial documents (will, trust, power of attorney, etc.) in order, or have that discussion with your children you have been putting off.

**Mastering the Art of Money**

Being in control of your finances does not happen by magic. It is a learned skill. Most people can't do it by themselves and, unless you are educated in the financial industry, you probably don't have the time or desire to struggle with the overwhelming amount of information out there to figure out which parts work for you. So, how do you begin to learn and apply the skills it takes to grab a hold and take charge of your finances? Here are some good tips to get started:

1. **Assess Your Situation and Build a Plan for the Future** – *Where are you financially?*

   If you don't know where to start, you will never get where you want to go. This step is probably the hardest and it starts with a budget. The website www.Kiplinger.com has a great budget sheet you can download from their website, but you have to put pen to paper and actually write down where you are financially. When I did this for the first time with my husband, we were about $400 a month short....no wonder we could never pay the credit card off and it kept getting bigger! What an eye opener for us, because we thought we were doing great. With a few small changes, we were able to get on track.

2. **Build Your Financial Team** – *Who is going to hold you accountable?*

   For you, this may be as simple as having a girlfriend help you cut back on your Macy's spending. Maybe you need to get your husband

and children involved in the household finances. Or you need to coordinate your CPA, financial advisor and lawyer for a meeting so they don't give you opposing advice. The most important piece here is communication. First, you need to tell your peers exactly what your expectations are of them. Second, you can't get mad when they call you out on your behavior. When your girlfriend scolds you for buying those new shoes, don't forget you asked her to help you control your spending!

3. **Read** – *Are you setting an example for your kids?*

   There are millions (okay, maybe millions is an exaggeration) of "money" books out on the market today. They're not all boring, believe me! Some actually use English words we can all understand! Brian Tracy, Steven Covey, and Suze Orman are just a few examples of authors who are money pros. Find one you believe in or who has your same values. Make sure it is easy to read and understand so that you can actually learn from it. Read newspapers and magazines. ***Money*** magazine is great, as it has short articles and is easy to understand. Check out financial sites on the internet. Smith Barney, Fidelity, and Women and Co. are just a few sites that have great information. Turn off the TV and read.

4. **Embrace Opportunities to Learn** – *Are others within your circle of influence in the same position?*

   Never turn down an opportunity to learn something new. Most companies or financial advisors put on free seminars or workshops specifically for women. You might even get a free meal out of it and meet a new group of peers who are in the same position as you.

Local colleges offer inexpensive classes during the day or evening. Start a money group for learning or investing – nothing like hands on experience!

5. **Ask For Help** – *What are you waiting for?*

   Reaching out for help and support is probably the most difficult step because some of us don't want to admit when we don't know what we are doing. You'll be surprised how many women will relate to you when you take that first step. Enough said.

Our society today is teaching us that one is never enough. It has to be bigger, better, and faster than our neighbor's and friend's. The message is, "If you can't afford it, finance it now and pay for it later!" And to top it off, we are never satisfied....we want more and think we deserve it! You need to stop, take control and just say no. You cannot spend uncontrollably and still have a good relationship with your money. You have to build a strong foundation to have a strong and healthy marriage, and the same goes for your money. We are all looking for the same things – stability and security for our future. Take control of your relationship with your money and you will live to your fullest potential financially.

*"Success is not the result of spontaneous combustion.*
*You must set yourself on fire."*—Reggie Leach

# ABOUT THE AUTHOR

## Tammi Polite

Tammi Polite is President/CEO of the Chameleon Company, a Personal and Professional Development Firm that specializes in relationships and professional development. A certified mediator as well as a trainer, Tammi was a Quality Assurance Analyst then a Human Resources Manager in a Home Care Agency with over 500 nursing employees before moving into coaching.

In addition to her work at Chameleon Company, where she delivers Train-the-Trainer programs in the areas of professional development, workplace relationships, diversity and coaching, and coaches individual clients on her signature brand of lifestyle congruence, she is a Human Resources Specialist at a Fortune 500 company. Tammi holds a Bachelor of Arts degree in Psychology from Fairleigh Dickinson University and is pursuing a Master of Arts in Marriage & Family Therapy as well as certifications in Christian Counseling.

*Contact*
The Chameleon Company
tammi@chameleoncompany.net
(917) 405-5617

## TWENTY-SEVEN

# DATING AFTER DIVORCE

### By Tammi Polite

Maybe you had the white dress, the two hundred guests, the requisite rice hurling, and open bar at the spring wedding. Or perhaps yours was a small, tasteful ceremony just for family, or even an elopement on a beach at sunset. Regardless of the attire, witnesses, or time of day, you thought that when you married your nuptials were for good.

And now here you are. Years, kids, careers, cross country and/or cross town moves and identities later, what once was is no more and you find yourself a divorced woman. To some, this might be cause for a deep depression, hysterics and/or a complete shut down of life activities while they cope with this reality. However, there are other women who are not given to such reactions. It is not because these women are stronger than everyone else. It is not because they don't feel pain or because they weren't in love, or because they know exactly what they're going to do next, or even exactly what happened in the marriage to cause its demise.

There are some women, of which I presume you to be one, that simply have too much going on to fall apart. Now let me be clear. I am not suggesting that an expression of anger, pain, fear or doubt is an indicator of weakness or emotional ineptitude on your part. However, there are some of us that do not have the luxury of shutting down our lives while we deal with the pain of divorce. And in some cases, equally painful and disorienting is the challenge of redesigning and re-identifying ourselves as sexual and relational beings.

So we do what we do. We go to work, we lead the volunteer activities, we take care of the kids or the grandkids, help out our neighbors, and we continue on. But somewhere in the labor-intensive marathons that are our lives, we must pencil in the time to address how, if at all, we are going to re-enter the seemingly treacherous waters of the dating pool and "get back out there". Or maybe you never took the time to think it through - you just did it. Either way, there's no harm in taking some much needed "you time". After all, if you're like me, you do some of your best thinking while a good tune is playing in the background and there is no one to put on a show for but you. So shut the door to your "quiet space", let the tunes play, and let's figure out the details to this integral part of you.

**I Can See Clearly Now**

Hopefully, you have had the time to assess what happened in your marriage. If you haven't – STOP. This is an integral step. You must invest the time and emotional energy to do this. The purpose is not to figure out whether or not your ex was wrong, or to validate any misguided feelings you may have about your unworthiness or ability to be loved. Instead, the benefit of looking back after the divorce is over is to assess the extent of the damages you incurred and understand where this has left you as it pertains to romantic relationships. Consider it like taking a drive down the highway. If, like me, you live even remotely near a major city, you're going to encounter some bumps or holes in the road. Some of them are small enough that you hit them and keep going. In a marriage, those can be compared to an argument over whose turn it was to pick up the dry cleaning or who left the back porch door open. Others holes are so large that you hit them, but it takes you a little while as you continue to re-acclimate yourself to driving comfortably. Those can be the larger events in a marriage – an illness, an infidelity or re-evaluation. But a divorce for some can be like a head-on collision. After the tires have squealed, the other cars have swerved out of your way, and you marvel at how slow everything seems to be happening while simultaneously musing at how you got in this predicament when just a second ago you were just driving along, you find yourself bruised, and battered a bit, but alive. Now, even though you are alive, and from what you can tell, you haven't sustained any life threatening injuries, wouldn't you still get out of the car, look at the road, the other driver, and try to figure out what in the world happened?

*Do not allow the defined time spans of the experts to completely govern your life.*

Granted, you may never look at the other driver and say, "Sorry, I veered off into your lane when I was looking for my cell phone." Or, "You know, this is the fifth head-on collision I've had like this! Every time I have a bad day at the office, I wreck someone else's car and hold up traffic for four hours!" But just like in that scenario, wouldn't it be nice to know that about your relationships?

*Where do I stand financially if I never marry again ?*

**Take Your Time**

If you are fortunate, after a divorce and as you delve into the lovely world of exploring new relationships, there will be all types of persons to advise you on what they did, what their sister Betty did, what their next door neighbor did, what their pastor says you should do, and most importantly, what they think you should do. At a point in your life when you may not trust your own opinions or emotions, it may be comforting to have so many people weighing in with contributions. But be mindful - your life, your actions and ultimate decisions, should not be based on an arbitrary clock or calendar designed by an expert. You are an expert in you. For some, six months may be seem like a minute and they may not be ready to take a trip to the mall, much less start dating. For others, six months may be an eternity.

No one knows you better than you. You date when you are ready to date. Not a day before or a day after.

**Girls Just Want to Have Fun**

There is no law against this. Not every date has to be an interview process for a marital relationship. In some cases, it might simply be for the purpose of..... brace yourself....... Here it comes..... wait for it...... fun! Yes, you have worked hard, done well, you are a beautiful woman, and you are entitled to enjoy yourself. There is no reason that you just can't simply enjoy yourself every now and then.

**Beauty Is Only Skin Deep**

This dating thing was a bit different when a cute pair of tight jeans and the right sweater was all it took to get ready. Although the years (and the salads every day) may have been kind to some of us, some women have added more to the lovely package that is them over the years. When dating, do not feel the need to all of a sudden dress like who you used to be, or dress like who you think you should be. Be honest with him and with yourself. If you know your feet cannot take four-inch heels, take them off! Put on the one-inch heels with the insoles and be comfortable! Because most men at this point in their life cannot deal with a crabby woman who is mean to everyone because her feet hurt. Let the real you shine through.

On the other end of the spectrum, although you may not have had to concern yourself with appropriate undergarments, flattering foundations for your face, or getting your nails done before, treat yourself now. The person you may have been married to before may have been content without those things and you still may be. Just be 100 % sure that you are presenting the best possible you to YOURSELF FIRST, as well as to any potential suitors. You and your previous spouse may have known what you looked like 25 years ago. This new man may not.

**Somebody Else's Guy**

The same scene is played in grade schools all over the world. Interchange age, class, gender and environmental norms such as attire and language accordingly, but the exchange pretty much goes something like this:

Teacher: *Children, stop that fighting right now.*
*(Teacher pulls children apart.) Why are you fighting?*

Student # 1: *Because she punched me.*
Student # 2: *Because she hit me first!*

Ever since we were little, we have been using the rationalization that if something has been done to us, somehow that makes it permissible for it to be done to another. Unfortunately, as children what we were not cognizant of is that both of us ended up with a black eye, a torn skirt, and a muddied shirt after rolling around in the dirt! The same, if not worse, happens when you're a grown-up. The simple answer to the question, "Well, she did it so why can't I?" is: Because you're better than that. Aside from statistical probabilities in your locale and your necessity to have someone on your arm at the next event where you might see your ex-spouse or any other person(s) to whom you might want to make it abundantly clear that you are attractive and desirable (including yourself), you deserve a whole man for the whole woman you are.

Kenya*, a 57-year-old medical professional recounts: "*We lived close to each other after the divorce. I would go out to a restaurant with my mother and he would be at the same restaurant with a date. Unfortunately, there were far more women willing to date a newly single 55-year-old man than men willing to date a 57-year-old grandmother. So when I met Theo**, *even though I knew he was married, it was just great to have someone to go out with – at first. But before long, I couldn't reconcile talking about the women that my ex-husband had run around with that knew he was married and then getting dressed to go out with Theo. Eventually, it ended. But the horrible part is, I had to go through that terrible period all over again. It was like getting divorced twice.*" * Names have been changed.

Even though your kindergarten teacher may have told you it was nice to share, that part of kindergarten etiquette cannot be applied to this situation.

**When Will I See You Again?**

So you did it! You went on a date. And it was not horrible. It was actually good. Ok, let's be honest, it was fantastic. He looked good, you looked good, your panty girdle didn't roll down and make a bump in the middle of your outfit, and you were able to find something on the menu that didn't make every biological function in your body go into overtime. You've hit it off.... Now what?

Depending on where you are in your life, this question may pose different challenges.

If you still have non-adult children in the house, be extremely mindful that they may not be on the same point in the process as you are. You may have grieved, denied, mourned, accepted, moved on, and come to a point in your life in which you are either ready to try love again, or you just want to go out and have some fun. Although your children may have accepted the divorce, it does not necessarily mean that they have accepted your need or desire to start dating. Refrain from introducing your children to anyone whom you have not identified as possibly being in your life as a consistent contributor and participant. You may even want to consider not disclosing to your children when you start dating. This is not lying – this is being a mature adult who chooses to be discerning about to what they expose their children. As one 59-year-old divorcee puts it: "*I went out when the kids went out. When the kids were home, I was home. I was divorced for almost five years before they ever saw me with a man.*" For some that may seem a little extreme. But to be sure, you do not want to exacerbate any feelings of hurt or confusion your children may be having by seeing their mom going out with different men.

If your children are adults, whether or not they are living in the house with you and depending on your relationship dynamics, you may want to have a candid talk with them about where you are in your life and what your intentions are. ***This is not to ask their permission.*** But it may alleviate fears, or in most cases, remind or educate your adult children that you are a well-rounded individual who must be considered in the totality of your personhood.

**Shop Around**

When you finally do decide that you are ready to make that one particular jump into a monogamous relationship, no matter the age, the stage or the number of grays, you cannot just pick up whoever is hanging around. First and foremost, know what you want! I strongly advise that every woman, ***regardless of relationship status,*** be able to articulate for herself and others her relationship requirements, need and wants.

**Essentially, Take Stock Of What You:**

**Require**

What has to be an absolute yes for you to even consider speaking to him? Race, religion, age group, marital status, sexual orientation, living arrangements?

**Need**

After you've spoken to him for a while, what do you need, based on what you know about yourself, to be happy with this person? Income, love of animals, acceptance of your children?

**Want**

What would be nice to have in a relationship with a man? Is there a particular characteristic that you have always desired, but never had? Or maybe there is one that you've experienced and grown to love.

Be sure that each item is in the right column or you could run the risk of getting into a relationship with someone who does not have what you really need. Or even worse, rejecting someone who does.

And then, go shopping! Wear comfortable shoes. This is an endurance sport, not one mastered by speed. Go up and down the aisles. But take your list with you. It will keep you tempered.

**She Works Hard For The Money**

Female baby boomers have made amazing strides and even more phenomenal accomplishments. But, to whom much is given, much is required. As a divorced woman, you must not only be mindful of your heart, but of your pocketbook. Do a fair and practical assessment of where you stand and what you can do. In addition to being a sound personal and financial decision, it also takes the pressure off of dating to be what it is not. Dating is not supposed to be a race to the altar. So ask yourself – where do I stand financially if I never marry again? If I do marry again? What assets do I have? What am I willing to share or divide? This type of financial auto-analysis will be useful if you do find someone with whom you decide to engage in a relationship.

**Sexual Healing**

Shhhh! Don't tell the kids (or in some cases, your ex-husband) but you like sex, too. Although, when you enter into the sexual phase of a relationship, it should be governed by your individual spiritual and moral guidelines. Know this: Men and women over 50 can and do have STI's (Sexually Transmitted Infections). An alarming number of baby boomers are contracting STI's and HIV infections as a result of not using condoms during sex. Plainly put – If you are going to engage in sexual activity you must wear a condom - EVERY TIME. It may have been a long time since you had to fumble around looking for one or sort through the aisles of your local pharmacy, but it is definitely worth it. Although the concern of creating another life may not be a factor, you must be concerned about protecting your own life and health.

Divorce is not the death of your life – it is the death of your past marriage. But it is not the defining fact of your life. Be realistic, but be optimistic. You are a beautiful woman on the inside and out. Use available resources like friends and family, local clubs and the Internet to meet people with similar interests and get out and enjoy your life. Do not allow your divorce to define you. ***Define yourself and introduce your defined self to the world.***

*Notes:*

# ABOUT THE AUTHOR

## Dr. Joyce Roland Ph. D. MSN

Dr. E. Joyce Roland is a doctorally prepared registered nurse with expertise in women's health from a holistic perspective (mental, physical and spiritual). She is currently an adjunct associate professor of nursing at North Carolina Central University, Durham, North Carolina. She is also president and founder of The Roland Group, a service that focuses on Wellness Training, Leadership Development, Stress and Conflict Management, as well as the mental, physical and spiritual health of women. She is a teacher, writer, and researcher in mental and physical wellness for women, and especially African American women.

Dr. Roland received a BS in Nursing from Winston-Salem State University, a masters degree in Nursing from Seton Hall University, South Orange, NG, and a Raleight, NC. Since 1978 she has worked as a nurse educator and research psychologist. From 1997 to 1999 she completed post-doctoral studies in Alcohol and Substance Abuse Epidemiology (as it relates to women) at the Alcohol Research Group, University of California, Berkeley (1997-99), and most recently completed research on post traumatic stress disorder among women veterans (2004-06). She enjoys working with women and young girls, teaching them self-care and self-improvement strategies and providing mid-career advice to women.

Her most recent community work has been with a Durham-based Rites of Passage program for African-American girls and volunteering with the Urban Ministries of Durham-a community agency for the homeless—teaching life skills development for women and preparation or re-entry into society. She likes to travel and has visited Mexico, Haiti and other Caribbean Islands, and most recently traveled to England, visiting Conventry Cathedral to learn more about strategies for promoting peace and reconciliation in the world.

Dr. Roland is a member of The Professional Woman's Network, a life member of Delta Sigma Theta Sorority, and a member of N.C. League of Nurses. She is an active member of St. Paul AME Church in Chapel Hill, NC serving on the Trustee Board and the Health committee. She also sings in the choir.

She is married to her husband, Lewis, and has three adult daughters: Leslie, Kaifa, and Lisa, and two beautiful granddaughters, Cameren and Asha.

*Contact:*

E. Joyce Roland, RN, PhD, MSN
125 Hidden Spring Drive
Durham, NC 27703
(919) 598-1917
jaylew@intrex.net
www.protrain.net

## TWENTY-EIGHT

# NOTES FROM A NON-BOOMER: A VIEW OF THE "BOOMER" PHENOMENON

**By Dr. Joyce Roland**

Let's begin by setting the record straight – I am not a "boomer". My contribution to this fabulous book for "boomers" comes from the perspective of a generation-outsider who has viewed societal changes from a perspective similar to that of Janus, the Greek god, who looked backward and forward at the same time viewing the past and the future. I feel privileged to give my insights from the vantage point of a woman who is not necessarily of this generation, but one who has benefited much from the social gains of this generation. I do feel quite privileged to have been invited to contribute a chapter to this "signature" volume by the "boomer" generation. Although I am not a boomer, throughout my life I have found myself identifying with or somehow being influenced by this grand group of people.

**Historical Perspective**

For the sake of this book and to give a historical perspective, I want to offer a backdrop of the social climate that existed just before "Boomers" became a political entity. I am in what I call a generation "time warp" – suspended between two generations. My generation, as far as I know, has no defining characteristics except that of the post-depression generation. I was born in the early 1940's. By 1944, my parents already had four children and my father was not eligible to join the army. (Too many children for the government to take care of in case something happened, I suppose.)

In 1946 when soldiers began to return home from World War II, the U. S. witnessed an explosion of new babies born; hence the term "Baby Boomers". These new babies would become known as the "Boomer" generation – an enormous, creative, powerful group of men and women.

**Personal Perspective**

To share a bit of my personal background, I considered myself just an average southern-born African American girl born in the segregated south who really came of age during this post-war period. As history informs us, this was a period in time where many social changes were taking place in the U. S. Graduating high school in 1957, segregation of public schools had already been outlawed in 1954, and "desegregation" was proceeding at a "deliberate speed", albeit slow. At the time, I did not feel I reaped many rewards from these societal changes. I still was not accepted at the University of North Carolina at Chapel Hill where I first applied for college. Public schools in my hometown were still very much segregated at the time I graduated, although the historical civil rights movement as initiated by Dr. Martin Luther King was already in full force.

However, young people (six years younger than I) were the ones who really ignited the glorious changes that occurred in the decades of the 60's, 70's and 80's. I found myself, as usual, on the outside looking in. I must say, however, that I was a part of the increase of African-Americans that did go to college. In fact, I was a second-generation college student. My uncle on my father's side had gone to college and become a teacher as a result of his status as a veteran.

As a young adult who came along at the beginning of these now infamous social movements (1954-1961), I really did not appreciate the changes that were taking place around me at the time. I readily appreciated that it was a new day, and my personal goal was to benefit as much as I could from these rapid changes. I wanted everything that was supposed to be coming to me and to be a part of the change and grab my piece of the pie, whatever way it was sliced. If it meant benefiting as a woman or African American, I wanted in. Consequently, I was an active observer and participant in many of the changes occurring as a result of the growth and expansion of the generation behind me. Although often after the fact, I had the opportunity to be in the mix and share in the opportunities of this "boomer" group.

Personal opportunities often came just after I passed a landmark age or as a direct result of some new change in the social order of things. Growing up in the years after WWII, I was witness to many changes in society. More people were going to college. There was no question about college in our house. My parents had already decided that each of us was going to college. No if, ands, or buts about it. From 1956 – 1986 my parents' mission was directed toward educating all six of their children. All six of us graduated college, plus a grandson whom they raised and took care of as their own. We all attended college, although my mother did not work outside the home at all during the early years. She would eventually go to work after she went back to school, receiving an Associates' degree (AA) that allowed her to work as a teacher's aide. My parents were my heroes and role models. They always taught us to believe that we could do anything we set our minds to, and we did that and more.

Being attuned to the changes going on in society, I was also alert to the changing times and the opportunities that existed. My career in nursing grew during these exciting times. During my early school years, there were few, if any, women doctors, journalists, lawyers, school superintendents, or even college professors, for that matter. Most women who worked then were either school teachers, secretaries, or nurses. I do remember, for one short period in high school, wanting to be a physician. But again, I saw no females in this role.

## Social Changes

The changing social climate that came after World War II, the Korean War, the Vietnam War and President Kennedy's assassination brought about more social changes than we could have ever imagined. So I grew up in the segregated south, attended and graduated from segregated high school and college, got married at 21 (a hold over from the post war period), and tried to find my place in the world. God smiled on me, I suppose, because during my sophomore year in college, I met my future husband.

My husband and I came from very similar backgrounds and cultures; therefore, we were pretty compatible with one another. In fact, his father and my father were entrepreneurs. Both owned and operated pool halls in the black community, and we found out later that they knew each other. So in many ways we grew up with the trappings of a middle class family, holding many of the same social and family values. We married five days after I graduated college, and I began work while he returned to college to complete his studies that prepared him to become a teacher.

During our first two years of marriage, I lived in one place while my husband lived in another. Then he graduated college and the next year he took a job in another state while I completed my first job as an instructor at a nursing school that hired me to teach right out of nursing school. Well, the fact that our lives took this turn was not that unusual. Many young people of that period were getting married and graduating college. During that time it could not be guaranteed to find work in the same town, especially if one graduated before the other. The long distance marriage, which may still be in vogue now, began for many young people of color long during this time, long before the trend was touted as a new lifestyle for the "boomer" generation. In those days, we went where the jobs were and many times that meant living our lives separate and apart for a while. My husband and I did that quite a number of times during our marriage. To make a bad situation worse, after living together as newly weds in Southern Virginia for about three years, we continued this lifestyle with my husband's move to New Jersey to teach, while I remained behind to complete a program of nurse anesthesia that I had enrolled in 1964. So here we were again – carrying on a marriage with hundreds of miles between us. But our relationship survived the challenges. I am proud to report here in 2008 that we have been married for nearly 47 years and have three adult daughters and two granddaughters.

As a new college graduate who came along at the nexus of these social movements (1961), I really did not appreciate the long-range impact of all the changes that were taking place around me. I wanted to be a part of the new movements and grab my piece of the pie, whether it meant benefiting as a woman or if it meant benefiting as an African American. Either way, I stood to gain. As it were, I was affected immensely by both descriptors. I must state, however, that the social influences came at me from both the generation ahead of me as well as the generation behind me.

The bottom line is, I witnessed and benefited much from many of the social changes emanating from the post war era. Now I realize I actual lived through historic social changes that benefitted many, many people, black and white, old and young, men and women. Although occurring usually after the fact, I had the opportunity, by way of preparation, to be in the mix, and to gently or vigorously press for my place in the puzzle of social change. My younger brother (who is a "boomer") emphatically states, "Luck is the junction where preparation and opportunity meet."

I began this reminiscence to discuss how my life and life choices have been influenced by the "Boomer" generation. Somewhere during my professional career, the term "Baby Boomer" caught on and gained popularity. This term was most likely coined by sociologists who study groups of people. As history tells us, many women during that time joined the workforce because the United States was short on workers with so many men being in the "war". This time provided an opportunity for some women to hone their skills in the work world, especially those who were not married or without other skills.

So what did it all mean? ...and what was all the hoopla about? The term is fitting in describing this new generation of men and women, who grew rapidly and benefited greatly from the gains of the war. This change in societal norms immediately set off a chain reaction of opportunities, discoveries, and life style changes, which this generation and succeeding generations enjoy even to this day. The impact of this group of "new births" after the war brought many changes. More schools were needed to house and educate the boomers and their children. More teachers were needed. Newer homes and suburbs were developed as a result of the post-war boom of industrial growth emanating from the war.

Although I was engulfed in and embedded by these societal changes, none of us realized the importance of this cohort of American offspring until the social order of things began to be recounted. We might consider these evolving changes in the social order of things as the serendipitous outcomes of the war. Women went to work, did not have as many children, and when the men returned, many women were reluctant to return to their former passive status in society. Many really found their own niche in life, rather than have it assigned to them by tradition. So, in reality, the 50s, 60s and 70s were about radical changes in society and the social order of things. Although the boomers may have precipitated these changes, and made what we see today possible, almost all segments of society, before and after, were afforded some of the rewards of living at this period, as well.

After the war, as new jobs became available for women, women worked in many capacities; they worked in factories, and did other work usually done by men. Having these jobs afforded these women newfound freedoms. They had their own paychecks; they did not have to work on a farm (if they chose not to). They learned to live on their own; therefore, many did not marry out of necessity, as might have happened before the war. The world for women was forever changed. And since women were affected by the change, so indeed, were men.

Meanwhile, I had taken my assigned place in society and was trying to become one of the elite, talented tenth described by W.E. B. Dubois. The African American community (referred to then as "Negro") was coming of age as a community, which worked hard to improve the lives of its own people. I, along with my family, lived right in the heart of a "Negro" (African American) community in Eastern North Carolina that afforded us all of the amenities of a community that were required to uplift and provide social prominence. Though somewhat insulated from the greater social events of that time, we had our own little community. On one corner was a drug store, and one or two dry cleaners; on another corner there was a grocery store in walking distance from my house. The community boasted at least two funeral homes within blocks of each other, several restaurants, (I lived next door to one) and numerous other black businesses, such as barbershops and beauty shops. North Carolina Mutual Life Insurance Company, then one of the nation's largest insurance companies for black citizens, was on another corner. Just about all the movers and shakers in our community passed my house every day, so much so, that we knew many on a first name basis. Of course, we, as children were not allowed to call any grown-up by their first name. And last, but not least, both of my parents had some level of importance in our insulated, segregated community.

My mother helped found a church that I grew up in and my father was a small business owner. My parents' primary goal was to ensure that their six children had a better life than they did. What I do remember most vividly about that period in history is that the social order rapidly changed from an agricultural society to an industrial one. I recall my mother lamenting that, as a result of us children not growing up on a farm, we had little knowledge of that way of life. She often said, "We did not know a horse from a mule or a donkey." We did indeed grow up in the city. She and my dad had been offspring of farmers and they knew the value (and limitations) of that kind of hard work. They imparted those values to us. So I would say as a result of that upbringing, I was always more or less tuned in to what was needed to make a better life for me and my family. I was not afraid of hard work. I worked as a teenager.

However, as the story is told now, youngsters six years or younger than I, "the Baby Boomers", were the ones who really fueled and ignited the changes that occurred in the decades following the war, the civil rights movement, and yes, two additional wars: the Korean War and the Vietnam War.

My generation was also part of the group that reaped many benefits from the Presidencies of FDR, Harry Truman, and Eisenhower. I have said that I was part of the generation of African-Americans that began going to college in larger numbers. I won't say we were the first, because all of our African-American teachers at that time were college graduates, and many had master's degrees from institutions such as N.Y. University, Columbia University, and Indiana University. They were just as intent on us becoming productive citizens of our communities and country as our parents. I think we believed the "hype" that education would redeem us and bring us more in line with American societal expectations. A number of us were anxious to attend college, and many from my community did attend and graduate.

Growing up in the years after WWII, changes were many. As expected, all my siblings did graduate from college, and during that time my mother did not work outside the home, and did not recommend it for her four daughters as a way of earning money. We were not allowed to baby-sit or work in the homes of any "white" families. You see, my mother was remembering her childhood and how black women were often denigrated and mistreated in such homes. Many times, it was because these women had no other means of removing themselves from these situations. They had no marketable skills. She (with my father's help) was determined that we would not be subjected to this kind of social mistreatment.

Consequently, my mother was my role model. She impressed upon me (us) the value of an education and controlling, to the degree that we could, our own destiny. She also modeled this value for us, her children. Going only as far as the 11th grade (which was the target when she attended public school in rural Eastern North Carolina), she returned to school, after having four children, to finish her high school diploma. She would eventually go on to the community college to receive her associate degree and work in the public schools for at least twenty years as a teacher's aide. She retired from the public school system with a state pension.

I, like her, returned to school after marriage and three children, to complete my masters' and my PhD degrees. I would not have thought it possible had not I witnessed my mother and many other women around me doing the same in the 70s, 80s' and 90's. You might say our motto was, "If it's worth having, its worth working for." So with my parents as role models, and the fact that they had four more children to raise after me (I was the second born), I took it upon myself to embrace any new opportunities that came along, especially if they followed new legislation or societal changes. Therefore, I lay claim to the changes that "Baby Boomers" helped bring about with their protest of the war in Vietnam in the 1960's. I witnessed also the sexual revolution of the 60's, which was the forerunner of many of the other social changes we witness today.

The Civil Rights Movement gave way to the Women's Movement led by Gloria Steinem and others. Even though I was not old enough to vote for President Kennedy in 1960, I was well aware of the impact his election as the first Catholic U. S. president. That was a social change of a significant magnitude during that era. His assassination in 1963 only added more fuel to the fire. More social changes occurred as a result of his assassination than we ever could have imagined. We witnessed Lyndon Johnson's War on Poverty and the passage of new Civil Rights legislation. Added to that was the assassination of Dr. Martin Luther King, Jr. and Senator Robert Kennedy in 1968.

Boomers benefited greatly from all these social changes occurring around them. Because of their massive presence and intolerance for the mediocre and inequalities, every time a protest was made by the "Boomer" cohort, some aspect of society changed. Society catered to the growing demands of this influential generation. Hospitals, schools and universities all over the country were made to recognize the value of all human beings, regardless of race, creed, or ethnicity. I attended a previously segregated hospital training program in Southern Virginia and became one of three student nurse anesthetists in training there in the early 1960's. I was one of three students: one Filipino, one White and one African-American. Although I did not realize it at the time, I was creating a legacy of my own for my children and their children to follow.

**Other Societal Changes**

Out of these massive social changes came other unexpected societal changes. We witnessed changes in the family. More and more divorces occurred in the new social order. These men and women remarried and brought their children with them. Thus was born new family forms: the blended family, and the like. Some women divorcees did not remarry – they made the term "single parent household" popular; many women never married, but had children – thus adding to the model of the "single parent" family. Women had all kinds of choices. More and more society changed to conform to the desires of the Boomer generation. Now the "Boomers" are ready for retirement. The question is: Will they really retire, or will they morph into some new social creature? Read their chapters. Many have found new callings in this time of multiple opportunities. All in all, being a part of this societal regeneration has been fascinating. I would not have missed it for anything. I say thanks to all for allowing this non-"boomer" to be a part of it. And...it's not over yet! The best is yet to come.

*Notes:*

## ABOUT THE AUTHOR

### SONJA SENHOUSE WILSON (SSW)

Sonja Senhouse Wilson is President and CEO of Break Through Development Group (BTDG), an organization that seeks to empower women emotionally, spiritually and physically by discussing and addressing issues that affect women in their personal and professional daily lives.

For the past three years BTDG has been charged with the mission to free women from low self image and improve heighten self respect. BTDG has achieved this by speaking, teaching and training in the areas of self esteem, prayer life and self image. BTDG has been invited to speak in New York, New Jersey, Connecticut and Oklahoma on issues affecting women.

SSW was born in Trinidad, West Indies and raised in the United States. She is a graduate of College of Mt. Saint Vincent where she received a dual Bachelor of Arts degree in Sociology/Communications Arts while she trained in Social Work. Social Work is where she developed an understanding of and a love for women of all cultures. She is a candidate for her MBA in marketing at Wagner College. SSW has traveled the world as a professional model and has graced the pages of Vogue, Cosmopolitan, Seventeen, and Essence and Ebony magazines. She has also been featured in many ad campaigns such as L'Oreal Cosmetics and Avon.

SSW is a member of The Professional Woman Network (PWN). SSW holds membership in other professional organizations such as National Professional Executive Woman (NAFE). She is active within her church and community and serves as a role model for children and youth.

*Contact:*
Break Through Development Group
P.O. Box 9306
Elizabeth, New Jersey 07202
(908) 294-2465
SonjaWilson3@aim.com

TWENTY-NINE

# 15 RULES FOR TERRIFIC CUSTOMER SERVICE

**By Sonja Wilson**

We who are "Boomers" have lived during a time in the past when there was really such a thing as terrific customer service. But, over the years, excellent customer service has almost disappeared. Customer service is critical in every aspect of our society. It's no secret that customers are the people who drive businesses and make companies wealthy. Without them, companies would just have a good idea and a brand, but no one to supply their goods or services to. All businesses, both large and small, need to attract customers, but that is only part of the equation. The question that businesses have to answer is how to build loyalty and how to create an experience that makes customers want to continue doing business with you over and over again. The answer is simple: develop a terrific customer service strategy.

**For a terrific customer service strategy to be implemented, three fundamental questions must be asked:**

1. As a customer, how do you expect to be treated?
2. When customers come to you, what should be their experience?
3. What do your attitudes, actions and behaviors say about your customer service philosophy?

These three questions take me back to the days when I worked for one of the largest telecommunications companies in the US. I started as a customer service representative where I had to deal with a large volume of clients via the telephone. My clients were big business consumers and very demanding. Upon accepting the job offer, the new hires were told, "You're going to work at the high-end of the rep world and it is important that you understand that this company prides itself on outstanding customer service. You will be working with our wholesale division, which constitutes 40% of our revenue. The reason why you have been chosen is because of your high test scores and your excellent performance on your simulated telephone interviews. You have what it takes to provide our customers with terrific customer service."

The telecommunications company that I worked for equipped each and every one of their employees with the necessary tools to be a success. Since it was a service driven industry and customers were the ones driving our business, I took my job seriously and I, just like my employer, prided myself on providing terrific customer service. My outstanding customer service gained me recognition, awards and promotions. To this day, I am appreciative of the incentive employee initiative program, where awards and recognition were recognized when top-notch customer service was provided. I would say this is a wonderful program to encourage your employees to provide terrific customer service.

**Rules for Terrific Customer Service**

**Rule 1. Always Start at the Top**. The CEO's attitude towards customer service is crucial to the quality of service that a company delivers. If the CEO thinks that customers are nuisances and who always want something for nothing, that attitude will surely permeate the company, and service will be less than terrific.

**Recommendation:** If you are a CEO, check your actions, attitudes and behavior in order to service your customers so they can keep coming back. If you're not the CEO, take responsibility to convince the CEO that customers are important; they are vital to the overall success of the company. Offer tangible suggestions.

**Rule 2. Educate and Train.** Emphasize and reemphasize the importance of customer service to all employees. It begins with the interview process and continues throughout the employment tenure.

**Recommendation:** Send employees to customer service training programs and seminars.

**Rule 3. Courteous Phone Conduct.** The way you and your employees interact with customers on the phone can create long-lasting relationships, or sever it permanently.

**Recommendation:** Good phone techniques include answering the phone with the name of your business, the employee's name, and a simple "How may I help you?" Improve phone skills by role-playing with other employees. Also ask customers for their name and then actually address them by name when appropriate. Although it may seem obvious, you'd be surprised how much of a difference addressing a customer by name can make. Another good way to make the customer service experience more personal is to ask for the customer's name instead of just a reference or a ticket ID. If there are a lot of people with their name, then ask for another personal piece of information like an email address or phone number. If all else fails, then use the reference or ticket ID.

**Rule 4. Hire Service-Minded Individuals.** Customer service is not a job for everyone. The ideal customer service person derives great satisfaction by helping people and solving problems. Keep customer service in mind during the hiring process and consider if candidates can meet your standards of service.

**Recommendation:** Once employees are on board, keep them focused on customer service. Test employees to evaluate their own customer service skills.

**Rule 5. Give The Customer Control.** I noticed that the best kind of customer service happened when management from the telecommunication company I worked for enabled its employees to put the customer in control. The requirement from management was to trust customers not to take advantage of the situation and to trust employees with this type of empowerment. Every time management took these high jumps, the quality of my customer service multiplied.

**Recommendation:** Do respond quickly to customer comments and complaints, especially when potential customers call or email with inquiries about your products or services. A rapid response is a must.

Late responses can annoy customers and prompt them to go to your competitors for their needs. Likewise, when existing customers contact you with a problem or a return, respond rapidly. Don't give them a sales pitch. Never give customers a sales pitch unless they're calling your sales department. Most customers that call for customer service, technical support, are not in the mood for a sales pitch.

**Rule 6. Show Gratitude.** Thank customers early and often. When customers make a major purchase or when they make an inquiry about your products or services, follow up with a sincere thank you.

**Recommendation:** Send a handwritten thank you note or an email. It would do wonders to create long-lasting relationships with customers.

**Rule7. Offer Money-Back Guarantees.** Keep customers impressed by offering unexpected extras.

**Recommendation:** Encourage customer feedback. Customers feel important when asked for their input. Ask customers to take a brief survey about your products, services and customer service.

**Rule 8. Accept Blame For Shortcomings.** When you take responsibility for your shortcomings, you are more likely to provide great customer service for these reasons: First, it's acknowledged that it's the company's fault and the company's responsibility to fix. Second, customers won't go through the irritating process of getting you to accept blame. (When I worked for my telecommunications company and circuits were not delivered as promised we had to recognize that it was our fault for not meeting the due dates and re-negotiate.)

**Recommendation:** Don't point the finger. This is the flip side of taking responsibility. A great customer service company doesn't point the finger. It figures out what the solution is, regardless of whose fault the problem is, and makes the customer happy. Great customer service companies don't shoot the messenger. When it comes to customer service, it could be a customer, an employee, a vendor, or a consultant who's doing the pointing. The goal is not to silence the messenger, but to fix the problem that the messenger brought so that other customers don't have a bad experience.

**Rule 9. Keep Your Commitment and Over Deliver.** The goal is to always delight your customer. For example, when the clients from my telecommunications company received their circuits ahead of schedule, they were more than ecstatic.

**Recommendation:** Purposely overstate the promise, and when service is provided faster than anticipated, you will always have a smiling customer. Have operating procedures, not scripts. You've probably called at least a few companies and you're sure the representative is reading a script. I think it's annoying and certainly not personal. Have standard operating procedures for common things like cancellations, frustrated customers, etc. to ensure the job is done properly, but never ask or train your representatives to read from an actual script or anything like it.

**Rule 10. Believe In Your Product Or Service.** You must have a quality product or unique service to sell to your customers. You must believe that your product or service is exceptional, not mediocre. You want to keep them coming back for more, so make sure they always get their money's worth.

**Recommendation:** Don't be afraid. One of the most common justifications for not giving terrific service is that your product or service is just as good or similar to others.

**Rule 11. Customer Service Must Serve As One Of The Pillars Of Your Business.** Customer service has as much to do with a company's reputation as sales, marketing, engineering, and finance. So integrate customer service into the mainstream of the company.

**Recommendation:** Reward your customer service heroes. They deserves all the accolades that a sales, marketing, or engineering department gets.

**Rule 12. Create Legendary Customer Service.** This is how we did it at the telecommunications company I worked for. If one of my clients wanted service by a specified due date and, because of technical difficulties, we were not able to meet their desired due date, I had to put several recommendations in action. First, I took responsibility by saying we were sorry service could not be met at their desired due date. Second, I didn't point the finger by saying it was the engineering department who had to design the circuit and they ran into problems. Third, I granted the customer control by offering to renegotiate another due date to their liking. Fourth, I under promised and over delivered. I believe this is the way to create legendary customer service.

**Recommendation:** Pull it all together.

**Rule 13. Keep Customers Informed.** Customers should never have to ask what you are doing. Let them know what's happening as you're doing something such as researching an issue. Extend keeping customers informed beyond the original communication, as well.

**Recommendation:** Be honest. Tell your customers what's the problem. For example, when will service be turned up and what you're doing to do to prevent it from happening again. Apologize profusely and offer compensation. Customers always feel appreciated when they feel you are going out of your way to keep them informed.

**Rule 14. Make Customers Feel Important.** Train your representatives to make customers feel important. If a customer makes a suggestion, the representative should note it and let the customer know they've noted it. Customers are often frustrated when they call customer service or support, so if you can make them feel good, you have achieved an important aspect of terrific customer service.

**Recommendation:** Ask them questions and keep the answers in mind. Customers feel important when they are asked questions. My favorite line when I worked for my telecommunications company was, "What's your level of technical expertise?" And if they said complete novice, I gave them some extra instructions and help. Anticipate the questions beforehand and provide the answers and clarification without being asked.

**Rule 15. Follow Up.** The biggest difference between acceptable and terrific customer service is how often and how well the customer service department follows up. If a customer makes a suggestion, follow up on it and give them a call or send them an email with the result. If a customer calls with a customer service problem and you believe it's resolved, send them an email or give them a call asking if their problem has been resolved to their satisfaction. Make follow-ups personal and sincere and customers will truly appreciate it.

**Recommendation:** There is Always time for Terrific Customer Service. Whether you are an employee, small business owner or a CEO, when you follow these 15 rules for terrific customer service, you are always going to WIN.

Globalization of many of the products available in the U.S and currently around the world shines a particular light on customer service. Some functions of customer service have been outsourced to third world countries where it is reduced to a concern about hourly cost. While the concern for cost is a valid one, it must take second or third place behind valued customer service. Valued customer service, product knowledge and cost must work together to meet the needs and concerns of the customer. After all, without the customer, there is no product demand.

**Here are a few proven tips for providing continued terrific customer service:**

**Politeness.** This tip should probably go without saying, but the truth is that many small and large business owners forget to say words like "please" and "thank-you" when dealing with customers. Simple manners go a long way to keeping customers happy.

**Empathy.** You don't have to agree with what your customers think, but it's important to let them know you understand where they're coming from. If your customer approaches you with a complaint, try saying things like, "I can certainly see why that would be upsetting to you."

**Consistency.** One negative customer service experience can erase several positive experiences, so it's vital you never allow yourself to slip up and be rude or inefficient.

**Make and Stick to Your Commitment.** Don't be afraid to make promises, but be sure you always keep them. Do everything to make it happen.

**Take Responsibility.** If a customer isn't happy with your product, service or demeanor, don't try to pass off the blame. Instead, apologize and accept full responsibility. If you can't give the customer what he or she wants, then ask for help within your organization.

**Ask For Feedback.** Talk to your customers and find out what you're doing well. Don't be scared to ask for advice on how you can improve your customer service.

Customer service affects all aspects of our society encompassing every industry. It is absolutely key not only for success, but for survival in the corporate universe. For women of all ages, it is time to reclaim the importance of professionalism and courtesy, bringing back the terrific customer service that was enjoyed in small towns of yesteryear when the needs of the customer REALLY came first.

*Notes:*

## ABOUT THE AUTHOR

### Carol Heady

Carol Heady is founder and president of Learning and Performance Solutions, a consulting practice specializing in professional skills training, management and leadership development programs, organizational development, and coaching. Carol's passion and niche is helping professional women, women business owners and entrepreneurs further develop their leadership and business management capabilities to accelerate personal growth and achieve greater business success. This is done through customized individual and group coaching programs, as well as public seminars and teleseminars. She brings 25 years business experience from a diverse background including: financial services, retail, and telecommunications.

Carol has an undergraduate degree in education and obtained her M.S. in Organizational Management and Human Resources from Manhattanville College. She is an Adjunct Professor at Manhattanville College where she teaches a graduate course on corporate training and development, and is a certified facilitator for three international training companies: Achieve Global, Omega Performance and Development Dimensions International. Carol is President of the Westchester/Mid-Hudson Chapter of American Society for Training and Development. She is a member of several professional associations including: International Coach Federation, Society of Human Resources Management, Toastmasters International, The Professional Woman Speakers Bureau, and the PWN International Advisory Board.

*Contact:*
Carol A. Heady, President
Learning and Performance Solutions
29 Ridge Road
Hopewell Junction, NY 12533
845-226-8047
www.learningandperformance.net
carol@learningandperformance.net

## THIRTY

# IT'S NEVER TOO LATE! GOAL SETTING FOR SUCCESS

**By Carol Heady**

*"You are never too old to set another goal or to dream a new dream."*
—C. S. Lewis

No matter your age or circumstances, achieving success is more a state of mind and a willingness to decide what you want and to take action toward that goal or dream. What I will share with you in this chapter is a proven process and some success principles that will help you achieve your goals. If you are reading this book at a time when you are also contemplating your retirement, next career, wanting to go back to school to earn that degree you always wanted, starting a business, or writing a book, whatever it is that you are contemplating, begin with the end in mind and know that it is never too late.

**The Seven Steps**

There are seven steps in this process that will make a difference in achieving your goals and creating the life or career you want. As we explore the seven steps, we will also consider some success principles that will help you move toward achieving your goals.

**Step One**

Decide what you want to accomplish. Identify or set your goal and write it down. *"The indispensable first step to getting the things you want out of life is this – decide what you want."* (Quoted by Ben Stein, actor and author; excerpt from *The Success Principles,* written by Jack Canfield and Janet Switzer.) Once you have decided what you want to accomplish, it's time to write the goal. There is a very effective method to writing powerful goals that will greatly increase your success. The method is using "SMART" Goals. "SMART" is an acronym for ***S****pecific,* ***M****easurable,* ***A****ctionable,* ***R****ealistic, and* ***T****ime specific.* Let's discuss each element of the "SMART" goal method. Vague goals don't get accomplished; being ***specific*** helps you stay focused on exactly what you want. Goals that are ***measurable*** will help you determine your progress. If a goal is not ***actionable*** you will greatly diminish your level of success. Goals that are ***realistic*** are attainable. Remember, goals are designed to help you achieve greater success with what you want to accomplish or achieve. Last, goals that are not ***time specific*** are not realized. If a goal is not time specific, it's a wish, not a goal.

Here are a few examples of a "SMART" goal:
*Increase revenues by 10% each quarter for 2008.*
*Lose 30 pounds over the next six months.*
*Learn to speak Spanish by the end of the year.*
*Read two business books per month for the next 12 months.*

Once you have written your goal, ask yourself if it meets the criteria to be a "SMART" goal. Is it well defined, can I measure my progress, can I begin to take some action, is it attainable, and do I have a timeframe for completion (Wish or Goal)? Successful people have disciplined themselves to use this method; disciplining yourself to use this method will greatly enhance your success.

**Step Two**

Have a vision of your goal. In other words, ask yourself what the success of this goal looks like. Imagine the goal already achieved and what that looks or feels like. So, if the goal is related to losing weight for example, how will you look at your new weight? Describe what it might feel like. Perhaps you will have more energy or a svelte body, or wear that bikini you haven't worn in years. This is your vision, so be as descriptive and vivid as you can – the more vivid, the more powerful the impact on achieving what you want. Another way to create the vision of your goal, in addition to using words, is using pictures. Find pictures in magazines that represent what that goal "looks like", cut them out, and post them on a bulletin board or refrigerator. Always be selective with your picture choice; it needs to reflect exactly what you want.

The power in creating a vision for your goal is that it reinforces a positive image, and therefore brings the experience to a sub-conscious level. The more we reinforce the image in our sub-conscious mind, the more we can expect to achieve. Napoleon Hill's famous quote speaks to this very important aspect of achieving what we want, be it personally or professionally, "What the mind of man can conceive and believe, it can achieve."

Another value in this exercise is that you are projecting a positive future state, and this has great influence over any negative thoughts or self-limiting thoughts that may creep into your conscious mind. In other words, it keeps that "negative inner voice" quiet.

**Step Three**

Make your goal known! Tell at least one person; more is better. This works for two reasons. One is that it raises your level of accountability. And second, it helps you achieve step six in this seven-step process.

Why would raising the bar on accountability matter? There is something quite motivating when it comes to having to tell someone what progress you have made. In my experience and in working with others, having someone to hold ourselves accountable to increases the likeliness that we will do what we said we will. While being well disciplined to work on our goals (taking action) is critical, stating our intentions to others holds us to a higher level of commitment and produces better outcomes/results. Jack Canfield, author of *The Success Principles*, suggests having 'Accountability Partners', for the very purpose of two people holding each other accountable for deadlines, accomplishing goals, and making progress. 'Accountability Partners' make an agreement on the goals that each person will be held accountable for and establishing a meeting arrangement. These meetings can be face to face or over the phone, and they can occur weekly, bi-weekly, or monthly.

**Step Four**

Identify what resources you need, if any. By resources I mean the "hard stuff", like money/capital, budget, space, land, a building, a particular type of transportation, printer; it all depends on your goal. Whether it's a personal goal or a career/job related goal, typically there will be some type or types of resources you will need to successfully achieve your goal. In step six you will begin thinking about what I refer to as the "soft stuff" (relationships); it's the "support system" you will have to help you achieve your goal. During step four, stay focused on the "hard stuff". Don't worry about the how as you begin to identify the resources; you will devote some thought to that when you start establishing action steps toward achieving your goal.

**Step Five**

What challenges or obstacles might you face in accomplishing your goal? How might you overcome them? These are critical questions to ask. By asking yourself these questions, you are "pre-empting" obstacles. This creates the opportunity to be proactive in overcoming a particular challenge. This also increases your success. In other words, you are preventing failure. Think of challenges or obstacles like a roadblock or detour; they present themselves (you see them) and you proceed with an alternative path.

There are two types of obstacles, internal and external. Most often, when we think about obstacles we immediately think about the external type. For example, lack of time, not enough resources, a particular person, or competition. The external obstacles (challenges) are typically the easy ones to identify, particularly the predictable ones like competitors (if the goal is business related). Other predictable obstacles might be the time of year, a spouse/partner's schedule or other commitments. Internal obstacles are sometimes more difficult to identify. These types of obstacles can be related to our beliefs, values, experiences, or self-concept. It's that inner voice challenging your self-confidence or self-esteem. It's the second-guessing or the doubting that you might do, or the fear of failing. Fear is a universal internal obstacle and manifests itself differently for each of us.

Internal obstacles are sometimes referred to as your "Gremlin" or self-limiting beliefs. Your "Gremlin" is that internal dialogue, sometimes referred to as "negative self-talk", in everyday life. When you experience the negative "self-talk", one of the best ways to overcome that obstacle is to begin practicing positive "self-talk". As soon as your inner voice begins the negative dialogue, immediately start talking positively about what you can accomplish, and that you will overcome any obstacle that is presented (real or imagined). In other words, you are replacing negative thoughts with positive ones and using positive language. This alone will increase your success. Think about any predictable behavior, that you are aware of, that may be an obstacle to accomplishing your goal. For example, do you have the tendency to be a 'devil's advocate' or do you doubt yourself. Simply being aware of the behaviors will enable you to think about what you might need to change or do differently to achieve your goal. Taming your "Gremlin" is a process and cannot be fully explored in this chapter, but begin paying attention to your inner voice and predictable behaviors that might be self-limiting and you will empower yourself to make a change.

**Step Six**

Ask, Ask, Ask... Expect to ask for assistance or help with achieving your goals. It's okay to ask for support in accomplishing your goals.

Women typically struggle with asking for help; successful people are not afraid to ask. The number one reason we don't ask is fear of hearing "no", in other words, rejection. If you think the fear of rejection will be one of your internal obstacles, write it down and ask yourself, "Is it worth the risk of asking?" What do you have to lose by asking? You have nothing to lose and everything to gain. Don't assume you are going to get a no. If wanting a mentor to be part of your support system is going to help you achieve your goal, the only thing you have to lose is the person saying "no." Be ready to ask more than one person. The person who says "no" might be able to recommend someone. You will never know until you ask.

Creating a support system is critical to success and that's what you are putting in place by asking others for help, assistance, expert advice, moral support, or whatever you determine you need to accomplish your goal. *"You've got to ask. Asking is, in my opinion, the world's most powerful and neglected secret to success and happiness."* (Percy Ross, self-made multimillionaire and philanthropist, excerpt from *The Success Principles*, written by Jack Canfield and Janet Switzer.) Think about if the role were reversed. If someone approached you for help or assistance to accomplish a particular goal, would you help that individual? My guess is, the answer would be yes.

There is a science to asking successfully. Here are five tips adapted from *The Aladdin Factor*, written by Mark Victor Hansen and Jack Canfield:

1. Ask with yes in mind, and expect the yes.

2. Assume you can (its okay to ask) and assume you will get what you want.

3. Qualify the person you want to ask. Are they the expert? Are they the decision maker?

4. Always be specific. Vague requests produce vague results.

5. Be persistent. If you get a no the first time, don't give up. Some people are going to say no. It's not a reflection of you; it simply means they have other priorities, commitments, or other reasons that prevent them from helping you.

**Step Seven**

The key to your success with this process is step seven. *Nothing happens until you take action.* Do not misunderstand me; the first six steps are necessary for your success, but if you don't take action, nothing will happen. Successful people have a bias towards action. If you don't take action, your goal remains a wish or a dream unrealized. You know the familiar quote about someone wanting to win the lottery, but they've never bought a ticket. "You've got to be in it to win it."

I will share a true story to further illustrate the importance of taking action. There is a woman in her late 70's who's always wanted to own a home. She and her husband have rented either a home or apartment for the 59 years of their marriage. Unfortunately, the first time they attempted to buy a home forty years ago, they didn't have enough money for the down payment. When they asked her husband's parents, they couldn't help them. The sellers tried to transfer the mortgage, but the bank wouldn't agree. She continues to say, "I want a house. I'm going to own a house someday, even if I only live in it for one day." The last time I spoke to her, she said it's too late to own a home. I told her it's never too late, but nothing happens until you take action. This story also illustrates the value of the other steps in the process, and if you don't practice all of them, your goal or dream remains unrealized.

Taking action doesn't require huge leaps. In fact, it's important to look at taking action in small steps. You can start with identifying just one action that would take you closer towards achieving your goal. Or you can list the actions you must take, pick one or two to start with, and as you complete each action, start another one. If you are a more visual person, an excellent tool for "chunking down" what steps to take is called a mind map (See sample diagram below). It starts with drawing a circle in the middle of a piece of paper and writing your goal in the center of the circle. Draw circles outside the center circle for each action step and connect them to the center circle with a line. Write the action step in each circle. For each of these circles, list the activities required to complete the action step. The most important aspect of step seven is to maintain in forward motion. Continually ask yourself, "Does this action take me closer to achieving my goal?"

**Mind Map Tool**

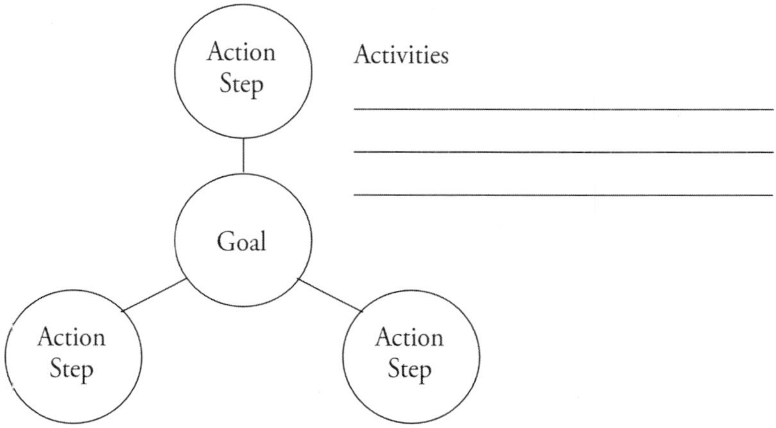

I will leave you with seven questions that mirror the seven steps of the **Goal Setting for Success** process. I promise, if you use the seven steps you will achieve your goals. Use the questions below to get you started on taking action toward achieving your goal or dream!

1. What do you want to accomplish? (Use "SMART" Goals):
2. What does the success of this goal look like?
3. Who will you tell? Tell at least one person (colleague, friend, peer, family). This raises your level of accountability.
4. What resources do you need to achieve your goal? (The "hard stuff")
5. What obstacles (include predictable) might you face? How might you overcome them?
6. What support system do you need? (Who do you want to ask?)
7. What one action will you take today, or this week, toward achieving your goal?

**My Motto: Start Small – Think Big!**

**Recommended Reading:**

*7 Habits of Highly Successful People* by Ken Blanchard

*The Aladdin Factor* by Jack Canfield and Victor Hansen

*The Success Principles* by Jack Canfield and Janet Switzer

*Taming Your Gremlin* by Rick Carson

*Notes:*

# ABOUT THE AUTHOR

## SELERIA JEAN WILLIAMS

Seleria Jean Williams is a licensed and certified speech-language pathologist in Pennsylvania and Delaware. She is Founder, President, and CEO of TPI Consulting Group, LLC, offering professional and personal development training, self-esteem and leadership development training, life style coaching, and professional consulting services for women. Seleria is a certified by The Professional Woman Network (PWN) as a Diversity Trainer with special emphasis in women's issues, diversity, and multiculturalism. She has been recently appointed to serve as a member of the International Board of Directors of The Professional Woman Network (PWN). Seleria is also a member of the Professional Woman Speakers Bureau.

As an independent contractor of speech-language services, she specializes in the treatment and management of neurogenic speech and language disorders, management of dysphagia and other swallowing related disorders, voice and diction improvement, accent reduction, and communication skills development. With over 28 years of experience in her profession, she is passionate about the health and well-being of today's woman with a special interest in empowering women to achieve optimal physical, emotional, and spiritual health. In addition to her experience as a Speech-Language Pathologist, Seleria serves as a mentor for children with special needs and serves on the Board of Trustees for Special Olympics for Philadelphia.

Seleria holds a Bachelor's degree in Speech Pathology and Audiology from Southern University A & M College in Baton Rouge, Louisiana and a Master's degree in Speech-Language Pathology from Louisiana State University. Her employment history includes experiences in public schools as a resource teacher, public school Speech-Language Pathologist; Clinical Rehabilitation Director various outpatient and sub-acute healthcare facilities; Clinical Coordinator and Classroom Instructor for the Speech-Language and Hearing Training Program at Tennessee State University; guest lecturer in the Human Behavioral Services certification program at Washburn University in Topeka, KS; and adjunct faculty member at West Chester University in West Chester, PA. Seleria holds membership in the American Speech-Language and Hearing Association, Delta Sigma Theta Sorority, Inc, Chester County Chapter of the Drifters, Inc., and at her church she is active in various church ministries, including the Mind, Body and Soul Ministry. Seleria serves as a role model for women and youth in the different organizations of which she holds membership. She currently resides in West Chester, PA., with her husband, Dr. John A. Williams and has two daughters, Mignon Cyrelle and Aria Nicole Williams. Seleria serves as a mentor for children with special needs and she serves on the Professional Management Board for her local university.

*Contact:*
The Total Woman Institute for Professional and Career Development
Seleria Jean Williams
P. O. Box 1732
West Chester, PA 19380-0058
(484) 252-6200
Email Address: info@tpiconsulting.net
www.tpiconsulting.net

## THIRTY-ONE

# AGING WITH GRACE AND DIGNITY

**By Seleria J. Williams**

**Aging**
By Bonnie Ruth Shaulis

*Growing old is but a state of mind.*
*You can enjoy your age or feel sorry*
*For yourself and sit around and pine.*
*You can make yourself feel happy or blue;*
*Whichever you choose is up to you.*
*Remember, you can be old in age but*
*Young at heart; you've gained wisdom,*
*Which can play a big part in whatever*
*New adventure you may want to start.*
*So quit trying to elude the age you are.*

*Accept it and reach for the stars.*
*Follow your dreams, although they may seem afar.*
*You've traveled life's road long enough to know the score.*
*And you can handle anything life could have in store.*
*Keep up the faith; it will open up many doors.*
*Believe in yourself and don't worry about your age,*
*For growing old is just another phase.*

You have heard the old adage, "Age is nothing but a number." Ruth Shaulis reminds us that we have an obligation to ourselves to enjoy life as we progress through those golden years of living. We should approach aging as a process for which we are well equipped to handle the highs and lows of what life offers us, no matter what phase of life we are living in. Aging is essentially the process of becoming older. Genetics and our environment often impact that process. For many of us, the thought of aging can be devastating. But, if we embrace the idea of healthy aging, the process can be as rewarding as giving birth to new life. In ***The Bucket List,*** a recently released movie starring Jack Nicholson and Morgan Freeman, two aging men from uniquely different social circles, both diagnosed with cancer, decide to team up and pursue adventures in life that they had put off in their younger lives. These two bright and witty gentlemen were given six months to one year to live. With faith and determination, together they set out in a desperate attempt to achieve their life dreams before they "kicked the bucket". Had they lived to tell their stories, I am sure they both would have agreed that their last year was probably the most rewarding journey of their life.

**What is Aging?**

Webster's dictionary defines **aging** as the process of becoming mellow, stable, or the process of becoming old. A check of any standard medical dictionary will define aging as "...the process of becoming old, a process that is genetically determined and environmentally modulated." If we think about it, the aging process begins the minute we are born. For many of us, if given a choice, we would prefer not to grow old. The fact still remains; we cannot prevent the process of aging. We are destined to grow old and we cannot turn back the hands of time. We can, however, with increased focus on healthy attitudes, experience longer and carefree lives.

**Taking a Closer Look**

What are your thoughts on aging and where are you in this process? Are you one of many who are afraid of the big 4-0? Are you fast approaching fifty and counting the number of gray strands in your hair? Are you overly obsessed with your weight? Are you concerned about your looks, your physical appearance, looking for sags, checking for wrinkles, or contemplating cosmetic surgery? Are you constantly asking your husband, significant other, children, or girlfriends, "How do I look?" If you answered yes to any of these questions, congratulate yourself on making the transition to midlife. This is what aging is all about, discovering facets in life that signify growth and maturity. Did you know that there is evidence that most people who reach age 65 are more likely to live to be 80 years old or older? The longer life span is attributed to the fact that today's seniors are now more informed about the benefits of healthier lifestyles. They are becoming more physically and mentally active, and they realize that they can enjoy the best of what life has to offer. What are your attitudes towards aging? Take a few minutes and answer a few questions. Let us see how prepared you are for approaching the golden years. The following questionnaire was based on a non-medical and non-scientific survey developed by Shirley MacLaine, documented in one of her articles, ***Health of Mind, Body, and_Spirit.*** What will your senior moments feel like? Remember to answer the questions as truthfully as possible.

Give yourself 5 points for every question that you answer **Yes.**
Give yourself 0 points for every question that you answer **No**.
Give yourself -5 points for every question that you answer **Sometimes.**

1. Do you cope well with stress?

2. Do you incorporate fruits and vegetables into your diet?

3. Do you avoid fatty or fried foods?

4. Do you sleep long enough and soundly?

5. Do you have a healthy sex life?

6. Do you limit your intake of caffeine?

7. Do you have a pet?

8. Do you minimize the amount of meat in your diet?

9. Do you believe in God?

10. Do you pray, meditate or visualize everyday?

11. Do you practice holistic or preventative health care?

12. Do you take vitamins?

According to MacLaine, if you scored 45 points or more, you will probably have an energetic and gratifying experience with your golden years.

If you scored between 30 and 40 points, you might have room for improvement, but you will probably still enjoy being a senior.

If you scored fewer than 30 points, you may want to consider an overhaul of your present lifestyle.

For many people, the thought of aging can be devastating. However, if you adopt a healthier lifestyle, you are much more likely to age well and live longer. We are now living longer with increased independence as a result of planning our futures early in life. We set goals, consult with our financial planners, strategically plan our retirement, sell our homes, move into retirement communities, and take pleasure in knowing that as we age, we can still have a future. If you develop healthy eating habits, increase the amount of physical activity in your daily routine, and learn to rest and relax with your hobbies and travel, you will find that you are on the right track for taking charge of your life as you age. An attitude of thinking young will make a difference in how you approach transitions in life.

**Taking Care of Yourself**

Preventative health care and practices can increase longevity and improve your quality of life as you age. Healthy practices such as maintaining a healthy diet, exercising daily, reducing stress, eliminating poor habits such as drinking and smoking are critical to expanding the potential to live for a lifetime. If giving up the booze is not an easy task, then limit it and drink in moderation (2-3 drinks a week). The ultimate goal is to take care of yourself early in life and, in doing so, consider these preventative measures:

- Get regular health check-ups.
- Drink plenty of fluids to maintain healthy skin and an intact digestive tract.
- Eat plenty of fruits and vegetables with high water content.
- Stick to a diet that is high in fiber and low in fat.
- Replace processed foods with complex carbohydrates, such as whole grains.
- Exercise regularly and stay physically active.
- Find humor in life…laughter is good for the soul.
- Love yourself and embrace the love of others.
- Accept changes in life by allowing yourself to let go and allow God to direct your path.
- Develop a positive attitude and be grateful for all things.
- Live for the moment and appreciate living in the now.
- Forgive others and relinquish resentment.
- Know your limits and plan ahead.
- Develop and maintain a strong network of family, friends, and colleagues, especially if you live alone.
- Incorporate safety habits that will prevent falls and injuries.
- Enjoy your journey in life and do the things that make you happy.

**Recognize the Signs of Aging**

Aging is the product of many factors that affect our health during the later years of life, and it is directly linked to aging of cells, reduced circulation, accumulated toxic build-up in our organs, changes in hormonal levels and balance, excessive body weight, decreased energy flow to the body, dehydration, and wear and tear of the body. Can you identify the signs of aging? Take a few minutes and write down ten tell-tale signs you have experienced that are related to becoming older and wiser.

**Things You Experienced That Confirm You Are Getting Older:**

1. ______________________________

2. ______________________________

3. ______________________________

4. ______________________________

5. ______________________________

6. ______________________________

7. ______________________________

8. ______________________________

9. ______________________________

10. ______________________________

Now, rank them from the hardest to cope with to the easiest to manage (with 1 being most difficult). Identify resources or tools that made coping with them easier. Are there any that you find to be unmanageable? Do you feel comfortable sharing the more challenging ones with friends and family? Are you getting medical advice for coping with the ones you have found to be challenging? It can be funny and often hilarious to know you are getting older:

- When you really pay attention to the Viagra ads on television
- When you start all of your conversations with "I remember when", but you do not remember the story
- When you go the mall and cannot find your car in the parking lot
- When you have more pills to take than there are hours in the day
- When you make a shopping list, and when you get to the market, you realize that you left the list at home

**Aging Gracefully**

Growing older with dignity and grace does not happen over night, and the experience will be different for each individual. However, you are the driving force behind your success to aging with confidence. Aging gracefully should be a natural process and a time in your life when you begin to feel confident about your life, your looks, your experiences, your well being, and your future. Your transitions through life over the years have withstood the test of time as you survived the excitement of growing up. You experience the ills of coping with life's demands, managing the highs and lows of menopause, and accepting the responsibilities and challenges of raising your family. Aging becomes a privilege and it is much to be desired. The key to embracing the process of aging is to take good care of your body early in life and protect your health from chronic illnesses and your body from injuries. Listed below are tips to help you live longer and happier. If you have not adopted them to your lifestyle, select three to five and begin incorporating them into your daily routine. Then assess whether or not the small changes you made have added value to your quality of life.

**Tips for Living Longer and Happier:**

1. See your doctor for regular check-ups and physical exams.
2. Find a hobby or sport that makes you happy and exhilarated.
3. Find time to walk and spend more time outdoors as weather permits.
4. Eat a balanced diet and take your vitamins daily.
5. Become a volunteer with a charitable organization of your choice.
6. Find a companion or buddy to share time with....someone to talk to about life, whether good or bad.
7. Consider getting a pet...at least you have someone to talk to that does not talk back.
8. Challenge your mind by filling out crossword puzzles, word searches, playing Scrabble or cards with family and friends.
9. Join a church or connect with a religious association.

10. Develop a strong support system of family and/or friends.

11. Do not sweat the small stuff.

12. Find positive things to watch on television, or read a book with positive story events.

By now you should have a different perspective and a more accepting attitude about aging and embracing the idea that you too can age with dignity and grace. Try to identify some reasons why growing older can be a fun and rewarding experience and share your conclusions with family or friends.

**Growing Older Can Be Fun Because:**

1. ______________________________

2. ______________________________

3. ______________________________

4. ______________________________

5. ______________________________

**Aging With Dignity**

As we begin to age, we soon begin to realize that there are things in our lives that matter more than life itself, and to the aging population, there is nothing more important to them than maintaining the love and respect of others while living a dignified life. In our most private moments, particularly as we age, our desires are to spend our last days with pleasant memories of life, cherishing relationships, and maintaining a sense of independence. As one begins to progress through the aging process, self-respect, self-esteem, and morale become as routine in life as waking up from a good night's sleep. Feeling valued and respected completes the cycle of aging. You may often hear our senior citizens say, "If I can't live the way I want to live, then what's the use of living." In this instance, they are struggling with the reality of losing control of their lives and not being allowed to make decisions about issues that impact their lifestyle. This is normal and we have to allow ourselves to listen with our hearts to do the things that bring inner peace, freedom and self-love. Aging is a gift from God. Cherish the moments and make good of each day. Dylan Thomas has expressed most eloquently a realistic approach to aging. He reminds us to...

*Do not go gentle into that good night,*
*Old age should burn and rage at close of day;*
*Rage, rage against the dying of the light.*
—Dylan Thomas

Resist the thought of "growing old", but remain active, eat healthily, read, play an instrument, write a book, make love, write a song, travel, engage in debate, discussions, and even arguments...hold on to your beliefs and convictions. Yes, you are aging and each day you do fewer things than what you were able to do the day before, the days when you were younger and more agile. There is grace and dignity that comes with maturity and aging. In the beginning, you were introduced to the concept of "the bucket list". Now, after reading this chapter, develop your own "bucket list". As you progress through life, make note of the items you have accomplished. By observing these accomplishments, you will find yourself feeling better and more fulfilled. And that is what aging with grace and dignity is all about. Enjoy the ride…cherish the moments.

**Resources:**

*Women's Encyclopedia of Health and Emotional Healing* by D. Foley and E. Nechas (1993). Rodale Press. Emmaus, PA.

http://www.shirleymaclaine.com/articles/health/article-275

*Notes:*

# ABOUT THE AUTHOR

**VIOLET MATHIS**

Violet Mathis is President and CEO of The V Factor. She specializes in international workshops, seminars and coaching for self empowerment. Her background is in dentistry and has been a Registered Dental Hygienist for thirty years. Opening her own management consulting company in 2000, Violet is a certified consultant for Bent Erickson & Associates, employment law and human resource specialist, as well as IPM (Integrated Performance Management). She is also a member of ADHA (The American Dental Hygienists' Association), SCN (Speakers & Consultants Network), as well as ADMC (Academy of Dental Management Consultants). She is a member of NAFE (National Association of Female Executives), ABR (The Atlanta Board of Realtors), and was the Governor of Who's Who International.

Violet has lived overseas and is an international author and speaker. She is a Certified Diversity Trainer, A Certified Life Coach, and a Certified Wellness Trainer. She has worked in the healthcare field, interior design, sales, and is forever volunteering for various social and charitable organizations.

Violet Mathis has a passion for people. She always sees the best in each person and has the ability to bring out their best qualities. She loves to travel and is always eager for more knowledge. Having a positive attitude is of the utmost importance in her life.

Violet is also co-author of "Women's Survival Guide for Overcoming Obstacles, Transition, and Change" and "Beyond the Body! Developing Inner Beauty".

*Contact:*
Violet L. Mathis
(678) 644-9499
vlmathis@bellsouth.net
www.protrain.net
www.pwnbooks.com

## THIRTY-TWO

# THE FALSE-SELF SYNDROME: HOW TO BE REAL AND AUTHENTIC

**By Violet Mathis**

Do you actually know who you are? Do you change depending on the situation? Are you the same person within your home and when you walk out your door? Have you ever met someone in any given situation, and upon meeting them in another, find them to be totally different? Do you find it difficult to non-assertively share your views with others? Are you trying to empress others instead of following your heart? Do you find yourself being a friend to someone to their face and then 'back stabbing' them when they aren't around? These are some tough questions and can be very difficult to answer at times. Can you remember a time in your life, whether it was in your childhood, your teens, young adulthood, or even now, when you were not true to yourself? This false self syndrome is difficult to keep, since you are always trying to measure up to expectations of others and continually living a lie. The false self will never gain independence.

As children we are innocent, loving, and carefree, and just accept ourselves for who we are without thinking about what others think we should be or do. The laughter and joy are just natural to most children. Growing up, we challenge authority because it in our nature to be curious and want to know how life works. Once we begin to be exposed to outside influences, our perception begins to change and we often times begin to believe that who we are is not either good enough or maybe not popular enough for what is expected of us. We may become our relationships, our job, or our home. If the nurturing of the child was not fulfilled, then you may be a survivor of childhood neglect. If only I could be better, maybe they would love me more, etc.

Sometimes there is a healthy false self, if in fact we can still be true to our beliefs and morals and not jeopardize our true self. On the other hand, an unhealthy false self believes it has been forced to comply with influences that are incompatible with one's true values and beliefs (feelings, values, needs and emotions). Your work, your relationships, your health, and all parts of your life should work harmoniously together creating a great synergy. This balance is not only healthy, but will enable you to be the best you can be.

Reality is something you create for yourself. You create your life out of the realities you have developed and learned from childhood. As a child, were you told you were bad? Were you good? Which one was it? This obviously creates a lot of confusion within.

Finding out just exactly who you are can only begin with the discovery of who you believe you are when no one is watching. What story do you make up about yourself? How would you describe yourself?

What are your likes and dislikes? What were your dreams growing up? What were your goals? How many of these have you achieved? Which have you achieved?

In some ways, it has never been harder to define who we are. Many of the traditional labels have disappeared. We may change employment regularly, marry up or down the social scale, marry much younger or older, or choose to hold different religious or moral beliefs than our family. We can be whoever we want to be, and often are encouraged to express this individuality and know which course of action feels right. But this tidy and stable identity doesn't fit the reality most of us experience. Most of us live our lives according to other people and society's belief's and values. No matter how hard you try to adjust and fit in, you will always be judged. So why not do it the easy way and simply be your authentic self.

I can certainly relate to literally putting on a mask or building a wall and not allowing others to really know the true me. What if they did not like me? What if I offended them? What if they knew how sensitive I was? What if I let them know how vulnerable I was? What if I did not measure up? What if they found out how insecure I was? What if I get hurt again? What if? What if? Most people actually have the same fears until they realize they have the option to do something about their feelings and beliefs and are able to fulfill their dreams or goals and actually move forward with their lives. Most people have some insecurity at different times in their lives. What about you? Think about some of the times in your life that you actually had to be someone other than your true self. Who you were was not compatible with your belief system. Remember, there is a fine line between being flexible and fake. Hiding your true feelings can feel false, and yet expressing them can be a high price.

Before you can determine your true self, you need to determine who you actually are and get to know that person. What are your core values? What keeps you grounded? What goals do you have? If others did not teach these to you, then you can certainly learn and continually evolve yourself. Once you know who you truly are, it becomes easier to stay true to yourself and others. Some guidelines might include the following:

| **TRUE SELF** | **FALSE SELF** |
|---|---|
| Awareness | Confusion |
| Positive Attitude | Pessimistic |
| Honest | Dishonest |
| Compassionate | Critical |
| Focused | Confused |
| Motivated | Indecisive |
| Loves Unconditionally | Loves Conditionally |
| Vulnerable | Appears Strong |
| Surrenders | Controls |
| Comfortable accepting complements | Uncomfortable accepting complements |
| Self-acceptance | Critical of self |
| Growing and has clear purpose of life | Stagnant and indecisive as to life's purpose |
| Balanced life | Unbalanced life |
| Spiritual | Believes in no higher power |

These are only a few of the characteristics of the True Self and the False Self. Once you determine where you are on your lifeline, it will be easier to move forward to being **The Real and Authentic You**. We evolve through many stages during our life. Liberating yourself is definitely exhilarating but may take time. You definitely are worth it!

Moving forward can basically be defined into three stages. This is when journaling is valuable. If you have not tried this, I would definitely recommend it.

**Stage 1:** You must work on the mind on a daily basis and it is truly the beginning step. From the first breath you take as a baby until you die, the brain is involved. You must nurture it with diet, meditation, knowledge, and challenges. It must stay engaged and active for survival. In order to nourish it, you might begin with self-awareness. Tao Tzu stated, "Knowing others is wisdom, knowing yourself is Enlightenment." Once you are aware of how you feel and why, you will be better able to begin the process of understanding and the opportunity to change the things you would like to improve about yourself. This allows you to actually know who you are and become the person you truly wish to be. Without this knowledge, it would be impossible to find the authentic you and to allow others to get to know you.

1. How do you feel?

2. What roll do you play with others in your life?

3. What feeling do you have regarding your entire life?

4. What will it take to restore you back to the real person underneath?

5. How do you begin to peel away the masks and layers you have learned over the years?

6. What tasks do you need to give up?

7. What ways did you learn to appease others while sacrificing your true self?
8. Do you feel you need to be all things to all people?
9. Were there times in your life when you had to be the "good little girl"?
10. Were you allowed to choose your career?
11. Were you forced to maybe go into a family business instead of following your heart?
12. What about dating and or marrying someone of your choice?
13. Were you always trying to measure up to someone's expectations?
14. Have you ever pretended to be someone you really weren't?
15. Have you ever felt you had to pretend to be someone other than yourself?
16. Have you ever lied in order to get what you wanted?
17. Have you ever cheated on something or someone for your benefit?

These questions can jump start your knowledge of who you really are. Awareness is the first step of getting to know the real you. As you grow in self-awareness, you are more able to fully understand why you behave as you do and why you feel like you do. This awareness enables you to realize the things you would like to change about yourself. Our beliefs and attitudes shape our views. By following your beliefs, are you getting what you want and where you wish to be?

Create a list of what you must have in your life. What has value to you? A few suggestions might be:

1. Respect
2. Intimacy
3. Learning or fun
4. Love

What is important to you in the following areas?

1. Family and friends ___________________________________
2. Career ___________________________________
3. Fun and recreation ___________________________________
4. Physical environment ___________________________________
5. Personal growth ___________________________________
6. Health ___________________________________
7. Money ___________________________________
8. Spirituality ___________________________________
9. Significant other ___________________________________

**Stage 2:** Once you have self-awareness, the next step is self-acceptance. This means being happy and content with who you are at this moment, even though there may be certain things about yourself that you would like to change at a later date. Remember, we are our own worst critics.

1. How often do you obsess over a certain part of your body?
2. When was the last time you gave yourself permission to not be all things to all people?
3. Are you judging yourself based on other's definitions of what is good or bad?
4. What if you gave yourself permission to accept yourself with the understanding that you would like to work on your weight, education, or whatever it is you wish to improve upon?
5. What are you afraid of?

What tape do you play in your head? The internal dialogue each of us plays can determine how we feel about ourselves. At some point in your life, you may have had a pivotal person who impacted your life, either positively or negatively. It may be necessary for you to forgive in order to move forward.

Other questions you might ask yourself:

1. What type of people do I enjoy spending my time with?
2. What do I enjoy about their company?
3. How does where I met them have an impact?
4. What are the values we have in common?

5. Why is it so important to have the approval of others?

6. Do I choose my friends by what I have in common or my differences?

**Stage 3:** Once you have accepted who you are, the next step is to keep oxygen flowing to the brain in order to keep it healthy. Any type of exercise is beneficial. What do you like to do? Find something you enjoy that you are likely to continue and will actually not feel like work or exercising. Find a friend to share your enthusiasm. Be open to new adventurers.

Be true to your core values and you will never stray far from **The True and Authentic Self**. It is not your abilities that determine who you are but the choices you make. Sometimes, you just need to stop and be still in the moment and think about who you truly are. You need to always tell the truth to yourself about who you are. Always consider your options and go with it peacefully and joyfully.

*"Your vision will become clear only when you look into your heart."*
—Carl Jung

Dr Phil McGraw, in his book **Self Matters**, states that you need to find yourself before life takes its toll in order to find your true authentic self. He believes that you must move beyond your fears and excuses to be your true person. Do not believe other's views of you to be total truth. You have the power and control to be the special individual that you were created to be. Take control!

Nurturing your mind, spirit, and body should be a priority in your life. Remember to put your oxygen mask on first in order for you to give to others. Your purpose in life is not to live by society's standards, but to be **Your True and Authentic Self**. If you live your life in awareness of who you truly are and stay true to your beliefs and values, life will be meaningful and fun. Listen to your heart and give only from the heart. By doing this, your will live your life with the glass always half full.

*God grant me the serenity*
*To accept the things I cannot change;*
*Courage to change the things I can;*
*And wisdom to know the difference.*
*Living one day at a time;*
*Enjoying one moment at a time.*

*Notes:*

# ABOUT THE AUTHOR

## Elizabeth Palm

This chapter is for every woman who feels challenged by the unexpected events life offers us. Life is full of different experiences and we all handle them differently. The biggest challenge is to do what works for you when times are difficult or a crisis shows up in your life. When you're dealing with unexpected events, take time to think it through before you make a decision, you can't cross a bridge before it's built. We must define ourselves first and allow that definition to sail us through those unexpected times in our life.

Elizabeth Palm, President of Palm Consulting Group, is a Certified Professional Consultant located in Southeast Michigan. Ms. Palm has a degree in Business Management and is certified in Human Resources. Her expertise includes corporate training, human resource support, and business management. Ms. Palm is an active member of The Professional Woman Network and serves as a senior member on the PWN International Advisory Board.

Ms. Palm is highly knowledgeable on issues regarding customer service, human resources, diversity, self-improvement, women's issues and professionalism. Ms. Palm has conducted training in both formal and informal settings nationwide for thousands of corporate employees including executive management teams. Ms. Palm has a passion for sharing knowledge and guiding others on their journey toward success. Her presentations are interesting, insightful, and thought provoking.

Ms. Palm is also a co-author for *Customer Service & Professionalism for Women*, *The Young Woman's Guide for Personal Success* and *Overcoming the Superwoman Syndrome*; available in the PWN library and www.amazon.com.

Ms. Palm is available as a keynote speaker, seminar leader, and consultant for groups, organizations or associations on a local, national and international basis.

*Contact*
Palm Consulting Group
PMB 343
19186 Fort St.
Riverview, MI 48193
(734) 282-8442
www.protrain.net

## THIRTY-THREE

# EATING ON THE RUN! HOW TO AVOID FAST FOOD

**By Elizabeth Palm**

Do you often find yourself out of time, looking for a quick answer, a quick solution, and a quick meal? Your life style is about keeping things moving, including yourself. While this chapter is not about dieting, consider for a moment that dieting might not be necessary if we took the time to balance our activities with moderation. There are many ways, or places, to stop along the way and quickly take a bite of something edible and call it a meal. Is this unconscious eating? Is it possible too many of us think we have eating issues, when the reality is we have other issues that affect how we eat?

There is no doubt; the fast food industry is a multi-billion dollar business. New fast food chains pop up like popcorn in even the most rural communities. This, of course, makes it easy for you to pull up to the drive-thru window and place an order. In addition, with so little time and so much to be done, why even stop to eat? We can just peel back the wrapper and get back on the road within minutes. Age knows no barriers; we can feed children, adults, and seniors on the way. Just pass those handy little individual bags/boxes around and keep going.

There are constant news reports and studies conducted identifying that this trend of rushed meals has a common result: the scale is tipping and it's not in our favor most days. Are you caught in the vicious cycle of eating unhealthy because you're in a hurry, starting a diet over again, and then fighting the exercise craze? What can you do to break the cycle? How can you avoid fast food when you're on the run?

**Time Awareness**

It is possible to take time out to eat better, make healthier choices, and save yourself from medical disasters, even if you can't give up the busy schedules. You can make it work! All it takes is a little strategy, planning, and preparation. The good thing is that you can begin right now! Grab a pencil! As you move through the rest of this chapter, write your ideas and thoughts down and half of the work is done. It's that easy to get started. No big diet to follow and no calories to count. It's about understanding what drives you to fast food! It's time to take care of yourself and build your strength up to enjoy your senior years.

If you understand what drives your decision-making process and why you have found yourself eating in a hurry, you can change the course of things to come. You don't want to spend the next ten years in the doctor's office; you want to be out there having fun, staying active and involved. There are probably just a few specific reasons you haven't taken the time to eat better. Identify this information and you can make minor modifications and create lasting changes in your eating patterns. What are the top three reasons you choose fast food?

1. ______________________________

2. ______________________________

3. ______________________________

There are occasions when we are moving through the day too fast and begin looking for short cuts or ways to save time. Fast food restaurants serve as a mainstay for saving time. Or at least that's the perception we buy into; there are a host of appealing options. How many of these meet your daily requirements for a fast meal:

1. You don't have to get out of your car.
2. You can eat it absolutely anywhere.
3. No extra work involved; just money.
4. You can take it back to your desk and eat while you work.
5. You've saved considerable time by not going into the restaurant.
6. You have saved a few dollars because you didn't order that yummy dessert.

Does this mean eating well is NOT a priority for you? Let's be realistic, there are enough issues to face as you age. Taking time to focus on a meal will do wonders for your health. Let's look at two fairly typical scenarios; ask yourself if this sounds familiar:

**Scenario # 1**

On Tuesday, you entered the local fast food drive-thru and there were only three cars ahead of you so you thought this would take a minimal amount of time. In reality, it took you about ten minutes to get there. You were in line for another four to five minutes (or more) while those three hurried people made their decisions after careful review of the multitude of options available to them. And it took you another ten minutes to get back to the office or home. So, the fast food trip took approximately 25 – 30 minutes, once you really think about it. Put it to the test; how much time do you really save by running out for fast food?

Favorite Location #1 ______________________________

Drive time to ________ Time in Line: _________

Drive time from ________

TOTAL: ________ Actual Time saved: _____________

Your Satisfaction Level (circle one): Good / Not Bad / Wrong Order

Favorite Location #2 ______________________________

Drive time to ________ Time in Line: _________

Drive time from ________

TOTAL: ________ Actual Time saved: _____________

Your Satisfaction Level (circle one):

Great / Good / Not Bad / Wrong Order

Most of us don't realize how much time we actually spend going through this process because we are in constant motion. Always thinking about the "next thing" we have to do or the "next place" we have to be.

**Scenario #2**

You travel, a lot! You seldom have time to even make it to the drive-thru. As a matter of fact, your meeting ran late, traffic is horrendous and you're ravenous. You'll eat anything. "Make that one bagel with cream cheese and a large cup of coffee, to go!" Now that's saving time, you'll be able to eat that on the plane or in the car while you're driving, no problem. Technically, it's a small meal, right?

Does this sound familiar? Are there things you could do differently? The answer is a resounding Yes! I think we can agree on one basic equation: Good Eating Habits = Good Health. As simple as that sounds, you know it's not easy unless you have a good starting point.

You could probably write lists of reasons why you don't prepare your own meals. Time is just one of them; yet if you really measured the time saved preparing your own meals, you might also realize another savings, money! Now don't get me wrong, today's fast food restaurants are changing and offering healthier options. It's worth a trip every now and then, *in moderation.*

I have learned it is never too late to start a good habit or two, especially with food. Once you build some momentum, you'll be up and running with these ideas and more of your own. So, let's begin with a quick evaluation of your current eating habits. Do you know what they are?

| An Eating Evaluation | |
|---|---|
| Y or N | |
| | Do you eat out frequently? |
| | _____ times a day multiplied by _____ times a week |
| | Do you cook? |
| | Do you hate cooking? |
| | Are you uninterested in cooking? |
| | Are you board with cooking? |
| | Is there food 'stock' in the cupboards? (Things you use often or repeatedly) |
| | Do you travel a lot? (By car or air) |
| | _____ times you travel a month or week |
| | Are you really busy or is there a priority issue? (Be honest with yourself) |
| | Is it too hard to decide what's for dinner every day? |
| | Can't get organized enough to use the crock pot? |
| | Does it take too long to prepare? |
| | Do you 'put off' your meals or 'forget' to eat? |
| | Do you eat less because you are dieting, again? |

Do you notice a pattern, or do you see anything in your answers that might reveal an opportunity for change? There are tremendous benefits to identifying or resolving your issues surrounding food. Let's take a look at the big picture: you clip coupons to save money, you exercise, you take care of other people (your parents, adult children, etc.), you run meetings with efficiency, and you solve problems of all kinds on a daily basis; you might as well eat better! It will support your efforts in so many ways. It is, without a doubt, the best way to feel more energized. Now, what else would you do if you had more energy?

It's time to stop the wheels of motion and sit through at least one meal a day without distractions, interruptions or rushing through it. It's hard to think of what to eat when you're in a hurry. Take a minute and write down a few menu ideas for those times you know are going to be busy. More times than not, if we put something in writing, it becomes easier to remember, so write out your three top food choices and then make sure to include them on your grocery list so they're handy.

**Breakfast Favorites**

1. ____________________

2. ____________________

3. ____________________

**Lunch Favorites**

1. ____________________

2. ____________________

3. ____________________

**Dinner Favorites**

1. ____________________

2. ____________________

3. ____________________

**Snacks And Mini Meal Ideas**

1. ______________________________

2. ______________________________

3. ______________________________

**Awareness Eating**

Take time to redefine your relationship with food. More importantly, think about what you say to yourself about food just prior to or directly after eating. Think about your last meal. Did you smell bitter or sweet aromas? Was it evenly heated? What colors did you see? If you only see brown (meats, sauces, etc.) or yellow (breading, fries, etc) food you could be off track.

It's time to raise your conscious awareness about yourself and your eating habits and come to an understanding about what really prevents you from eating better. Do the same reasons or excuses apply? You can raise your awareness level to avoid the hazards that come with eating on the run by making or scheduling time to eat and enjoy the experience. For instance, which of these statements have you made lately:

__ "I'm too busy" __ "I'll eat at my desk" __ "I'll eat later"
__ "I'll grab something on the way"

Are these common ways you answer the call to meal times? Do you skip breakfast or lunch on a regular basis? Are you filling yourself up with the latest meal supplement drinks? It's time to stop and get off the fast meal track. You are heading in the wrong direction if you frequently complain of indigestion, heartburn, or other digestive issues. All of which are most likely related to your eating habits. Frequent eating on the run can bring you to a screeching halt if you don't stop to smell the aromas of a good meal.

**Plans And Strategy**

There are several ways you can avoid the pitfalls of eating in a hurry. One way is to have a plan. For instance, when you know your schedule is going to be busy and you won't have time for a meal, bring a sandwich and a cup of soup. Another way might be to keep small healthy snacks handy.

Try this idea: buy the ready-made salads or salad kits from the grocery store, add some cooked chicken, and there you have it, a great meal in fifteen minutes without the temptation of fast food. This works great if you travel, too. Most grocery stores carry the ready-to-go type foods and they are usually better for you than a quick burger. Still can't avoid the fast food line? Try the following ideas:

1. Check fast food web sites for nutrition information.

2. Keep your menu selections to "small" sizes or half orders.

3. Order with options. Add the veggies – minimize the toppings.

4. Avoid menu items that are fried, breaded, crispy or saucy.

5. Order a cup of broth based soup and a half sandwich at the Deli.

6. Keep some good snacks in the desk drawer (fruit cups or granola bars).

7. Skip the buffet. Order specific items or a la carte.

8. Drink a bottle of water before you eat anything.
9. Avoid sodas and other sweet drinks. Choose water or unsweetened ice tea.
10. Order fresh foods and think color; minimize yellow and white foods.

Know what prevents you from creating a meal plan for yourself! The biggest obstacle when trying to avoid fast food is usually finding time to plan meals in advance. It's worth it to think ahead about your next meal. Once you get started, you will find new ways to make it easier. It's absolutely important, for your health, to take a few minutes a day to plan your meals; especially if you know you're going to run short on time. Here are a few additional tips to help you with your plan:

1. Flexible Options (Put a small cooler in the car for those road warrior days.)
2. Healthy Choices (Get pre-cut/mini cups of fruits and veggies to snack on.)
3. Easily Prepared (Buy bags of frozen meats and veggies for last minute stir fry's.)
4. Good Cookware/Tools (Stock sharp knives, microwave dishes, storage containers.)
5. Money Saver's (Use coupons and discount deals.)

**Avoid These Hazard Zones:**

1. Skipped meals (causes mid-day slumps or over-eating)
2. Substituting food with vitamins (too much of a good thing is not good)
3. Eating in the car (this is not how you define multi-tasking)
4. Waiting until the last minute ($11^{th}$ hour decisions create unwanted 'waists')
5. Cheap eats from the local drive-thru!

When it comes to time and convenience, YOU don't have time to deal with the health problems caused from eating fast foods on a regular basis. Take small steps to reach your goals. Try one of these ideas:

1. Add One Day: If you eat in the cafeteria three times a week and bring your lunch the other two, try turning it around. Simply add one more day of bringing your own lunch.
2. Take Inventory: If you're not sure if the cupboards are stocked with the basic staple items you need to throw a quick meal together, take inventory. Keep a note pad or index cards handy to jot down what you need so you don't forget.
3. Plan Ahead: If you're traveling, visit the websites of those fast food restaurants and plan your meals in advance. Do they have healthy selections such as salads or yogurt on the menu? *Write out your own menu and stick to it.*

4. Love bagels? Get the mini bagels at the grocery store and avoid the big ones at the airport or coffee shop.

It's not always easy to switch gears and make your own food when you've been living it up in the fast lane. Most of the people I spoke to on this subject agreed they could stop solving the world's problems for thirty minutes to focus on a meal. Can you? Your internal self might thank you.

Remember to keep fresh fruit on hand and always take two or three pieces with you to eat throughout the day.

Eat to build your body up, not break it down. Enjoy your food and you'll enjoy longevity. Cheers to your good health and may all your eating habits be good ones!

**Recommended Reading:**

*Serves One: Simple Meals to Savor When You're on Your Own* by Toni Lydecker

*The Best Life Diet* by Bob Greene (Foreword by Oprah Winfrey)

*Notes:*

# ABOUT THE AUTHOR

**Jennifer Higgins**

Jennifer Higgins, President and founder of Get Yourself Coaching LLC, is dedicated to helping her clients reach their goals in their personal and professional lives through one-on-one coaching, inspirational retreats and specialty seminars. Jennifer offers her clients the leadership and experience gained from over 25 years of professional management experience in a number of corporate environments, tempered by a down-to-earth, practical style.

Her diverse background and life experiences have created in Jennifer a passion for helping people and groups "get out of their own way", removing obstacles and building momentum in order that they may capitalize on their unique and special talents. Jennifer graduated from the University of Massachusetts at Amherst with a Bachelor's Degree in Spanish, spending a year abroad studying the language and culture in Sevilla, Spain. Over the course of her career, she has experience working in large corporations and also working for small business owners, which gives her a personal appreciation for the opportunities and challenges facing many working women today.

She has dedicated much of her free time to youth soccer, serving two terms as President of her local youth soccer club. Jennifer brings her corporate America meets soccer Mom perspective and sense of humor to her coaching and retreats.

In addition to her years of professional experience, Jennifer is also the author of The Heart of a Leader, a book that takes a fun and practical approach to helping identify and nurture the leader that is within all of us.

Jennifer lives in Florida with her husband and two children. You can learn more about her coaching, retreats, and purchase a copy of her book by visiting her website at www.getyourselfcoaching.com.

*Contact:*
Get Yourself Coaching, LLC
P.O. Box 901
Lutz, Florida 33548
jhiggins@getyourselfcoaching.com
www.getyourselfcoaching.com

## THIRTY-FOUR

# NOT ALL BABY BOOMERS ARE CREATED EQUAL

### By Jennifer Higgins

Depending on the definition you ascribe to, the Baby Boomer generation includes those born in 1946 and stretches as far as 1965 by some estimates. The start of the Boom can be equated to World War II ending, a lot of soldiers coming home, and not coincidentally, lots of babies being born. However, 20 years is a long time to label an entire generation – perhaps even more so as the rate of change in the world increased more rapidly with each passing year as technology allowed things like television to transform how we lived and experienced both everyday life and defining events that would become a part of our psyche and culture forever.

As someone born in 1960, I always felt I was born ten years too late. I've felt that way since I was about 18 or 20 and could appreciate all that I "missed" by being too little during the 60's to appreciate them, as elementary school students aren't exactly up on what's going on around them in the world and current events. I mean I missed all the war protests, the start of the women's movement, the assassinations of the Kennedys and Martin Luther King, Jr., the Beatles, Woodstock – I really felt I missed all that great history, yet here I was, labeled a Baby Boomer, just the same as someone born in 1950 who actually "experienced" all that great history. So I have to ask, "Who gets to decide how to name and categorize a generation?" The answer, as I understand it, is both the demographers and number crunchers of society, as well as anyone willing to come up with a better name. This understanding has all come home to roost now as the first Baby Boomers begin to collect Social Security. When that story came on the radio, the irony of the fact that I was driving to work was not lost on me – nor was the timing of how many more years I'd need to work before I could even sniff at Social Security. So here it was - a very significant mile-marker for the oldest of the Baby Boomers, and here I sat in traffic with at least forteen more years of work stretching out ahead of me before I could even think about Social Security and what might be left when I actually get there.

Shortly after that story on the radio, I was at a seminar where the "get to know each other" exercise required each of us to fill out a sheet with something about each of the other people in the class. Jim and I met over the question about finding someone who had written a letter to the editor. It turns out that Jim had written a letter to the editor in 1968 to protest the Vietnam War. My radar hummed as I knew I was meeting yet another person whose experiences I wanted to have lived myself and who would remind me that I was born ten years too late. During the course of the week, Jim shared with me how profoundly he was shaped by his experiences of the 60's, particularly 1968 (of course!). That was the year he turned 18, registered for the draft, experienced the shooting of Martin Luther King, Jr. and Bobby Kennedy, graduated from high school and gave the valedictory speech -- protesting the Vietnam War-- witnessed the protests at the Democratic National Convention in Chicago, and saw his older brother go off to and be killed in Vietnam – all before we ushered in 1969. I didn't have a lot to add to the 1968 discussion, as I was all of 8 years old, in 3rd grade, living a very normal suburban life, totally clueless about all the political awakenings and protests that were going on around me -- hardly the same Baby Boomer experience, I lamented.

So, as I prepared to write this piece about being born ten years too late, I came across something called "Generation Jones". A sociologist named Jonathan Pontell wrote a book, *Generation Jones*, in which he describes those born between 1954 and 1965 as Generation Jones, separate and distinct from the "Mature" Baby Boomers born between 1946 and1953. Born in 1958, Mr. Pontell said he never felt like the experiences of the Baby Boomers resonated with him. So he set out to understand how the events and changes that were to characterize the 1960's were really what shaped those of Generation Jones, who were young children through early teens during that same timeframe. The name Generation Jones comes from both the anonymous nature of the name Jones, as the generation had not been unidentified before, and the slang term "jonesin'" meaning to crave something – in this case, a generation of unfulfilled expectations as compared to those of the mature Boomers.

World events were certainly different being experienced as an elementary schooler rather than someone coming of age. I am too young to remember anything about John F. Kennedy's assassination or even the assassinations of Martin Luther King, Jr. and Bobby Kennedy. What I remember about the world news in the 60's was every night talking about the Vietnam War and the de-militarized zone and children starving in Biafra. I was too young to appreciate the gravity of the events and how they would change and shape history from the moment they happened onward. For me, the first real event that I can truly say I remember was the landing on the moon in 1969. The whole neighborhood stayed up all night to watch it. For a nine year old, maybe that's why the event is so permanently etched in my brain – all the neighborhood kids up all night, watching Neil Armstrong take one small step for man and one giant leap for mankind. I was old enough to feel and be a part of an experience that almost anyone alive at the time can remember and can compare notes on. The other "big news event" for Generation Jones was the Watergate Hearings in 1973. I remember coming home from school every day and seeing the hearings on all three TV stations. From a 12-year-old's perspective, I really would have rather watched "Let's Make a Deal"– seeing a bunch of men sit behind big tables asking questions all day didn't do it for me. My generational experience was shaped by the Watergate break-in, the hearings, and ultimately the resignation of President Nixon. Perhaps this helps explain one of the hallmark characteristics of a Generation Joneser as being generally cynical about government!

Being born in the 60's meant that us Jonesers had a very different music experience than the older Boomers. I completely missed out on the Beatles, as they had broken up before I even had a clue what Rock and Roll was! My first music memory was listening to my AM clock radio and hearing "Tears of a Clown" by Smokey Robinson and the Miracles and recognizing that as a song I liked. To this day whenever I hear it, I can picture myself lying in my bed waiting until that song came on, hoping it did before the sleep feature turned the radio off for the night. Having no older siblings and parents who were into Herb

Albert and the Tijuana Brass, I was totally clueless about a lot of music until middle school. So it was up to a friend with an older sister to introduce me to the Beatles. Watching the newsreels of girls screaming when they got a glimpse of the Beatles live is fine for me – that is not something I feel I missed out on experiencing in person. I certainly understand why the Beatles stopped touring – they couldn't be heard and couldn't hear themselves for all the screaming girls. So I'll take my experience of slow dancing to "Hey Jude" played over and over again at Friday night parties – telling our parents that the song wasn't over yet – and loving the fact that either they couldn't tell or indulged us in our ploy to dance a little longer. While the older Baby Boomers got the Rolling Stones and Beatles, Woodstock and the Monterey Pop Festival, Janis Joplin, Jimmy Hendrix, Bob Dylan, and Eric Clapton, all me and Generation Jones can claim is disco. Yes, disco was great to dance to and anyone in their 20's during the disco craze that didn't try to dance to it and imitate John Travolta's moves on the dance floor missed out on a great ride. The movie "Saturday Night Fever" steam-rolled into our lives in 1977 and things were never quite the same. It wouldn't replace Woodstock, but everyone went to discos where DJ's played all the Donna Summers and Tavares you could dance to under the requisite disco mirror ball. Who didn't learn to do "The Hustle" and dance it every Friday and Saturday night? And for good measure, Michael Jackson taught everyone a dance move or two. Who doesn't remember watching the "Thriller" video's first run on MTV in 1983?

Movies were another big part of the Generation Jones experience. "Saturday Night Fever" was huge, as it combined a movie with a whole lifestyle of the disco and the dance craze that it set off. There was the "Star Wars" trilogy, the "Indiana Jones" trilogy, "American Graffiti", "The Big Chill", "The Blues Brothers", and several of the James Bond movies. I remember the scene in "The Spy Who Loved Me" when the whole audience gasped as Bond skis off the cliff – only to have his British flag parachute unfurl to the roll of the opening credits. I also remember my own scream as I joined the audience's screaming when the head rolled out of the hole in the sunken hull in the movie "Jaws" and Richard Dreyfus nearly killed himself getting to surface. I remember how the "Jaws" music made your skin crawl because you knew the shark was somewhere out there and I remember friends confessing that they couldn't swim in the ocean for years after they saw "Jaws". By 1978, I was off to college where I saw "Animal House" my first weekend away from home. Toga parties abounded every weekend thereafter. And of course, who can forget the cult classic "Rocky Horror Picture Show". Although it premiered in 1975, by 1978 when I first saw it, it still didn't have the cult following that was to come. At my first viewing, you could actually see and hear most of the movie – although I remember being shocked when many in the audience jumped up and did the "Time Warp" in the aisles when the song came on. I would go to see the movie several more times, but never heard as much of it as that first time.

The power of TV cannot be overstated in its impact on the Baby Boomers and Generation Jonesers. For the first time in history, everyone could see and experience the same event at the same time. Today that power and impact has been lost between reruns and syndication and the ability to record and Tevo anything you happen to miss, but during the 60's, 70's, and 80's much of the events and icons that would help shape and define us were experienced through television. By the time us Generation Jonsers we were old enough to sit in front of Saturday morning cartoons, advertisers had perfected their craft enough to make us consumers from the start. From the Friday night fare of the Brady

Bunch followed by the Partridge Family, we segued into a full lineup of Saturday morning in front of TV with cartoons. Little did we know our little minds were being indoctrinated with the need for the latest cereals like Quisp and Quake – the tie about which one to choose at the store to be broken by which cereal had the best toy displayed on the box. (That toy, however, was fiendishly hidden at the bottom of the cereal, and of course could only to be extracted by pouring out the entire contents of the box as soon as it was opened. Unfortunately, the cereal never went back in the box as neatly as it was when you first opened it!) That sugary cereal was all the energy needed to allow my sister and I to watch as much "Scoobie Doo", "The Monkees", "Wacky Races", "Lancelot Link: Secret Chimp", "H R Puffenstuff", and "Johnny Quest" as we could stand without taking a break until sometime well after noon. As I grew up, TV still played an important role. Every high schooler had to be able to quote lines from the weekend's Saturday Night Live to be considered cool. There was "Mork and Mindy" introducing Robin Williams to the world. I was attending the University of Colorado at Boulder at the time and the entire city shut down when that came on as if Mork was going to walk in and watch with you. Then there was "Dynasty" and the Carrington family feuds. All homework would stop and we would all meet in someone's room to have a Dynasty party and watch the show. It truly was a must-see so that you could participate in discussions the next day. And who didn't cry watching the final episode of M.A.S.H. or watch when Rhoda got divorced? And of course, there were the classics like "The Rockford Files", "All In The Family", "Maude", "Hawaii 5-0", and "The Jeffersons". And what girl didn't have a huge crush on Tom Selleck as "Magnum PI"?

The power of the shared experience through television made us all feel a part of something bigger than ourselves, like watching the US beat Russia in hockey in 1982. When the game ended and the US won, I remember going out in the snow covered walkways of the huge dormitory complex at UMASS/Amherst and seeing US flags unfurl from windows 20 stories up. And I remember hearing thousands of voices raised in celebration of what would come to be known as "The Miracle on Ice" and would unite Americans around a single great event for years to come. In 1984, I remember watching Joan Benoit win the first ever women's marathon in the Los Angeles Olympics and Geraldine Ferraro accept the Vice-Presidential nomination on the Democratic ticket with Walter Mondale. I truly felt that I was watching history being made and I imagine it was the feeling that those born early in the Boom generation must have felt many times during the 60's. That feeling that you are truly witnessing something that will change you and world, or at least your part of it, forever.

So, when I tell my children stories about the fact that cartoons were only on Saturday mornings and that you only had three channels to choose from, and that you actually had to get up from your chair to change the channel, I know I sound old to them, but that's me and my generation and that's the fabric of my growing up that made me. In the course of this writing, I have come to realize that whatever you experience growing up, it is yours and it is what helps mold and shape you. There are personal events that only you experience and there are bigger events that you share with a community, and part of the generational experience is figuring out how big the community is that shared that experience. Whatever those events and experiences are, they are what make and shape us. Regardless of how we are labeled, we grew and experienced life that was going on around us and life that was happening to us. So I vow to no longer wish I were born ten years earlier – whether I'm a Boomer or Joneser doesn't much matter. What really matters is how I choose to take what I have now and share it with the world. My lesson in all of this is to embrace your history because it's yours and tell it to anyone who'll listen after first listening to her history. Each of us has a history that makes us interesting, some of it shared with a community and some of it very personal, and that history helps us and others understand where we're coming from and where the other person is coming from. Perhaps if we spent more time trying to understand the personal story rather than tagging everyone as a Boomer or Joneser or Generation X'er, we'd find the world a more civilized place to be.

## ABOUT THE AUTHOR

### SATHEDIA BUSH

Sathedia Bush is the President of Lifetime Professional Institute which is a personal and professional training organization. She is committed to helping others achieve personal and professional excellence. She has over 27 years of experience in the federal and corporate community where she has held numerous leadership and management positions and gained extensive knowledge and experience in management, negotiations, training, contracts, marketing, and public speaking.

She interacts proactively with academia, local and national professional communities and has built cooperative relationships with businesses throughout the United States. She provides guidance and direction for local, national, and international small businesses. Sathedia regularly briefs Fortune 500 companies, senior government executives and leaders of professional organizations.

Sathedia Bush has worked as a professional model and as the admissions director for a well-known modeling and etiquette school. For the last three years she has helped develop small businesses into successful companies that can compete in a global work force. Sathedia has a passion for sharing knowledge and helping others succeed. As a professional speaker and certified trainer, she conducts seminars and workshops in etiquette, dressing for success, and professional image.

Through her affiliation with The Professional Woman Network, she has obtained certifications in Branding and Image, and Women's Issues and Diversity. Sathedia earned a bachelor's degree in Business Administration from Louisiana Tech University and a master's in Business Administration from Incarnate Word University in San Antonio, Texas. Sathedia is a member of The Professional Woman Network and the National Association of Female Executives.

*Contact:*
Sathedia Bush
Lifetime Professional Institute
P. O. Box 591753
San Antonio, TX 78259
sgbush11@sbcglobal.net
(210) 885-1058

## THIRTY-FIVE

# SOCIAL ETIQUETTE: WHAT TO DO AND WHEN

**By Sathedia Bush**

Have you ever gone to a social event where you felt you did everything wrong and were unsure of what to do or say? People often judge your character on how you handle these social situations. To help us determine the appropriate behavior in certain situations, we turn to the rules and guidelines of etiquette. Do keep in mind etiquette is more than rules; it is treating others with respect, consideration, and honesty, while using common courtesy.

My grandmother (who lived to be 103) said her secret for a long, happy life was to always treat everyone the way she wanted to be treated. If someone treats you rudely, smile and treat them with kindness. During a recent trip, I encountered a reservation agent early one morning who was truly beginning to have a bad day. I politely smiled while she snarled at me; I continued to be kind and courteous with a big warm smile. After a few minutes, she softened and smiled as well. What could have been a bad experience ended positively. (I am sure the customers behind me were thankful.) If you treat others with kindness, they will generally return the favor. Try it; it really works!

To build relationships and have a social network, you must learn to be sociable. Let's take a quick true and false quiz to see if you are a model of good social manners:

( ) When introduced to someone, you should offer a smile, good eye contact and firm handshake.

( ) If the invitation says R.S.V.P. and you are not attending, there is no need to reply.

( ) At a formal dinner, your water glass is to your right and you should pass food to the right.

( ) You received excellent service; there is no need to tip, just say "thank you."

( ) Jan's hair is beautiful. You think it's a wig. It is okay to ask.

( ) It is okay to forward the e-mail addresses of others without their permission.

TEST ANSWERS: 1. True 2. False 3. True 4. False 5. False 6. False

## Introductions

It is important to make graceful introductions when appropriate. It is rude and inconsiderate to allow someone to stand awkwardly silent without making an introduction. Introduce men to women, younger people to older, and a lower ranking person to a higher ranking person. An easy way to remember this rule is to mention the name of the woman, older person or higher ranking person first. For instance, in a formal setting you would say, "Mrs. Best, I would like to introduce Mr. Stone." If everyone is on a first name basis, you would say, "Jan Best, may I introduce you to John Stone." When you are making introductions, state their names clearly and offer some information about each person to get the conversation started. If you encounter individuals in a deep conversation, do not interrupt simply to force an introduction.

## Introduction Tips To Remember:

1. When attending social events, make an effort to meet people you do not know. Do not hesitate to introduce yourself by saying, "I don't believe we've met. I'm Jan Smith." Self-introductions do not require a courtesy title before your name. If you are at a business event, it is appropriate to say what firm or organization you are with.

2. Do smile, make eye contact and look approachable. It is a proven fact that people react positively to smiles, even babies. Smiles are disarming and make you appear approachable and friendly. If you can stand during introductions, always stand and shake hands firmly without squeezing. A proper handshake lasts about three seconds with two or three pumps; palm-to-palm with your

hand perpendicular to the ground. If your palm is upturned, it may subconsciously signal submissiveness and a downward palm, dominance. At social events, hold your drink in your left hand to avoid damp, cold handshakes.

**Conversation Skills**

Methods of social interaction can be in many forms. The most basic social interaction is the conversation. A challenge for many, the main point to keep in mind is that conversation is two-way communication. You are sending and receiving information that involves both listening and interchange. A good conversationalist is usually a very good listener.

When you speak, pay attention to your volume, tone and rate. Avoid speaking in a monotone, use correct enunciation, and eliminate vocalized pauses such as, uh, err, and um. When talking with someone, really listen, showing genuine interest, and keep good eye contact. Be aware of your body language; non-verbal communication is very powerful. In fact, the majority of our messages are communicated non-verbally and through facial expressions. Dr. Albert Mehrabian, a noted researcher, found the total impact of a message is about 7 percent verbal, 38 percent tone and inflection, and 55 percent nonverbal expressions. In a group setting, remember to address everyone within the group, not just one or two people.

**Conversation Tips:**

1. It is rude to interrupt and one error people often make in conversations. Never ask prying or embarrassing questions such as how much things cost, what someone makes, if their hair is really

theirs, or if they go to alcohol anonymous. Do not gossip or use profanity. Steer the conversation to an interesting topic, getting the attention away from the gossip.

2. Know when to talk business and when to talk pleasure, and do not talk about your health or the health issues of anyone else. Avoid off color jokes, and controversial or emotional subjects.

3. Do not hold long, loud conversations on your cell phone in public.

**Letters, Notes and E-mails**

Our approach to communication is constantly evolving; we may write letters, notes, e-mails or text messages. When a personal **letter** is appropriate, write about what you have in common with the recipient, keeping the tone conversational. Personal letters are often more touching than conversations. And remember, they may be kept for years for many eyes to see.

**Notes** can work magic when you are thinking about someone or for a special occasion. When sending notes, here are a few points to remember:

1. Know your relationship with the recipient. Is the recipient your intimate friend, someone you would like to know better, or someone you barely know? Is the occasion sharing joy or are you offering condolences? This will determine the type of note or card you send.

2. When writing an informal note with a monogram in the center of the page, do not write anything on the front of it. Place a short note inside, under the fold.

3. Within a week, send handwritten thank-you notes if you were an overnight guest, dining guest or received a gift. When traveling on vacation, do not wait until you get back home to send the thank you. If you can, try and send the note within 48 hours, or as soon as you get to your next location. A thank-you note expresses gratitude and makes others feel appreciated, and it is good manners. Failure to promptly send a thank-you note is considered a social insult.

4. There are greeting cards for almost any occasion. When selecting the cards, do use discretion and tact and always think about the person you are sending the card. You would not want to send a "get well soon" card to someone with a terminal illness. When sending pre-printed special occasion cards, personalize the card with a short handwritten message.

**E-mail** is ideal for casual correspondence and is used by everyone from children to grandparents. When sending e-mails, do not forget your "Netiquette." Use the subject line, be clear, brief, use the lower and upper case letters, and correct grammar. All capital letters LOOKS AS IF YOU ARE SHOUTING. Use the spell checker and delete any unwarranted messages. Read your e-mail before hitting the send button, printing it out, if necessary.

1. Do not pass around e-mail addresses of others without their permission. Do not send the latest joke or chain letter to everyone on your e-mail list. Use the BCC when sending to multiple recipients.

2. Do not include gossip, send financial or sensitive information, or get too romantic in e-mails.

**Formal and Informal Invitations**

Today's hostess may invite guests in writing, orally, e-mail or on the internet. Formal invitations should be engraved, mailed, and may include a reply card or be marked "R.S.V.P.", meaning, "*Répondez s'il vous plait,*" (French for, "Please respond.") Informal invitations can be purchased fill-in cards, written on informal notepaper, or written on a folded monogram note. Invitations should include when the event will start and end, appropriate attire and location of the event. Invitations are usually sent two weeks before the event. On occasion, some casual invitations are sent with a week's notice, and more formal invitations, such as weddings, are sent one month before.

**If You Are The Recipient, You Should:**

1. Reply promptly in the manner the invitation is received. If it is a formal invitation, the R.S.V.P. should be to an address, never a telephone number. If you are unable to attend, briefly state the reason for the refusal in your reply. Two common reasons are previous engagement and out of town. It is not necessary to include the hour and place, but be sure to include the date. If a telephone number follows the R.S.V.P on an informal invitation, it is proper to promptly reply by telephone. If the R.S.V.P. is omitted on an informal invitation, it means your hostess is assuming you will attend if you are able; a reply isn't necessary. You are only required to respond to "Regrets only," if you are not attending.

2. Do not be late or too early when attending events. Arrive at least 15 minutes early.

3. If you bring flowers as a gift, have them already arranged in a simple vase. Good gifts to bring are exquisite gourmet foods and wines. If you break something, offer to pay for it.

**Appropriate Attire**

If your invitation is to a formal event, it normally means very dressy formal eveningwear. Formal attire rules are similar to black tie, although slightly less dressy. When you receive an invitation that reads "Black tie," in conservative areas it means tuxedos for men and formal floor-length dresses for women. In some parts of the country it means a dress or attractive evening suit of any length or style. When an invitation reads "White tie," women must wear a floor length gown and their best jewelry and men full evening regalia (black tail coat tuxedo, white tie, vest and shirt). For informal or semi-formal events, women may wear a dressy suit in evening fabric, a short cocktail dress or a long skirt and blouse. Once required, gloves are now fancy accessories and may be worn whenever one wishes. If you are invited to a dinner or cocktail party and you are not sure what to wear, ask the hostess what is the appropriate attire.

**Name Tags and Corsages**

1. If you are wearing a nametag, place it on the upper right side of your chest about four inches below the shoulder. This makes it easy to see when shaking hands during introductions.

2. When you wear a corsage, you may pin it to the left shoulder, to the waistline of a dress, to a purse or make it into a wristband.

**The Entertaining and Dining Experience**

The dining experience requires a whole set of etiquette procedures, and gives the hostess and guest an opportunity to show off good manners. The fundamentals of setting a formal table and informal table are similar. When setting a table, solids are to the left and liquids are to the right. A simple way to remember this is bread, meal, and water (BMW). Place the dinner plate one inch from the edge of the table. Flatware is aligned at the bottom and placed in order of use from the outside in. Forks are placed to the left of the place plate and knives to the right, with the cutting edge toward the plate. The oyster fork is the only fork placed to the right across the soup spoon or parallel with the knives. The dessert fork and spoon are above the dinner plate, with the bowl of the spoon facing left and fork below facing right. Place glasses in order of use, the glass farthest to the right is a sherry glass, white wine glass is next, behind the white wine glass is the red wine glass, the largest glass is the water goblet which sits above the dinner knife, and behind it to the right is the champagne glass. The butter plate is placed above the forks with the knife across the top, handle to the right with the edge of the blade toward the user. The napkin is to the left of the forks or on the dinner plate. Let's look at a formal and informal table setting.

**Formal Table Setting**

**Informal Table Setting - Bread, Meal, Water (BMW) Placement**

**Basic Table Manners to Remember:**

1. If you have not met your dinner partners, introduce yourself and talk with those on each side of you. Keep your purse, briefcases and other foreign matters off the table. Place your napkin lengthwise on your lap with the fold facing your waist. Use your napkin only to dab food particles discreetly from around your mouth. Say excuse me and place your napkin on your chair when you must excuse yourself during the meal. After the meal, place the napkin loosely, not refolded, at the left side of your place setting. Never place the napkin on your plate. You can rest your wrists on the table, but no elbows on the table.

2. So your hands will not warm your wine, hold wineglasses where the stem and the bowl join.

3. Dishes will be presented at your left and passed to the right. Never reach over someone's plate; ask for the items to be passed to you. Do not begin eating until all the people around you have been served, or as instructed by the hostess. Use your silverware for its specific use from outside in. Do not wipe your silverware with your napkin. If not clean or you drop it, request another from the waiter or hostess. Once used, utensils do not go back on or touch the table. During the meal, the knife is placed at the top of your plate with the sharp edge facing toward you. Cut your meat, fish or chicken bite size one piece at a time. Completely chew and swallow before you cut another piece. At the end of the meal, place your knife and fork side by side at **10/4**; the knife facing you with the sharp blade in and fork tines up to the left of the knife. This signals you are finished. Do not rearrange your place setting.

4. If you must complain in a restaurant about cold food, wrong orders, dirty silverware, etc., do so courteously with a warm smile. Do not make a fuss. You may get the servers attention by looking at the server and quietly saying "Waiter" or "Waitress." If they are across the room, you may raise your hand no higher than shoulder level to get their attention.

5. Place the pad of butter on your bread plate; break a small piece of bread and butter separately using your butter knife. Do not put your coffee spoon in the sugar dish. If there is no saucer, leave the iced tea spoon in your glass, not on the tablecloth. You may place sugar packets on the tablecloth or under the coffee cup saucer.

6. When you have food in your mouth, do not talk or drink. Chew with your mouth closed.

7. Turn off or silence all electronic devices before entering a restaurant. If you forget to turn off your cell phone, and it rings, immediately turn it off. Do not answer the call.

8. If you need to remove gristle, bone or seeds from your mouth, remove it the way it entered and place it discreetly on your plate. If you cannot remove it discretely, or you must burp, blow your nose, pick your teeth, groom, put on make-up, or perform other bodily functions, excuse yourself from the table and go to the restroom. Never use toothpicks in public.

9. The rule of thumb is the person that does the inviting usually pays. You can make it clear by arranging to pay beforehand, or telling your guest, "I would like to buy you lunch."

## Tipping

10. Tipping is a preference and is given when an individual performs a service for you. Carry cash for tips, and when giving the tip smile and say, "Thank you." For excellent service, tip 15 to 20 percent of the before-tax amount to waiters, waitresses or bartenders; hairstylists and manicurist 15 to 20 percent; doorman $1 or $2 per bag; if he hails you a cab $1 or $2; parking valet $1 or $2; taxi trips 50 cents or 15 percent of the meter reading for longer trips.

## Miscellaneous Manners to Remember:

11. Always remember to be courteous and say "thank you" and "please" when appropriate.

12. Do identify yourself when answering the phone or placing a call, enunciating and speaking clearly. Leave brief messages on answering machines, speaking slowly and clearly when you leave your number. Do not call a personal residence before 9:00 a.m. or after 10:00 p.m. If you dial a wrong number, apologize to the person who answers. It is rude to just hang up.

13. Nothing is more unacceptable socially as poor grooming and hygiene. Be neat, clean and well groomed at all times and never wear curlers or chew gum in public. If you smoke, be considerate of others. When flying, do not fall asleep, snore or snuggle on the stranger next to you. If they do not want to talk, leave them alone and keep quiet; and that goes for the movies and theater. Cover your mouth when you sneeze in public and say, "Excuse me."

14. If friends split, say nothing about their partner; support your friend by listening. When a friend has a terminal illness or someone close to them dies, promptly let your friend know you are thinking about them. Do what you can to comfort and assist them with sensitivity.

There are many situations you will encounter in a lifetime. Where there are no rules or guidelines, think about how you would like to be treated and let common sense, respect and consideration for others be your guide. Relax, be yourself, and keep smiling!

**Recommended Reading:**

*Amy Vanderbilt Complete Book of Etiquette* rewritten by Nancy Tuckerman and Nancy Dunnan

*The Etiquette Advantage in Business* by Peggy Post and Peter Post

*The Art of Civilized Conversation* by Margaret Shepherd with Sharon Hogan

*Notes:*

## ABOUT THE AUTHOR

### Micki K. Jordan, MLDR

Micki Kremenak Jordan is a mentor, trainer and coach. She has held a variety of corporate management positions over the past 25 years. She has participated on Visioning and Strategic Planning Teams, Leadership Teams and in Training and Development of staff.

Micki has a Bachelor of Science Degree in Sociology from the University of Iowa. After several years in the corporate world she obtained her Masters of Arts in Leadership from Bellevue University, Bellevue, NE. Micki is certified in Diversity Training, Public Speaking and Professional Coaching and holds the Certified Insurance Councilor Designation. She is a member of the Professional Woman Network (PWN) serving on their International Advisory Board and the National Association of Female Executives (NAFE).

Her passion is assisting others to recognize their true potential. She has written chapters entitled "Living Your Values" and "Mirror Image", that may be found in the PWN publications *"Women's Survival Guide for Overcoming Obstacles, Transition and Change"* and *"Women's Journey to Wellness: Mind, Body & Spirit."* She also has chapters entitled "Super Vision" in the book *"Overcoming the Superwoman Syndrome"* and "Are you a Shadow or a Light" in *"Women as Leaders: Strategies for Empowerment & Communication"*. Her latest chapters are "Macho Man: The Importance of Character" in *"The Young Man's Guide For Personal Success"* and "Being You: Eliminating Outside Influences" in *Emotional Wellness for Women Volume III.* All books are part of the PWN library.

This chapter is dedicated with lots of love and hugs to my parents, Ruth Kremenak, and the late Charlie Kremenak. Their lives demonstrate how to remain ageless as you journey through life. I learned how to enjoy and explore the world around me while never being satisfied with the status quo. It is also dedicated to my husband, John. Without his support and encouragement these chapters would never have been written.

*Contact:*
Micki K. Jordan
863 Gleamstar Ave.
Las Vegas, NV 89123
702-463-5786
mk.jordan@yahoo.com

## THIRTY-SIX

# FOREVER YOUNG: BABY BOOMERS REDEFINE AGING

**By Micki Jordan**

*"Youth is not a time of life;*
*It is a state of mind.*
*It is not a matter of rosy cheeks, red lips and supple knees;*
*It is a matter of the will, a quality of imagination, a vigor of the emotions.*
*It is the freshness of the deep springs of life."*
—Samuel Ullman

There are 78 million boomers born between 1946 and 1964. Research is showing that this is an ageless generation. Boomers tend to look and act twenty years younger than people use to act at the same age. Many within this group want to do as much as possible and to get as much as they possibly can. Many are not thinking of retirement, but of changing careers. Their attitude comes from their spirit and determination. They are determined to actively enjoy more years than prior generations. Lifestyle interests involve health and fitness activities.

The Boomers are the first generation to grow up with an emphasis on exercising. They continue to enjoy the same sports they participated in in their 20's and 30's. You will find them on ski slopes, playing pick up basketball games or touch football on Sunday. They will be found playing soccer or company sponsored softball. Tell them they are "too old" for the game and they will laugh at you. Often times they are in better shape and more competitive then the younger players on the team. They are driven to compete.

*"Age is only a number."*—Lexi Starling

The Boomers are reaching a new stage in life. As more are approaching retirement age, it is actually a different time of "re". It is a time for redirection, reinvention, and rejuvenation. Many are rekindling their dreams from their youth. There is a determination not to get old.

Through out their lives, their most dominant characteristic has been their youthful attitude toward life. Youthfulness means continuous exploration and reinvention. It is the opposite of acting, thinking or being old. For the Boomer, being old involves closure; it involves convention and tradition. Being old would mean being pigeonholed by one's age. Youthfulness involves innovation and energy. It means being open to new possibilities at each stage in life.

No matter the year they were born all Boomers believe in these things:

1. **Youthfulness** – an ageless involvement with an active, spirited and exuberant life.
2. **Impact** – having a mission to make a difference.
3. **Possibility** – continued personal development built upon the feeling of empowerment.
4. **Fun** – the spirit of life is to have fun. It is central to the Boomer lifestyle.

*"I'm not denying my age, I'm embellishing my youth."*—Tamara Reynolds

**Youthfulness**

To maintain their youthfulness, the Boomer wants to remain flexible, adaptable, curious, questioning, discovering and continually learning. Age, it is felt, should not be a limiting factor on the endless opportunities available. It isn't age that stops you, it is your belief you can't that does. Can't isn't part of the Boomers thought process, just as old is not. Because the Boomer doesn't want to live long being old, they remain in an age-less middle age. They would like to be in their middle age for as long as possible. This approach is what allows them to handle their lives.

Naomi Judd said, *"Sixty is the new 40…or less."* The Boomer feels they are just "too young" to do nothing. They feel the need to stay active, and by being active, they will maintain their youthfulness. It might be said we are growing "whole" instead of growing old. We are entering the youth of our older age.

What are you doing to maintain your youthfulness?

1. ______________________________

2. ______________________________

3. ______________________________

4. ______________________________

5. ______________________________

*"Don't grow old, no matter how long you live."*—Albert Einstein

**Impact**

A big part of a Boomer's life is staying engaged. There is a belief they can have an impact and that they can make a difference. The Boomer does not feel that aging will or should slow them down in what they want to do. They believe as an individual they can make a difference. They also have a strong sense of personal responsibility. They are determined to leave the world a better place.

The Boomers have the highest rate of volunteerism of any generation. They volunteer more for the social interaction than from a sense of obligation. They volunteer because of social, self-development, self-esteem or because of leisure focused motivations. The favorite volunteer activity is working with youth, being involved in 4-H or scouts or youth sports. Their reasoning comes from the opportunity to try something new, the unpredictability of young people, and the opportunity to provide information or to mentor someone. It also is an opportunity to be involved in something that makes you feel good.

In what ways would you like to make an impact?

1. ______________________________

2. ______________________________

3. ______________________________

4. ______________________________

5. ______________________________

*"Beautiful young people are accidents of nature, but beautiful old people are works of art."*— Eleanor Roosevelt

**Possibility**

The Boomer is passionate about what they can do. They bring "passion" to those things they "feel" are important to them. It is as if they are heading into a second adulthood. It is the time where many are starting a business, launching a new career, following a dream that has been waiting for them to pursue. The traditional thought of retirement and having idle time is not part of the Boomer's make-up. They don't recognize retirement

The future holds another life opportunity, not the prospect of reducing life experiences. They will work and play until they are no longer able. It is time to redirect their focus. It is time to rediscover the dreams of their youth and what was their heart's desire. It is time to re-evaluate what is important in their lives and to go for it.

What do you want to do in your second adulthood?

1. ______________________________

2. ______________________________

3. ______________________________

4. ______________________________

5. ______________________________

*"At twenty we worry about what others think of us; at forty we don't care what others think of us; at sixty we discover they haven't been thinking of us at all."*— Author Unknown

**Fun**

Boomers believe if you are engaged in your life and you are having fun with your life, you will be healthy. Good health is about feeling vital, feeling invigorated, feeling alive.

To them, health and wellness is a combination of physical, emotional and spiritual fixes. It is this fix-it mentality that leads them to believe whatever remedy will be needed will be available when the need arrives. They reason that problems can be fixed, but they cannot recover lost time or missed opportunities.

Rather than just trying new restaurants, you will find the Boomer off to a new country. Their idea of being active is to be running, skiing or traveling. Boomers are buying RV's and are off to explore the country. There are Adult Camps and Elderhostel programs for the travelers. There are Adult Sports Leagues. Entire communities are being developed for the Active +55 Adult. These communities have recreational facilities, clubs, restaurants, trips, and shops, all designed with the Active Youthful Boomer in mind.

Several web sites are being developed that are devoted to the Baby Boomer; web sites for the singles, for health and beauty tips, and online clubs. There are places for trivia and blogs for communicating. If you can think of a subject involving the Boomer, you can probably find it online.

What are some activities you would like to do for fun?

1. ______________________________

2. ______________________________

3. ______________________________

4. ______________________________

5. ______________________________

*"Remember, you don't stop laughing because you grow old. You grow old because you stop laughing."*— Benjamin Franklin

**Forever Young**

Age is an attitude and that attitude is a frame of mind. The Boomer is continually going through a process of repurposing their lives. They will reinvent whatever rules necessary to get what they want. A desire to stay involved drives their passions. Because of the number of Boomers, some 78 million or one in four Americans, their force and influence cannot be ignored. If all of the Boomers in New York City started their own city, it would be the fourth largest city behind New York, Chicago and Los Angeles. Their youthfulness is part of a multifaceted attitude about their life. Being youthful involves not acting or thinking or being old.

By not getting old, the Boomer has found they can stay connected and influential. They can continue to matter, which is critically important to them. Following fads is not their style. They are not conformists. They will find new, original ways to continue to evolve. They are not followers. Their aim is to continue to have impact, not to surrender. Their future involves reengagement, not retirement. The Boomer is not uncomfortable with change or trying something new.

Wanting to get something done now, they take care of their immediate needs. They don't want to wait for the future; they want to be making a difference for themselves today. They feel there is too much left to accomplish. The Baby Boomer will age, but be assured they will NOT get old!

**Websites for the Boomers Enlightenment and Enjoyment:**

www.naabw.com – National Association of Baby Boomers

www.boomerwomenspeak.com

www.bbhq.com – Baby Boomer Headquarters

www.babyboomernews.com

www.fiftyandfuthermore.com

www.boomspeak.com

www.boomergirl.com

www.eons.com

www.boomj.com

# ABOUT THE AUTHOR

**PAMELA THOMPSON**

Ms. Thompson's nearly thirty years' experience in education spans teaching grades K through 12, guidance counseling and administration. She has instructed in literature, public speaking, writing, and drama. Her strengths are in research, development and presentation, and she has been recognized for her work in professional development and incentive programs. A self-taught artist, Ms. Thompson enjoys teaching other adults to draw as well as continuing to develop her own skills, recently winning a regional award for mixed media art.

Thompson is a new addition to the PWN family and is in the process of developing a seminar business geared to the boomer generation going through new transitions. In addition, she plans to offer her writing and artistic skills to other PWN members by editing, revising, ghost writing and illustrating their self -published books.

Ms. Thompson brings experience, knowledge and entertaining wit to her presentations, accessing the mind-body-spirit connection while managing to stay grounded and practical in her approach.

*Contact:*
Pamela Thompson
613 8th Avenue
Dayton, KY 41074
thompson.pam@insightbb.com
www.protrain.net

## THIRTY-SEVEN

# ROLE MODELS FOR INDEPENDENCE

**By Pamela Thompson**

My father used to go to Saturday matinees in the late 30's to watch two cartoons, a newsreel and a Tom Mix double feature. Adding a soft drink and a bag of popcorn, he still had a nickel change from his quarter when he returned home. The rest of the day he played "cowboys" with his brothers, no doubt running off his sisters who were "girls" and therefore technically eliminated.

With the advent of television, it was inevitable that cowboys would find their way to the small screen, as well. We boomers watched The Lone Ranger, Hopalong Cassidy, the Cisco Kid, Sky King and everyone's favorite, Roy Rogers. But something was different about Roy's program. Roy had a grown woman on the show, and she didn't stay home on the ranch cooking for the hired hands and raising a bunch of kids. She was a COWGIRL!

Yes, Dale Evans was very likely the first independent female role model we boomer girls had. Our mothers had some independence during WWII working in factories, waiting for our fathers to return from the front, but by the time we were born most of our moms were full-time housewives and mothers. Television reinforced this traditional role with characters like June Cleaver, Donna Reed and Jane Wyman.

How exciting, then for us to see a bonafide cowgirl on television! She rode a horse; she shot a gun; she lassoed bad men. All my life I was taught to fear big animals, guns and bad men because they might hurt me and here was a woman who looked fear in the face and said, "DRAW PARDNER!"

In addition, Roy and his sidekick listened to Dale's ideas. She often came up with the plan that the men carried out with her assistance. It was fun to watch this woman outsmart crooks and thieves with brains over brawn, and she always had a spunky retort and a wink to go with it.

Our mothers, while working in the factories during the war, had donned male attire to do the job. However, once back home most returned to housedresses and aprons, encouraged by the aforementioned June Cleaver and friends. Dale Evans had her typical cowgirl attire and it did include a fringed skirt, but when riding Buttermilk, chasing bad guys or climbing over rough terrain, she wore pants! I wasn't even allowed to wear pants on the playground at school, so this was pretty neat to me. Even when she wore a skirt, she might be shooting a rifle. There is a joke that says, "What is so great about Fred Astaire? Ginger Rogers did everything he did backwards and in high heels!" So, what is so great about Roy Rogers? Dale did everything he did wearing a skirt and flawless makeup!

Today, women who are role models for independence have a true Cowgirl Spirit. What are the qualities of this spirit? Let's reflect on Dale and find out.

**The Cowgirl Spirit**

**She Is Courageous. Dale bravely faces life and her opponents. She doesn't give up when the going gets tough.** Don't ever think for one minute that Dale wasn't afraid when she was backed into a corner, but courage is not the absence of fear. It is bravery in the face of it. What is easy for one person may take great courage for another. We each must travel our own trails, and whether you need courage to go back to school, start a business, leave a bad marriage, or just to retire and rest awhile, you can be afraid and do it anyway. Cowgirls are courageous.

**She Is Honest. Dale stands on the side of truth and justice.** If you have ever been tempted to be dishonest or have fallen prey to it, no doubt you saw some disadvantage in the end. Maybe you even got away with it, but you knew that you had compromised your integrity. That is a high price to pay. Honesty starts on the inside. Know yourself and be true to that self. Take off the masks. The bad guys don't want to be recognized for who they really are, so they hide behind masks. You are not "bad" but you may not want your true self known out of fear of rejection or low self-esteem. When you value yourself first, others will honor that integrity in you. Cowgirls are honest.

**She Is Loyal. Roy knows she's "got his back."** Along with honesty comes loyalty. We know to whom we owe our faithfulness. We don't switch sides depending on the advantage it may give us. We play fair and square and stay true. This is the Cowgirl's Code. Cowgirls are loyal.

**She Is Skilled And Wise. Dale had to learn to rope and ride and shoot. She uses her skills and wisdom to be successful.** If you have a dream, then to follow that dream you may need to learn more skills. If you have a desire to heal the sick or to save the environment or to teach the elderly to read, you may have to sharpen your skills. On the other hand, wisdom comes with age and experience. This you have. Combine this with your newly acquired and practiced skills and success can be yours. Cowgirls are smart and wise.

**She Takes Calculated Risks. Dale, being skilled and smart, trusts herself to make wise choices.** If we are wise and skilled, we then can trust our decisions. So often we women second and third and fourth guess ourselves out of fear of being wrong or offending others. But at this point in our lives we usually are less concerned with the opinion of others and use our skills, wisdom and courage to move forward. Cowgirls take risks.

**She Doesn't Limit Herself. Dale doesn't say she can't just because she is a woman or in a certain time or place.** We may feel a bit out of touch with the pace of life in these times and want to excuse ourselves and hide. I resisted being computer literate as long as possible and finally had to "be brave and smart" and get with the program. It can be intimidating to try new things, but the advantages can be amazing Cowgirls are unlimited.

**She Is Confident. Dale knows she has what it takes to accomplish her tasks.** All of us will experience failure, but we use those failures as points of learning and sources of wisdom. Thus, even failure contributes, in the long run, to our confidence. Cowgirls are confident.

**She Has Heart. Dale is willing to accept help, and she compassionately helps others.** Many are able to give help but are too proud to receive it. See how gracious and grateful others are at your giving and how much joy it gives you. Allow yourself to receive graciously and gratefully and know you are still giving by the joy that is expressed. Cowgirls give and receive compassionately.

**She Is Forward Thinking And Open Minded. Dale knows it takes all kinds of people and ideas to tame the Wild West.** As you journey the trails of your life, you will meet many interesting characters. They won't all look like you or think like you or believe as you do. But the sheepherders and the cattle ranchers have to figure out a way to get along. Put a fence around your land, but put gates in it. Cowgirls are open minded, forward thinkers.

**She Is Spunky. Dale can laugh at herself and the ironies of life.** Then, of course, on some days everything can go wrong. So, you go to bed, cover up your head, and in the morning laugh it off. Amidst all of these sterling qualities, one can become overly serious and pressure oneself to be the "Darling of the West." Be spunky – laugh! Cowgirls see the humor in life.

So we see that the Cowgirl Spirit is not limited to a bygone era or a geographical place. As we look back in American history, other names of "official Cowgirls" easily come to mind: Eleanor Roosevelt, Rosa Parks, Kathryn Hepburn, Florence Nightingale, Clara Barton, Margaret Sanger…and more recently Gloria Steinem, Sally Ride, Oprah Winfrey, Condoleezza Rice, Hilary Clinton, Anita Hill… and you can add many more who have influenced and continue to influence women of all ages. Of course, in our own towns, churches, organizations and families, many more cowgirls tackle the open ranges before them: teachers, nurses, lawyers, doctors, pilots, ministers, scout leaders, counselors, therapists, librarians, bankers, and others.

We are all still cowgirls in our hearts. I can look back in my memory to my red and white cowgirl outfit at age eight. I had a white hat, a pistol, and lots of fringe. When we were eight years old, we had all of those cowgirl qualities, didn't we? Weren't you brave, and loyal, and honest, and confident and spunky? I was. But I lost some of that over time. It may not be the Wild West anymore, but we could use a little of that Wild Cowgirl Spirit that our foremothers had. So, let's build our confidence by getting back on that horse and check our own cowgirl qualities by completing these sentences.

**Exercise:**

I Have The Cowgirl Spirit Because:

1. I am courageous when_______________
2. I am honest when _______________
3. I am loyal when_______________
4. I have the skills I need when _______________
5. I use my intellect when _______________
6. I am wise when _______________
7. I make wise decisions when_______________
8. I make smart choices when _______________
9. I take calculated risks when_______________
10. I don't limit myself when_______________
11. I am confident when _______________
12. I have compassion when _______________
13. I receive compassion when _______________
14. I am forward thinking/open minded when _______________
15. I am spunky when_______________

I'll bet you didn't know you had so much cowgirl spirit! Of course, you might just be a tenderfoot in some areas, so let's finish these sentences to see where you may want to spruce up a bit.

**Exercise:**

To Have More Cowgirl Spirit:

1. I want to be more courageous about ______________________
2. I want to be more honest about/with ______________________
3. I want to be more loyal to ______________________
4. I want more skills in ______________________
5. I want to use my wisdom in/for ______________________
6. I want to take more risks in ______________________
7. I want to stop limiting myself in/about ______________________
8. I want more confidence in/for/with ______________________
9. I want to have more compassion toward ______________________
10. I want to be able to receive more ______________________
11. I want to be more forward thinking about ______________________
12. I want to be more open-minded about ______________________
13. I want to be spunkier when ______________________

All of this leads us to say, I want to be more independent. I want to be more ME. I want to be a 21$^{st}$ Century Cowgirl!

Many of our independent women role models have been members of our own boomer generation. We have looked at our contemporaries and said, "If she can, then why can't I?" Our own friends and family and coworkers along with great women of the past and present have inspired us. We, in turn, will inspire others with this spirit of independence. Each day more women are stepping out independently to make an impact on society. Our future should no longer be in a man's world. Nor do we want only a woman's world. We need to be "pardners," just like Roy Rogers and Dale Evans (who kept her own last name by the way!).

Shortly after this book is released, we may have the first woman President of the United States of America. That beats Dale Evans by a country mile! If Hilary doesn't make it, she will have blazed a trail for others to follow, quite often in hostile territory. If she does make it, she has a long hard ride ahead, but she'll be fine. She's a Cowgirl!

"Happy Trails to you!"

*Notes:*

# ABOUT THE AUTHOR

## Leanne Norwood

**Leanne Norwood** is president and founder of Synergy Consulting Group; an organization specializing in improving and enhancing the lives and images of their clients.

Leanne is certified in areas such as self-esteem, image and branding, coaching, and marketing strategies. She's an active member of Professional Woman Network offering training and educational seminars worldwide. The workshops and seminars consist of topics such as: Women a Journey to Wellness; Branding and Image; Leadership & Empowerment Skills; Professional Woman Coaching Institute; and Professional Presentation Skills.

Leanne Norwood is President and Founder of Supermom Network which is dedicated to the improvement and well-being of today's moms. She has written several newspaper articles on the issues and challenges today's mothers face, and is in the process of taking this organization globally with inspirational articles, specialized gift items and several books.

Leanne has a diverse financial background consisting of more than twenty years in the financial arena. She is a public speaker, a real estate investor, expert in foreclosure investing, and has written and published '*Real Estate Wealth Toolkit*'.

She is president of the local chapter of Business Network International. Leanne teaches self-esteem awareness to women's abuse shelters in hopes that women will change self destructive patterns of abuse. Her passion is helping others understand and improve their thought process so they can become all they were meant to be.

She attended both Rochester Institute of Technology and the University of Houston where she studied Management Technology and Marketing. Leanne has several awards and honors for her contributions as well as her talents. Her third book '*Emotional Wellness for Women Volume II* and fourth book '*The Young Man's Guide to Personal Success*' will be published in 2008.

*Contact*
Leanne Norwood
(865)680-4410
leanne@cascadesmortgage.com

## THIRTY-EIGHT

# A COMMITMENT TO THE EARTH

**By Leanne Norwood**

It's spring at last and the sights, smells and sounds are like a welcoming friend after a long journey. Spring is the beginning of fragrant flowers, blooming trees, the smell of rain, and the awakening of God's creatures. Summer is the season of relaxation, sand under your feet, the sounds of the ocean rushing to the shore, and children playing and laughing long into the night. Fall is the season of rich, warm colors adorning the trees, hay rides and picnics in the warm midday sun, star gazing in the clear night sky, and animals scurrying to prepare for the approaching cold. Winter is the time for roasting marshmallows in the fire, holiday celebrations with loved ones gathered round, curling up to a good book on a comfortable chair, and the simplicity and peacefulness of the warm indoors.

I truly love our four magnificent seasons and the uniqueness of each one. It would be wonderful to always enjoy God's miracles, but our climate is changing at a rate that may cause these miracles to end. Our world as we know it is changing faster than any other time in history. Our temperatures are rising faster than our world can adjust and the results could be catastrophic to our environment, health and planet. God's miracles are slipping away.

We call this rapid change in our planet global warming. Put simply, global warming is a term used to describe a gradual increase in the temperature of the Earth's atmosphere and its oceans. Scientists say that the earth's temperature may rise by 2.5 – 10 degrees Fahrenheit in just a few years. This would put our temperatures at the highest levels in thousands of years. Studies determined that eleven of the last twelve years have ranked among the eleven warmest years on record. The 1990's were also ranked as the warmest decade on record. But it is not the temperature rise that makes global warming dangerous; it is the speed and its causes that are responsible. Nature is not responsible, humans are and therefore, humans must work together to find a solution.

We are only now understanding the consequences of our "taking the world for granted" way of life and the results are far more devastating then ever imagined. So let's understand what we are doing wrong so we can start learning what to do right!

Global warming is caused by gases released into the atmosphere that trap heat near the earth's surface. This is commonly referred to as the greenhouse effect. This is very similar to an enclosed greenhouse that traps warm air and maintains a certain temperature and humidity level so plants can grow. We are emitting a layer of gases that is also stopping the heat from rising and is therefore warming our environment to an unsafe temperature. But we are not only trapping the warm air, we are trapping unsafe gases as well.

If we continue with this trend, it is highly predictable we will face major environmental and health consequences, which may not be reversible. Some of these predictable events include:

1. Rises in sea levels of as much as three feet, which would flood many countries where millions of people now live.
2. Reductions in rainfall, which would cause crops to die off.
3. Melting of many glaciers, which would affect water supplies everywhere.
4. Increased storms such as hurricanes and increased intensity and frequency.
5. Extinction of animals and plants that cannot adjust to new climates and habitats.
6. New health problems due to changes in temperatures, humidity, and pollution.

So what are we doing wrong? Well, to understand what we need to do right, we first need to understand what we are doing wrong. As I said, global warming is caused by gases being released in our environment. Here are the top two major contributors to the greenhouse effect and global warming.

- Industrial carbon dioxide: This is the biggest culprit, producing 60% of the total gases. Coal burning power plants are the largest U.S. source of carbon dioxide pollution. They produce 2.5 billion tons every year. Automobiles are the second largest source of carbon dioxide, producing 1.5 billion tons annually. The United States produces over 21% of the world's carbon dioxide.
- Residential carbon dioxide emissions are second, producing over 22% of the total emissions. These emissions come from burning

of natural gas, fuel and propane. Household electricity use is also a major contributor. The average U.S. household generates over 45,000 pounds of carbon dioxide each year. Studies indicate that household emissions are often at least as much as those given off by our cars.

Now that we understand what we are doing wrong, we need to focus on what we need to do right. We also need to understand that change happens only when we make it happen, and our world is at a state that change needs to happen quickly. This is a good time for you to understand if you are feeling like you can't make a difference and anything you do won't matter, please stop and understand this simple concept; no single person will stop global warming alone, but by working together and doing your part, you can make a difference. Together, we can change a world! When people unite and call for change, then change isn't just possible, it's unstoppable.

I am purposely not elaborating on the things we've done wrong to this point because we can't change them. We all know we have a world that is not as healthy as it once was and we all share in the blame and responsibility for it. As women, we feel an even greater need to fix the things that are wrong, and we will go to great lengths to rectify a wrong situation, especially if it affects our families. If we do nothing, our children and grandchildren will surely live in a world with increased health risks, poorer air to breathe, and a host of other negative conditions to face. We owe it to them, to their children, and to future generations to proactively correct what we and past generations have done wrong. We have the ability, fortitude and willpower to initiate change. We also have compassion and love and those are mighty forces to be reckoned with. So it's time we lead our households, our circle of influence and ourselves to bring about the necessary changes. Each of us must work smarter and contribute more. To change the world, we most assuredly have to change ourselves.

Here is a list of things we can all do to help change our environment.

**Change Your Light Bulbs.** There are now highly efficient fluorescent light bulbs that last for years, use a quarter of the energy of regular bulbs, and actually produce more light. The cost of these bulbs will be higher at first, but remember there are two other price tags to be concerned with: what you save in energy costs over the bulb's lifetime and what you improve in the environment over the bulb's lifetime. Here's the impact this would have: If every household in the U.S. replaced a burned-out bulb with an energy-efficient one, it would eliminate more than 13 billion pounds of carbon dioxide from entering the atmosphere, which is equivalent to taking a million cars off the road for an entire year. Are you starting to see "the light" on how a small change can make a huge difference?

**Control Your Home's Temperature.** What's the difference between 68 degrees and 70 degrees? Well, you're probably saying 2 degrees and wondering why I'm asking. By changing your thermostat just 2 simple degrees, you can change your electric consumption by 10 percent! Remember that the second leading contributor to global warming is household electricity use, so just a small change in temperature can have a huge impact on our world.

**Beware Of Your Refrigerator.** Your refrigerator is by far the single biggest user of electricity in most houses. It accounts for anywhere from 10 – 15 percent of your electric bill. Again, changing your refrigerators thermostat by 2 degrees will make a huge impact on your bill and our environment. Make sure the doors seal properly, keep the coils clean, and most of all, tell your family to decide what they want before they open the doors. I don't know what is so fascinating to children to make them open the doors and stare inside for hours, but it is a reality nevertheless. Tell them how they can also make a difference by not leaving the doors open while they decide what they want.

**Drive Differently.** This was a hard one for me, as I have been a "hurried" mom for many years. It was all about getting from one place to another as quick as possible. The truth is that anything we can do to improve the fuel efficiency of our cars will have a huge impact on our climate. Changing your driving habits may very well have the single biggest effect on global warming. Combine multiple errands or stops into one trip. Car-pooling is also a great way to keep car mileage down. Keep your car "healthy" by changing the oil when due, tuning up the engine regularly, and checking tire pressure will make a huge difference, not only in our climate, but in our wallet, as well. Learn to slow down. By changing our speed and aggressive driving habits, we can make a big difference and save lives as at the same time. Try to learn to enjoy the trip and just slow down!

**Stop Buying What You Don't Need.** We need to start paying attention to how we spend our money. We need to stop spending just to spend. Every time you buy something, energy was used in making that product. The less you buy, the more you save, energy wise. The old saying "less is more" is absolutely true. The less you buy, the more our world improves. A wonderful side benefit to this is that we might actually have more money! Now that is a novel idea; don't spend everything we make. I think I'll try it!

**Control Your Water And Its Temperature.** Many of us just love those long, hot showers or baths where we barely leave enough hot water for anyone else. If this sounds like you, then try shortening those showers and turn the temperature down a couple of degrees so it doesn't take as much energy to heat the tank. You can also use the energy cycle on your dishwasher and try washing a few dishes by hand so you conserve water and heat. I have found that it takes less time and energy to just wash the dishes in the sink than it does to fill the dishwasher, run it and then empty it. Washing your clothes in warm water, not hot, will help, as well. These three changes can change your energy bill by as much as 50%.

**Unplug Those Lamps, Appliances And Electronics When Not In Use.** Don't just turn off the TV, VCR, coffee pot, etc. – unplug them. Appliances are still using electricity when plugged in, even though they are off. You can save as much as 12% on your electric bill by unplugging things you don't use regularly. Americans alone pay $1 billion a year to power our televisions and VCR's while they're turned off. We use another 1,000 kilowatt hours a year per household by leaving our toasters, coffeemakers, hair dryers, computers, and cell phone chargers, to name a few, plugged in. Unplug to undo!

**The Three R's.** Reduce, reuse and recycle. It takes less energy to manufacture a recycled product than a new one, so if you buy recycled, you help conserve energy. Reuse everything you can, especially those plastic bags from the store, plastic containers you would normally throw out because they cost so little to replace, and plastic and glass bottles you can put to good use after they are rinsed out. Reuse everything you can and come up with other ways to reuse other things in your household. Reduce your purchase power. Don't buy things just to buy them; have a real need for it before you spend your money. Don't clean out your closet and give it to charity so you can replace everything you bought. Always be asking yourself if this is something "I need" or something "I want". If you can do without it, then do so. Remember, everything produced creates energy and is very likely emitting carbon dioxide into our atmosphere. Do your environment and checkbook a favor and reduce your consumption.

**Buy Organic.** There is more than one reason to buy organic. First, it is healthier for you, since it does not use chemical pesticides. Most foods we eat have chemical pesticides sprayed unto the food and into the ground to kill pests. On average, American farmers spray a billion pounds of pesticides on crops each year. When pesticides are used, they not only kill the pests, they kill the microorganisms that keep carbon contained in the soil. When these microorganisms are gone, the carbon is released into the atmosphere as carbon dioxide. Secondly, when the organisms are gone, so are the natural fertilizers in the soil, so chemical fertilizers must be used to replace what is missing. So let's sum this up: I can eat healthier foods, eliminate carbon dioxide from the air, and eliminate chemical pesticides and fertilizers from my diet all by eating organic? What's not to understand about this?

**Stop Using Paper.** Stop the junk mail. Deforestation, cutting down of trees, is responsible for 25 percent of all carbon emissions released into the atmosphere through burning and cutting of millions of acres of trees annually. You can stop much of this by "going paperless" and stopping junk mail. Opt out of as many solicitation mailings and paper catalogs as you can. On average, American households receive 41 pounds of junk mail per year per household. Simple things like communicating by internet instead of faxes or letters can make a big difference. Reuse the backside of paper for notes or shopping lists, etc. Eliminate as much paper as possible from your daily use. A nice side effect of this is a greener world with more beautiful trees to enjoy.

This list contains only ten things you can do to make a difference in your world. With a little more research on your part, you can learn of many more "little" things you can do to cure our unhealthy world.

Read and re-read this list until you are doing all of them. I think you can agree, there is nothing on this list that is difficult, inconvenient or impossible to do. Make this a family affair and educate everyone on what they can do to help. We can make climate friendly choices in our personal lives and we can influence our families, as well. By changing our habits and influencing others to change theirs, we are changing our world one woman at a time. The more we get involved to bring forth change, the safer and cleaner our world will be for our kids and grandkids. We have a voice and we make a difference, one woman at a time.

Remember, we are at this point from one mistake at a time. We can correct this point by one positive action at a time. I pray every day for a better world and together, He will hear our prayers. God's miracle will survive; we will survive.

## ABOUT THE AUTHOR

### MYRALYN STEWART MILLER

Myralyn Stewart Miller is CEO and President of the Stewart Miller Institute For Excellence, Inc. and the Stewart Miller Communication Institute for Excellence, Inc. Myralyn Miller is a speech pathologist, educator and entrepreneur who received her Bachelor of Arts Degree in French Liberal Arts and a Master of Arts Degree in Speech Pathology with a minor in Linguistics. Myralyn did extensive studies in supervision, administration, leadership, speech pathology and accent reduction.

Myralyn Miller is ASHA certified and licensed in the state of Florida and works extensively with children, youths and adults addressing communication disorders and dysphagia. Myralyn has conducted numerous workshops and in-services addressing swallowing, communication skills, developmental milestones, vocal abuse behaviors, accent enhancement, and reimbursement issues.

Myralyn Miller, as an entrepreneur, offers communication skills training at the Kids' Toolbox for Success Summer Camp for children with day and residential programs.

In Myralyn's free time, she creates children's stories, therapy games and speech activities. The proceeds from her themed wall-hangings and totes support scholarships for the summer camp programs. Myralyn is a contributing author five books published by PWN Publishing dealing with communication skills and aging parents. Myralyn served as a board advisor for the Port Gibson Mental Health Center and is an International Advisor of the Professional Woman Network.

*Contact:*
Myralyn Stewart Miller, MA, CCC-SLP
Stewart Miller Institute for Excellence, Inc.
410-09 Blanding Blvd, #303
Orange Park, FL 32073
(904)-537-3629
Stewart Miller Communication Institute for Excellence, Inc.
410-09 Blanding Blvd, #221
Orange Park, FL 32073
678-849-3494
myralyn@smfsuccess.com
www.smfsuccess.com
myralyn@stewartmillercommunication.com
www.stewartmillercommunication.com

THIRTY-NINE

# ROLE REVERSAL

**By Myralyn Miller**

Caregivers are in such demand. As life expectancy increases, changes can be anticipated in social, vocational and medical status. Functional decline, illness and/or disease are possible, which will require personal care. In most cases, the Baby Boomers, considered active, youthful and family oriented, will assume the role. For some, the role of caregiver may become an unwelcome or daunting reality in unchartered waters, while others may view the opportunity as a way to initiate, provide and/or oversee quality care for their elderly parents. Several questions are raised that call for reflections about reversing roles with parents. Why do I have to do this? What is involved in being a caregiver? How will my parents relate to me in this role? The answers depend on your relationship with your parents, your willingness to accept this role, and your perceptions of your capabilities to assume this role. Hopefully thought-provoking reflections about the information, responses and realistic situations will guide you to answer those questions honestly, as you consider embarking on this adventure.

This chapter is dedicated to my parents, Dr. Alfred Stewart, Sr. (90) and Mrs. Iona J. Stewart (88) who demonstrated amazing strength, dignity, fortitude and unrelenting spiritual faith during their daily medical, social and vocational challenges, while they struggled to hold onto their independence and maintain an intact family structure on their own terms. My siblings, Rosalyn, Danita and Edmond courageously walked this path with me as we learned from each other the importance of maintaining a loving family relationship based on a mutual respect of everyone's contribution through shared decision-making while constantly focusing on our parents' safety, security and comfort according to their wishes.

*"Your mother wants me to cook... This is not what I thought it would be like... I don't know what to do."*—Daddy, April, 2006

Daddy's voice was cracking. I knew he was crying; but he did not admit it. I thought, "What can I do to help?" Mama cooked and did all of the chores since age seven and she continued that through the years. At 86, then, she had to be tired. For a few years, when we came home, we cooked, cleaned and filled the refrigerator. At first we thought nothing of it because we thought that it was time for us to "give back" and wait on our parents. We wanted to pamper them. Little did we know that this began the progressive journey on the unmarked path of role reversal with our parents. The journey took us from frequent visits to mail-ordered gourmet meals to part-time assistance to 24/7 care. We experienced the gamut of emotions; but our commitment was steadfast in making sure our parents, who displayed very different personal care and medical needs, were comfortable and safe through creative problem solving, finances, family conferences, and medical consults.

**How Well Do You Know Your Parents and Your Siblings?** As a caregiver, direct or indirect involvement with others is inevitable. Success is dependent upon your siblings' strengths, weaknesses, likes and dislikes, communication skills, medical status and financial constraints. In an informal survey of adult children who assumed the role of caregiver, 78% received support from siblings while 12% did not. Support included periodic visits, money, respite and shared tasks. Stressful situations seemed frequent according to 88% of the informants; but 40% felt that indifference or the sense of being alone at times to manage the parents' care seemed to create ill-feelings, frustration and anger toward the sibling(s). In the midst of schedule conflicts, family obligations, opinion differences, historical disagreements, finance constraints, work status, personality, and medical issues, stress and unexpected emotions may occur. How you respond to these challenges is important. Your relationship with your siblings will have a consequential impact on your parents' care and/or their response to it. What is important? You want to know what role is best suited for each person involved by anticipating the communication style, attitude, emotions and/or behaviors that may occur during different events throughout the day. Collaborating, resolving issues, follow-through and task completions while maintaining an emotional balance are necessary to be effective during day-to-day activities.

**Discovery Information Assessment:** Determine who will be most effective in the day-to-day care of your parents. Using the checklist below, note how each person responds or reacts to daily routines, topical discussions, or unexpected changes. If the conclusions drawn are based on truthful observations, your data analysis will reflect critical information for judiciously selecting the ideal person for a given situation, task or event to manage your parents' care in a timely and efficient manner. Put **Yes** or **No** by each question.

| | | | | | |
|---|---|---|---|---|---|
| | Are they secretive? | | Are they defensive? | | Do they seem selfish? |
| | Are they trustworthy? | | Do they appear aloof? | | Do they undermine? |
| | Are they fair? | | Do they gossip? | | Are they talkative? |
| | Can they problem solve? | | Are they domineering? | | Are they engaging? |
| | Are they reliable? | | Do they have transportation? | | Are they flexible? |
| | Are they cooperative? | | Will they follow MD's orders? | | Are they cooperative? |
| | Do they attend church? | | Are they reclusive? | | Are they passive? |

**How Well Do You Know Your Parents?** Often, decisions are made based on discussions from years ago on the assumption that those wishes will not change. The following interview questions, presented in the book, *The Christian Women's Guide to_Success,* are being re-visited to confirm that certain wishes about care may change. As Daddy's care needs changed sometimes on a daily basis, knowing what he wanted and how flexible Mama would be during her care was important.

**Interview with Dr. & Mrs. Alfred Stewart, Sr. (12/22/07)**

**Daddy, do you feel up to answering the same questions I asked you a year ago?**

**Daddy:** "Oh! My answers have changed since then."

1. **What are you concerns about aging?**

   **Mama:** "I thank the Lord I'm aging."

   **Daddy:** "Aging can be a blessing. It can be a curse."

2. **What are your blessings?**

   **Mama:** "I'm blessed with four children. I haven't had to pull out any from jail...I'm still healthy. My husband is in pretty good shape. I'm retired and I'm comfortable."

   **Daddy:** "Everything I have attempted blossomed until this year when all of this (sickness and oxygen deprivation) was hung on me. I wondered if I did something wrong...But maybe before it's over, I'll understand. Maybe...I'll wait for that day. I never had problems. They were solved instantaneously...I am now completely inundated with helpless situations. I still believe all of this will come out of the washing and I'll be cleansed..."

3. **What are your needs?**

   **Mama:** "My needs are sufficiently supplied. I eat what I want. I am comfortable..."

   **Daddy:** "I'm not sure. I have to rest and wait... and there'll be something much better than I can ever do."

4. **What is it that you do not want to do?**

   **Mama: "**Well, I don't do what I don't want to do. I pay someone to do what I don't want to do. I am comfortable with my home that is paid for."

**Daddy**: "I don't want to do anything that gives me a negative relationship with my life's ultimate Guide (God)."

5. **How does your day impact your eating?**

**Mama:** "I eat like I want to. How often? I eat regularly. I try to eat two full meals. I don't like all that eating... My husband is the same."

**Daddy:** "No, it's not the day at all...Loss of taste, loss of mouth digestibility...That's the whole problem... I can't seem to eat much. I try hard... As I chew, my stomach gets full. That's strange, too."

6. **What was the reason for your last doctor's visit? When was it?**

**Mama:** "I don't remember going to the doctor. It might have been going to get my heart and blood pressure checked."

**Daddy:** "It was for discussion...not treatment...What should we do now? It dealt with mobility and getting around and that's when I got the motorized wheelchair."

7. **What is the greatest concern you have?**

**Mama:** "I really don't have one. I'm in my own home. We have a peaceful home...I have missed something I can't find; but I don't worry about it."

**Daddy:** "That I will not miss my Heaven's goal. That's it. I have no other concern. Well! There is a concern. My physical...a physiological concern. I had said whatever was loaned to me would be in place before I march out. I may miss out on that. If I can leave everything in place when I walk away heading for another family life, a spiritual family life, there will be no load on my shoulder."

8. **How do you feel about someone coming to your house to give you assistance?**

   **Mama:** "Well, I'm comfortable...We have someone coming in to help us."

   **Daddy:** "I think it's beautiful. I can't do it, now."

9. **What modifications need to be done to your house to avoid accidents and keep you comfortable?**

   **Mama:** "I don't know of anything because when we discover something, we get it fixed. You have to ask Alfred...Have you come home because of an accident?"

   **Daddy:** "We've removed loose rugs from the floor. Yesterday, you fixed that (transfer shower seat) seat in the tub...Keep needful, purposeful things and get rid of things that have no utility. No matter how attached we were to them when we were younger, get rid of them because we have no use for them...and to me, the sooner, the better."

10. **What would lead you to consider an alternative living arrangement?**

    **Mama:** "I don't know. I have all the comforts I need. Whatever I need, I can hire someone to do the work..."

    **Daddy:** "I would truly have to need that...As long as I don't need it...I'd rather struggle with my needs in this house, even if I have to cover the cost...But if Medicare and some others would do that, I would be happy. I would rather cover the cost until I became a pauper. I wish the same thing for my wife, if she has the same orientation. But, if I can survive and stay active and live within my home, I would."

My heart was full as their comments not only confirmed the inevitable, but reflected very diverse thinking and concerns with significant changes in care that needed to be considered. One seemed to be in denial of circumstances while the other was more spiritual and in tune with them. The picture was clear about their needs, wants and wishes. Listen to them and observe their response and participation behaviors throughout the day. Your credibility as their advocate will be evident as your astute observations result in prompt care plan modifications, if needed.

**Financial Considerations**

Costs can be unbelievable, whether services are provided in-home or at a facility. Very few persons have the deep pockets required to cover the hourly rates that agencies charge for personal care or sitting services. For example, agency fees ranged from $648.00 a month for 12 hours of light housekeeping a week to an estimated $9,408.00 a month for housekeeping, personal care and total care as a live-in. Calculating the yearly cost was an eye-opener. My parents saved all of their life to assist them in their golden years to pay for services that they may otherwise not receive in a timely manner. The down side is the risk of losing quickly everything they saved because of the ineptness of the bureaurocratic and unwieldy medical system. This was a major concern area.

Having, a working knowledge of your parents' financial status and portfolio is necessary in order to organize bank accounts, stocks and bonds, safety deposit boxes and monthly/quarterly bills. Having Power of Attorney (POA) in place is an invaluable tool in handling business concerns timely, when they cannot physically or cognitively take care of their own business. The results of the discovery assessment will give you an idea about their willingness to share their personal and financial information. The following questions need to be answered in order to coordinate and/or manage your parents' financial obligations.

1. What financial arrangements are in place for your parents' care?
2. What is your parents' monthly income?
3. What are your parents' assets and liabilities?
4. What funeral/burial arrangements have been established?

**Searching for Resources:** Many are not prepared to set in place the necessary resources for personal care services and equipment because they do not know where to begin the search. Additionally, locating dependable, competent, and trustworthy caregivers for your parents can be a daunting and time-consuming task, as leads and interviews may go nowhere. Several approaches can make the search less stressful and more productive. Consider the following:

1. Contact admission directors and social workers at hospitals and long-term care facilities for a list of personal care and home health agencies.

2. Communicate with the social worker to discuss discharge plans from a hospital or skilled nursing facility to ensure rehab services, equipment, and products are scheduled prior to your parent's discharge.

3. Get referrals from caregivers in the skilled nursing facility or hospital. All resources or contacts can be a source for a potential in-home care provider.

4. Be honest about your parents' condition(s) and the type of care you need.

5. Interview potential caregivers with open-ended questions and role-play situations to gain insight about their communication skills, attitudes, emotional stability, and caregiver competence.

6. Be astute to avoidance, dishonesty, potential abuse and diligence. Any response that raises a red flag is a reason to tread cautiously with the hiring process. You are not looking for a friend. You want someone to provide quality care.

**Information Gathering Task for Personal Care Assistance:** Every contact is an opportunity to network and put out feelers for a personal care assistant. Be prepared to discuss your search needs and gather information through targeted questions, such as the sample questions listed below. Mark questions that seem appropriate for the service you are seeking to keep you organized and focused on gaining specific answers in order to select the ideal candidate for the job. Record the date, time, information and the person supplying the information in your log book. Transfer pertinent information to a chart (sample below) for comparison to make sound decisions.

| | |
|---|---|
| | What services do you provide? |
| | Does any insurance pay for this? |
| | Do you provide Alzheimer's and Dementia services? |
| | What is included in housekeeping? |
| | Is there medical staff to handle emergencies? |
| | How often are your programs scheduled? |
| | Is the same person scheduled for each visit? |
| | Do you provide transportation to your facility? |
| | Where are you located? |
| | What is your schedule? |
| | What is the cost? |
| | Do you take vitals? |
| | What do you not do? |
| | Describe a typical day. |
| | What are your business hours? |
| | |

| Company/ Name | Service | Cost/Fees | Hours | Caregiver Qualifications |
|---|---|---|---|---|
| Angelic Friends | Personal care, light housekeeping, cooking | $14.00/ hr; minimum of 4 hours | Meets clients' needs | Non-medical; primarily non-licensed; licensed CNA upon request |

**Organize Data:** As caregiver, make every attempt to move seamlessly throughout the day. Create schedules and charts that increase inter-caregiver communication with recorded data as a visual reminder of each day's events about your parents' care and how the day was managed. Make a separate chart for medication, doctors' contact information, appointments, meals for the day, personal care, oral intake, liquid intake, visitors, social activities, etc. Include reasons for any duplicate care, the occurrence of an incident such as slipping on the rug, and comments about how your parents participated during this care, i.e., "was pleasant to caregiver". Add clarity to your documentation. Keep the information accessible for review by siblings, the physician, case manager and/or home care providers to answer inquiries about changes since the last visit.

**Caregiver Challenges:** Baby Boomers are stepping up to the plate and feeling their way through the dark to care for their aging parents, while your parents are counting on them to allay their fears, keep them safe and make them comfortable. Unfortunately, this role reversal carries with it challenges that do not have a how-to manual for troubleshooting, a one-stop location for services and equipment, or a stress-free guarantee. Any situation may impact your lifestyle, your coping skills, your communication effectiveness or your emotional balance. Keeping a daily challenge diary is suggested for collecting situational data for reflection and to change behaviors that yield more effective consequences in similar circumstances. Review the list below and categorize each challenge by placing **(W)** for Work, **(PC)** for Personal Care, **(M)** for Medical, **(C)** for Communication and/or **(EW)** for Emotional Wellness. You may note a pattern and realize that someone else may be better suited to handle that situation while you work on coping behaviors.

___ Not enough time in the day

___ Managing doctor's appointments around work

| | |
|---|---|
| ___ Absences from work | ___ Lost wages |
| ___ Making parent comfortable | ___ Hiring competent and caring persons |
| ___ Internalizing emotions | ___ Uncorroborated swallowing decline |
| ___ Observing declining status | ___ Accepting the inevitable |
| ___ Difficulty chewing | ___ Getting your parent to take medication |
| ___ Witnessing husband do CPR | ___ Witnessing father's death |
| ___ Funeral arrangements | ___ Your parent's grief |
| ___ Insufficient oral intake | ___ Refusing home health services |
| ___ Getting your parent to use the walkie-talkies | |

Reflect on one of the challenges with regard to the impact it has on you and write your response to each question.

1. What about this particular issue makes it a challenge? _________

   ______________________________________________

   ______________________________________________

   ______________________________________________

2. What are some things you could do to minimize or prevent this from being a challenge for you? ______________________

   ______________________________________________

   ______________________________________________

   ______________________________________________

3. What behaviors will be required of you to do this?___________

   ______________________________________________

________________________________________________

________________________________________________

**Engaging Activities:** Communication and social skills play a major part in your parents' daily interactions. A part of your role as caregiver is to ensure that your parents participate in engaging activities that take into consideration their medical status, wants, needs and skills. This may give them a purpose each day, shift their attention, and facilitate their physical, emotional and/or mental health, even if it is for five minutes. The following suggestions can trigger recall of your parents' hobbies and interests as you create a list of activities for their daily communication and social calendar. Have your parents place a mark by the activity they want to do. Schedule diversion activities with their participation; but accept last minute changes or refusals for any reason.

| | | |
|---|---|---|
| Quilting | Computer Tasks | Low Impact Exercises |
| Scrapbooking | Word Search Puzzles | Personal Care Appointments |
| Outings | Diary Entries | Writing Letters or Notes |
| Watching Movies | Golfing | Reading |

**Caregiver Problem-Solving Task:** This is your practice in managing challenging issues and problem solving. Read the situations described below and write a solution for each. **Hint:** Review the chapters written on elderly/aging parents in *The Christian Women's_Guide to Success* and *Emotional Wellness Vol. 1* for suggestions, tips and resources to facilitate decision-making. What is your split-second decision?

1. Your mother has a 9 A.M doctor's appointment today. She has a history of undressing and putting clothes in different locations in the room, if left alone. It's 8: A.M. She's dressed, but not you.
____________________________________________________________
____________________________________________________________
____________________________________________________________

2. Your father complains of a dry mouth; but he has a 1000cc liquid restriction.________________________________
____________________________________________________________
____________________________________________________________
____________________________________________________________

3. You're ready to begin your twelve-hour drive back home; but the person who provides 24/7 coverage has not arrived or called. Your mother is ambulatory, expresses her needs and wants well, and only requires cuing during personal care. ________________________
____________________________________________________________
____________________________________________________________
____________________________________________________________

4. Your father is weak in part due to muscle wastage; but the caregiver places the wash pan, soap and washcloth on the bedside table and walks away. His daughter walks in to say good morning and finds him crying while holding the washcloth. ________________________
____________________________________________________________
____________________________________________________________
____________________________________________________________

5. You need to make a quick trip to the store; so, you leave your mom who has a history of fainting and not breathing, alone at home.____________________________________________
   ________________________________________________
   ________________________________________________
   ________________________________________________

Problems and split-second decisions can occur at any time as you manage day-to-day changes in your parents' medical, social and personal care. How you solve problems and communicate will determine your effectiveness and the outcomes you achieve. Listen to your parents because they are counting on you to be supportive as their advocate, and to help them deal with any healthcare, financial, or living accommodation issues. Keep vigilant. Do your best and have no regrets. This may be your final journey with them during their transition.

*THE JOURNEY CONTINUES!*

*Notes:*

# ABOUT THE AUTHOR

## Kathy Ryan

Kathy Ryan is President and founder of Pinnacle Coaching Group LLC. Pinnacle Coaching Group is committed to helping people reach new heights in their personal and professional lives through specialized one-on-one coaching, restorative retreats and customized group workshops.

Kathy is an accomplished coach, facilitator, trainer, and author with more than 20 years of Human Resources management and coaching experience. She has enjoyed success in environments as diverse as the highly structured world of corporate insurance and the fast paced, fluid atmosphere of entertainment and hospitality. As a Coach, Kathy creates a partnership with her client that empowers them to identify their deepest values, remove obstacles, release worry and fear, and challenge limiting beliefs so they may enjoy the life of their dreams.

With Pinnacle Retreats, Kathy has designed inspirational programs to help nurture and promote emotional and physical wellness. Participants have the opportunity to reconnect with their own unique purpose and to truly listen to their heart's desires. Pinnacle Retreats give you the chance to step out of your busy life and to replenish your spirit. Retreat topics include the power of visioning, handling times of transition, restoring balance, reducing clutter and practicing extreme self care.

A Dickinson College graduate, Kathy received her bachelor's degree in Psychology. She has been coaching for over 20 years, and graduated from Coach U, the oldest coach training institute in the country. She has expertise in using a variety of coaching techniques, such as the Myers-Briggs Type Indicator (MBTI) and 360° Feedback. She earned a Lifetime Certification as a Senior Professional in Human Resources, and is a member of the International Coaching Federation, Society for Human Resources Management, The Professional Woman Network, and National Association of Female Executives.

*Contact:*
Pinnacle Coaching Group LLC.
P.O. Box 772377
Orlando, Florida 32877
(407) 932-0682
kathy@pinnaclecoachinggroup.com
www.pinnaclecoachinggroup.com

## FORTY

# VISIONING: CREATING THE LIFE OF YOUR DREAMS

**By Kathy Ryan**

If you could have any superhero power, what would it be? Would you choose the freedom to fly through the air like Spider-Man, the ability to get people to tell the truth like Wonder Woman, or would you want to try out Superman's ex-ray vision? These are all exciting options! But what if I told you that within each of us lies a power so great that it would rival any of these choices? And better yet, you already have access to this awesome power and you can begin to use it today! I'm talking about the power of Visioning, and it is a process that will help you to create the life of your dreams. Now that's a super power worth having!

**What is Visioning?**

The process of Visioning is based on the fundamental belief that if you can imagine in your mind what it is that you want, and believe that it is possible for you to have it, then you can attract what it is you desire into your material world. Once you begin to understand and practice the concept that "thoughts become things", and commit to taking whatever action is necessary to support the creation of your desires, you are well on your way to achieving every goal you set for yourself in life.

The process of Visioning is really quite simple and it accelerates the achievement of any goal in a number of very important ways:

1. It jumpstarts the creative powers of your subconscious mind.

2. It focuses your brain, which activates your *reticular activating system* (RAS) and you begin to notice things and resources that were always there, but you may have missed them before. For example, have you ever decided to buy a specific brand and make of car, only to see it everywhere on the road, when before you never saw one? That is your brain's RAS in action.

3. It acts as a magnet and begins to attract the people, resources and opportunities to you that you need to achieve your goals.

There are a number of ways for you to begin to use Visioning to create and attract your heart's desires. In this chapter, I am going to take you through a two-step process of visualization and creating a vision board. Each step is easy to do, and when used in conjunction with one another, these tools are an incredibly powerful creative force that will accelerate the achievement of your goals and success in life.

**Step One: Visualization**

For many years, researchers have studied the effects of visualization on success. Olympic athletes were tested to see exactly what brain functions they used when performing their event in real life. These results were compared to the athlete's brain waves when they just "visualized" performing that same activity. What the researchers found was astounding. The brain used the exact same process for both activities! In other words, there was no difference to the brain between visualizing something and actually doing it. That is the key to using this super power of ours, creating something in our imagination is just as powerful as doing it in reality.

To harness the power of visualization, you need only spend 10-15 minutes a day creating the visual image of what you want in your mind. Here are some things to keep in mind, in order to maximize the effects of this process:

1. Make the images as clear and detailed as you can. To enhance the effects, add sound, smells, tastes and feelings to your visualization. The more feelings, excitement and energy you can create during your visualization, the more powerful the results will be.

2. Visualize your goal as if it has already been achieved. For example, visualize yourself standing on the porch of your dream home, leading a meeting in your new job, or slipping into that new dress - four sizes smaller than you currently wear! Remember to feel the feelings of the experience, as well.

3. Write down in your journal, or on index cards, your goals and objectives. Review them, affirm them, and visualize them every day.

**Visualization Exercise:**

Let's go through an exercise that will help you to focus on your heart's desires. In your journal or notebook, write down your thoughts as you take a look at five key areas of your life: health, relationships, career/business, spiritual and finances. For each area, use the questions provided to reflect on your current condition, positives and opportunities for change. Use the sentence in bold and italic at the end of the section to help you write an affirming phrase or statement that best describes what your desire or wish is for that area of your life. For example, in the area of health you might write, "I have an abundance of physical and mental energy and I look and feel great. I am perfectly healthy and I am at my target weight of 145 lbs." Let's begin.

1. **Health** – What is my emotional and mental health? Do I have a positive approach to life? What mental activities do I engage in? What are my dominant emotions? What is my current level of physical health? How active am I? Am I at a weight that is appropriate for my age and physical type? How do I feel about my body? ***My dreams and desires have been accomplished in this area. What does it look like?***

2. **Relationships** – Who are the five people I am closest to and what is their attitude toward life? Do they bring out the best in me? Do I have any "toxic" relationships? How do I interact with family members? Are my relationships with friends and family where I want them to be? Is my relationship with my significant other in a healthy place? Is there enough romance in my life? Is there a relationship that is broken or one that I am missing? ***My dreams and desires have been accomplished in this area. What does it look like?***

3. **Career/Business** – Does my current job/position fulfill me? Am I appreciated? Am I satisfied with the money I earn? What is my work environment like? Do I love this type of work? In what ways do I contribute to others? In what way is my work important? If I knew I could not fail, what position/business would I pursue? Am I still growing and learning? ***My dreams and desires have been accomplished in this area. What does it look like?***

4. **Spiritual** – How connected do I feel to a higher power? What kind of spiritual practice do I engage in? What do my religious or spiritual beliefs bring to my life? What places or activities help me to feel inspired and uplifted? Do I feel at peace? ***My dreams and desires have been accomplished in this area. What does it look like?***

5. **Finances** – What is my approach to money management? Do I have a plan for growing wealth? Do I routinely put money into savings and retirement accounts? Do I carry any debt? Do I impulse spend? Do I have a track record of making wise money choices? Do I have the money I need to make my dreams come true? ***My dreams and desires have been accomplished in this area. What does it look like?***

The affirming phrases and statements that you write for each area above are the images you should focus on during your visualization process. Now take 10-15 minutes every day and visualize each of your statements. Make sure you feel the feelings of what it would be like when this dream comes true to increase their impact. Remember to visualize what it ***does*** look like in the future once you achieve your goals and dreams, not what it ***will*** look like.

**Step Two: Vision Boards**

Vision boards are an outstanding way to keep your subconscious working on creating the life of your dreams. Your creative subconscious does not think in words, it thinks in pictures. When you give your brain colorful and emotionally compelling pictures to manifest, it will immediately get to work attracting and seeking out all the necessary elements to bring those pictures to life for you.

Creating a vision board is a very personal process. It is a visual representation of what you want in the future. It represents your dreams, your goals and your ideal life. There is no right or wrong way to create a vision board. Some people's boards are a collage of overlapping photos, clippings from magazines, and hand drawn messages that almost jump off the board at you. While others prefer a more orderly look, using only a few photos and phrases. Find your own style. There are no rules. Your board can reflect several goals to be accomplished or focus on one area of your life. The look and method is very much a personal preference. What follows is my suggested process for creating a vision board, but feel free to deviate from the instructions if at any point they don't work for you.

Before we begin though, I would like to say a quick word about your "inner critic". During the creative process, you must fight that little voice inside your head that says, "Why am I doing this? I'm not creative. People will laugh when they look at this. This wish will never come true, how dare I even think it. I will never have that." Nonsense! Silence your inner critic, or at least try to ignore it. There are no mistakes in this process, so you cannot fail. You don't even need to share your board with anyone if you don't want to. Your negative self talk will usually crop up when it is time to make a commitment and glue your items down, so be ready for it and move through any anxious feelings quickly.

***Supplies:*** (Depending on your style, choose from the suggested list below.)

Glue stick, scissors, snapshots, photo mounts, art paper or poster board (18x24 inches or larger), cork board, push pins, colored paper, a variety of magazines with lots of pictures in them, greeting cards, felt pens, markers, rubber stamps, computer for printing specific images, relaxing music, large table

**Creating Your Vision Board:**

1. Since this is going to be your board, your first task is to find an image that represents your true self. It can be a symbol (such as a rose, an animal, or a logo, or it can be literally a photo of yourself that you are pleased with). This will go in the center of your vision board. Once you find it, put it aside.

2. Choose a theme or focus for your board. Do you want it to represent several areas of your life, or just one? You do not need to choose a time frame. Once you complete your board, you will find that the universe will bring those dreams to you in its own time. Some will happen very quickly, almost immediately, while other desires will take time. Trust that the process works, and let go of needing to manage the timeframe.

3. Be clear about the desires being represented. Use your affirmative phrases and statements from the Visualization Exercise to help you. Keep the final picture of the life you want to create in your mind as you complete the next step of this process.

4. Search for images and words, captions and phrases that express your goals and dreams. Your focus should drive your choice of pictures and words. Grabs what jumps out at you. Don't edit your choices because you think it is out of your reach. Separate the images from the words and place them in a pile to the side.

5. Starting with the images, select the ones that best represent your focus statements. Base your decision to use an image on whether the picture directly relates to your theme. If an image doesn't really fit, put it aside for use on a future board. Place your final selections next to your board. Don't glue or secure them yet.

6. Now you can look through the words and phrases to see what ones best support your images. You can use the words as captions for an image, or to make a statement. As before, they should relate to and support your theme or focus. When done, place the words to the side of the board.

7. Time to assemble! Don't panic. This is a very intuitive process. We were all born with the ability to compose a picture that says what our hearts want to say, so trust your intuition, or sixth sense, here. Place the symbol (or photo) of you in the middle of your board. Allow the images and words to find their place around it. Play with moving your images and words around, trying different combinations and locations. You may find that you do not have room for everything you've chosen, and that's ok. It is better to use only the images and phrases that really say what you want, than to have a collage full of distracting, irrelevant or redundant items. Look at your use of space and make sure your board doesn't feel too chaotic.

8. When you feel good about your final design, begin to glue (or pin) your elements down. When you do this step, you are making a commitment to your dreams and to yourself. Do not allow your inner critic to keep you so serious that you lose your joy in the process.

9. Sit with your board. Does it need anything more? Know when you've done enough.

10. Display your vision board in a place where you will see it every day. This is critical to your success. Each day reinforce the image of your future by looking at your board and practicing the visualization process discussed earlier. Write in your journal or explain to a supportive friend, in the present tense, the details of the story your vision board is telling. Be careful though, and protect your dreams. Do not share your collage with people who tend to criticize you!

**Pulling It All Together**

The final part of the Visioning Process may actually be the most difficult aspect of reinforcing your dreams. This is the part where you relax and let go. Trust in the creative process and have faith in all of your hard work. You must release your attachment to the outcome, your need to plan and manage the means to your goals, and let go of your worry and negative beliefs. Just as a farmer trusts that nature will take care of growing the seeds he has just planted, so must you be patient and have faith in the process. Where would that farmer be if he dug up his seeds after just two days to see what was happening? Be grateful for what you have now and what you know will come your way in the future.

Believe in magic and miracles. Keep your heart and your eyes open to the signs and messages along the way that may be pointing you in the direction of your dreams. The Law of Attraction will draw people and opportunities to you that will move you further down the path towards your dreams than you could have ever imagined. Your responsibility in this process is to recognize these signs and to take action. Visualizing alone is not enough. Without action on your part, your dreams will never become reality. That might mean that you need to take a risk, try something new, or do something different. Change is not often easy, and sometimes in order to make room for your new dreams, you will have to let go of something or maybe even someone.

Don't forget to gather a support team around you. Look for people who are positive and have your interests at heart to help you through moments of self-doubt and confusion. Many people have accelerated their success by using a Life Coach. A Life Coach can be an essential part of your team, helping you to clarify your desires and keeping you focused on your goals.

Now, celebrate your success! This is not the end. There are many more dreams in your heart just waiting for you to shine a light on them. You can repeat this process over and over again on your journey, each time moving you closer to your heart's desires. I can see you living the life of your dreams already, can't you? Of course you can, you've already imagined it!

*Notes:*

# ABOUT THE AUTHOR

**PAMELA COWAN**

Pamela Cowan is the owner of a financial planning practice, Cowan Financial, LLC. Her key focus when working with clients is to educate and assist them in making better decisions in their lives especially as it relates to their finances.

Ms. Cowan is a graduate of the University of Toronto with a Bachelor of Commerce degree in Finance and Economics and a minor in Political Science. She has many years of experience as an accountant and later as a consultant in the computer software field which included international travel. In addition, she has conducted training for adults in accounting and computer applications. Her passion for teaching, led her to a career as a planner to be better able to assist and teach people on a more personal level.

*Contact*
Cowan Financial, LLC
2041 Stockmeyer Blvd.
Westland, MI 48186
(734) 722-5227
Pamela.A.Cowan@gmail.com

## FORTY-ONE

# THE MIDAS TOUCH: MONEY SAVVY AND ACCUMULATING WEALTH

**By Pamela Cowan**

The best way to become money savvy and to accumulate wealth, like any successful venture in life, is to become knowledgeable about financial issues, make an honest evaluation of where you are personally, determine where it is you want to be, and finally prepare a strategy for how to get there. In other words, you need a plan.

**People Don't Plan to Fail, They Fail to Plan.**

Planning, at a high level, incorporates these activities and further examines your budgeting, debt management, investing and saving, protection, and long-term goals, such as retirement and estate planning. Everyone has a reason to plan. Do you own a home (or do you want to), do you want to provide for your children's education, are you saving for your retirement? What kind of retirement do you want? There are as many reasons to budget, save, and invest as there are people in the world, but unless you have a clear goal, even if it changes in the future, it is difficult to set a path or course towards it. For some, you may have been too busy living life to think about setting clear priorities and goals, but taking the time to do this will help with more than just your finances. Setting priorities in your life makes finding the discipline to budget and save much easier when you are clear on what it is you are working toward. I believe in 'writing it down' and seeing things in black and white. The information I will present is not new, nor is it intended to be comprehensive and specific to your particular situation. For a complete comprehensive financial plan, I recommend you seek assistance from a licensed professional who has the proper training and tools to correctly advise you. In the meantime, let's look at some key pointers to increase your knowledge and give you some wealthy ideas.

First, you need to know where you are. Forget about regrets about what little you've done to date or how poorly your investments have done, let's truly look at where you are. The average Boomer has held several jobs and consequently may have several old retirement funds with different investment firms, not to mention other bits of money here and there. Pull out all of your investment statements, bank accounts, and old 401k or pensions plan statements you have languishing in drawers. Your old 401k plans can be rolled over into an IRA and/or rolled into your current plan. I like rolling the old ones into one IRA. First, you will stop paying fees at all of those firms and you will have more fund and investment options by not limiting yourself to those available in your current employers' plan. The same is true about paying fees with many different bank accounts. Consolidate all the little pieces.

Next, we are going to create a budget. The initial exercise of creating a budget is actually less of planning what to spend as getting a good handle on what you are spending. Only then can we make choices and begin to prioritize. If you don't know where to start, type 'financial planning' into any search engine and you will be presented with many tools, budgeting worksheets and plenty of free advice. The greater the period of spending data you have, the more meaningful and more realistic your budget numbers will be. Why? Because some expenses, like car and home insurance, may not be paid every month. Holidays, vacation and birthdays may only happen once a year, but your data will be skewed if you only look at a month with little spending activity. Likewise, you may need to adjust your budget for the method in which you are paid. It is easier to start with an annual number and adjust to reflect a monthly income amount. Use this method also for the infrequent expenses previously mentioned. I prefer the spreadsheet versions of budgeting tools, as they have the ability to automatically spread expenses for you, such as annual items, and will also list your debts in a more realistic fashion when budgeting. Many people do not pay off their entire balance each month, so you need to be able to enter your minimum payments as part of your budget. You can better start to address your debt when you can see it all listed, including the outstanding balance, interest rate and minimum payment.

After collecting all of this data and preparing your budget, or at least your current spending patterns, you can start to make more informed decisions and perhaps better choices in how you spend your money. This is also the first opportunity you will have to truly plan. What do you have left over that you can begin to use towards your goals, or do we first need to address any debt. Remember to allow for an emergency fund in cash, or a cash equivalent that you can rapidly access, which could cover at least 3 to 6 months of expenses. Without an adequate sum of money set aside for unexpected events and expenditures, you are going to pull out your credit card and be back in the same position; conquering the debt rather than building wealth. Budgeting is not about deprivation, but more a healthy assessment of your goals and priorities versus your past spending patterns and habits. It is a time to differentiate between needs vs. wants. To accumulate wealth, you will need to exercise some discipline with your spending, but now you can see if impulse buying, eating out or whatever is your weakness.

Remember, life has many cycles and phases. Give yourself credit for what you have achieved to date, especially if you are currently in one of those phases when your spending is not where you would like it to be and your saving is non-existent. Many give up because they do not feel they can make a sufficient difference in saving toward their future, so they do nothing. A little saving can go a long way. If you haven't, get started today, however small the amount may seem to you. It may be time to circle back to the earlier comments on writing it down, realizing where you are at, and clearly stating where you want to be.

While accumulating your wealth, you need to address how to protect it. You and your spouse need to have disability plans in place in case of an unexpected illness or accident. One prolonged absence from gainful employment can wipe out your life savings, or worse if you are unprepared for a permanent disability. Remember that any payments from your employer provided plan will be taxed unlike a private plan that you pay for. Consequently, the plan, which often covers 60% to 70% of your income, will be net of taxes and may be coordinated with social security. You would receive only a percentage of your income less taxes and the portion attributable to social security. This translates into a substantial drop in pay. Adequate life insurance must be in place for both of you, also. A sudden death would seriously affect not only the attainment of your financial goals, but limit your opportunity to provide for you and your family's future.

In addition to all of the changes Boomers have made on the political and cultural landscape, they have also affected the way society views retirement and the expectations associated with it. During the last 20 years, pensions have almost become extinct and retirement savings are more and more important. The Boomer generation has no intention of sitting around knitting socks. Boomers travel, not only for leisure, but to visit children and family who are no longer around the block. They are more active, more involved, and are living longer and fuller lives. Volunteering and philanthropy also play a large role. All of this takes money. There is a greater need to become focused on the Number. The Number you say? To summarize, I'll use the title of Lee Eisenberg's book; *The Number, What Do You Need For The Rest Of Your Life, And What Will It Cost*? Eisenberg's book is an excellent study of all things related to prepping for and enjoying your retirement. He incorporates humor with an honest assessment of the changing landscape and Boomer attitudes, which makes it a worthwhile and enjoyable read.

While this is not the forum to discuss what is important to you or what your retirement will cost, some guidelines may be in order. In the past, we often assumed that we would need approximately 80% of our current income in retirement. These figures were derived based on the assumption that your clothing needs and commuting costs would be lower during retirement, as well as other work related habits such as eating out for lunch. For many, these cost savings are not being realized, as they are doing other things and spending their money *differently.* In an effort to shed some light on how to derive your number or cause mass hysteria, as the case may be, let's look at a simple and conservative example.

Let's pretend that you decide you can live on $40,000.00 per year in retirement. We are all aware of the effects of inflation, so in the second year of retirement, that amount will need to increase by the rate of inflation, and so on. Prices go up, so our income must go up by the same percentage. Let's use 4%. I know that seems high given the recent cost of living, but everything runs in cycles and a couple of decades earlier the average rate was twice that. Let's also assume that you expect to be retired for 25 years or until age 90, not really unrealistic. Further, you are a well informed Boomer and realize that your money will still need to be invested so that it can continue to grow and last for your entire retirement, so we'll assume your investments are earning on average 8%. Finally, we come to this realization at 45 years old giving us 20 years to prepare for our *number.*

Step by step, I'll describe the process, but we'll skip the math. Determine what $40,000.00 will be, inflation adjusted, in 20 years, or the future value of $40,000 at 4%, which rounded is $87,645. Next we need this amount for 25 years, adjusting for inflation and taking into account it will be invested earning on average 8%. You aren't going to remove 25 years of money and leave it in cash; otherwise you would need a whole lot more cash. So, we will need approximately $1,445,286 saved when we begin our retirement assuming we do not plan to have part time job. Next, we look at how much money you determined you had already saved from those old 401k's, pensions, savings that you had marked for retirement, and any funds that you would receive from Social Security (check your annual statement). Let's assume nothing, so we can easily figure out what we need to save each year, as long as we have it invested and are earning on average 8%. On a level basis, you would need to be saving $31,583 per year.

At this point, you are feeling 1) not so bad knowing that you've made a great start, and with a little tweaking will be able to eat and visit the grandchildren in your golden years or 2) are completely overwhelmed and can't believe the size of those numbers. Perhaps you are even ready to get some help determining how close you are to your number.

We are told repeatedly to start early with our savings and retirement plans, which is good advice, but how do we do it? First, it should go without saying that if you have a 401k or other retirement plan at work, you should be enrolled in it. It is the easiest way to save, as the money is removed pre-tax and before it gets into your hands. Most firms have a matching policy to encourage you to invest. If possible, plan to have the maximum allowable amount deducted over the year to fully fund your plan. If you are over fifty, most plans allow for catch-up or extra amounts that can be contributed.

Many retirement plans use mutual funds as their investment vehicle. Whether investing in your retirement plan, IRA or other savings vehicle, mutual funds are an easy method to utilize. At a high level, you should own a few funds representing an asset allocation spread between stocks and bonds. Stock mutual funds are further classified, at a high level, by the size and/or type of company held in each fund; large, mid, small and international. How will you know which percentage to put in each fund? Every fund company and most of those online sources mentioned earlier will have a risk tolerance questionnaire that you can complete online, or some suggested asset allocation percentages, which you can follow. The return of the different types of mutual funds will fluctuate independent of each other. By holding different kinds of funds, we smooth out our returns so that the positive performance of some investments will neutralize the negative performance of others.

Most fund families will also have a fund that will do the asset allocation for you. It will be labeled appropriately as conservative, moderate or aggressive blend. Some now also have a number, actually a year, which you choose as closely as possible to the year you would be retiring. The fund manager will change the allocation within the fund over time to a more conservative blend as the retirement year approaches. If you are still nervous about selecting the right fund family, don't be; jump in. Studies indicate that 92% of an investor's returns are due to the asset allocation, not picking the best fund family.

Market risk comes with investing, which means there will be volatility in your returns. It is more important to be aware that the fluctuations are going to occur, rather than investing too conservatively. Too conservative a portfolio may not outpace inflation, thereby increasing the risk of outliving your assets. Long-time horizon investors aiming to build wealth can wait out the inevitable ups and downs of the stock market. The stock market cycle has typically been seven years, so you will experience at least three cycles in a typical retirement. The key to long-term success can lie in a balanced asset portfolio – neither all stock, which makes a person too exposed to bear market risk, nor all bonds and cash with scant potential for upside appreciation.

A big part of being money savvy involves tying up your own loose ends and making proper arrangements for your final wishes and your estate. One of my roles as a financial planner is to force people to have conversations about things they don't want to think about or talk about. We don't do it to annoy you. Death is a part of living, and by properly recording your wishes and looking after your affairs, you can save those left behind a great deal of anguish. After all, it is your stuff we are talking about. If you don't document it, the government, in the form of a probate court, will be very happy to make those decisions for you in a very public and very costly manner. In addition, a will can establish guardianship for any minor children. Should anything unexpected happen to you and your spouse, adequate consideration should be given to who would raise your children in your absence.

In order to avoid probate in all but the smallest estates, you would require a trust to be prepared by an attorney. It is also the only method that lets you exercise control from the grave. A trust allows you to benefit one or more desired beneficiaries, take advantage of the investment expertise of a trustee, avoid probate, protect assets from creditors, and achieve income, gift or estate tax savings. You will need to review your situation with a financial planner or attorney to determine whether a trust would be appropriate for your situation, and if so, which type of trust should be created.

Continuing with our 'you are mortal and your parts wear out' conversation, you should give some consideration to purchasing a long-term care policy. As we age, just looking after ourselves, dressing, eating and bathing can become difficult. You or your partner may eventually require more assistance with day-to-day living. In fact, no age group is exempt from facing the risk of needing long-term care. Waiting until you are 65 or older to think about long-term care issues can be too late. The population in need of long-term care is diverse in age and level of disability. A majority are over age 65 (57%), however 43% are below 65 years of age. As you age, the probability you will need care, either at home or in an institution, increases. At ages 65-74, 12 % of all people need help with care tasks. At age 85 and over, 70% of all people need help with activities of daily living and long-term care.

Boomers have typically spent a great deal of money fixing up their nests to their liking and/or have purchased that dream retirement home. Having a long-term care policy in place will allow you to stay in it longer. These policies allow for the proper nursing staff to come to you, so don't think about it as only buying a nursing home stay. The greatest fear among female Boomers is outliving their money. The sudden or unexpected requirement for skilled nursing care or stay in a nursing home facility will deplete your wealth faster. The cost of long-term care generally ranges from $30,000-$100,000 per year, depending on region and level of care. Often, one spouse will become stricken with a debilitating disease, which leads to admittance to a long-term care facility. The second spouse essentially depletes all savings and is often left in poverty, in addition to being alone and without a backup plan when they need more care themselves. If none of these scenarios has you thinking more seriously about getting a policy, realize that without one, you will be relying on family for assistance.

The whole experience does not need to be looked at with dread. Many people will make a gradual adjustment. When caring for your home and each other becomes somewhat taxing, couples can opt for a senior living community. Many of these communities include units from completely independent living to more services and more care as your needs change. Remember, as we age we become more resistant to change, and I think that these communities offer a logical and comfortable choice when your own home is no longer a viable option.

Finally, I want to clarify that in only one article I cannot possibly fully or fairly discuss all the aspects of these important topics, but I can only hope to peak your curiosity. From here you can determine that you need more information or realize when you may need help.

To become a licensed financial planner requires a series of rigorous courses, exams and ongoing training and certification, and for good reason. We help people with some of the most important financial considerations and decisions they will make in their lives. In this industry we are truly baffled at the number of people with neither the time nor the inclination, computer tools, or math skills, who prefer to address these decisions on their own. Many pay more for cable TV service than the fees charged for the preparation of a financial plan and the ongoing advice of an advisor. What is the value to you of seeing your child walk across the stage collecting their degree or knowing that you will be comfortable in retirement? I hope, priceless!

Becoming wealthy involves more than having a large investment balance. Good health, great relationships, a healthy attitude and outlook, and the ability to share and be grateful for what you have achieved are an even greater component. Then, you are truly wealthy.

**Recommended Reading:**

*The Number: What Do You Need for the Rest of Your Life, and What Will It Cost?* by Lee Eisenberg

# ABOUT THE AUTHOR

## Dr. Stem Mahlatini-Marks

Dr. Mahlatini is President and CEO of Global Coaching & Consulting Services, LLC (GC&C), a service that focuses on inspiring, and empowering people to lead stress free lives by stabilizing the mind, body and spirit through counseling and coaching. GC&C's services also include a focus on promoting eldercare work/balance. GC& C provides specialized trainings to employers and community organizations on developing innovative, cost-effective approaches to preventing and resolving eldercare/work conflicts. Dr. Mahlatini is an Independent Licensed Psychotherapist who conducts individual, family, group-counseling services to clients of diverse backgrounds from ages 8-99. In addition, She conducts workshops and seminars throughout the United States and abroad. Dr. Mahlatini's passion is to empower and inspire youth and adults in overcoming obstacles that hinder their everyday success through her counseling and coaching services.

Her knowledge of business and mental health counseling is supported by her fifteen years of experience working in corporations, hospitals, nursing homes and as an Employee Assistance Professional. Dr. Mahlatini's work includes working with adolescents involved with the department of Juvenile Justice, critically ill patients as a heart transplant social worker, elderly patients as a consultant and therapist, Superintendent and Quality Assurance Manager with the Department of Juvenile Justice as well as a middle school teacher. She has been a trainer and consultant in all the positions she has held, experience which has been a blessing and motivator in presenting seminars in her own practice.

The oldest of seven, Dr. Mahlatini was born in Zimbabwe and came to the United States in 1986 to pursue her education in Boston Massachusetts. She received an Associate's Degree in Business from Middlesex Community College, Bachelors Degree in Business from University of Massachusetts Lowell, a Masters Degree in Social Work from Boston University and Doctor of Education Degree from Nova Southeastern University. Her accolades and one of her lifelong dreams include Co-author of four upcoming PWN books. Dr. Mahlatini truly believes that she is at the onset of an annointed journey that will take her globally where she is destined to impact many lives young and old.

Dr. Mahlatini-Marks is married to her husband, Harold "Tim" Marks, the love of her life and has continued support from her parents, Benjamin and Idah Mahlatini in Zimbabwe, as well as siblings and in laws around the world. With an exuberant passion and dedication to empowering, inspiring as well as helping other people excel, Dr. Mahlatini-Marks is available as a youth consultant, mgt consultant, key note and conference speaker to small & large organizations, leadership teams, hospitals, professional associations, civic & public organizations, school systems & youth groups on a local, national and international basis.

*Contact:*
Global Coaching & Consulting Services, LLC
75 Fox Ridge Court Suite C
Debary, FL 32713
Telephone: (813)431-5154
Email: Drmahlatini@globalcoachconsulting.com
Website: www.Globalcoachconsulting.com

## FORTY-TWO

# WHO ARE WE? UNDERSTANDING THE BABY BOOMER GENERATION

**By Dr. Stem Mahlatini-Marks**

Not too long ago, while walking in the park, I was stopped by a woman who from all appearance looked like she was entering her golden years. Sensing my uneasiness, she smiled in an apparent attempt to ease my nerves and proceeded to ask me one of the strangest questions that I have ever heard. "Are you a Baby Boomer?" That question was strange to me on two fronts; I had never been asked that question before, and I had no clue what a Baby Boomer was. As I contemplated a response to the question, a sudden rush of cynicism overcame me. So, before I uttered a response, I chose to ask a question of my own. "Why did you ask me that question?"

With a slight grin on her face, she said that a Boomer was someone who was born between 1946 and 1964. True to form, I asked another question. "Why me?" Because you appeared to be a kind and warm-hearted young woman. I have been living a long time, so I am a pretty good judge of personalities," she said. With such flattery, I was not about to disappoint her, so with a huge smile on my face, I told her that based on her description of a Boomer, I am a Boomer.

As I stated at the outset of this chapter, I had never been asked that question before. Therefore, I wasn't sure how I should respond, but I was disarmed by her gentle and peaceful smile. Moreover, I come from an island that does not believe in too many labels, especially labels relating to people. In addition to that, on my island, personal stuff remains personal for the most part. But as my inquisitive friend was about to leave, I asked her if I could ask one more question. She replied, "Yes, you can, but you would have to walk with me as I continue my daily three mile exercise." "Wow!" I replied. You walk three miles a day. That's awesome, I wish I could do that, but I am too busy working to walk three miles a day." "You should", she replied. "It would make the world of a difference to you, especially for you, Boomer.

So what's the question?" I replied, "You told me that a Boomer was someone who was born between 1946 and 1964. But is that all there is to a Baby Boomer? From what I have been told, the time of one's birth is the major distinguishing factor, but from my experience as a member of the Greatest Generation, I would say that there might be a few other things that distinguish one from the other." Then she said, "You are a Boomer if:

You grew up on the Beatles.

You love the real Michael Jackson.

You grew up with Martin Luther King.

You know who JFK is.

You have less energy than you had about ten years ago.

You have more to look back on than to look forward to.

You start to dye your hair.

You have less interest in sex.

You are beginning to understand the importance of a relationship.

Professional development means more to you today than yesterday.

You are more concerned about stocks and bonds than you were about ten years ago.

It takes you longer to get out of bed than it did a few years ago.

I immediately became introspective; everything she said resonated with me. I could no longer deny that I was indeed a Boomer. I thanked her for her insight and waved her goodbye. In my solitude, I started thinking about my life and where I go from here. Before going any further, let us learn some more about the things that matter to the Boomer woman.

For example, Boomer women have had more choices today than the women of yesterday had. The Boomer woman even has a chance to become the first female president of the United States. The Boomer woman is faithful, loving, and hard working. She is creative, entrepreneurial, daring, and even commanding. Despite the diversity of backgrounds that she comes from, she continues to use her experiences to her advantage. The Boomer woman is wise, sensitive, and compassionate. She enjoys making a difference and does not let her age or the term Baby Boomer slow her down.

**Retirement**

One of the goals of the Baby Boomer generation is to find the best strategies available to sustain the joy and enthusiasm of the youthful days. She strives to make mindful choices that encourage personal growth and creativity. Those choices supply the momentum to rejuvenate the spirit, the body and the mind. The advances in medicine erase the fear of early death from the minds of the Boomer, enticing the Boomer to delay retirement. In fact, for most Boomers, retirement is a foreign word. Gone are the days of Bingo, shuffleboard, and golf. Baby Boomers love to keep busy. They love to stay involved and continue earning, but without the stress and pressure of a traditional job. Essentially, most Baby Boomers are finding themselves working as caregivers to their parents and children. Their concerns range from finances to relationships and health. This certainly is not the ideal way of being family-oriented. Actually, many have little choice but to care for their aging parents and remain on the job. According to the Natural Marketing Institute, 93% of boomers state that exercise is integral to good health, but only 27% do it regularly and only 21% do it infrequently. That means 53% don't bother at all. What other mixed messages are we sending out?

Baby Boomers are the first generation who will live on average into their 80s. An avalanche of octogenarians is approaching. Now there are 9 million Americans 80 or older. By 2050, there will be 31 million, according to US Census Bureau estimates. In 2000, there were 250,000 people worldwide over 100. By 2050, there will be 3.8 million. The study also reveals that men and women envision retirement very differently. Men are more likely to view retirement as a time to enhance primary relationships, while women plan to become more involved in their communities. It would appear that these views pose possible disagreements in many households. As a result, many of the Baby Boomers cannot picture themselves quitting all forms of work, to play golf and travel in their RVs. Rather, they see themselves as transitioning into part-time work at their chosen profession, starting a new business, or learning about a new trade or industry. Those boomers who do see retirement in their future see it as beginning at 70 or 75, not the traditional 60 to 65. In other words, they plan to live longer and postpone old age.

The money earned during years of hard labor will help fund their lifestyle and they won't be tapping into their retirement nest egg until well past 70. This means that retirement planning as we know it today will need to be revamped to fit the Baby Boomer Generation. Their concept of financial freedom is the point at which they have the ability to move on to the retirement they envision, no matter what age. One will notice that the Baby Boomers are unwilling to make the financial sacrifices that a traditional leisure retirement would require. Hence, they are willing to work longer, even if it means less hours at reduced pay, rather than deny themselves today. Boomers say that their ideal life plan in retirement includes work. However, they are seeking new ways of combining leisure and work, which means there are more entrepreneurs and small business owners.

Talking about business, the beauty of Baby Boomer women in business is their collective spirit of collaboration. The baby Boomer women realize that 9-5 is not the only option they have. They certainly can be on their own and still afford to fend for themselves. Rather than being intimidated by a potential business competitor, they will often seek out ways to cross-promote, pool resources, and support one another. They understand that there is enough business for all of us, and the more they work together, the greater the demand for their particular product or service. And this is a good thing...when you carefully select the women with whom you align yourself. We definitely have seen 'at play' with our fearless leader Linda Ellis Eastman, a woman who has operated a successful network and empowered all of us to be entrepreneurs and authors.

Finally I would like to share this story, which is a reminder that we do not have to wait until we reach the baby boomer years to be our best and live our dreams.

**The Limit Is Me_**

One day, all the employees reached the office and they saw a big sign on the door on which it was written: "Yesterday the person who has been hindering your growth in this company passed away. We invite you to join the funeral in the room that has been prepared in the gym." In the beginning, they all got sad for the death of one of their colleagues, but after a while they started getting curious to know who was that person who hindered the growth of their colleagues and the company itself. The excitement in the gym was such that security agents were ordered to control the crowd within the room. The more people reached the coffin, the more the excitement heated up. Everyone thought, "Who is this person who was hindering my progress? Well, at least they died."

One by one, the thrilled employees got closer to the coffin, and when they looked inside it, they suddenly became speechless. They stood nearby the coffin, shocked and in silence, as if someone had touched the deepest part of their soul. There was a mirror inside the coffin: everyone who looked inside it could see themselves. There was also a sign next to the mirror that said, "There is only one person who is capable to set limits to your growth: it is YOU. You are the only person who can revolutionize your life. You are the only person who can influence your happiness, your realization and your success. You are the only person who can help yourself. Your life does not change when your boss changes, when your friends change, when your parents change, when your partner changes, when your company changes. Your life changes when YOU change, when you go beyond your limiting beliefs, when you realize that you are the only one responsible for your life. The most important relationship you can have, is the one you have with yourself."

Examine yourself; watch yourself. Don't be afraid of difficulties, impossibilities and losses. Be a winner; build yourself and your reality. The world is like a mirror. It gives back to anyone the reflection of the thoughts in which one has strongly believed. The world and your reality are like mirrors in a coffin, which show to any individual the death of their divine capability to imagine and create their happiness and success. It's the way you face Life that makes the difference.

## ABOUT THE AUTHOR

**JANE DENNER**

Jane Denner is the principal of Inner-States, LLC which is dedicated to the evolution of the whole person –mind, body, and spirit- substituting patterns of success for those of past failures. Emphasis is placed on nutrition and emotional awareness. Ms. Denner is a Certified Professional Consultant and Holistic Health Counselor with over thirty years of experience in the field of natural healing. She is an active member of the Professional Woman Network and serves on its International Advisory Board.

Ms. Denner uses practical exercises to demonstrate that which we hold in our minds can either hold us back or move us forward. Jane provides seminars and coaching to support and guide individuals over the obstacles they encounter on their paths. Inner-States, LLC programs help individuals navigate while focusing on nutrition, self esteem and building healthy relationships. Private one-on-one as well as small group coaching sessions, workshops and seminars for all individuals of any age are available. She is passionate about healing through physical and emotional self awareness and strongly believes in being her own example. Jane Denner is a native of Canada and resides in Massachusetts with her family.

*Contact:*
Inner–States LLC
P O Box 474
Concord, MA 01742
[617] 605 6205
Jane777comcast.net
www.protrain.net

## FORTY-THREE

# LIVING A LOVING LIFE

**By Jane Denner**

*"The secret of health for both mind and body is not to mourn for the past, worry about the future, or anticipate troubles, but to live in the present moment wisely and earnestly."* —Buddha 483 B.C.

### Return to Innocence

As a child, I remember being filled with a joy and natural appreciation of life. A favorite pastime was to lie on the grass, looking up at blue sky, and feeling a private yet paradoxically universal connection to a wondrous planetary consciousness. Over time, however, this experience of the universe was replaced by the emptiness of being perpetually conditioned by a hierarchical society that primarily instilled feelings of imperfection and sadness. I, too, began to substitute arbitrary value judgments for the natural flow of living. At some point, however, during my some fifty plus years of life, more often than not seeing life as a victim through a landscape of fear and uncertainty, I realized that I had a choice – to return to the joy of my youth, and to regain the control, power, and freedom commensurate with the perfection and happiness residing at my core – free of fear and exulting in the possibilities inherent in the innocence and wisdom of our immutable spirit – indeed to regain innocence, with its intuitive wisdom and courage. Challenge patterns of emotional negativity; always strive to experience the ultimate energy of your inherent possibilities. Sculpt your highest self, realigning your mind, body and spirit into one undefeatable, and therefore undefeated, entity. Find the spiritual warrior within; knowing thy true self is essential to happiness.

**"Live Slow"**

I recently saw the words "Live Slow" printed on the back of a tee shirt and was instantly reminded of the incredible power of living, fully conscious and focused, in the present, rather than in an external world of "artificially inseminated" imperfection and fear, which sadly had become my predominant, driving energy. Our natural state of being is joy; it is far better to be "pregnant" with joy, love and the possibilities of self than with the pervasive negativity, fear and rejection which society is too willing to make our legacy.

When we "Live Slow", we practice the body, mind-alignment which maximizes clarity. It is through emotional awareness that we connect our now aligned body and mind to our fundamental innate consciousness, and realizing the power to control your world by remaining grounded in the present and trusting your innate intelligence. Remember well that the longest, most important journey begins with "one small intention" – embrace your courage, wisdom, and ultimate divinity, and it will become your natural path, as well.

**Compassion**

*"Out of suffering has emerged the strongest souls; the most massive characters are seared with scars."*
—Kahilil Gibran, novelist and poet, 1931

The natural sibling of our inherent joyful state is "compassion". By being kind and compassionate to ourselves first, and seeing beyond the egocentric distractions that generate our suffering, we begin the journey to self-love and freedom, without which we cannot experience the joy. By taking the time to carefully explore the cause and effect matrix of our suffering, we will come to understand that it is hidden in the illusions of our desire, comprised of the "**imperfect** and the **temporary,"** which collectively delude us with the false promise of filling up our perceived emptiness. Awareness of how the mind operates requires the diligent practice of turning on, and tuning in, to our spiritual energy – trusting our intention to move to an aligned mind, body and soul living completely in the moment – the perfect and permanent energy that is the homeostasis of our being. The proverbial "empty cup" will fill itself through a path of purposeful, compassionate intention and action. It can never be filled, nor indeed fulfilled, with the bottomless promise of attachment to an immediate gratification borne of the" temporary fixes" inherent in the pursuit of the external world.

What do you desire?

________________________________________

________________________________________

Do you feel more desire for these things when you are under stress? When are they most prevalent?

____________________________________________

____________________________________________

Describe your feelings of neediness.

____________________________________________

____________________________________________

What happens in your mind when you cannot have what you desire – what emotions are you feeling?

____________________________________________

____________________________________________

Do you substitute another desire to distract or sooth you from the pain of not getting what you wanted originally – such as food, television, computer, sex, drugs or spending? How do you habitually act out your survival tactics?

____________________________________________

____________________________________________

Once we are able to step outside of ourselves to witness existentially what happens to the mind when it cannot have what it impulsively, and repetitively, believes it desires, humility is born and with it, empathy for our own condition. It is from here, in that moment of suffering, that we have an opportunity to expand beyond the five basic sensory perceptions of sight, smell, hearing, taste and touch, and become multiplex in our sensations. By using our intention and will to align ourselves with our souls, we become instantly aware of our heart energy and our intuition begins to expand. Thus, the ineffable journey of self-exploration begins as we open to the indescribable realization that the Earth and Universe are our most perfect training ground for theevolution, if we stay vigilant through the higher state of self-awareness which, most truly and enduringly, fill the "half empty cup" with the highest energy – love.

**Forgiveness**

It is only from truly experiencing compassion for yourself that you begin to become cognizant that all humanity is afflicted with the same matrix of illusive and impulsive desires that causes the "unevolved you" so much pain and suffering. When we compassionately care for others by aligning ourselves with the higher vibrational energy of our basic goodness, we act as a "tuning fork" – effectively assisting others subconsciously to oscillate at the same frequency. And, when others experience this higher vibrational range, they will connect with the vital force resonating from their heart's center. Thus, they begin to attain, as the Bible teaches us, "a peace that passes all understanding", as the mind is momentarily still and their authentic selves – soul energy – remains. Such conscious interactions amplify a deeper reality/intimacy, which brings joy to giver and receiver alike. Compassion then transcends, and ultimately defuses, our own and others' entrenched anger and hurt. In essence, all life is divine and is fueled by the same energy source – separation is an illusion, oneness is the reality. When we are finally able to release our perceived unjust treatment by others and understand it to be simply an inevitable by-product of a previously unevolved, unexamined consciousness, we all heal and grow together.

Conversely, resentment binds us emotionally to our "perpetrators" and we stay imprisoned in our suffering. Forgiveness is the key to freedom from energetic bondage. Your sadness is rooted in the assumption that others' conduct is meant to hurt you personally. This is most frequently not the case.

*"The weak can never forgive. Forgiveness is the attribute of the strong."*
—Mahatma Gandhi 1948.

**Gratitude**

When you experience the holiness of who you are, you will begin to experience gratitude in all areas of your life. As you begin to see more "life" in the present, find the courage to confront your fear and pain by directing your inner "will" to go beyond them, ultimately selecting "love". You will begin to feel the true wonder of such personal transformation. Life becomes "living art" and you become the co-creator, the author of your vision, as the spirit of love is able to move freely through you. You are truly a "work in progress", whether or not you are conscious of this fact. But when you do realize what has happened to you, you will be filled with admiration and gratitude for the opportunity, and the gift that has been presented to you.

*"I would maintain that thanks are the highest forms of thought, and that gratitude is happiness doubled by wonder."*—G K Chesterton 1936

*Notes:*

## ABOUT THE AUTHOR

### PHYLLIS S. QUINLAN, RNC, MS

Phyllis S. Quinlan resides in Flushing, New York. She has over 30 years experience in the healthcare industry with 25 years at a management level in emergency services, acute care and long term care/ short-term rehabilitation settings. Phyllis is also a consulting Feng Shui Practitioner and has practiced this complimentary therapy since 1999. She is presently pursuing her Doctorate Degree in Healthcare Administration at the Warren National University.

Phyllis is the president of MFW Consultants To Professionals, a Consulting Firm serving the educational, personal coaching, and managerial needs of individuals and organizations. As a certified legal nurse consult, she also serves as an expert witness to many attorney-clients.

Phyllis is a contributing author for the following PWN publications: *Overcoming the Superwoman Syndrome, You're on Stage: Image, Etiquette, Branding, and Style, Woman's Journey to Wellness: Body, Mind and Spirit, A Woman's Survival Guide to Overcoming Obstacles, Transition and Change, "Women as Leaders: Strategies for Empowerment and Communication" and "Emotional Wellness for Women Volume I".* As member of the PWN International Speakers Bureau, she is available internationally to assist the individual client and/or organization with professional development needs. Phyllis' most cherished role is that of godmother to five fabulous young women.

She dedicates this chapter to the memory of her late mother Madeline Walsh Quinlan, her cherished friend and colleague, Dr. Robert Curran, MD, and the wonderful nurses & staff of the Good Shepherd Hospice in Port Jefferson Station, New York.

*Contact:*
Phyllis S. Quinlan, RNC, MS, CLNC
147-20 35th Avenue Apt.#2B
Flushing, New York 11354
mfwconsultants@mindspring.com
718.661.4981
www.mfwconsultants.com

## FORTY-FOUR

# HOSPICE: THE GENTLE GOODBYE

## By Phyllis S. Quinlan, RNC, MS

Just after dawn on December 11, 2007, my mother went to God. There was a beautiful peacefulness that fell over that bright, winter morning that seemed perfect. Mom had battled several chronic, debilitating diseases that slowly robbed her of her energy and physical function. Her mind was always clear and her determination to live to see her grandchildren grow and to be with her husband of 59 years was intact. Unfortunately, her body had betraying her. Mom and I were very different. Our life's journey together could best be described as rocky, but the journeys end was her last gift to me.

It began one Thursday evening when I went to visit my parents. Mom had just come home from yet another unavoidable hospitalization. She was out of immediate danger, but the likelihood of a relapse and perhaps a challenging surgery was weighing heavy on her mind. She looked tired, frail and was having difficulty speaking. I could sense she was in pain although she characteristically denied it. As I sat down next to her, she looked me right in the eye and in a clear voice said, "I'm too weak to live and too strong to die. I want to go to God." She went on to explain that she was done taking her medications, had seen her last doctor, and had been to the hospital for the last time. If those declarations weren't enough, she asked me, "What are you going to do?" I knew immediately what she meant. She wanted me to take control of this out-of-control situation. She was entrusting me to help her live her last days in comfort and dignity. She wanted me to ensure that her transition from this life would be as gentle on her husband, children, grandchildren, and family as possible. The best solution was to arrange for hospice services.

I was the nurse in the family and I tried my best to collaborate with mom's private doctor. We spoke so often that we were on a first name basis for many years. Dr. Bob had grown very fond of my parents and their relationship. Our common goal was to keep mom comfortable and out of the hospital. Once my mom's wishes were clear, my role was then to ensure that those wishes were carried out. First, I helped my dad understand and accept her decision. Next, I call Dr. Bob and explained her request. He was very supportive. We both knew that the only treatment he could offer her was palliative. Clearly, in his medical opinion, Mom had less than six months to live. He made all the arrangements from his office. Finally, it was now time to call my sister. The inevitability of losing our mom to death was here. Thankfully, as in all things pertaining to our parents, we would do this together.

The next twelve days were exceptional. Mom was peaceful with her decision. She enjoyed her days with Dad, her visits with her grandchildren, and her messages from family and friends. Although she refused to take any more medication, she did allow the hospice nurse to obtain an order for pain meds so she could be truly comfortable. The hospice team arranged for a priest to come to the house. She received the sacraments of Holy Communion and the Anointing of the Sick. Mom prayed her rosary daily and in a few days slipped into a coma.

For twelve days the angels from hospice supported my family through the process of letting go. They immediately responded to phone calls and answered endless questions. Nurses came daily with supplies, understanding, and support. Their presence and professionalism allowed me the opportunity to be a daughter and not a nurse. On the day that Mom died, it was the hospice nurse that we called first. She came right away, pronounced her and walked us through the next step.

**The Value of Choice**

I have been a nurse for 30 years now. For the majority of my career I practiced in critical care and emergency trauma units. I fought death constantly with knowledge, skill, medications, and technology. I had limited success. During the last 10 years however, my focus has shifted from the length of one's life to a profound appreciation for the quality of one's life. High tech healthcare has its place when lives need to be saved. However, death does come to us all.

Hospice services allow for the care of loved ones to take place in safe, familiar surroundings with those they love close by. It empowers the patient through their last days, and offers them the respect of honoring their choices and the dignity of privacy. Hospice care assists the family during horrific moments of anger, regret, and grief that under less supportive circumstances could seriously challenge the family's unity.

It's important to understand that hospice is a philosophy of care rather than a specific place. It is an option for people whose life expectancy is six months or less. Treatment outcomes are based on pain and symptom relief rather than pursuing curative measures. This approach enables the person to live his/her last days with dignity, grace and support. Hospice affirms life and does not hasten or postpone death. Hospice care focuses on all aspects of physical, social, emotional, and spiritual well-being. There is no age restriction. Anyone in the last stages of life is eligible.

**Hospice Care Services**

1. **The Interdisciplinary Team:** Team members include doctors, nurses, social workers, counselors, home health aides, clergy, therapists, and trained volunteers who offer support based on their areas of specialty. The team provides a comprehensive palliative plan of care aimed at relieving symptoms and giving social, emotional, and spiritual support.

2. **Pain Management and Control of Symptoms:** The goal of these services is to help the patient to achieve comfort while allowing them to remain alert enough to make important decisions and remain in control.

3. **Spiritual Care:** Since people differ in their spiritual needs and religious beliefs, spiritual care is individualized and never forced.

4. **Home Care and In-patient Care:** Hospice care is typically centered in the home. However, it may be necessary to admit the patient to a hospital, extended-care facility, or a hospice in-patient facility. The hospice team can then facilitate this transfer and stay involved

in the patient's treatment. The team can also facilitate resuming in-home care when appropriate.

5. **Family Conferences:** The hospice nurse or social worker facilitates these conferences. They serve to help family members stay informed about the patient's condition and what to expect. Family conferences also provide an opportunity and safe forum to share fears, feelings, talk about expectations, and learn about the process of dying.

6. **Bereavement Care:** Bereavement is the time of mourning following a loss. The hospice team works with surviving family members to help them through the grieving process. The team can refer family members and friends to other professional services, if necessary. Bereavement follow-up services are provided for at least a year after the loved one's death.

**Hospice Care Settings**

Approximately 80 to 90 percent of hospice services are provided in the home. But, it is important to know that if the patient in a nursing home, hospice services can be offered there, as well. Hospitals that treat seriously ill patients often have a hospice program, too. Some hospitals have a dedicated hospice unit, while others have hospice teams who visit patients in any unit. Lastly, many communities have independently owned hospice centers that feature in-patient care, as well as home care hospice services. Independent hospice centers can benefit individuals who do not have family caregivers.

**Who Is Eligible For Hospice Care?**

1. You are eligible for hospice care if your doctor has certified your prognosis as not longer than six months. This applies to anyone of any age. Should you be blessed with improved health and no longer need hospice care, you will remain eligible to reapply for hospice care if it is necessary in the future.

2. While the majority of hospice referrals are cancer related, hospice is not exclusively for cancer patients. People with terminal neuromuscular diseases or any end stage disease can also benefit greatly from the services. It is not uncommon for people with Alzheimer's to be referred to hospice when they are in the final stages of the illness.

**Are Hospice Services Expensive?**

Hospice care customarily costs less than conventional care in a hospital or nursing home. This is because with home hospice, you pay only for the specific care that you need. In addition, volunteers may often provide many services at little or no cost, such as telephone support, meal preparation and running errands. Most private insurance plans, Medicare and Medicaid cover the services.

While patients usually pay out-of-pocket for any services not covered by insurance, hospice services can be provided without charge if you have limited funds. If you are unable to pay, most hospices will try to provide care using funds raised from community donations and charitable foundations.

## Closing Thoughts

Hospice care truly provides for the gentlest of goodbyes. It allowed me the space and time to be able to cherish my last moments with my mom. I look back on those days in peace, not pain. And I will always be grateful for the last gift my mom gave me, her trust.

**References:**

National Hospice & Palliative Care Organization

http://www.nhpco.org/custom/directory/main.cfm

Center for Medicare & Medicaid Services

http://www.cms.hhs.gov/center/hospice.asp

National Association for Home Care & Hospice

http://www.nahc.org/

# ABOUT THE AUTHOR

**Dr. Karen B. Wasserman**

Dr. Karen B. Wasserman is a licensed Clinical Psychologist (Indiana and Ohio), a Registered Nurse (Missouri and Ohio), an experienced consultant, and Life Success Coach. Whether working with special populations such as adults abused as children, people with bariatric concerns or individuals with chronic illnesses, Dr. Wasserman's focus has been on teaching others to find personal empowerment, to feel good about themselves, and most importantly, how to maintain positive self-esteem! Her goal throughout her career has been to help others to be about the business of enjoying life and find the joy around them.

Born and raised in the Midwest, Dr. Wasserman received her Doctor of Psychology (Psy.D.) degree from Wright State university, School of Professional Psychology in Dayton, Ohio. As an Air force spouse, she has lived in Texas, Germany, and along the Gulf of Mexico. She is a founder, and co-owner for nine years , of Fairhaven Clinic, Inc., (Private Mental Health) in Biloxi, Mississippi. She and her spouse also owned and operated a small book and gift shop nearby. Besides enjoying visiting her two children and collecting antiques (especially McCoy Pottery), she is an avid gardener. With her husband and a very small cat, she now makes her some in Olde Worthington, a suburb of Columbus, Ohio. This is house number fifteen!

*Contact:*

Dr. Karen Wasserman
696 Oxford St
Columbus, OH 43085
(614) 296-3522
drKarenB@columbus.rr.com
www.protrain.net

## FORTY-FIVE

# KEEPING THE FAITH: THE POWER OF HOPE

**Dr. Karen Wasserman**

"*For I know the plans I have for you . . .plans to give you Hope and a future.*"—Jeremiah, 29:11

We bandy the word Hope around a lot. "I *hope* this looks alright; my hair is okay; my suit is not too wrinkled; I know the right answers; I will not be too tongue-tied to talk to her/him." "I *hope* the baby is all right; we stocked the cabinets with enough provisions; we have enough fuel to go through the mountains." Hope pervades our speech and our thinking. In the early history of humans, we probably did not have a lot else to rely upon. We began to notice other forces involved besides our own, and often those forces were much greater than ours! To what could we/would we attribute this considerable differential in power? It began to dawn upon us that, while humans know only finiteness, cause and effect, beginnings and endings, there was something that came before and that continued beyond a single life or a generation. What was this? What did it mean?

Thousands of years later, we are no closer to tangible proof of the power of creation, in the eyes of some, than we ever were. For others though, we have not seen and yet believe. We KNOW there is more than just what we can see, hear, feel, measure, taste, smell or prove, beyond reasonable doubt, before a court or board of scientific enquiry. There are strange wonderful, indefinable/inexplicable things that happen to everyone and no one, yet have a complete explanation for these events. Have you ever 'felt' there was someone looking at you and turned around to find someone was staring at you? How did you know? No one can say, but the majority of us have had this experience. Humans experience this universally, yet this phenomenon is not explainable or provable by the scientific method. We cannot measure what is happening, only we absolutely KNOW it happens and so have faith in it.

Did we not all read, "Once upon a time . . ." and wriggle with anticipation? Did we not HOPE that there would be something wonderful and interesting that came after? And were we not enthralled the first time we heard the classic fairy tales and our imaginations began to blossom? Certainly we were likely captivated, and with each story we looked forward to the next chapter or verse. By the middle phase of our lives, though, we have likely experienced some rain, some cloudy days, perhaps some emotional or personal misfortune, lost a loved one, been downsized, or even seen our savings disappear as a business went bankrupt. By this time, we have had some struggles. Perhaps we have had personal health issues, sibling conflicts, been separated from loved ones by distance or war? We, "Boomers," are also known as 'The

Between Generation," with sometimes aging parents to care for, while still raising our own children, or even having 'grown' children moving back in with us after they experienced a calamity.

So what did we do? How have we coped? How did we find the wherewithal to put one foot in front of the other; to get out of bed for yet another day? What did we do if overwhelmed by grief or exhausted by competing priorities? What has kept our spirit intact? No doubt there have been days we felt 'spacey,' or 'out of it'; days we felt numb or baffled by all of it. Most have had times they just felt like they did not know where to start to unravel the snarls in the skeins of life. Yet, we were bolstered by **hope**, based on **facts** that have been the same for all of life as we know it. The sun does come up again; rains do not last forever; flood waters will recede; houses come and go; people move away and new neighbors arrive. We are still here! Common wisdom suggests that "90% of life is just showing up." So, we can be of good cheer, we're still here! So what of being faithful, depending upon hope and enduring, even allowing ourselves to be reassured? How does the Power of Hope become woven into life?

Consider that we cannot see wind, but we can see the effects of it. And where does wind begin? We see the stars and track them, but none know their origin – oh, we have theories abounding, but not the sacred, "randomly assigned, double blind study" *proof* of any particular theory. How do we attempt to explain and understand these amazing elements of our existence? We cannot generate or produce a blizzard or a hurricane, so is this mass hallucination, magic, trickery, or the sheer force of the Universe that reaches out to us? And, who/what created that Universe, at least the part that we do know about? How do I determine my reason for being here, and dare I rely on the power of Hope? (I didn't study for this section of the test!)

Likely, the subject of faith now enters our thinking. Do we not have faith that the sun will come up in the East and set in the West? Has it not been so since the beginning? Do we not expect the moon to have certain predictable phases and that certain signs in the skies can help to predict the weather? Of course we have these expectations and have been telling each other about these events, remarking that signals are different from different vantage points on the Earth. While we think we are quite clever, all of these things occur without our slightest intervention! This is the onset of faith, of that upon which we can rely, of what we can anticipate, of what is assured and thus 'of hope.' We have faith that, "Gravity is the Law!" Water usually runs downhill and warmth causes that which is cold to change states and ice to become water or vapor! Faith then is an essential of hope. While none of us can predict an absolute outcome, we hope/anticipate the best; do take it on faith that the people who put up the power grids and communication satellites know what they are doing and that we will not forget how to find our particular home in time for dinner. We recognize that at first humans were nomadic hunters and gatherers. Then, someone of faith *hoped* that putting seeds in the ground for a period of time and watering them, (and yes, watching them and talking to them) would result in young plants that would be like their parents. We do not have to discover this again now; it is part of our collective memory and knowledge. This experiment in faith and putting hope into action enabled humans to build more permanent dwellings/groups, and ensured a stable source of food without the necessity of packing everything up and moving it from place to place. Eureka! No more cardboard boxes, no wrapping paper or tape necessary! Ahhhh, the power of hope!

Gardeners may remark, "*Who plants a seed beneath the sod, and waits to see, believes in God.*" "*It all began in the Garden.*" "*Thyme began in a garden.*" Gardening, like building or traveling to new places, is activity that relies on the interaction of humans with faith in our Creator, the workings of the Universe, and putting hope into action. One could insert astronomers, sailors/mariners, or YOU here, as well! Humans have faith that no blizzard lasts forever, that summer's heat has a purpose and changes buds to fruit as temperatures cool and leaves begin to change color and drop. As a group, we have faith that change occurs with regularity, if not with absolute predictability!

Our American culture seems to require/expect/anticipate absolute predictability, and our national, irrational idea is that if something does not happen exactly on time, exactly the way it 'should' when it 'should', or in the correct order or place, then a terrible calamity will result; a catastrophe will have occurred! What if you did not receive the latest e-mail or voice message? What if you did not choose the 'best buy' and purchased some inferior brand? Each of us has his/her list of 'too awful to imagine.' What are your absolute 'horrors', that if they did/do not occur as planned, a genuine catastrophe will result? For instance:

1. My child must attend the right school or ________________
2. I must have a 6-figure income by ______________________
3. ____________________________________________
4. ____________________________________________
5. ____________________________________________

Now, as you peruse your list, how many of these events actually rise to the level of catastrophe? Maybe you need to re-examine your definition of catastrophe? A friend once said about her wedding, "It went pretty well. After all, no one died, nothing caught on fire or exploded, and the Earth is still spinning through space." Pretty good analysis, based in reality!

When the parents or grandparents of many Baby Boomers lived through the Great Depression AND World War II, hope was severely tested. We ask what kept them going; how did they not lose heart during the depression, when some worked all day for $1.00 or had to eat lard sandwiches because there was no real food? How did they keep hope alive while news of the war and far away loved ones was slow in coming and rationing was everywhere? How did they summon up the faith to keep going in the face of a war lasting for years, putting cardboard in the bottom of their worn shoes and women daily going into arms and aircraft factories, instead of dusting, sweeping or baking? All this is difficult for us to imagine, as we can purchase furniture in a grocery store, buy a gallon of milk while we fill a prescription, or download music at any time, while having the world's news at our fingertips. We have not had to "go without." We have no experience with rationing, being out of contact with one another for prolonged periods, not having enough gas or tire tread for travel, and cannot imagine a city without shopping malls.

This "Greatest Generation" did accomplish their hope of maintaining our freedom, democracy and way of life. They did keep the battles "over there," away from our shores and streets. We did walk on the moon, go on after Kennedy was shot, and exited Vietnam. We *did* survive rock 'n roll and may yet survive rap. How is our faith being tested now and how do we keep hope alive? We consider global warming, another Ice Age, terrorists, university shootings, cell phone use that may be as deadly to us as cigarettes, and that the future of our Medicare coverage is a big question. We struggle to actually define what our hopes are and now search for the means to realize them. Where is our faith, our hope? What hopes will we put into action?

Some of us feel depressed that we did not accomplish certain goals. Does this mean we had no faith, that we abandoned hope? Perhaps it represents instead, being 'becalmed' for a while in the sea of life, and that for the moment we have no wind to fill our sails and do not know when or from where the wind may come. We do as other mariners have done; we wait and become bored perhaps, and may muse or dream. This can be a perfect opportunity to determine a different direction, to caulk any leaky seams we've found, or even to bail, if we are taking on water! Other opportunities reveal themselves through our social support network. Another person might ask you about your mood, apathy or lack of energy. Do you dismiss these questions and return nothing but a lazy pat on the head? "Oh, I'm okay; it is just a tough day, but I'll be fine." This is akin to giving them a pacifying-people-biscuit. "Here, be a nice little person and go away please, so I can wallow in my misery a little longer." Others are trying to share their hope and faith with you – faith that situations can/do improve, and yours can too. They are reminding us of what Winston Churchill said, "Never, Never, Never give up. In no thing, great or small. Never give up." Or as the ski instructor related, "When I was 9, my father and some friends took us up to the top of the mountain, expecting us to ski down. We were above the clouds and could no longer see our village. My knees were shaking and my mouth was so dry. I looked around and saw all these other people talking and laughing as they got off the lift and headed down towards the clouds below. It occurred to me that they expected to ski down the mountain.

I determined that if they were able to get to the village, then so was I, and took off that moment." By their deeds, words or actions, others have provided inspiration and motivation for us. Therefore, we do not need to be mighty to have hope, but merely to be observant, embracing what is before us, and to consider the possibilities. The power of Hope is transferable and tangible!

What is your measure of faith that others want to help you? Are you afraid you'll be/feel beholden to them? Are you so focused on being independent, you cannot accept the Universe's offer and demonstration of energetic assistance? Was your focus on self-pity or tallying misery? Did that obscure what was happening around you? Did you lack faith in the other person's genuineness, not believing they really meant to help you? How do you tread that line between being gullible or naive, of being trusting, or "perfectly" self-sufficient? Where is your faith that the other person can accept you, as is, without perfection and without requiring a 'pay back?' Perhaps you consider such an idea 'idle hope', or are suspicious? Perhaps you think faith is only for fools, since one must make his/her own way in the world; it is 'dog-eat-dog,' we say, or 'early bird gets the worm' (an idea that always makes one squirm); or 'get out of bed early in the morning and the first punch of the day is yours!' Maybe, perhaps, you are afraid of hope or afraid to hope? Or maybe you are just afraid to let go of where you are (or where you think you are), because you are not quite sure of the direction or outcome? What if you have set your aspirations too low; have settled for less, rather than risk being disappointed or feeling lost? Maybe you lack experience in hoping, or is it practice that is lacking? Are you concerned with status quo? "Don't rock the boat." "Quit while you're ahead." "That is just impossible; only a magician can make that happen."

Whatever our beliefs, it is fitting to stop, slow down, assess the situation, look for a guide, seek inspiration, not be in motion every single second of life. No one can live your life better than you. No one else has your experience and understanding. Even if others have different hopes and dreams, goals and views of the Universe, we can learn from them as they are learning from us. People have accomplished many astonishing things before we came on the scene, and there are many other miraculous discoveries to be made. When a stone drops into the lake, no one knows when the ripples end. Without knowingly or planfully doing so, you may have inspired someone today, just by being you. Watching you, someone may be able to go forward for another day and another, until they come to the end of their life's journey, and most of us do not know when that will be either! So we keep searching, keep learning and keep trying.

What has brought you this far is a combination of hope, faith and dreams, with a lot of hard work in between. Maybe you never thought you would live to see 40, 50 or 60? (Linda Evans was the first to tell us, "40 isn't fatal.") You might be thinking, how could anyone be that old anyway (especially me!)? Must be an antique and really out of touch. But now you have seen, been and experienced living through some major challenges, but not ALL of them! As people approach retirement age, they do often stop to take stock of themselves. Some are surprised by how much they have been through, and some feel they are just beginning a new adventure. Consider your plans and *hopes* for this part of the journey. Are you where you wanted to be, or was that particular part of your initial dream not realistic? Maybe things have turned out even better than planned. Children survived to adulthood, married and are having families. You achieved your degree and began your own company. You may have turned corners on paths you did not know ever existed. You have changed and the world did, too. By this time, we recall that "back in the day" it was different, and now a new horizon lies in an unknown area. Both the rising sun and the setting sun provide lovely light. Now you wear a few scuffs and scrapes, maybe have some missing body parts, a little thicker skin, and an 'odd'/enhanced, or totally different hair color than when you were 20! Perhaps you pierced a part of your body not generally shown, or endowed yourself with a tattoo, known only to you and that sky-diving, bungee-jumping, amateur-sleuth group with which you associate?

Or maybe, just maybe, it is difficult for you to imagine not being so busy? What if you are feeling so "not needed," or not respected at this time? Did you plan for this supposed inactivity? Certainly not! So let your faith guide you, now that you know a thing or two and can apply that prior experience and knowledge to this situation. What is in front of you to do? Is it time to re-invent yourself? The soul does not age, so your hopes and dreams may be the same OR different. You are certainly equipped differently than you were initially! What is our/your Hope-Power? How is this power going to be manifested in the now?

Maybe you have taken the adage 'age and treachery will always overcome youth and skill' to heart. Maybe you will kick over the traces, wear a red hat and a purple dress and embrace whoever you are? Or, now may be the time to take naps, paint pictures, compose poetry or invent a dryer that sorts and folds? There is no guarantee that our hopes and dreams will be fulfilled. But there is also nothing that says they cannot be. Entertain them as you would a favored guest. Those you find suitable you keep around, because now that you know more, you can do more! You can scoff at 'agism', recognize 'spin' for what it is, or sort out the likely from the possible. You can plan projects, or not. But, you can rely on the faith that has sustained you thus far; the Creator or the

Higher Power of the Universe has had an intention for this little planet and for all our souls. Since the soul does not age, we don't necessarily feel differently inside ourselves than we ever did, although the image in the mirror can be a surprise. We are at a different event-horizon and can have, yet, some hopes to realize before we go "out beyond the rim." (Babylon 5).

We can rest assured that in faith we have traveled this far and we can continue. We can take time to smell the roses (and lilacs and gardenias) and enjoy our chosen route. (Or maybe this is still the detour?) Faith has helped us to realize many hopes and sustains us yet. If your faith falters and you have hit a stone wall, or your hopes seem crumpled or somewhat faded, look around you and see if you can enumerate all that you have accomplished so far. Do not gloss over the "little" things, such as cooking dinner for your family or caring for your pet, watering the plants, fixing the lawn mower, picking up your father's packages at the Post Office or donating to a good cause. It is not the amount spent, nor the number of minutes recorded. It is that the acts were accomplished by you. These do not represent sugary, empty-calorie reassurances, but real events. You can feel the difference within yourself. Our Creator had faith to put us into this Universe; now is our time to make our Hope-Power tangible. And by all means, visit the ***DEPARTMENT OF SUNSHINE AND RAINBOWS.*** The invitation indicates: *HOPES RESTORED! FAITH UPLIFTED! ENTHUSIASMS RENEWED!* Hope is tangible, so "Keep the faith, baby!"

Dedicated to my parents, Betty Varner Boling and Kenneth G. Boling, who were both veterans of World War II, with gratitude for their inspiration and hopes realized!

# ABOUT THE AUTHOR

## DR. DARLENE SILVERNAIL PHD LMHC CAP

Dr. Darlene Silvernail PhD LMHC CAP is a Corporate and Professional Trainer. She has been working in the mental health field for over twenty-three years with extensive experience developing and implementing quality assurance protocols. Dr. Silvernail has been a past nominee for the Robert Woods Foundation Award (1997) The Best Practice Award (2000) and nominated three times for the Sun Sentinel Community Leadership Award (1999-2004).

Dr. Darlene Silvernail is the President and CEO of Professional Enhancement Services and the Founder of ICU, International Coaching Unlimited with clients in the USA and abroad. She has assisted numerous companies in expanding and enhancing their businesses. Her mission is to help you reach your vision and achieve your personal, business and professional goals and to take you, your company and your employees to a higher level.

She is a member of the Professional Woman Network and has co-authored two books.: Emotional Wellness for Women Volume III and The Baby Boomers Handbook for Women.

**Other Memberships**

Certification Board Addiction Professional, Professional Woman Speakers Bureau, American Academy of Health, South Florida Society of Trauma Based Disorders, NAADAC and FADAA, CBAPF and NAFC, American Mental Health Counselor Assoc, Coalition for Batterer's Intervention Programs, PB County Victim Advocacy Advisory Council, Mental Health Association, Palm Beach County Domestic Violence Council and Palm Beach County Human Trafficking Committee Pride Probation Advisory Council.

Dr. Silvernail is available for seminars, workshops, keynote addresses and Corporate and/or personal coaching.


*Contact:*
Darlene Silvernail PhD LMHC CAP
International Coaching Unlimited
PO Box 18745
WPB Florida 33416
1-888-90-Coach
ICUCoaching@aol.com
www.ICUCoaching.com

## FORTY-SIX

# UNDERSTANDING THE BABY BOOMER GENERATION

**Dr. Darlene Silvernail**

The baby boomer generation is a modern slang term describing the population born between 1946 and 1964, which had its origin in the increased births (77 million babies born) after World War II. The peak boomer births were between 1952-1957. Baby boomers are now between the ages of 47 and 62 years old. The first baby boomer turned sixty on January 1, 2006.

By 2015, those aged fifty and older will represent 45% of the U.S. population. By 2030, according to projections, we expect to see 57.8 million baby boomers still living and 54.9% will be female. The boomers will then be between the ages of 66 and 84. In 2006, there were 7,918 people turning sixty each day, and 50% of these were women.

**The Birth of the Boomers**

The following chart shows the number of U.S. births from 1940 to 1964, the Baby Boomer years: (in millions)

| | | | |
|---|---|---|---|
| 1946 | 3,411 | 1956 | 4,218 |
| 1947 | 3,817 | 1957 | 4,300 |
| 1948 | 3,637 | 1958 | 4,255 |
| 1949 | 3,649 | 1959 | 4,245 |
| 1950 | 3,632 | 1960 | 4,258 |
| 1951 | 3,823 | 1961 | 4,268 |
| 1952 | 3,913 | 1962 | 4,167 |
| 1953 | 3,965 | 1963 | 4,098 |
| 1954 | 4,078 | 1964 | 4,027 |
| 1955 | 4,097 | | |

The 1950's and 1960's were well known as decade that defined who the boomers were. Oh, the nostalgic memories! **I can still remember the trends and fads of the time:**

1. Poodle skirts and saddle shoes
2. The mini-skirt and Twiggy!
3. The garter belts, thigh-high stockings and fish nets
4. '57 T-birds and sneaking into the drive-in theaters
5. Tie-dyed t-shirts, hip hugger bell-bottoms
6. Leave It To Beaver, I Love Lucy, Ed Sullivan, Twilight Zone and MASH

7. Mooning and streaking
8. Elvis Presley, vinyl records and 8-track tape decks
9. The Twist with Chubby Checker, The Jerk and the Bump
10. American Bandstand
11. Beatles, Jimi Hendrix, Grateful Dead, Tower of Power, Santana and the Drifters
12. Woodstock

**It was also a time for great political and social changes:**

1. Martin Luther King and Malcolm X
2. Watergate scandal
3. Gloria Steinem, Angela Davis, Patty Duke
4. Kennedy assassination
5. The birth control pill in the 60's
6. The turmoil of Viet Nam
7. Militant Black Panthers

These political times greatly impacted my life and personality. Boomer women were demanding equal rights as they discarded their girdles and garter belts and burned their bras. It was during this era when the civil rights legislation brought new opportunities for women. We were attending graduate school and working at well-paying careers. We had demonstrated the ability to balance home, children and careers.

It was also during this time when many of us began our gender-bender missions. We were challenging the stereotypical image of the 50's. I entered the military in the 70's, which was during a time when women were not totally accepted serving the country, even though we played an important role in the Viet Nam era. After the military, I entered law enforcement and again pushed the gender role stigma. At the time of my law enforcement career, there were only five females in a department of three hundred men. As female boomers, we were accessing many non-traditional roles and employment opportunities that had previously been considered male-only positions.

Baby boomer women are now better educated, more independent, and have actually surpassed men in obtaining higher education. Men earned 508,424 bachelor's degrees in 1975; however, by 1991, women had far surpassed the male figure earning a total of 599,045 undergraduate degrees. That same year, women surpassed men in the number of master's degrees obtained: 156,895 for men and 181,603 for women.

Women often make more money than their partners. A baby boomer average income is reported as $71,400. If we include values of homes, the average net worth of the boomer generation is $550,000 each. Did you know that boomers own 62% of all large Wall Street investment accounts? And we boomers still dine out approximately 4-5 times per week.

The boomer women who are now turning 50 viewed this time as a time for new opportunities and self-actualization, both for personal growth and for career advancement. Women today feel approximately 7-10 years younger than their real age. You Go, Girl!!!

Women today feel 7-10 years younger than their real age. Move over, Jane Fonda! The female boomers have fueled the fitness revolution for the past thirty years. In the 70's, we discovered jogging for life. Women then pressed forward in the 80's with aerobics and in the 90's with kickboxing. Today, we find our 50 and 60-year-old bodies welcoming the softer side of fitness, such as mall walking, yoga, tai chi and Pilates. Oh, don't let me forget my much-needed weekly massage!

Today's medical advancements have also added a new twist to the Mid-Life Crisis stage. (Yes, we female boomers have our own version of mid-life crisis and even our own version of Viagra! Ladies, did you know that Viagra-type medication is consumed every three seconds by our male boomers?) We have spent serious dollars on face-lifts, Botox, tummy tucks, coaches, trainers and counseling. Boomer women no longer look at the change of life as a curse or a negative milestone. We now embrace it and welcome this exciting period in our lives. We are still setting trends, and chronological and biological ages no longer mesh. Youth is a relative term! I am as young as I feel.

**The ME Era**

I am still working on "me." It is my desire to continue to pursue self-discovery, self-improvement, and self-actualization. As a result, I strive for knowledge, love to travel, and want to be stimulated intellectually, physically and spiritually. I hope to continue looking for adventure. Yes, during the day I put on my business attire and carry my briefcase; but, on the weekend, there's a good chance you will see me riding one of my two Harley's while wearing black leather and some lace (smile)! Nearly a third of Harley Davidson riders are now 50 years of age or older. It's also why travel that involves exotic destinations and/

or novel experiences is at an all-time high. Don't get me wrong! I must absolutely have my spa vacations as well. We gals must be pampered! Based upon life-span theories, we have entered the Integrity vs. Despair stage of life span, described by Eric Erikson, a well-known lifespan development theorist.

| | | |
|---|---|---|
| Generativity vs. Stagnation | Middle Adulthood | Adults are willing to have and care for children and devote themselves to work<br>***OR***<br>they become self-centered and inactive. (Middle adulthood brings real major life changes. Becoming a grandparent, loss of a child or husband (death or divorce), changes in career, empty nest syndrome or aging parents) |
| Integrity vs. Despair | Old Age | Older people reflect on the meaning of their lives and accept death with dignity<br>***OR***<br>they feel despair for unaccomplished goals and failures.<br>(As people get older, they must come to terms with the approach of death. People who have gained full maturity by resolving earlier stages possess the integrity to face death with a minimum of fear.) **(Broderick)** |

Eric Erikson had his views on mid-life and argued that a person must accept and face major crisis in life to accept one's own mortality and destination. Contributing to how we cope and expose ourselves are often our own self-made crises. Many of us in this phase of development have challenging professions; some, like myself, have made significant changes. Job satisfaction peaks in middle age when some are more productive, but take on major life changes. I sold my three treatment centers and toxicology lab to reduce life stressors and went to work for someone else (Uncle Sam) because I had to re-evaluate my life choices and the need to prepare for retirement. I wanted less stress at this stage of my lifespan.

It is in this stage of our development where we should be able to look at our accomplishments. As older adults, we can often look back on our lives feeling contentment and a sense of fulfillment. This has probably brought a deep sense of life's meaning. Ask yourself, what have you contributed to life? This is a feeling Erikson calls **integrity**. Some adults may reach this stage (55-65 years old) and feel **despair,** seeing their experiences perceived as failures. They may fear death as they struggle to find a purpose to their lives. Do you feel a sense of satisfaction-integrity? If not, it's not too late. Complete the following:

1. Take a moment to reflect and list several of your memorable experiences. ______________________________________

   ______________________________________________

   ______________________________________________

   ______________________________________________

2. What have your accomplishments been? ________________

   ______________________________________________

   ______________________________________________

   ______________________________________________

3. What kind of life have you lived? ______________________
____________________________________________
____________________________________________
____________________________________________

4. What would you still like to achieve? __________________
____________________________________________
____________________________________________
____________________________________________

5. What changes in you life are you willing to make? ________
____________________________________________
____________________________________________
____________________________________________

The majority of boomers are in good health; 77% report being in good/excellent health. We are living dramatically longer than our ancestors, so we will have to support ourselves longer and earn more money to pay the bills, often including health insurance premiums. A female who survives to 65 can expect to log another 15 years, on average. Are you ready for this financially? More and more females prefer the challenge of the workplace to the quietude of retirement. Many have watched friends, relatives and co-workers take early retirement, only to encounter boredom and despair. AARP found that 69% of people ages 45 to 74 were working, or planning to work, in some capacity after retirement.

Married boomer women are more than six times more likely to share responsibility for savings and investments compared to their mothers' generation. How financially secure do you feel? Fewer boomers may be as secure in retirement. It has been reported by AARP that nearly half of boomers have a traditional pension plan, 50% have a 401(k) and 50% have an IRA. Nearly 70% of boomers have employee or retiree health insurance. And, about one third have long-term care insurance. One-third of the Boomer population says they plan to take Social Security when they turn 62; the rest plan to take Social Security at age 65 or later. In the past, those who took Social Security early did so for health reasons.

Most surveys will agree that 76% of baby boomers intend to keep working and earning in retirement, although many say they will "retire" from their current job/career at around age 64 and then jump into an entirely new job or career. There is information on Social Security and what we female boomers need to know! Ladies, it is not too late to plan and prepare. Refer to the following link for info: http://www.genpolicy.com/2006_journal/index_articles.html

Also, explore the following site for information that will help calculate your estimated SSI payments: http://www.ssa.gov/OACT/quickcalc/index.html.

I am at the stage in my development where I just want to "putz"! My retirement vision is to teach a few classes online and travel. My bank account, on the other hand, screams, "Please buy my book!"

Did you know that many employers are afraid of the potential future shortage of skilled employees? This is one of the major reasons why they offer unusual perks to keep us baby boomers on the job. They don't want a large and experienced work force to walk out the door. More and more employers are hiring an increased number of part-time workers and empowering them to create their own personalized, flexible work schedules. Ladies, play your cards correctly and negotiate a flexible work schedule to meet your lifestyle and needs.

I am just not ready to retire, and you won't get me into a nursing home (shoot me first!). Seniors not content with nursing homes are forming new retirement communities that reflect their interests, desires and needs. I also do not want to be homeless and a bag lady. It is a fear that lurks in the back of every woman's mind. Can I survive the next decade at the lifestyle I am accustomed to?

Interesting Boomer Facts: Some Famous Female Boomers

| | | |
|---|---|---|
| Suzanne Somers 10/16/46 | Michelle Pfeiffer 04/29/58 | Madonna 08/18/58 |
| Duchess of York, Sarah 10/15/59 | Patty Hearst 02/20/54 | Meryl Streep 06/22/49 |
| Cheryl Tiegs 09/25/47 | Tanya Tucker 10/10/58 | Vanna White 02/18/57 |
| Dorothy Hamill 07/26/56 | Patty Hearst 02/20/54 | Oprah Winfrey 01/29/54 |
| Hillary Clinton 10/26/47 | Princess Anne 08/15/50 | Chaka Khan 03/23/53 |
| Whoopi Goldberg 11/13/55 | Princess Caroline 01/23/57 | Farrah Fawcett 02/02/47 |
| Melanie Griffith 08/09/57 | Sharon Stone 03/10/58 | Roseanne 11/03/52 |

**Informative Boomer Weblinks**

The National Association of Baby Boomer Women, http://www.NABBW.com
http://www.BoomerWomenSpeak.com

AARP Magazine has some tips for retirement. http://www.aarpmagazine.org/.

Bring back childhood memories with "Mothballs in My Attic" www.mothballsinmyattic.com

**Resources:**

*The Life Span: Human Development for Helping Professionals* by P. C. Broderick & P. Blewitt (2003). Upper Saddle River, NJ: Pearson, Merill, Prentice Hall.

Census facts http://www.census.gov/popest/national/ (U.S. Census).

AARP: www.aarp.com

*Feminism's Generation Gap* by Stephanie Herman, Vol. Two, Issue Nine (May 22, 1995) and Issue 10 (June 14, 1995) of CGX.

Journal of Women & Aging, the multidisciplinary quarterly of psychosocial practice, theory, and research, Volume: 11 Issue: 4

## ABOUT THE AUTHOR

### JO ANNE WHITE, PHD

Jo Anne White, PhD, is President and CEO of Doc White Consulting Services, LLC, a corporate consulting and training company strongly committed to excellence and achievement. As a personal & business coach and corporate trainer, she empowers and inspires women, their families, businesses and corporations to achieve greater health, wellness and success.

Her expertise in training and coaching has motivated organizations, groups and individuals to be more effective and successful, and to create more satisfaction in their lives and businesses. Corporate clients include hospitals, banks, universities and organizations that desire the best in Team Building, Strategic Planning, Image, Performance and Achievement.

Formerly a professor at Temple University's Dept. of Education, Dr. White developed educational and training programs for several University departments which included the Institute on Aging and the Special Education Department. She's also been featured on the Internet and in local, national and international publications including Web MD, Woman's World and Women's Day. Doc White has appeared as a frequent guest on radio and television networks such as NBC and CN8, World Talk Radio and WYSP.

Jo Anne White, PhD has presented many seminars that she designed specifically for baby boomers. Her talent is to gather together women of different ages and experiences to foster community and personal and professional growth. She's been counseling women and their families for over fifteen years. As a certified hypnotherapist and therapist, she specializes in an integrative and holistic approach to wellness. Doc White currently resides in New Jersey.

Jo Anne White, PhD is a member of The Professional Woman Network (PWN) Speaker's Bureau PWN Author's Bureau and a contributing author in: Emotional Wellness for Women: Volume II & Volume III.

**Additional Books:**

Sense Your Way to Life Satisfaction

How to Love: Secrets to Lasting Relationships

*Contact:*
Dr. Jo Anne White
Doc White Consulting, LLC.
PO Box 176
Haddonfield, NJ, 08033
856-795-5854
1-877-DOC-WHITE
joanne@drjoannewhite.com
www.docwhite.org

## FORTY-SEVEN

# CREATIVE AGING

**By Jo Anne White, PhD**

Baby boomers like us have been defying convention and setting new perceptions and models for living, loving, working, parenting and more throughout our lives. Now in mid-life, once again we have that same opportunity and responsibility to create a new paradigm for aging as we face our own aging process. Some of us, in our early sixties, question the old structures of retirement and volunteerism, health and longevity. We're finding our own direction when it comes to outdated stereotypes that don't match how we feel, think and behave. This is an exciting time to create our own beliefs, images and realties of aging for us and to pave the way for future generations: our children, grandchildren and great grandchildren. Attitudes, lifestyle and goals during midlife set the stage for aging. They significantly affect its outcome and life quality. Decisions and perceptions are crucial to what lay ahead in the continuous shaping of your future. You have the ability to make adjustments immediately that will impact the rest of your life.

Choose the **Tenants of Creative Aging,** described below, to ensure an enjoyable, fulfilling and successful ride.

**Tenants of Creative Aging**

**Time To Let Go:**

Before we can creatively claim or reclaim ourselves, the first task is one of letting go. To move from one life stage to another is not always easy, but runs more smoothly when you know what to anticipate. During this shift or life transition, adjustments are necessary. They may be accompanied by some discomfort and real sense of loss and temporary confusion. You look ahead to a future that's still vague and undefined. You glance back to the past that you can never return to, except in your memories. It's a perfect time to release whatever stands in your way of aging according to your own standards and your own potential. Naturally, there's some reluctance and sadness when you must say goodbye to a certain physical or body image that can no longer be maintained, especially when many cultures extol youth and beauty that is age-conscious and limiting. You've grown up with negative stereotypes about aging and older people. Maybe you've even harbored some of your own. There was a time when a woman who was forty or fifty or sixty years old seemed ancient to you, but alas, no more. Now you are there and you don't feel aged or ancient, nor do you look the part. You have a responsibility to banish aging stereotypes, both personal and cultural, and be rid of them forever!

The first myth that we've grown up with and even voiced is that we're not responsible for what happens because it's all in the genes. Let go of this false notion that usurps your power. Instead, don't blame genetics for your circumstances. Genetics only accounts for less than one-third of what happens to us as we age. What's more encouraging and within your immediate control is how you're living. Leave behind the outdated idea that aging always represents a decline in creativity, ability and action; research states otherwise. Some of the most creative individuals began late in life and their most significant contributions occurred after age sixty-five.

To let go, you have to make peace with your past. Are you still holding onto past hurts, disappointments or anger towards another person or a situation? If yes, now is the time to approach them differently and with forgiveness. Forgive you, the other people, and events from the past and say goodbye to those feelings that weigh you down. They limit you and prevent you from moving forward with emotional and mental ease. Find a way to heal those past hurts and resentments within you and make amends with them. You don't need to carry that extra baggage with you on your way to creating your future.

**Time To Revive Your Lifestyle:**

Your lifestyle is significant in how successfully you age, so examine if your lifestyle is suitable for the long haul. If not, making changes can, in many instances, positively reverse the direction you're headed in. Decide upon physical, mental, emotional and spiritual goals to enhance you and better equip you for expected and unexpected life events.

1. **Take care of your physical body.** Examine your eating, sleeping and physical exercise patterns and make way for new habits that support healthy and hardy aging. So what if you can't eat like a twenty year old; now you include healthful choices that bring about staying power and personal endurance. The adage about moderate living still has appeal, so follow it often. You've already heard plenty about how physical exercise can improve health, your mind, and slow down the aging process, so take action to introduce more

physical activity into your schedule. Personalize it to fit your needs, body type and interests in such a way that you won't abandon it at the first chance you get.

2. **Mental exercise** is additionally important to sharpen your mental skills, such as memory, performance and reasoning, and to keep them functional. It's vitally important to find activities that require different types of thinking and mental processing. Challenge yourself with mental tasks that require usage of your brain. Choose activities of interest to you that not only use your brainpower, but are also aimed at having fun. There are numerous clubs, classes, entrepreneurial pursuits and more that can satisfy any palate, so experiment and find what suits you. You're not just preserving what's already there; you're also expanding your capacity. Your brain can make new pathways to learning, regardless of age.

3. **Emotional Balance** is about resolution. You have resolved or are in the process of resolving your past with your present. It's also all about attitude. Your feelings about you, your life, aging and your future affect how well you'll age. If your expectation and view of you and your future lack optimism, shore up your attitude about aging. You can change it. Any limitations that you place on you can be lifted. Envision you living a satisfying and enriching life while you set the stage for inner calm and personal strength. Your life experiences account for how you view present challenges. Hopefully, you've acquired the wisdom, even temperament, and a faith that you can face each situation with confidence. Remind you of all the past victories that you've won and the hurdles you've crossed. Acquire a graceful and realistic acceptance regarding change and aging, without glossing over what can happen. At the

same time, hold true to a determined, undefeated image of you, regardless of life's surprises. Expect that the surprises will be many; anticipate them with interest, rather than dread. Tell yourself that you are capable of handling whatever appears. When you do, you'll create more inner calm, trust and resolve.

4. **Spiritual Nourishment** can be sustained inside churches, synagogues, mosques, or in nature walks, quiet reflection, meditation, prayer and loving communion with others and a Higher Power. How you receive your spiritual sustenance isn't important as long as it revives you and recommits you to a better, more loving and tolerant you, and opens the window to compassion and a feeling of wholeness and faith. Now, more than ever, spiritual belief and spiritual practices can keep you strong, add to your health and well-being, and give you the anchor to face any situation. Your faith leads to a deeper understanding and sense of purpose in your life, and a heartfelt connection to others, the universe and the world around you. It also supports a healthier, less stressful and longer life. Include ample spiritual activities that uplift you and others. Make a commitment to unify your spiritual practices with conscious action and choices that promote the highest expression of your humanity.

**Time To Embrace and Cultivate:**

1. Authenticity
2. Creativity
3. Friendship and Companionship

4. Mentoring
5. Positive Role Models
6. Community and Civic Engagement
7. Productivity
8. Acceptance
9. Passion

You decide what to embrace as you move forward in midlife and beyond. It's important that you seek whatever's going to support and sustain you in all facets of your life. To be authentic means that you're not deceiving you about you, and about how you're living. Authenticity connotes honesty in word and action about what's really important to you. You live close to your truths and values; you feel good about your choices that are compatible with your beliefs. Creativity is also necessary to design your present and future. Not only does it feel good and keep you young in heart and mind, creativity promotes problem solving skills, motivation and practical life management. It can add to your sense of purpose, autonomy and social interaction. Creativity comes alive in the kitchen, travel, conversation, interaction, and in many forms of personal and professional expression. Creativity may surface because of loss or newfound pleasure, or can be a continuation and expansion of early interests that still sustain you. Express yourself, too, with friends and companions, old and new. Never lose sight of how important your friends, family and social engagements are to healthy aging, and in creating a life that is filled with depth and meaning. Life is not fully lived without passion. Find activities, people, ideas, causes, travel, new careers, etc. that fire up your passion and are also pleasurable. Passion is most alive when you're living and doing what brings you joy and personal satisfaction. Experiment with this, because your passions can change as you age and as your interests broaden and your life experiences increase.

Teaching younger generations from your wealth of life experience is one of the most rewarding activities that you can embark on. Everyone involved benefits. Here's where you have an opportunity to change views about getting older by being a positive influence on young people. Find women to mentor, and help them fulfill their dreams with your support and encouragement. If you've never been mentored, find someone who can mentor you. Who are your heroes? Make sure that you seek them among older people so that you have something and someone to aspire to. They can be famous people or people in your own life from the past or present that you look up to and admire. Search for the special qualities in the people that inspire you and change those limiting notions you have about aging.

Continue to be active in work, leisure, and in some form of community service that you look forward to. Make sure that your mind, heart, talents and interests are involved. Rewards come by being productive rather than idle, no matter what your age. Life is more meaningful when we engage in activity that's purposeful and helpful to other people, as well as to us. We realize that with aging come expected and unexpected events, and we learn how to handle them and move on. We recognize that there may be new losses and grief that accompany aging, as friends and loved ones depart and as changes take place in and around us. Sometimes those life changes are limiting, or may appear so. This is when learned acceptance for what is can be valuable. Acceptance doesn't mean that we give up or abandon our hopes and dreams. We persevere and keep constant faith in our ability to thrive, and to discover new methods to move ahead, regardless of what we face. We don't diminish the realities of what's happening, yet we're able to take charge as best we can without retreat or defeat. New dreams or new ways to realize those dreams may have to be created. Often, what's created anew out of despair or tragedy can lead to fulfillment and peace.

**Time To Reinvent and Discover You:**

1. Recreate Yourself.

2. Revitalize Your Relationships.

3. Redesign Retirement.

4. Redefine Volunteerism.

5. Revisit Your Views on Aging.

6. Recommit to Lifelong Learning.

Aging can be an exciting continuum of your lifelong journey as you embrace you in a novel way. You've learned more about you and have come to accept and value who you are. Continue to seek and discover new activities, interests, or hobbies and travel that give your life meaning. Maybe it's another career that beckons to you and you respond passionately. It's not unusual, as we age and live longer, to have several different career pursuits that are successful and enjoyable. Remember that you're creating what you want to include into your life design. Arrange time for family and social engagements that deepen your relationship to others and to you. Make a commitment to lifelong learning. It's never too late to learn something that you've always wanted to, like a musical instrument or a new language. Make time for it now. Your capacity for learning doesn't have to diminish as you age, so keep your brain cells thriving.

Redefine what it means to be old for you and for others, and realize that aging is really based on how you see you. Plan for your retirement: financially, physically, socially, and in all ways, rather than letting it take you by surprise. Nowadays, retirement may mean gradually easing out of a particular job or career, or can mean changing your career completely to suit you, your time and new interests. It doesn't have to mean boredom or lounging around in front of the television. Aging and retirement can be as vitalizing and tantalizing as you decide them to be. You can design them any way that you desire. View volunteerism differently, as an opportunity and a call to service and civic responsibility. Think what a wonderful and continuous contribution you can make to your community and to your world and take action.

Creative aging thrives on the confidence and understanding that you've gained by living through all the different experiences that shook you to your very core, or awed and uplifted you with their beauty and uniqueness. It takes courage to age creatively. You've learned to accept and transcend life challenges, and continue to keep a sense of hope and gratitude for the present and the future. You see the opportunities and possibilities all around, not diminishing, but expanding, as you open your heart to your own wonder and majesty.

**A. Age Enhancing Activities:**

1. Become eco-conscious: take responsibility for the planet.

2. Be responsible to your community-at-large in the form of service and contribution.
3. Develop a true sense of community that matters to you.
4. Create physical, mental, emotional and social activity that you feel good about.
5. Mentor someone.
6. Be grateful every day and don't be shy to proclaim it openly.
7. Be inspiring and inspired.
8. Explore a new interest or hobby that is motivating and rewarding.
9. Cultivate your relationships and love more deeply.
10. Find ways to love and accept you more each day.
11. Live, love, work and play passionately.
12. Keep your mind and body active.
13. Open your heart to the spiritual side of living.

**B. Age Reflection:**

1. Identify your views about growing old.
2. What age stereotypes do you need to let go of?
3. Who or what do you need to forgive from your past?

4. What fears or concerns about money and loss interfere with your upbeat attitude about aging?
5. Develop a financial and life strategy to defeat those fears.
6. How do you continue to challenge and grow your mind and you?
7. What steps do you take each day toward aging creatively?
8. How well do you care for your health?
9. What actions do you take to age healthfully?

**C. Creative Aging Survey:**

Rate yourself with honesty and kindness:
Never Sometimes Always

1. I take active steps to be more creative.
2. I act responsibly for my health and well-being.
3. My life has meaning and satisfaction.
4. I love and accept myself.
5. Every day I am grateful.
6. I contribute to others and to my community.
7. I creatively plan for my retirement.
8. I tend lovingly to my significant relationships.
9. I look forward to the future.

Note: Include these creative aging ideas into your life more often. If never or sometimes is your rating, step up your creative aging program right now.

**Recommended Reading:**

*Awakening at Midlife* by Kathleen A. Brehony

*Boosting Immunity: Creating Wellness Naturally* by Len Saper and Nancy Faass

*Creativity and Successful Aging* edited by Adams-Price

*Emotional Alchemy* by Tara Bennett-Goleman

*The Mature Mind: The Positive Power of the Aging Brain* by Gene Cohen, MD.

*Notes:*

# ABOUT THE AUTHOR

## TAMERA SWAN MASON

Tamera Swan Mason has always been a multifaceted individual who wears many hats. She is currently the Administrator and occasional lecturer for the Unity Center of Christianity in Baltimore, Maryland, a non-denominational New Thought organization. Educationally, she holds a Master of Public Administration degree from the University of Baltimore, a Bachelor of Science in Metaphysics, and is currently studying with the University of Metaphysics in conjunction with the University of Sedona. She will receive her Master of Science in Metaphysics in 2008, specializing in metaphysical counseling and training. As a certified trainer and member of the Professional Woman Network, Tamera has combined her knowledge of diversity and women's issues with metaphysics in assisting her to enhance her counseling activities.

She has authored two books; *How to Start And Operate a Home-Based Business* and *Mail Order Mania*. She offers her services as a workshop facilitator in the areas of Board Leadership Training and Small Business Management. She presently contributes as an adjunct professor, teaching business subjects at a local college.

Five years ago she started a mail order company called White Swan by promoting her own line of personal care products for women. Her products are known as "Wild Rose" because of their unique rose fragrance.

Tamera advises women to follow their dreams. There are many challenges that women face in life that will take them away from their timetable of accomplishment. But the women who ultimately succeed are the women who continue to strive and never give up no matter how long it takes their dreams to come to fruition.

*Contact:*
Tamera Swan Mason
White Swan
PO Box 303
Randallstown, MD 21133
www.metamorphosis10@comcast.net
www.whiteswanproducts.com
(410) 521-4249

## FORTY-EIGHT

# LIVING A LIFE OF THANKFULNESS

**By Tamera Swan Mason**

**Reminiscing**

Yesterday, I ventured down into the basement to begin to clear away a lot of old items and furniture that had been stored away for many years. While pulling through the many boxes, I came across a box of old dresses that I had not seen in years. They were my dresses, beautiful little organdy and cotton dresses that I wore as a little girl. There were two of them in a box that my mother was saving for my little girl. Unfortunately, my little girl is now a young woman with little girls of her own. I smiled when I saw those dresses and remembered how I hated them. There was a faded, wrinkled, pink cotton dress with tiny pink flowers. It had very exquisite smocking on the bodice, a little white peter pan collar, and a full gathered skirt with a large white sash that tied in the back making a big bow. There was also a gray and white organdy dress with a white tuxedo front and a peter pan collar made out of white pique material. I remembered going to Sunday school all dressed up in those dresses with black patent leather shoes, white socks, matching hair ribbons, and little white gloves. Oh yes, there was also a matching black patent leather pocketbook to match those shoes. As I stood there reminiscing, I remembered how my mother labored over those dresses. She was an excellent seamstress and we, my sisters and I, always had nice dresses for church.

While I hated those dresses when I had to wear them, today I find them, even in their present condition, very beautiful little dresses. Beautiful because mother made them, and beautiful because she was loving and caring enough to take care of us the way she did. They are beautiful because I have learned over the years to give thanks and be thankful for everything that comes into my life.

**We Have Forgotten The Little Things!**

With so much at our disposal, our society has become spoiled, thankless, and unforgiving. Our society has forgotten the little things in life that meant so much to generations of old. We are a generation that expects to have everything without having to do very much to acquire it. In our "throw away" society, we have become so accustomed to being able to experience all the latest technological advances and financial rewards, that we often forget to give thanks to all those who came before us and made them all possible. As a nation, we celebrate Thanksgiving on the fourth Thursday of November each year. Do we ever stop to consider what this day really means outside of the family gathering, for some people, and the feast that is usually prepared?

Living a life of thankfulness probably sounds very religious, and in a sense it is. When we think of giving thanks, we often think of God or a Supreme Being. However, being thankful is more than being religious. It is a thought process that is usually developed in us from childhood to respond to someone's act of kindness for us or whatever gives us pleasure. It is one of those qualities like honesty and respect that parents teach their children early in life. It is a unique quality that helps to shape and mold our character.

When I am driving along in traffic and someone wants to enter my lane, and I let them in the flow of traffic, usually he or she will wave or offer some kind of response to say, "Thank you." As a child, I was taught to always say "thank you" when someone did something nice for me. Our society has forgotten how to say "thank you." It is a small gesture that warms the heart and lets the individual know that the kindness displayed was appreciated.

**Why be Thankful?**

In your quest to live a life of thankfulness, you must first be honest with yourself. Ask yourself, am I really thankful for all that I have, or do I simply expect to live a certain way, and expect to be privileged to certain things? Do you feel that life owes you, and you don't have to give thanks? This seems to be a rather acceptable attitude among young people today who have not had to work very hard for what they have. Maybe this is the reason why thankfulness is such an antiquated attitude.

Living a life of thankfulness is also being forgiving and casting off many useless and unrewarding thoughts and feelings that you hold in your heart about others. These unforgiving gestures only harbor relentless thoughts of pain and suffering and do nothing to add to the pleasure of life. In fact, these emotions take away from the pleasures you could be experiencing. When you learn to let go of these attitudes, you will discover how much better your life will flow.

When you look at your life and the lives of others, do you say thank you that "I am me" and not that other person? You may admire some of the attributes this person has, but does he or she have your talents and abilities? The fact that this individual may be very athletic, and derives great pleasure out of mountain climbing, skiing, surfing, etc., does not make him or her any more of a person than you are. That individual probably would not enjoy many of the activities that you enjoy. You may be very satisfied sitting quietly, relaxing with a good book. He or she would probably find that very boring. The point that I am trying to make, and one that we must all understand, is that whatever you are and wherever you find yourself in life, never forget to say, "Thank you." Thank you for the opportunity to experience whatever that may be. When you show your gratitude to someone or something, you are displaying an act of thankfulness.

When you live a life of thankfulness, you will be surprised at how you will elevate your acceptance of others. Your understanding and tolerance of others will increase, and you are less likely to complain and be impatient. Understanding the human plight, as it is, you will be able to see beyond the petty disturbances that plague many, and you will find that your life becomes a more peaceful and rewarding existence. You will draw to you individuals who wish to be in your company because of the attitudes you display.

One of the things we must be aware of is the reaction of others. In many instances, you will not receive the same kind of response in return, or any response at all. Do not allow this to upset you. You can only be responsible for your own actions and not those of others. If you are kind and gentle and the other person approaches you with anger and hostility, it does you no good to follow their lead. Remain calm and let it go.

**Life's Many Challenges!**

How can I possibly give thanks when I am driving along in my car and someone in the next lane crosses over into my lane, hits my car, and causes an accident? I am un-nerved, my car is damaged, I may have been harmed physically, and I am in a state of shock! Where are the thanks in this? In the world in which we live, we fight a constant battle of worldly challenges. No, it is not a good thing that someone was not paying attention and caused an accident that unfortunately may have caused great harm to both parties and probably passengers as well. The initial and human reaction, once the shock of the accident has subsided, is one of anger and reproach. But the individual who has learned to live a life of thankfulness is able to put those feeling aside and get on with the business of moving forward to correct the situation. This does not mean that this individual will not have these feelings. They are natural, normal reactions to a situation of this kind. However, he or she has learned that anger and hostility will not help the situation.

It may be difficult to understand how thankfulness plays a role in such an event. The normal person will be outraged for months. Consider the inconvenience of not having a car while it is being repaired, (if it can be repaired), or having to utilize a rental car and dealing with the insurance company. There may be a possible physical condition as a result of the accident, and medical bills, not to mention constant visits to the doctor, and the possibility of not being able to work for a while etc., etc. The list could go on and on. But the individual who has learned to live a life of thankfulness is better able to take these occurrences in stride. It does not mean that the individual is thankful that this has happened. It simply means that he or she is able to deal with situations in a more civil and constructive way. Thank goodness my car can be repaired, thank goodness my injuries were not worse, thank goodness my insurance will cover the cost of the repairs, etc. It could have been worse.

Living a life of thankfulness is not being pious and existing from a level of blind trust, it is an understanding from a deeper level of consciousness. As stated earlier, thankfulness is a process that is developed and grows deeply into the fabric of your being. It is an understanding of the nature and the laws of the universe and how they operate. We will always have challenges in our lives, some more serious than others. Being thankful is a positive attribute that can only bring forth well-meaning and positive results. Should we not strive to bring forth well-meaning and positive results in our lives and in the lives of all concerned?

Living a life of thankfulness is always remembering to be kind, to think of others, and to be aware that you do not live in this world alone. It is opening up your heart to those around you when they need help, and being willing to express gratitude for being able to be of service. When friends and family members seem to be facing a challenge, how many times have you said, "How can I help?" In reviewing the situation, after providing the assistance needed, remember how thankful the individual was that you were there to be of service. And think about how you felt in receiving their thanks. This act of kindness brings home the fact that we must all learn to live together and be of service to one another.

Living a life of thankfulness is an indescribable heartfelt emotion that opens up the floodgates of sunshine and truly adds another dimension to everyday life. It reminds you that you are a wonderful individual, alive, alert and enthusiastic about life. Living a life of thankfulness is simply being thankful for who you are, and the life you live.

*Notes:*

# ABOUT THE AUTHOR

## Sharyn Lynn Yonkman

Sharyn Lynn Yonkman is the founder and principal consultant for Lynn Consulting Group, a personal and professional development training organization. Lynn Consulting specializes in career advancement skills for the professional woman, helping her in achieving personal excellence. As a passionate advocate of women's Self-empowerment and life balance issues, Sharyn offers special expertise in dealing with transition and change in the workplace, as well as programs designed for those of the baby boomer generation.

As former CFO of several high profile retail and hospitality companies, Ms. Yonkman has gained valuable in depth financial and managerial experience in the corporate community providing the knowledge for cost effective solutions for todays business challenges. Programs available include: Interactive Sensitivity and Diversity Training: Superior Customer Service in Retail and Hospitality; and Handling Conflict Fear and Transition.

One on one individual life balance coaching is available in addition to group sessions. Highly customized curriculum is offered to meet your specific organizational needs. Ms. Yonkman is a Co-author of *Remarkable Women*, an anthology project with Marci Shimoff of "*The Secret*", and actress Jennifer O'Neil. Additionally, she is an author in several of the PWP library books, including *Becoming The Professional Woman* in which she addresses overcoming fear ; *Overcoming the Superwoman Syndrome,; You're on Stage! Image Etiquette, Branding & Style; A Woman's Survival guide for Overcoming Obstacles, Transition and Change,* and *Beyond the Body! Developing Inner Beauty.* She is currently completing a self-help book for baby boomer women facing the challenges of moving from the first act of life to the second, and would love to hear input from her fellow boomers on how they feel. Please contact her at the info provided below.

Author, trainer, motivational speaker, and life balance coach, Ms. Yonkman is available internationally to help the individual or organization with their professional and personal developmental needs.


*Contact:*
PO Box 1266
Ventura, Ca 93002
805.677.3117
www.protrain.net
Lynnconsult@ yahoo.com

FORTY-NINE

# GETTING OVER GETTING OLDER: FACING OUR CHANGING FACES

**By Sharyn Lynn Yonkman**

**Talking 'Bout My Generation**

This is dedicated to my fellow Baby Boom sisters, we who came of age in the 60's, and now are in (or are rapidly approaching) our 60's. We, the generation that did not trust anyone over 30, who preached anti-establishment values, and are now purchasing anti-aging products. We, the wearers of mini skirts, who are now trying out mini face-lifts. What lessons or gifts from the 60's do we take into our 60's?

**Time Of The Season**

The 60's were a time of idealism, a time of flower power and free spirits. It was a time that gave us a glimpse of what was possible, a time when we were there to change the world and we used our music to convey the message. It, and we, were a ground breaking and revolutionary agents of change.

**It's The Same Old Song**

The question is, as members of that glorious hopeful generation that was determined to change the world, did we change the attitude we have toward aging, or are we still just singing the same old song?

**Who Knows Where The Time Goes?**

When did we stop being the ones that turned heads when we walked through the door, and instead became the ones that had to go into their heads to now be considered interesting and attractive?

Saying goodbye to where we have been, whom we have been, in order to move on to life's second act, is the challenge now facing the baby boom generation. How do we take our collective generational wisdom and face life's second act? And that includes dealing with our changing faces.

**Oh, Oh, Pretty Woman**

When asked if she had any regrets about her life, Eleanor Roosevelt is said to have replied, "Just one. I wish I had been prettier."

Numerous studies have been conducted and endless books and articles have been written that provide us with information about the power of beauty, and how others respond to those who possess it.

Beauty has the power to attract and influence others, for it is found that people believe that which is beautiful is good. We superficially, and often times erroneously, associate positive qualities to people who are good-looking, and negative qualities to people who are not.

Beauty standards change with time, cultures, and what society wants or needs. Across the ages, beauty has been a major factor at the core of how women are valued, and therefore treated. In many cultures and eras, beauty was central to their survival. Pretty women attract strong protectors, and that includes good providers.

Youth is generally acknowledged as beautiful. Unfortunately, it seems to have become the only form of beauty that is acceptable in today's culture.* This, my sisters, is something that we must change.

*For an in-depth look at this subject, please see my chapter, ***How The Media Portrays Women*** in PWP's *Beyond the Body! Developing Inner Beauty.*

**Just Like A Woman**

Many fear, and not without good reason, the loss of their youthful attractiveness. Images of youth abound everywhere, and with them the powerful message that young equals beautiful. We are assaulted daily with advertisements to look younger and thinner, along with the pressure for a woman to look young in order to compete in the workplace and social arena. It is no wonder that so many of us are fearful about (and unable to accept) our changing appearance.

**What's Going On?**

A study found more than 80% of women who where 50 years old and older have resisted or restricted some type of activity due to feeling badly about their aging appearance. These activities, listed below, are those that women believe society (and themselves?) are less accepting of.

1. Wearing revealing clothing, especially bathing suits
2. Being photographed
3. Looking in the mirror or being viewed naked
4. Being intimate
5. Flirting and dating

And you? Do you find yourself avoiding things you once did because you feel badly about your appearance? Take some time to think about what you might be avoiding and why.

**It's All Over Now, Baby Blue**

Aging, one of the most natural processes in the world, seems to be perceived as taboo in our culture. This perception, however, is not reality. Getting older brings many advantages not available to the young, not the least of which are knowledge, wisdom and self-understanding.

**Kind Of A Drag**

For most, our internal prime is later than our outward prime. I think the universe does that purposefully, for can you imagine how powerful we would be if our primes synced up? Unlike that pesky collagen, inward qualities are not depleted by age. For most of us, they are enriched.

Baby Boomers have not matured into midlife reconciled with being old. We are the generation that is determined to stay youthful at every stage of life. Our generational, youthful mindset is not only about change, but also about a life-long journey of self-discovery. We refuse to be pigeonholed by the established rules of age. After all, weren't we the generation that believed rules were made to be broken?

**Time Has Come Today**

Some of us may have a memory of an event that shocked us into realizing that not only had our outward appearance changed, but also that people interacted differently with us because of that change. Let me share an incident that brought this home to me, literally.

The day my first co-authored book, *Remarkable Women*, was delivered was an exceptionally happy and important day for me; a day where I felt all-powerful and unstoppable. When the young UPS delivery guy came to my door with 46 boxes (weighing 28 lbs. each) and told me he wasn't allowed to bring them inside, he called his supervisor to get permission to help me deliver them into my home. He explained to his superior that the boxes were heavy and that he felt badly having me carry in all those boxes for, as he described to his supervisor, "Well, you know, she's older."

**You Can't Always Get What You Want**

But if you try sometimes, you get what you need. What? Could he possibly be describing me? I was angry and humiliated at the same time. Fortunately, that plucky youthful rebel I once was (apparently still am) rose up inside me and I sprang in to action, carrying those 46 boxes as quickly as possible, amazing the delivery guy (and myself), so I would not seem so frail, feeble, and, yes, old. Later, after a much-needed visit to the chiropractor, I wondered, when did I go from being an object of desire to a man, to an object of compassion or concern?

**Piece Of My Heart**

The loss of beauty (like any loss) is a type of death, and the fear of losing our youthful beauty is about fearing the demise of the power that beauty provided. Holding on to any sense of loss can lead to depression, so we must face the changes time has wrought, and embrace the fact that life is all about changes. As we mourn this loss, we can slowly begin to let go by losing attachment to our perception of beauty.

**Stages to process when dealing with change:**

Mourning – acknowledge loss, then letting go
Reunite – with your true self
Refocus – on your future, with courage and creativity

**Turn, Turn, Turn**

There comes a time for all of us when it is imperative for us to say goodbye to who we have been, in order to move on to who we will become. Too much energy placed upon "I was" thinking is of no value, and obsessing about your lost youth is a waste of your valuable energy.

**I Can't Get No Satisfaction**

If you try to hold on to your youth, you will sooner or later discover that it is not a satisfying activity. Worrying about aging is only likely to make getting older more difficult than it needs to be. Since all this worrying and attempts to stop the passage of time are an exercise in futility, why not make peace with the process and do your best to accept the reality of aging?

**Nowhere To Run To Baby, Nowhere To Hide**

This is simply not true. We can, and should, go inside to deal with our changing outside appearance. It is the first stop along the way to finding out who we will be.

Letting go is the lesson of life's second act. This lesson includes the gathering of knowledge, intensive self-examination, and unconditional self-acceptance.

| |
|---|
| Accept first INTELLECTUALLY<br>Then deal EMOTIONALLY<br>Finally ADJUST self-image |

*"How many cares one loses when one decides not to be something, but to be someone."* —Coco Chanel

**Wake Me, Shake Me, When It's Over**

The gift of age is the realization that time is not limitless – therefore, we should be more mindful in every moment, not living in or for some idealized future, but realizing that <u>this</u> is the future. Realizing your mortality should not be heard as a funeral church bell, but more like a bell that begins a boxing match. It's the sound that tells you to "Wake up little Suzie, and come out fighting."

**Feed Your Head**

By life's second half, our intellect has greatly developed, and it wants something more interesting to do than to obsess about one's appearance. It's a time when the more we place attention and energy inside our heads, the better the outside looks. When we get in touch with our true self, our inner beauty reveals itself.

**Looked At Life From Both Sides Now**

Letting go of the old is the first and most crucial step in the process of second act growth, for this necessary detachment creates the space needed for new insights and opportunities to occupy and grow.

Very often middle age people become invisible. This can be a difficult and painful reality to accept, especially if you were accustomed to a certain amount of power and attention due to your physical attractiveness. This threat of invisibility can make one feel that they have vanished from sight; that they no longer exist. Do not despair, however, for there is a good news/bad news aspect to all this.

When people stop seeing you, noticing you as they once had, they lose control over you. We gain a sort of freedom from being defined by others opinions of us and no longer need to worry about what others think. This frees up our valuable time to spend it on activities that are truly meaningful to us, and allows us to find and be our authentic selves. As we age, there are hormonal changes in our brain that help free us to care less about the opinion of others and more about our growth as a person. The freedom associated with this ability to be under the radar, so to speak, is incredibly empowering and much like the personal freedom we fought so hard for in our youth.

I told you there was good news in this.

**Eve Of Destruction?**

Not even close! Aging is not the end of living; it's the result of all our life's experiences. A time when one can sow what we have reaped. Just as we had love-ins in the 60's, it is now time for us to take that love, that unconditional love, and place it in us. We must love ourselves from the inside out.

**You're So Vain**

A certain amount of vanity can be healthy and useful in dealing with our changing faces. Looking "cared for" does tend to increase ones self-confidence, and working at being the best you can be at any age is certainly a worthwhile undertaking.

**I Feel Free**

In our 60's, many women have hit their vanity limit and simply no longer care as they once did about their appearance. Why should they? Self-confidence allows them to look great naturally, and the desire to reinvent ourselves in ways that are not related to our looks takes center stage. And that, my friends, is part of what drives us to live and thrive.

**Foxy Lady**

Remember back in high school when someone was trying to describe a blind date? When asked what he or she looked like, would reply, "They have a great personality." That usually meant that the individual being described was not very attractive. Well, we are most certainly not in high school any longer, but there is a lesson to learn from this observation.

As our physical prowess is reduced by age, we need to develop a "presence", a power, that isn't physical to replace it. The second half of life attention grabber is tougher to attain than the effortless youthful one. For many of us, it takes work to develop that charismatic magnetism that holds so much appeal. It is now time, if we have not as yet done so, to be the one with the terrific personality.

**Time In A Bottle**

Inner beauty is a radiance that cannot be bought in a bottle. When you realize that you are a fascinating, fabulously interesting creature, you can stop worrying about the outside and knock them out with the presence of what you have inside.

**Spirit In The Sky**

Instead of looking at growing older as a time of loss, why not see this as a time of growth, especially in the spiritual and emotional arena? Connecting with your own spirit by living your passion and being engaged in the world with compassion and service to others is one of the best beauty secrets there is.

**Do You Believe In Magic?**

Much about beauty is perception, and personal confidence can go a long way in helping you to perceive your beautiful self. As we age, confidence, character and personality play a larger role in beauty. Remember that old adage, beauty is in the eye of the beholder?

Start by convincing yourself that you are everything you ever were in the beauty department, and then some. Soon others will follow suit. We may well be sabotaging our appeal with too little self-esteem and hang-ups about our appearance.

**Good Vibrations**

Put the Law of attraction in action for yourself.* Accept yourself for the beautiful person that you are. Create your own reality. If you believe you are beautiful, your body language will improve, and others will notice and be attracted by your confident vibration.

* For an in depth look at this subject, please see my chapter on ***Creating The Life You Want*** in PWP's *Women's Survival Guide for Overcoming Obstacles, Transition & Change.*

**All Right Now**

People who laugh and smile are very appealing to those around them. Happy people are beautiful, and it doesn't hurt that optimism boosts your immune system and, therefore, increases your life expectancy. Make a concerted effort to truly appreciate yourself and love the person the passing of time has revealed. People who like themselves are much more attractive than those who do not.

**The Beat Goes On**

And so shall we, fellow sisters of the 60's, for a very long time to come, facing all the upcoming, exciting changes life has yet in store. We, the generation that broke the rules and demanded change must find our way home to a new mindset on aging. We will face these changes, sometimes quietly and alone; but remember, it is always much more satisfying when we **Listen to the music** and do it **With a little help from our friends.**

Peace and love (your face, yourself).

# ABOUT THE AUTHOR

## AHMON`DRA (BRENDA) McCLENDON

Ahmon`dra, President of Brilliance Inc., is an international speaker, facilitator, motivator and author. She imprints an indelible impression upon your heart and makes you smile, laugh, cry and contemplate the deeper issues of life. She arouses in each listener a passion to commit to his or her higher purpose with her grace, power and spirit.

With twenty plus years in the human services arena and an MSW from San Francisco State University, Ahmon`dra has developed a highly successful program called P.L.A.N.E. – "Passionately Living A New Existence." She has spoken to thousands of young adults in North America, Europe and Africa on how to create a powerful future by staying devoted to their dreams, trusting their intuition, boldly taking risks and asking for what they want.

She is a Certified Facilitator for Motivating the Teen Spirit Inc. a teen empowerment program that conducts transformational workshops, and leads the international program, Core Value Training as a Senior Instructor. Ahmon`dra is a recipient of the "Speaking with an Active Voice" grant sponsored by the American Medical Women's Association and Pharmacia Corporation.

A contributing author to the best selling book *Chicken Soup For the African-American Soul*, she was featured as a keynote speaker for The Monster Diversity 2003 Leadership Program in the United States.

Passion and magnificence exude from her presence with an amazing energy of wisdom, healing & love as she creates, flies and soars! Get clear on your life and passions with the energy and excitement of Ahmon`dra

*Contact*
Ahmon`dra (Brenda) McClendon
Brilliance, Inc.
484 Lakepark Ave pmb 485
Oakland, California 94610
ahmondra@brillianceincorp.com
www.protrain.net

FIFTY

# SAYING GOODBYE: DEATH, GRIEF & LOSS

**By Ahmondra McClendon**

Life is like a beautifully written book containing thousands of wonderful stories. Imagine that every person you love has a chapter in your book of life. There's a beginning story that represents the first time you met, a middle story that portrays all the experiences you've shared, and an ending story called ***death,*** where they dêpart and you say good-bye.

Although no two chapters read the same, they all have one thing in common – the ending. It doesn't matter how old you are, where you live, or how much money you have, ending that chapter can be painful. It is painful because that last good-bye is final. There will be no more laughs, or hugs. No more long walks or talks. Everything that you once shared with that person stops.

The end may come quickly and unexpectedly, or it might arrive with advanced notice and fanfare. However death appears, its presence signals a change in life. Everything that was familiar becomes unknown, and everything that was comfortable becomes unbearable. The time has come to begin a new story without that person, but how is that done?

Death is a constant in life, and you have no choice as to whether someone will die. You do, however, have a choice in how to experience that loss. You can sink into depression and live a life of sadness, or you can accept the finality of it all and move forward through the transition.

To reject death and push away grief is to get stuck in the pain and suffering of bereavement. Lapsing into denial is a set-up for a long-term relationship with grief.

Learning to treat death and its traveling companion grief as temporary houseguests just passing through, will lesson their impact and shorten the stay. Gaining the ability to accept the end and feel the pain creates a sense of peace inside the loss. Cherishing past experiences develops the courage to embrace the future with hope, and begin a new chapter in the book of Life.

It is my intention in this chapter to present new liberating beliefs on:

- The old superstitions about death, loss and grief
- Healing past hurt, pain and anger
- Saying good-bye powerfully

*To complete the exercises in this chapter, you will need a journal, preferably one that has pockets on each page. This journal will be your "Book of Life".*

**A New Paradigm**

The old superstition that death is bad and only brings pain does not serve you, nor does the belief that sadness is the only by-product of loss and grief. How you choose to experience death, loss, and grief can liberate or enslave.

Creating a new paradigm and placing death in a different perspective brings enlightenment. Death provides the opportunity to acknowledge a blessing: the gifts that those you love left behind. Your focus should not be on, "*the loss of a loved one*", but rather on "*the commemoration of a loved one*".

It is more powerful to spend time acknowledging a life than highlighting a ***loss.*** The writer and speaker, Iyanla Vanzant once wrote, "*People come into our lives for reasons, seasons and lifetimes.*" Honoring the contributions made, and embracing the time-shared gives us a sense of continuance.

For instance:

1. Although the time was short, the **reason** they came was powerful and it shifted your life.

2. How beautiful that **season** was they spent with you, and how you grew from it.

3. What a magnificent life you have lived because of the influence from a **lifetime** of love and wisdom.

## The Commemoration

**Exercise #1**

This exercise is designed to honor the loved ones who contributed to your life before they departed. (Use your "Book of Life" for all entries.)

- Make a list of those you want to honor.
  (Assign a separate page to each person in your book. Write only one name at a time because you may need to use more than one page for some people. Complete the entire exercise for one person before moving on to the next. If the journal has a pocket, insert a picture or memento)
- Assign them a life category; reason, season, lifetime.
  (Write the category beside their name)
- List the gifts they gave to you.
- Write a Thank You letter expressing your gratitude.

Example:

*(Remember it is not the length of time they were with you; it is how their presence supported your growth)*

Julian > **A reason** (In my life for 1 week and departed.)

The reason you came into my life was so that I could learn how to show unconditional love, express compassion and forgive.

Dear Julian,

Thank you for allowing me to be with you for the short time you were here. Through your presence, I learned so much about myself.

Laura > **A Season** (In my life from childhood to young adulthood.)

You were with me through the seasons of biggest growth so that I could develop courage, make those tough decisions of adolescence and become independent.

Dear Laura,

It is with deep love and gratitude that I say Thank You for helping me through the hardest times in my life. Even though I wish you were still here with me, I know that your work was done and completed right on time.

Mom > **A Lifetime** (In my life from birth until middle age.)

A lifetime of devotion was your gift to me. It is because of you I learned how to stand tall, do my very best, live with integrity, and always be of service to others.

Dear Mom,

Thank you for giving me everything I needed to be the wonderful woman that I am. I am truly a blessing to the world because of your training and leadership.

*The next time a loved one departs, use this exercise to honor their life and ease your way through the transition. Put just as much energy into celebrating their life as you will put into mourning their death.*

**Healing Through Closure**

Living a full and satisfying life requires constant personal growth and development, and personal growth and development is in direct proportion to the amount of closure in your life. Creating endings to life stories establishes a foundation for healing because each experience of saying good-bye heals hurt and anger, and paves the way for forgiveness. No matter how painful creating closure might be, it releases you from grief and increases your capacity to love.

## The New Ending

***Exercise #2*** (Examples are included in italics within exercise.)

This exercise is designed for to you identify the relationships that need closure and write endings for those stories.

- List the love ones you have strong feelings about.
  The relationships in which you feel the need to create closure.
- Write down the first time you met.
  *You were my big sister, but I didn't meet you until I was 5 years old.*
- Write down incidents you vividly remember (good & bad memories).
  *I remember us going to a soccer game and having a great time.*
  *I remember coming to your house and seeing you and your children crying because your husband had beaten you.*
- Record the last time you saw them and what you said or felt when you heard they had died.
  *The last time I saw you, you were lying in a bed, black and blue from being beaten by your husband. I told you that I could not stand to see you like this. I was going away and not coming back because it hurt too much to see you in pain. Fifteen years later, when I heard you had died, I was devastated and overcome with anger, grief, and guilt. How could I have not been there for you?*
- Make a complete list of all the feelings you have.
  (If you have unresolved anger or rage, stop complete the forgiveness exercise and return. You can also complete the exercise to resolve any anger you have towards yourself.)
  *I have love and respect for you, and I am ashamed and angry with myself for how I abandoned you in your time of need.*
- Describe how the connection with them has influenced your life, and what strengths you have developed.
  (Remember, you gained strength from this relationship, even if it brought you

pain. You may have learned endurance, tolerance, patience, or perseverance, you may have become more independent and more determined, or you may have learned to protect yourself.)

*Your presence in my life has made me a more caring and empathic person. I no longer make decisions solely based on my needs; I take into consideration how my decisions might impact someone else. I have more patience, more tolerance, and more empathy. I am more committed to helping those in need.*

- Compose a new chapter ending. Highlight how the future will look as a result of the connection with them.

  *You are gone, but not forgotten. I will always keep you in my heart. I apologize for abandoning you and ask for your forgiveness. I have made a decision that I will not allow what happened between us to be recreated with your children. I will be actively involved in their lives, and I will always be there for them, showing love and support. Through my experience with you, I have learned that no matter what happens, family is most important and I will never turn my back on them. I will make sure that your children and grandchildren receive the love that you would have given them if you were still here. I will keep your memory alive!!*

## Forgiveness

### Exercise#3

***(This work will not be done in your journal, but on a separate sheet of paper.)***

Answer these questions:

1. Is the anger I am holding hurting them or me?
2. Do I want to continue to be in pain?
3. Would I be happier and healthier if I released my anger?
4. Am I ready to heal this hurt and release the pain?

Make a list of the experiences in which you were hurt, or in which you hurt someone else. Anger toward ourselves will also keep us stuck in bereavement. This letter can also be written to release any anger you hold toward yourself.

(This exercise can be completed alone or with another person. If it is done alone, you can use a picture of the deceased, or you can stand in front of a mirror.)

Complete the letter below and read it out loud. After reading, destroy (burn it, shred it) it as a physical demonstration that you are ending this chapter in your life. (Remember, this exercise in not for the other person, but for you. Just because you choose to forgive doesn't mean you condone or will forget their actions. It simply means you are ready to release yourself and move on. If you still feel anger or hurt, seek professional help to support you further.)

**Forgiveness Letter**

*Dear Step-Dad, I am writing this letter to express my feelings of hurt and anger toward you. I have spent many (days, years) years being angry toward you because of your molestation toward me. I feel that is was wrong for you to rob me of my safety. Today I am ready to move on with my life and release my feelings of anger and hatred. I realize that I am responsible for my happiness, and therefore I choose to not hold anything toward you and to forgive you for the pain and suffering you created in my life. I am complete with you. Good-bye.*

**Forgiveness Letter (to self)**

*I am writing this letter to express my feelings of anger and disgust toward myself. I have spent many (days, years) years being angry and self-destructive toward myself because of how I treated my best friend the last time I saw her.*

*I feel that it was wrong for me to not stop what I was doing and convince her to not leave town with that man.*

Today I am ready to move on with my life and release my feelings of anger and guilt. I realize that I am responsible for my happiness, and therefore I choose to not hold this tragedy toward myself and to forgive myself for not stopping her from going and preventing her murder. I am complete with myself.

**Adieu**

The time has come to say good-bye to the ones you love. Saying good-bye doesn't mean that you forget your loved ones. It simply means that you finish their story in your book of life. You make a conscious decision to let them go with love. Unfortunately, it doesn't signal the end of the pain; it only signals the beginning of healing.

It is your choice to begin the journey forward through the pain and out of bereavement. You will still grieve, and sometimes it may feel like you are stuck, but if you have earnestly said good-bye, you will still be moving… just very, very slowly.

Sometimes the pain of losing someone can be so devastating that you are unable to move to a place of saying good-bye. This is especially true when a loved one's departure leaves you with ***unanswered questions***.

1. Maybe they took their own life and left no reason why.

2. Maybe someone took their life and you never found out who did it or why they did it.

3. Maybe your loved one just vanished and you don't know if they are alive or not.

4. Maybe they were the victim of an accident or a senseless crime.

However the question was asked, there was *no answer*. There is only a gaping hole and you have no idea how to close it. The good news is that the hole can be closed. The other news is that only you will know how long it will take before the hole begins to shrink.

The following illustration is designed to provide you with a real life example of what saying good-bye to pain and grief can look like. Remember, the *power is in the decision to move forward*; the actual demonstration will look different for each person.

**Saying Good-bye**

Example: Saying good-bye to grief and hello to life.

*Two days after my 21st birthday, my best friend and roommate was found brutally raped and murdered. Her killer was never found and no motive for her death was uncovered.*

*Her death threw me into the depths of depression and despair. I went from a fun loving extrovert to an introverted loner. Everyone believed I was okay because I still managed to function.*

*For ten long years I lived in a very dark and lonely place. I was immobilized with pain, and I fluctuated between being suicidal and homicidal. One night while finding myself, once again, stretched out on the floor crying uncontrollably, I had a moment of clarity.*

*What was this pain and grief doing for me? What was it doing for my friend? I realized that my actions were not honoring her life or mine. I made a decision to celebrate her life instead of mourning her death. From that day forward I took my focus off the pain and put it on the joy.*

*I organized a 10-year memorial service to honor her life. That day I remembered the wonderful years she was with me, and I said my final* **Good-bye.**

*When I feel the old painful thoughts or feelings trying to creep in, I immediately pull up a good memory. On special days such as her birthday (which is Halloween) I do something fun and special. On days when I miss her (even after 34 years) I touch my heart and softly whisper, I miss you.*

Honor your loved ones by acknowledging the blessing they were to you in life. Embrace the pain of their departure, and then make a conscious decision to move forward, carrying them with you in Mind, Body and Spirit.

# ABOUT THE AUTHOR

## CHRISTELL ENGRAM-BENSON

New Beginnings to empower your mind, body and spirit…

Ms. Christell Engram-Benson, was born to enjoy life, and rises above all seemingly limitations. She believes that all of her changes are easy to make and is just a thought away. With the help of God and determination we learn what true love is by first learning to love and accept ourselves.

Ms. Engram-Benson is the president and founder of Chrysalis and Company L.L.C.

As a passionate entrepreneur, motivational speaker

Ms. Engram-Benson focuses on providing educational and relaxation initiatives that specialize in promoting health and wellness in the workplace and corporate arena.

Ms. Engram-Benson is a concert pianist and is the Director of Music for her church in Great Falls, Mt. She is also the host of her local television morning show, **"New Beginnings"**. As a visionary her hopes are to somehow give others focus to their **"New Beginnings"**

while sharing weekly affirmations, and her guest sharing. Speaking and thinking positively to empower the mind to do more, believe more, to make a difference in their lives and others.

Ms. Engram-Benson is a graduate of Florida College of Natural Health. And is the mother of five adult children. She is a facilitator for seminars and innovative solutions designed and tailored specifically for the goals and objective of your organization for Team Building, Diversity Issues, Women's Issues, Self Esteem and Communication Skills. She is a member of the Professional Woman Network (PWN) and is a certified trainer and has Co-authored **Women's Journey To Wellness Mind, Body, and Spirit** as well as **Emotional Wellness For Women Volume I.**

Giving back to her community has involvement with numerous non-profit local and national organizations where she continually develops others in areas of pursuing their passion. Ms. Engram-Benson exudes a compassionate presence along with a passion to mentor and help others and feels she is on an endless journey and has assisted many to discover their authentic selves in creativity thru change and growth.

This chapter is dedicated to all that have played apart in my life in helping me define and develop my authentic self and to all that are developing their on unique self to be all that they can be. Our Love is Limitless….

*Contact*
Christell Engram-Benson
Chrysalis and Company L.L.C.
New Beginnings Consulting Group, Inc.
1027 1st Ave. S.
Great Falls, Mt. 59401
(406) 868.6797
Chrysalis59401@yahoo.com

**GUEST AUTHOR**

# NEVER GIVE UP

**By Christell Benson**

**ABOUT YOURSELF—Giving Up Is Not an Option…**

As a child, my mother would say, "Christell, you can't see for looking." Or, "It didn't get legs and walk away,"…letting me know it was an object, to keep looking, and I would find it. She would also say, "you can't see the trees for the forest". Well, I finally understood that the trees, actually, were the forest.

These little sayings would truly frustrate me when I would be at my wits end trying to find something that I knew was there, but just couldn't locate to put my hands on.

These subliminal witty messages and principles serve me today. When they are decoded, they really meant, NEVER GIVE UP. The answer is always there. YOU JUST NEED TO HAVE PATIENCE WITH LIFE IN ORDER TO LEARN ABOUT WHAT YOUR SOUL NEEDS.

It is these principles that I apply to my life daily that keep me looking for the gifts and hidden treasure that I know I possess. Somewhere in the process, a foundation was beginning to be created in me.

I recently spoke to a group of about 65 people who were so wonderful, so full of life and vigor. They captured my heart and we seemed to connect, so we all enjoyed the company of each other. They were the lovely ***Senior Citizens Foster Grandparent Group – Very Important People***. What a joy they were. The sparkle in their eyes and the delightful smiles carried the room to a level of undeniable energy, filled with anticipation along with wisdom and understanding. I spoke about ***Sink or Swim Emotional Survival*** – from the book I co-authored ***Emotional Wellness For Women Volume II.*** It was as if every one of them were there to learn something new about life, and it really didn't matter that they were in the winter of their lives.

During this time as I spoke on this subject of survival, I again realized a few things about emotional wellness. Let me explain to you that much of my life had been consumed with avoiding pain, to the point that my need to survive had become a reaction, rather than a choice. That's not uncommon for any of us, if we think about it. My early experience of life had taught me this, so I thought that I always had to GIVE UP a part of me in order to get love, a pattern I have learned to recognize and change, because I know now it was diminishing my self-esteem, and self-love.

Ironically, as I looked into the audience, I began to see what role these foster grandparents were in, which is a very important one, as they become nurturers to those that need help in some area of their lives. Their mission was to somehow help children discover love for themselves unconditionally. As I continued to share my thoughts, my eyes sought out a beautiful elderly lady and it was if we both knew our hearts were agreeing. I asked the question, "Where has the time gone?" Her response was, "In my hair, on my hips, in my stride." We both giggled. Afterwards, a gentleman wrote a note and shared it with me. I have kept it to read when I needed to hear his words which he so kindly took the time to write to me.

***He said in the note*: "*You made the statement that you're so glad other people never gave up on you. Key: The most important thing that happened to you is, YOU NEVER GAVE UP ON YOURSELF.*"**

I use a mirror with all my students. I have them look in a hand-held mirror, and I tell them that no matter what anyone else tells them - that their best friend is in the mirror. The person in the mirror is the only one who can make changes and gain great results. The gentleman from the audience said, "The rewards I have received over many years are so great it is beyond belief! The mirror doesn't lie!"

***This gentleman took the time to give me wonderful enduring sound bytes that I can once again replay in my mind over and over again. This is when I say Heads On - Apply to the Mind. What an inspiring moment. I was reminded that the most important relationship you will have is the relationship you have with yourself.***

*"Have high regard for yourself. Be your own best friend."*—Leon Nacson

*"If you always do what you have always done, then you will always get what you have always gotten. If you want something that you have never had, then you need to do something that you have never done. If you always think the way you have always thought, then you will always get what you have always gotten."*—Author Unknown

**Are you giving up? It depends on what you're giving up.** How do you Love thyself? Let me count the ways.........

**If you're giving up bad habits**, I would say, please do. It is time for change. We must grow.

**If you are giving up toxic relationships**, I would say - ASAP, quickly before it poisons your heart.

**If you are giving up programmed clutter and mental garbage,** I say it's about time to release the thought patterns that are just not working. Have a spiritual cleansing that will start out with honoring and accepting yourself; another new beginning will find your true authentic self, the awesome treasure that lies within YOU.

My mind goes back to how simple things that are said can stay there to remind you where to place your values. Listen to this: I was about nine or ten years old and I guess I was just coming into the "knowing" of myself and interacting with other peers my age, when someone said to me, "You think you're cute, don't you?" I didn't know how to respond to a comment like that. I just said, "No, not really." It bothered me to the point that I said something to my father when he got home. (Mind you, my father was a very proud Bahamian man that left me with so much when he left for his higher calling, so soon.) Well, when I repeated to him what this woman had said "You think you're cute don't you?" He chuckled and said, "Well, if you don't think it, who will?" I thought about it for a minute. Coming from a conservative modest home, I knew how to answer such a comment in the future without hesitation, to this very day.

*"You are beautiful, no matter what your mind tells you. That is a fact. If you are aware of your own beauty and accept your own beauty, the opinion of others doesn't affect you at all."* —Don Miquel Ruiz

**'Know Thy Self' Awareness**

Living in an independent state of mind or choosing autonomy is a state of being: both must be chosen willfully and daily by our thoughts. Whatever is in your soul will set up the circumstances and experiences of your life. Believe it. Always remember that you may not always succeed, but at least you tried.

The errors account for something and are a common element in life, but how we avoid them is to learn through experience. With that said, sometimes poor judgment has made us feel as if we have failed ourselves, and others, at crucial times. And because we remember our failures and would never want to hurt others or to be hurt ourselves, our emotions begin to react indifferently to what is really happening. So, we stop believing in ourselves, and we try working through all the clutter by not taking action or making any decisions, only to avoid failure or errors that might happen, which is a great injustice to ourselves, and of course very distressing. Experiences tend to heal you or cripple you in your soul. The conclusion should always be," I will learn and will never *Give Up*." Find the treasure that is within you.

**Give Up The Fight With You.**

Discover love. Love yourself. Love others. Finding love and maintaining our own dignity is something we often struggle with. Experiencing the struggle is setting in motion the creation of finding out that you *Can't Give Up*.

We fight with ourselves constantly. We want to do all, be all, give all, but it's impossible. You will wear yourself out. There was a time in life when all I sought was approval and acceptance, and like a junkie, became unsure of myself when that "fix" wasn't delivered.

A traumatic brain injury a few years ago didn't help me become confident, either. It seemed as if life was going from bad to worse. I was in a whirlwind, struggling to keep what little was left of myself. My memory was scrambled and emotions were explosive. There was a time when staying in denial was my safety zone, so I thought. That sink-or-swim syndrome began to set in motion a powerful realization that made me come to the decision that I couldn't give up.

I had too much to live for; I had to learn to live for myself. I became willing to let go of all of the negative self-talk and started to shed everything that had taken it's toll on me. I faced the journey of sorting through all the dirty laundry, cleaning out the closets, and took a closer look at all my decisions, examining all choices, refusing to give in to fear and confronting them, instead. I was determined I would learn how to **love my self**, because I was worth loving. Pretty soon, I began to see a little clearer and my authentic self began to come into focus. I was "becoming". I knew that I could *Never Give Up*; it was not ever an option.

You don't have to have a traumatic physical injury to bring you to the beautiful treasure within yourself. But, you do have to:

- Tell yourself the truth about yourself - face you. Only then can your life become real.

- Write your vision, your goals.

- Write down what inspires you.

- Write down what you really expect from yourself and from others.

I have learned that everything that I am, I am because I made it through the past, and because I never gave up on me.

*Notes:*

# ABOUT THE AUTHOR

## KATHLEEN J. PENLEY, MBA

Kathleen Penley is owner of **The Penley Practice**, a management consulting firm specializing in strategic and operational planning and performance improvement. She assesses organizations to identify performance gaps, tailors solutions to align the management system, and coaches leadership in the execution of the makeover. Kathleen's work has taken her around the world, consulting, training, and providing the overall management required to ensure customer success.

Kathleen has been a key note speaker domestically and internationally. Prior to consulting, she was a senior banking executive and a corporate quality manager for a national insurance company. She has taught strategic planning and organizational behavior and development for a university MBA program.

The Department of Commerce Malcolm Baldrige National Quality Award selected Kathleen to be a Senior Examiner for five years. She is on the Executive Global Advisory Board of the Euro-American Women's Council whose mission it is to strengthen the status of women in the global marketplace. She was a member of the Board of Directors of a national credit union and a charter member of the Strategic Planning Institute Council on Benchmarking. She has an MBA and a Chartered Property Casualty Underwriter (CPCU) designation.

*Contact:*
Kathleen Penley
561-352-6366
kpenley@attglobal.net

**GUEST AUTHOR**

# CLEANING HOUSE

**By Kathleen Penley**

Honey, I can't find my keys! Where are my glasses? I know I put those documents in a safe place…now where was that? Sound familiar? Ever wish you could just wave a wand and p*resto!* Your home office would be free from papers and clutter, or you could enter your garage and find what you need without fear of something toppling over on you? Our homes are filled with things that we think we may need one day. And we are wasting valuable time and energy searching through these old things to unearth what we need today.

Thoughts that cross our minds when we try to purge our space of clutter:

1. I'm saving this for my children.
2. I'm keeping this "just-in-case".
3. I can't get rid of that because Susan gave it to me.

4. I remember the day I got that, or this holds so many great memories.

Stop! Let's do ourselves a favor and rid our lives of excess things, simplify our existence, gain back time, and enjoy the ensuing sense of freedom and power from taking control.

**Concept of 5S**

As a process management consultant, I coach organizations in Lean Six Sigma. Lean is a mindset of waste reduction that has as one of its foundations the concept of "5S", which stands for: *Sort, Set in Order, Shine, Standardize, and Sustain.* It had its beginnings in the early 1900s and is often attributed to the work of Frederick Taylor, the father of scientific management, and Henry Ford, the automaker, in their efforts to make things easier, more orderly, and more consistent. These techniques were scrutinized, refined, and popularized by Japanese scientists, engineers, and managers.

The principle behind this tool is to generate and maintain a well thought-out, clean, safe, and efficient environment to yield the highest level of performance (in your case, living!). This means eliminating excess belongings and employing a good dose of self-discipline to maintain orderliness.

**Benefits**

To extricate myself from the clutter nightmare, I applied this concept to our home. What I found was a whole new sense of empowerment. As we transition to a new phase in our lives, it is time to clean out the old to let the new in, both mentally as well as physically. I encourage you to apply the business concept of "5S" to your living space to obtain this energizing independence that prepares you to take on new challenges. This chapter will provide you with proven steps and tools to help you clean out the muddle in your life to make room for the new.

As organizations have received payback from the implementation of "5S", we, too, can achieve benefits by scaling back our belongings and creating order.

1. Less space is required. The kids are gone and some of us want to downsize our living space so that we have less upkeep and can travel whenever we want. We can do this only if we have a system in place for minimizing what we hang on to.

2. Not having to search for things – By removing excess items, and establishing a place for those we keep, we know right where they are. Track it – How much time in the day do you spend looking for things?

3. Reducing the things we need to buy because now we can find them. Do you find yourself saying, "They used to be right here…?" Then, read on!

4. Things last longer when we take better care of them. Our mothers used to tell us not to wad things up or leave them on the floor. Once again, they were right.

5. Enhance your chances of selling your home by de-cluttering the space.

6. Decrease your stress and frustration levels.

7. Take greater pride in your home and control over your life.

## Getting Started

So let's get started on our new habit for a lifetime. Following is a description of how to embark on this journey followed by a discussion of the 5 steps:

1. First, pick a room you want to confront – ultimately you need to do them all. However, we do not want this to be overwhelming, which would end with you throwing up your hands and going shopping (for more clutter, of course). The room may be the kitchen, your home office, the garage, your closet, or maybe even your computer.
2. Take a picture of how it looks today. Hold it – don't clean it first. Shoot the reality.
3. Envision how you want it to look. Draw a picture or describe it in words. If it is your closet, your vision may be to walk into it without tripping over shoes and purses that have accumulated on the floor, or that you will be able to find that favorite outfit without having to fight with all the other clothes in the closet that you haven't worn in ages.

## The 5Ss

Now that we know where we are and have a good idea of where we want to be, we can start with the first "S":

1. **Sort:** The purpose of this step is to determine which things are needed now and perhaps the immediate future and what can we remove. Once we have determined our current projects, we clear

the area so that it contains only what we need or use now. The mantra of this step is, "When in doubt, throw or move it out."

How many of you are keeping things because you think your children may want them? Yet, we have all heard people ask, "Why did they keep all this junk?", when it was actually kept for those who ask the question. Our treasures are not theirs. We had boxes of college books our children used. Turns out, after all these years, they don't want them. The books are out of date. And, they aren't in that line of work any more. Clean up now. Give them the things that are meaningful while you can both enjoy it, and throw or give away the rest. Cleaning house is about taking care of things that we need to do, not leaving it for our children or others to manage when we are gone.

This can be a painful and emotional step. It's difficult to let go of things that brought us so much joy in the past. Consider keeping only one thing that reminds you of those times and heave the rest. I recommend that you get a good friend to help with this. It needs to be someone that is forthright and decisive. It's not helpful if they say, "You're not going to throw that away, are you?"

It may be easier to give away a cherished item that is no longer useful rather than throwing it away. For example, if you are removing professional clothes from your closet, give them to an organization that assists women getting into the work place. Or have a garage sale. Or use my sister's favorite, eBay!

a) *Examine each item and decide to keep it, throw it out, give it away, or sell it.* Mark each item accordingly and establish a staging area to put each group so that when you are done sorting, there is no question as to which things are going to be tossed and which are going to be sold. Throw things away right now! If you wait, you may find yourself "second guessing" your decision. Questions to ask include:

i How often is this used? If the answer to this is not known, then put a "red tag" on it that contains the following information:

Item Description:

Quantity:

Date Tagged:

Date Used: ________________

________________

________________

Location of Item:

Disposition:

Keep close: ____________

Store: ____________

Throw away: ____________

Donate/Sell: ____________

Review your red tags after one month to determine which ones you use:

Rarely – determine whether to keep it or not. If you decide to keep it, store the item in a container clearly labeled with the date of last use and the contents and put it in an out-of-the-way place. Examples include holiday ornaments or seasonal items.

b) Monthly or occasionally – Again, store the item in a clearly labeled box with the date last used. Put this box in a location that is out of the way but easy to get to.

c) Weekly or daily – Put these items within easy reach to minimize motion and searching.

b) **Tip:** Three dangerous words to challenge when your inner voice is talking to you: "Just In Case." If you find yourself keeping things "just in case", ask yourself why. How often do you need it "just in case"? Most likely, by the time you get around to using these items, they are obsolete, out of style, or no longer viable. Change that little voice that is telling you to get more "just in case" to "I'm free!" (Unless, of course, it is your favorite lipstick and then buy all you can because you know it will be discontinued!)

**c) Tip:** Take a moment and determine what items you would want to take with you in an emergency. We always think we would have time to work this out but that time is now. In a medical emergency or natural disaster, we have to be prepared and act fast. This is particularly important as we age. Make a checklist of your vital documents, medicines, photographs, heirlooms and valuables. Set aside two plastic containers to hold these critical items. Perform a test run to determine if you are able to hoist the containers into the car when they are full!

2. **Set in Order:** Now that we have decided what to keep, we need to determine the best way to arrange our things to minimize motion, keep things in good repair, and find them when they are needed! The mantra here is Ben Franklin's, "A place for everything and everything in its place."

    a) *First, draw a basic map of where everything is currently.* This highlights all of your possessions needing a "place".

    b) *Next, determine where you want to put things and draw a future map.* Consider the vision you developed when we started. You may want to re-arrange your kitchen to minimize motion, putting cooking utensils within easy reach of your working area. In the garage, you may want to store tools near the workbench, arranged in the sequence they are used rather than haphazardly tossed in a box across the room.

    c) *Make it visual.* The key to being able to find things is to put them back in the same place each time you use them. Make it easy to do this or you will be back in the same state shortly. Be creative! For example, a friend of mine in San Francisco had a small kitchen with high ceilings. She loved having dinner parties, but needed a way to accommodate all of her things while making the most of her space. First, she built shelving up to the ceiling. She then bought rectangular baskets and placed clever labels on each one so that she knew what was in it. Following the "Sort" step, she put the items she used rarely in baskets on the top shelf, those she used occasionally on middle shelving, and those she used daily at a level for easy reaching. The result was an attractive and efficient use of space at a low cost. Other visual approaches include:

i. Color coding – this works particularly well with filing your important papers or in a home office environment.

ii. Label drawers, cabinets, storage closets, shelving – for example, post a picture or label where cleaning supplies go in your supply cabinet. You will know exactly where something is when you need it and an empty space will alert you to when its time to restock.

iii. Install a shadowboard, a device used in the "Set in Order" stage to organize tools, materials, and other paraphernalia. A shadowboard contains outlines of each item to show where it should be stored. It can be posted on a wall or can be used to organize a drawer. The purpose is to let you know immediately where things belong and when something is missing or hasn't been stored properly.

    I travel almost 75% of the year so I wake up in strange places all the time. To minimize getting ready time and the frustration of having toiletries all jumbled in a canvas bag, I developed a hand-drawn shadowboard on a towel that contains outlines of all my toiletries in the sequence I use them each morning. When I arrive at the hotel, I pull out the shadowboard towel and set out my assorted creams and makeup according to the outlines. I know which things I need to use. They are in order so I don't have to think about what comes next, and I don't forget the essentials! No more wasting time digging for the elusive mascara in the darkest corners of the bag.

a. Toiletry Bag b. Shadowboard Towel c. Stress-Free Application

Think about how you can arrange things to simplify your life.

3. **Shine** – The purpose of this step is to clean the area and keep it looking like your vision. Determine the best way to keep the area de-cluttered and safe with everything in its place.

    a) Post a picture of what it should look like.

    b) Take the last 15 minutes of your day to make sure things are in place – e.g., keys are in the second drawer in the front.

    c) Clean things off the desk and put them away in the color-coded files so that you start fresh in the morning.

    d) Throw papers away that you are not going to use any more or that are already stored in the computer (Keeping hard copies "just in case?" Consider using a backup on external hard drive.) Keep the shredder nearby.

e) Erase computer files that you are not going to use so that they don't take up valuable space and clutter your computer desktop and backup files.

4. **Standardize** – The purpose of this step is to make sure that the order and efficiencies gained are maintained on a regular basis. Make a list of the "cleaning" that needs to be done, responsibility for doing the cleaning (if there is more than one of you), and when each item on the list should be done.

| **5S Shine Schedule** | | | | |
|---|---|---|---|---|
| ***Room*** | ***Item*** | ***Task*** | ***Frequency*** | ***Responsibility*** |
| Garage | Gardening Tools | Place tools on shadowboard | Daily | Kathleen |
| Closet | Cleaning Supplies | Replace empties | Weekly | Dennis |

Include as tasks periodic inspections of equipment such as fire alarms, fire extinguishers, and batteries for electronics. Also, if there is more than one of you, rotate assignments.

**Tip:** For travelers, this is a helpful tool for those that come in and take care of your home while you are away. They know where to find things. As I am often away on business, I have someone to clean my home. I provide pictures, shadowboards, and other tools to indicate where things go, otherwise, I find (or not find as the case may be) that things are nicely put away but I can't locate them!

5. **Sustain** – The purpose of this step is to ensure that you keep up your good work and don't let it slide. This is where the self-discipline really needs to kick-in. Once you have "stabilized" your area, determine how you are going to make sure that it doesn't return to its former character. Institute some easy rules to guide you. One rule that many follow for keeping their clothing closet manageable is when you buy a new pair of slacks you must identify some piece of clothing to remove. Mark your calendar when monthly or quarterly cleanings of the garage or attic are due. And when you go to buy those must-have souvenirs, ask yourself how long will those hold my interest. I overheard a husband and wife on vacation indicate that one souvenir would last a week and another three months at best. Is the delight of the moment worth adding to the clutter when you return home?

   Use a checklist to assess the effectiveness of your program and make necessary changes. Here is an example of an abbreviated 5S assessment:

| "S" | Description | 1 | 2 | 3 | 4 | 5 |
|---|---|---|---|---|---|---|
| Sort | 1. There are no unnecessary items in supply cabinet. | | | | | X |
| | 2. Quantities are accurate, no "just-in-case" supplies. | | X | | | |
| Set up | 1. All items are on shadowboard. | | | | X | |
| | 2. Anyone can tell normal from abnormal. | | | | X | |
| Shine | 1. Everything is put away, nothing on desk. | | | X | | |
| | 2. Floors and flat surfaces are free of clutter. | | X | | | |
| Standardize | 1. Everything is labeled correctly, labels are intact. | | | | | X |
| | 2. Equipment manuals are organized, easily accessible. | | | | | X |
| Sustain | 1. Pictures, procedures are up to date. | | | | X | |
| | 2. Received compliments. | | | | | X |

1 = non-compliance, 5 = total compliance. The higher the score, the higher the compliance. In the above example, it looks like we need to spend more time on "Shine" and challenging our purchases.

To change a habit, we must change behavior and reinforce the change. Recognize when you and your family have standardized and gone through at least one 5S cycle and celebrate! Discover where you will apply the next 5S cycle!

**Give Yourself the Gift of Freedom – Start Today**

A "clean house" clears our minds so that we can focus on what we want to do rather than being scattered, wasting motion, time, and energy. It also prepares us for disasters by helping determine what is vital before an emergency occurs. Our children will be thankful that we didn't leave them with a pile of "junk" to sort through. Our friends and family will be pleased that things are in order in the event they need to take care of something, and your mind will not be preoccupied with how things look. And it relieves a burden from our shoulders. This new, unencumbered verve readies us to seek new opportunities such as writing a chapter in a book.

*Notes:*

## THE PROFESSIONAL WOMAN NETWORK

Training and Certification on Women's Issues

Linda Ellis Eastman, President & CEO of The Professional Woman Network, has trained and certified over two thousand individuals to start their own consulting/seminar business. Women from such countries as Brazil, Argentina, the Bahamas, Costa Rica, Bermuda, Nigeria, South Africa, Malaysia, and Mexico have attended trainings.

Topics for certification include:

- Diversity & Multiculturalism
- Women's Issues
- Women: A Journey to Wellness
- Save Our Youth
- Teen Image & Social Etiquette
- Leadership & Empowerment Skills for Youth
- Customer Service & Professionalism
- Marketing a Consulting Practice
- Professional Coaching
- Professional Presentation Skills

If you are interested in learning more about becoming certified or about starting your own consulting/seminar business contact:

The Professional Woman Network
P.O. Box 333
Prospect, KY 40059
(502) 566-9900
lindaeastman@prodigy.net
www.prowoman.net